To Dirk & Suzanne
Christmas 1993
Part of the summer of 1903 or 1904
my Father John Adrain Epping & my
Mother Emma Elisebeth, my
uncle Albert and Aunt Belle Rahles
camped at Arch Cape alone
with we five children, Dorothy,
Adrienne, Carl, Bud and I — as
I was practically blind at the time
I could not give David or Alma
facts, only hear say. I do
remember two tents and huge
trees down to the sand

Love
Grandmother

D1571475

Arch Cape Chronicles

A Bit of

Oregon Coast's

Past

By David and Alma English

To Berkeley III
Alma Jo English
David K. English

Co-published
    David and Alma English
    P.O. Box 90
    Arch Cape, OR 97102
       and
    Frontier Publishing
    Seaside, OR 97138

Lithographic film service
    Darryl Schmidt, Trademark
    6217 Roosevelt Way, Northeast
    Seattle, WA 98115

Photograph and page layout
David English

Cover photos by David and Alma English

Front: A view looking at Bird Rock through one of the Arches.
Back: Castle Rock at sunset.

Text via an *Apple Macintosh IICX* using *Microsoft Works,* Version 2.0,
and for final layout, using the *Aldus PageMaker* program, Version 4.0,
by David and Alma English

ISBN 0-939116-38-3

Library of Congress Catalog Number 93-72487

Acknowledgment

Jan Tarr for her writing and proofreading; Bridget Snow for her inspiration and encouragement; Travis Tyrrell for furnishing records and information on the water and sewer systems and for the Fire Department; Mike Graham for his unselfish help with the Fire Department story; Brian McDonough, Jack Foster, Mike Graham, Kent Price and Gordon Hauck for help with the three water system stories; the late Jim Dennon for helping me find photographs at the Clatsop County Historical Society and for giving me his book, *The Schooner Shark, Shark Rock, and Cannon Beach*; the Oregon State Department of Highways; the Columbia River Maritime Museum; Jim Markham for his story, *Kelps in Clatsop County;* Jim Richmond for his help on the geology story; John Markham for his story, *The Natural History of Arch Cape;* Kent Price for his homestead and plat maps; Gwen Carney for her brochures, old maps, records and news clippings; the *Oregonian, Seaside Signal* and the *Astorian* newspapers and to all who contributed photographs and stories.

The co-author and his inspiration, Bridget Snow, 94 years young.
David English photo.

Table of Contents

Prepages

Nature and Environment

Growth of Arch Cape

People Who Made It Grow

People Who Made It Grow (Continued)

Dedication

To Salvador Mardesich
my friend

who volunteered to edit these pages

Introduction

This book is for all who have walked the two to three mile ocean beach between Hug Point and the Arch Cape headland and enjoyed its unparalleled beauty. Castle Rock guards the west while the nearby steep hills of the Coast Range block entry from the east. Only elk, deer and bear found their way to this narrow strip of flat land now occupied by homes east of the dune line. Recorded settlement in Arch Cape is less than one hundred years old. The area wasn't appealing to Native Americans because the territory was rugged and inaccessible. Besides, their livelihood depended on the abundance of salmon that nearby rivers provided. Consequently, the Tillamook, Nehalem and Columbia rivers and their tributaries along with the Clatsop Plains flatlands were far more desirable.

Arch Cape derives its name from the two arches found just behind the headland south of Arch Cape Creek. If hikers ford the creek at low tide, walk between the headland and the "haystack" rock to the west and then keep close to the cliff for a hundred feet or so, they will see the arches. The arches disappeared for a time following the tunnel construction. Vibrations from the blasting combined with an unusually wet winter loosened rubble from the top of the cliff and, in 1940, covered the arches. In 1947, when I married Alma and brought her to Arch Cape, we intended to walk through the arches. We climbed the rubble pile and found a small opening that framed Bird Rock to the south. The rock that fell was a softer rock and since has eroded. When exploring the area, you can see the scar at the top of the cliff. Today, it is an easy walk through the arches and you will see a number of boulders lying on the sand at the south side. Perhaps in another thirty or forty years, they too will be gone.

Castle Rock, the sentinel standing offshore, has an Indian legend attached to its name. Native Americans told it to Captain William Warren, an early resident in the area. Captain Warren repeated the story about a beautiful Indian princess from the Tillamook Indian tribe on Neahkahnie Mountain. The North Wind desired the princess and took her to his home on Castle Rock. Angry Indian braves pursued him. The North Wind turned and blew his hardest until the narrow strip of land that connected the rock to the mainland crumbled and fell into the ocean. The braves fell to their death and since then, Castle Rock has been unreachable.

Hug Point, too, has a story. Early records claim the name "hug" came from the first travelers who risked "hugging" the rock to negotiate that obstacle rather than climb overland to reach the other side. Old photographs show foot and hand holes carved at the south side. These holes permitted travelers to reach a ledge that followed a level fracture line between layers of sandstone. When the road was blasted out about 1908, that ledge disappeared, but the holes getting to it are still there and the fault line where the ledge used to be is still visible.

Homesteads were available in the Arch Cape area between 1890 and 1900. Seven claims were filed in those years from Arch Cape Creek to Hug Point. Joseph Walsh's claim was north of Arch Cape Creek, Section 30, Certificate Number 4376. Harry (or Henry) Bell, a civil engineer in Astoria was next, also Section 30 with Certificate Number 6061. Then came Robert C. F. (Jack) Astbury, Section 19, certificate number 6379. Astbury was a civil engineer who laid out the Elk Creek Toll Road for the owner, Mr. Herbert F. Logan, and he also surveyed homesteads in the area. Clark W. Carnahan settled just north from Atsbury, Section 19 with Certificate Number 6062. Then, Lydia A. Austin, Section 19, Certificate Number 4424, located just south of Hug Point and Sam Adair, Section 18-19, Certificate

Number 6356, settled near Hug Point State Park.

Four subdivisions developed from the homesteads:

Cannon Beach Park — This includes the Joseph Walsh, Harry Bell and Edith Watson homesteads. Watson's homestead was east of Highway 101 up Webb Avenue (now Mill Road). Frank A. Row came into title August 6, 1906, to most of the property. The first subdivision was made November 24, 1906, by James Finlayson as trustee and the extension was made August 26, 1926, again by Mr. Finlayson. This subdivision is in south Arch Cape and begins up the hillside south of Arch Cape Creek, north to the creek between the Carney home and the Huss home and east of the highway to Fifth Street. The entire territory, according to county plat maps, is divided into lots, but few homes exist east of the highway other than those up Mill Road.

No Name Area — The area between Cannon Beach Park and Kent Price Park was never officially platted. The properties' south border began at the north border of Cannon Beach Park and ended somewhere between Marshall and Columbia Avenues on the north. Dow Walker owned most of the area in the 30's. Wilber Markham laid out the streets and property sites and surveyed the area. Later, Ernest White purchased all of Mr. Walker's property. Ocean Road, just north of the Deli, runs east and west right down the middle of this tract.

Kent Price Park — This subdivision is part of the Robert C. F. Astbury homestead. J. M. Shank purchased the property from him September 12, 1932, and later sold to Kent A. Price September 4, 1945. Mr. Price subdivided it, named the subdivision Kent Price Park, and installed a water system. Kent Price Park is west of the highway just south of Columbia Avenue to Maple Street on the north.

Arch Cape Park — This subdivision is part of the Clark W. Carnahan homestead. He subdivided on June 22, 1908. It extends from Maple Street on the south to Larch Street on the north. Much of the subdivision is east of the highway. There was an unusual feature for this tract. Early maps show a right-of-way at the ocean edge for a railroad. One can only speculate just how that rail line would negotiate the Arch Cape headland. Later maps set aside the same space for a public park.

Cannon View Park — This subdivision is part of the Lydia Austin homestead. Charles Kirschner and Henry Hano purchased the property on June 6, 1906, and sold it to Mr. and Mrs. Rudolph Kissling on September 21, 1925. In September, 1945, Paul Sullivan bought it. He took Mel Goodin as a partner and they subdivided the property. Mel Goodin bought Paul Sullivan's interest shortly thereafter. Cannon View Park is the narrow strip of ocean front commonly called the "Flats." A private road separated beachfront homes and a single row of homes east of the road.

Little development has occurred between Cannon View Park and Hug Point State Park, the popular beach lined with sea stacks, caves and secluded beaches.

The Arch Cape beach was important to travelers going from Seaside to the Tillamook Bay area after the turn of the century. It was a natural stopping place to rest after negotiating Hug Point and before heading up the formidable Neahkahnie Mountain. Accommodations were available for travelers at the *Arch Cape Hotel* where there was feed for the horses and a barn to protect them from the winter weather.

Sam H. Webb, a realtor from Astoria, sold lots in the Arch Cape area in the late 20's. A 1931 plat map, titled **Cannon Beach Park and Extension, Revised**, covers an area from Arch Cape Creek at the south to one block north of Hug Point Avenue (now Markham Avenue) and from the ocean eastward about 2,500 feet. Sam Webb had grandiose plans for the area. Several interesting features show on the plat map: a wide boulevard and parkway on Walsh Avenue (now named Leech Avenue), a site reserved for a hotel on the south side of Arch Cape Creek, and an area reserved for the hotel beach between Walsh Avenue and the creek. On the map, the coast highway turns east as though planned to wind around the Arch Cape headland (See the plat reproduction on page 14). The depression doomed Mr. Webb's project and growth was very slow in the Arch Cape area in the 30's.

Much growth occurred in Arch Cape during the next thirty years. In January, 1966, a temporary committee of Arch Cape residents sent letters to neighboring home owners inviting them to attend a meeting to discuss forming a community group, based on the Nea-Kah-Nie Community Club. It was to have by-laws, officers and dues, and its purpose was to help in seven distinct areas:

1. *Lower fire insurance rates.*
2. *Devise a tsunami warning system.*
3. *Create a closer relationship with the County Planning Commission.*
4. *Police our beach and residences.*
5. *Request county attention to our roads.*
6. *Improve sanitation.*
7. *Lower the rate of speed on the highway through Arch Cape.*

The organization continues to address these and other community issues. The Community Club which began February 12, 1966, still meets in the hall of St. Peter the Fisherman Church in Arch Cape. The original committee forming this club consisted of Walter Weibensen, Chairman; William Kane, Betty Snow, Lowell Hawkins, Eleanor Simmonds and Floyd Scott.

One of the items on their agenda was accomplished in 1987 and is so unique it deserves special mention. This is the community warning system, also known as COWS, which the fire department purchased for the Cannon Beach and the Arch Cape areas. It is designed to warn against tsunamis. This solar powered system, also used in Holland, Finland and Alaska, is tested in Arch Cape periodically on Wednesday evenings. Wherever you are in Arch Cape, if conditions are favorable, you will hear cows mooing. This sound comes from two speaker sources. Startling as thunder, it seems to come from the sky. When you stop laughing, you hear a voice telling you "This is a test and in case of an emergency you will hear a loud siren followed by instructions." It is reminiscent of the early 1900's in Arch Cape when real cowboys moved cattle from Clatsop Plains to Tillamook and herded them down the Arch Cape beach. One of these tsunami tests occured December 2, 1992, when Dr. Melvin Beemer, a veterinarian was visiting from Ames, Iowa. He called us and asked where those sick cows were. He was serious. We explained the COWS warning system to him and he had a good laugh.

In September, 1984, the club, now known as the **Arch Cape-Falcon Cove Beach Community Club,** asked Mary Goodall Ramsey to write a history of the Arch Cape area and unanimously voted to back Mary financially. Mrs. Ramsey and her husband had been residents in Arch Cape since 1973. Mary was a former journalist with *The Oregonian* and *The Oregon Journal.* She had previously written a history of Lake Oswego called *Oregon's Iron Dream,* published in 1958, and she was enthusiastic about writing the Arch Cape story.

Mary collected a number of publications, pamphlets, news articles and photographs. She also interviewed local residents. According to an article dated December 6, 1984, in the *Cannon Beach Gazette,* her first effort was limited to the story of Arch Cape, but as she became involved in the project, she stated "we are so bound to our neighboring communities that I had to spread my scope." Mary wanted to include the north Oregon coast and the Native Americans that populated the area.

Unfortunately, in the spring of 1987, Mary had a disabling stroke and in September of that year she sorrowfully decided that she lacked the energy to continue the project. A letter from Mary Ramsey dated September 10, 1987, to George Cerelli, President of the Community Club, tells of her research regarding the Arch Cape history project, which she wished to become the property of the club. She stated in the letter that she could not do any writing and asked that all of her material be put under lock and key until it would be used in a serious manner. Her research and materials were boxed and stored in a locker at the Arch Cape fire station.

In May, 1988, a committee formed by Bridget Snow asked that we take over the task of completing Mary's dream—writing the Arch Cape story. Mary's boxed research materials were removed from the fire station and inventoried. Mary had collected many photographs and names. We told the committee that we are not writers but would take on the task. In February of 1991 we sent a letter to all property owners asking them if they had anything to contribute to the story. Many did and the *Arch Cape Chronicles* story is the result: a collection of family recollections, of area development, a scientific record and a history of this bit of the Oregon coast from the Arch Cape headland to Hug Point. Every effort has been made to verify the information in this book for historical accuracy. Many stories in this publication are memories from second and third generation family members. Wrong dates, wrong facts and wrong names will occur. For this, we apologize.

David K. and Alma D. English, 1993, Arch Cape, Oregon.

The following six pages, including the photo below, will help the reader understand Arch Cape. The arches at the south, the road around Hug Point at the north and Castle Rock at guard a half mile to the west makes this area very precious to those who live here and for those who have yet to experience a place like Arch Cape.

The above photograph, a postcard by someone named Coe, date unknown, has a July 27, 1907 Portland, Oregon, postmark and shows Hug Point before the road was blasted around the point. The carved steps where the girl stands led to the ledge at the top of steps used by early-day travelers to negotiate the point when tides prevented traveling around Hug Point. Emil Gelinsky wrote on this card the following message to his mother, Elizabeth Gelinsky: "Rose City Tent, July 27-07, Sat 8:30 am. Dear Mama, Everything all fine on this end of the line. Eat 3 meals every day and have a good sleep every night. I go to bed as soon as the sun goes down or from 8:30 to 9 pm. Regards to all, Your son Emil." Could Emil have named his Arch Cape tent site "Rose City" because Portland was called the "Rose City," even back then? Eugenia Dooley collection.

This early-day Woodfield photograph shows the outer part of Hug Point and part of the ledge where travelers "hugged" the rock when traveling around the point. Later, a road blasted out below the ledge allowed wheeled traffic, both horse-drawn and gas-powered vehicles access to the Arch Cape area. Eugenia Dooley Collection.

An old postcard photograph shows the south exit when looking south. Compare this view with the photograph on the previous page. Photo source unknown. Eugenia Dooley collection.

This early-day "Sand" postcard photograph shows the roadbed at the central part of the Hug Point road. It looks the same today. Author's collection.

The steps carved into the basalt and sandstone to reach the ledge around Hug Point are still there at the south entrance of the Hug Point road. The co-author, Alma, stands beside them in 1992. David English photo.

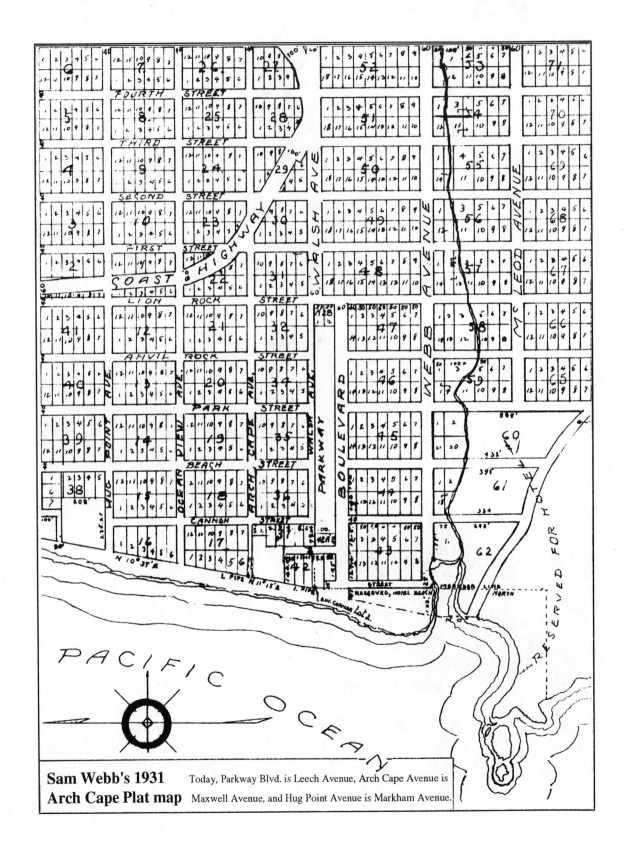

Sam Webb's 1931 Arch Cape Plat map   Today, Parkway Blvd. is Leech Avenue, Arch Cape Avenue is Maxwell Avenue, and Hug Point Avenue is Markham Avenue.

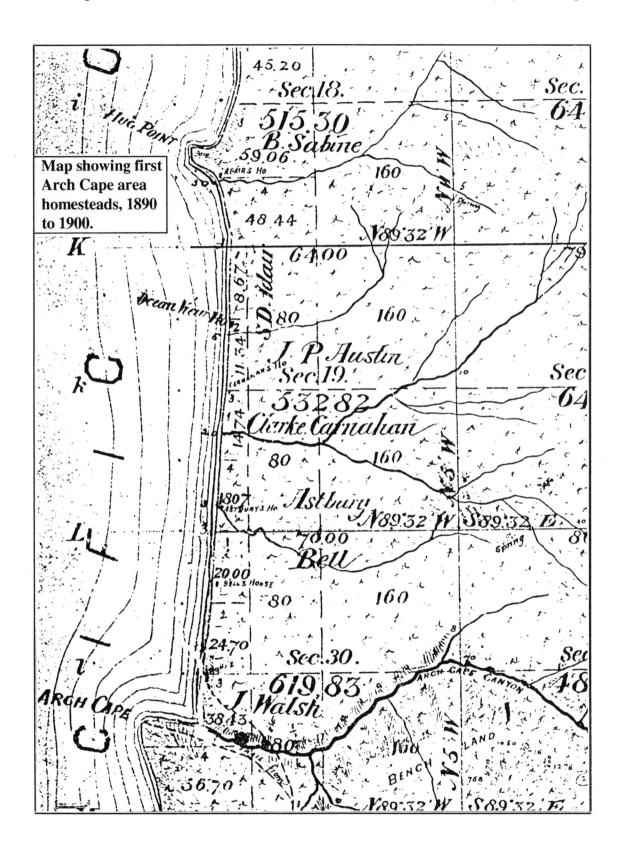

Map showing first
Arch Cape area
homesteads, 1890
to 1900.

Brian McDonough Photo

A silent sentinel stands Arch Cape
Watching wind and water roar
Violently as if to rape
The bounties of the fruited shore.

The waves along the beaches roll
Sand and silt and weed and rocks,
While happy couples stroll
And a scavenger his meal stalks.

The graying cedar-sided houses bleached
By wind and rain and sun and sand,
Witness the flotsam and jetsam beached
By Neptune's hoary hand.

Castle Rock leans into the wave,
Braces its feet against the shore
Lest it succumb to a watery grave
As the sands that have gone before.

The gnarled, twisted trees are bent
Leeward, toward their lumbered kin
As their grasping roots are rent
From the earth's moss covered skin.

The morning sun is in the sky,
The Harpy wind lost at sea,
The air is filled with sea birds' cry
And laughing childrens' shouts of glee.

Peace again befalls the Cape,
Queen Vic* once more at rest
Mindful of her narrow escape,
Mindful too, She stood the test.

Don Mitchell

*A popular name by many for Castle Rock

A north view of the arches shows an easy walk through them before rock tumbled down in 1940 and left the huge sandstone boulders you see there today. People drove automobiles through the arches toward Cove Beach in the 20's and 30's when conditions were favorable. Tides, especially in the winter months, create large tidal pools between Arch Cape Creek and the arches and make the walk through the arches difficult. Starfish, mussels and barnacles are there all of the time and when tides are low, many varieties of animal and plant life, including kelps and sea grasses, can be observed. Photo source unknown. Authors' collection.

Falls Creek between Hug Point and Hug Point State Park. Photo source unknown. Authors' collection.

The Arch Cape Cannon

The Arch Cape cannon history begins with the construction of the schooner *Shark*, built at the Washington, D. C. Navy Yard, at a cost of $23,627, and launched on May 17, 1821. The *Shark* had 2 masts, weighed 198 tons, was 86 feet long, had a 67 foot 4 inch keel and a 24 foot 9 inch moulded beam. The depth of her hold was 10 feet 4 inches. She carried 12 guns, 10 of which were 18-pounder carronades, and 2 were 9-pounder "Long Tom" guns. The design required a crew complement of about 70 men. The *Shark* was one of 4 vessels built at the same time: the *Alligator* was built at the Boston Navy Yard, the *Dolphin* at the Philadelphia Yard, and the *Porpoise* at the Portsmouth Navy Yard. The decision of the government to suppress piracy in the West Indies led to the construction of these small fast schooners which were inexpensive to maintain and man. They were designed by a Mr. William Doughty and based on the lines of the famous Baltimore clippers.

On May 11, 1821, the Navy assigned Lieutenant Matthew C. Perry to command the *Shark* and prepare her for a cruise. The *Shark* joined the West India Squadron, then under the command of Commodore James Biddle, cruising in the West Indies to fight piracy and slave trade. Lieutenant Perry was succeeded by Lieutenant Thomas H. Stevens July 29, 1823. During this period, the *Shark* captured or assisted in the capture of several pirate vessels, including the *Bandara de Sangre*. She then returned to New York in the summer of 1824.

During 1826 and 1827 the *Shark* cruised off the coast of Africa and in the West Indies combating slave trade under the command of Lieutenant Otho Morris. In the latter part of 1827 and the early part of 1828, she patrolled off the New England coast and then again in West Indian waters with Lieutenant Isaac McKeever in command. She sailed the coast of Africa again from 1828 to 1832, first under the command of Lieutenant Samuel W. Adams and later under Lieutenant Ralph Voorhees. The *Shark* was then transferred to the Pacific Squadron in 1833 and was the first U.S. war vessel to pass through the Straits of Magellan from east to west. She assisted in protecting American interests in turbulent South America and along the North American coast during unstable times in California. Her commanders in succession during this period were Lieutenant Abraham Biglow, Commander Aloysius Dornin, Lieutenant Henry Eagle, and Lieutenant Neil N. Howison.

On April 1, 1846, Lieutenant Howison received orders from Commodore Sloat to proceed to Honolulu for repairs, coppering, and the loading of provisions in readiness to ascend the Columbia River as far as the Willamette. According to specific instructions from Commodore Sloat, Howison was to visit the valley of that river with a party of officers to "obtain correct information of that country and to cheer our citizens in the region by the presence of the American flag." He was also to take a survey of conditions in The Oregon Territory relating to the Canadian border negotiations then in progress. His reports would assist in formulating a decision on the location of the boundary between England and the American lands. Great Britain wanted the border to be the Columbia River and the United States wanted the border to be 54 degrees, 40 minutes latitude. This was the reason for President Polk's slogan, "54-40 or fight." Unknown to the *Shark's* crew or to the residents of Oregon, Washington D. C. had already settled the border at 49 degrees latitude by treaty on June 15, 1846.

The *Shark* arrived about 30 miles north of the mouth of the Columbia on July 15.

Lieutenant Howison's chart for the entrance to the Columbia River was based on Lieutenant Wilkes' 1841 exploration and chart, the first official American survey. Howison was warned that the sands at the entrance of the river had shifted since then and he spent considerable time exploring before crossing the bar. They sailed to Astoria and stayed from July 19th to the 22nd, explored that area, and then went on to Fort Vancouver, about 100 miles up the Columbia River. The vessel returned down river six miles to the mouth of the Willamette River in an attempt to sail to Oregon City. The shallow bar prevented the *Shark* from entering the river. Crew members in a small boat did visit Oregon City, and Howison returned with the schooner to Fort Vancouver.

Lieutenant Howison's orders were to come out of the Columbia not later than September 1. He left Fort Vancouver August 23, but did not reach Baker's Bay, near the bar, until September 8. The next day he observed the bar and prepared for the crossing. He made the attempt on September 10th, which resulted in the loss of the schooner because of unpredictable wave, current and wind conditions. In an effort to get the ship off the south spit, the crew chopped down the three masts and jettisoned the cannons. When she began to break up, the crew took to life boats and all on board were eventually saved. A court of inquiry was held and no blame was imputed.

The shipwrecked officers and crew immediately began the construction of winter quarters in Astoria. Officers and men constantly explored the beaches from Point Adams, which is near Hammond, and southward down the coast. They searched for articles from the wreck worth salvaging, but seldom found even a spar, since Native Americans had already found what wreckage came ashore and stripped it of its copper and iron fittings.

Lieutenant Howison received information through Native Americans that part of the hull with guns upon it had come ashore south of Tillamook Head, about twenty or thirty miles down the coast from Clatsop Spit. He sent Midshipman Simes to visit the spot. He reported that the deck between the mainmast and the forehatch had been stranded near the mouth of Shark Creek and that three of the carronades (short light iron cannons) adhered to this portion of the wreck. He succeeded in getting one of the carronades above what he thought was the high water mark; the other two were inaccessible because of the surf. Simes realized it would be utterly impracticable to transport any weighty object over the mountain trail to Astoria so made no effort to recover them. The one he did rescue sank in the sand.

The site and time of the Arch Cape cannon's discovery is well established. The portion of the wreck with the three carronades washed ashore in front of the Austin House. Mr. J. P. Austin had acquired a homestead of 320 acres just south of Hug Point in the early 1890's, where he and his wife built a hotel. The Elk Creek Hotel, located on the north side of Elk Creek close to where the Ecola Creek Lodge is today, was the only other hotel in the area and was the terminus of the Elk Creek Toll Road to Cannon Beach in the 1890's.

The Austin House was a low rambling structure on the site now called Cannon View Park, commonly referred to as the "flats." It was the first Cannon Beach Post Office, established in 1891 and closed in 1901. Mail carriers from Nehalem and Seaside met there to exchange mail sacks for the return trip. The property had a mountain creek flowing to the ocean and that is where the cannon was re-discovered. In 1898 one of the mail carriers found the cannon there in the sands at the mouth of Shark Creek in front of the Austin House. The irony of the story is that Mr. Austin had been sure he would find a cannon near his house but he died four years before its discovery.

The January 29, 1898, *The Daily Astorian* carried this story: "Mail carrier Bill Luce, who carries the mail between Nehalem and Cannon Beach, while on his regular route yesterday, saw a funny substance in the creek on Cannon Beach in front of Mrs. Austin's house. It did not look like a rock, and upon investigation he found the cannon from which Cannon Beach derives its name." John and Mary Gerritse's team of horses dragged the cannon out of the sand and then John placed it on timber blocks in front of the Austin farmhouse, fifty-two years after the *Shark* had been lost in 1846.

Ownership of the cannon changed several times. Mr. Mel Goodin purchased and platted the land known as Cannon View Park in 1945. He graded the area in preparation for home sites and the cannon was in the wrong place. George Van Vleet, of Van Vleet Logging Company, gave one acre of land to the state on which to place the cannon as a memorial; Mr. Goodin, who then owned the cannon, donated it to the public. The Oregon State Department of Highways prepared the site, moved the cannon and pedestal, and placed a historical marker on the east side of Highway 101. The cannon is displayed a short distance south and east from the original location where Jim and Lydia Austin had their Cannon Beach Post Office.

On April 12, 1989, *The Daily Astorian* published an article regarding the Arch Cape cannon and indicated that the Clatsop County Historical Society and the Heritage Museum in Astoria wished to display the cannon under cover and in a secure environment. On April 13th, Director John Cooper and Steve Kann moved the original cannon and capstan from the Oregon State Highway site to the Heritage Museum. The purpose was to protect the cannon from weathering and vandalism.

An Arch Cape Community Club Committee, chaired by Barbara Shaw, with committee members Mamie Markham and Irene Tyrrell, established an agreement with the Clatsop County Historical Society that an exact replica of the cannon be put in the original's place. At the May 19, 1989, Falcon Cove-Arch Cape Community Club meeting, Mr. Cooper said he would guarantee the return of the cannon to the community. A sign placed at the bottom of the State's Historical Marker explains that the original cannon is at the Heritage Museum in Astoria and spells out the terms of the agreement between the Community Club and the Historical Society. "At such time as the community of Arch Cape has a suitable, secure, and accessible public building, it is the intent of the Clatsop County Historical Society to place these items again in the area where they washed ashore." The replica is now in place.

The preceding material came from Chappelle's *History of the American Sailing Navy*, The Clatsop County Historical Society, The Oregon Historical Society and *The Daily Astorian*.

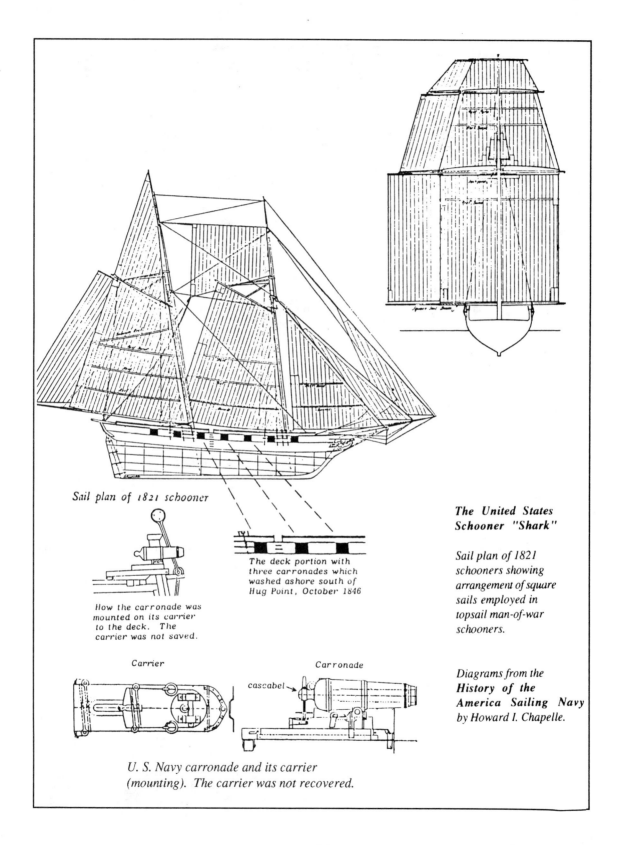

Sail plan of 1821 schooner

The deck portion with three carronades which washed ashore south of Hug Point, October 1846

How the carronade was mounted on its carrier to the deck. The carrier was not saved.

Carrier

Carronade

cascabel

U. S. Navy carronade and its carrier (mounting). The carrier was not recovered.

The United States Schooner "Shark"

Sail plan of 1821 schooners showing arrangement of square sails employed in topsail man-of-war schooners.

Diagrams from the **History of the America Sailing Navy** *by Howard I. Chapelle.*

Pauline Steabb (Mrs. Frank Dow) at age 13 standing by the cannon in front of Mrs. Lydia Austin's house (then the Cannon Beach post office) in 1898. At left is John N. Griffin, whose homestead was nearby. (Clatsop County Historical Society Photo Number 5546-015, courtesy of the Cannon Beach Library.)

Ann Lensrud at the highway cannon site in August, 1944, 46 years after the cannon was found by mail carrier Bill Luce in front of the Austin House. Ann Lensrud photo.

Paul Bartells, a long-time brick mason in the Cannon Beach area, constructed the concrete base for the cannon in 1929. It was mounted on the base by the property owners, Mr. and Mrs. Rudolph Kissling that same year. Mr. Mel Goodin purchased the property and developed the "Flats," Cannon View Park, in 1945 and the cannon was in the way so it was moved to the present Highway 101 site. The Oregon State Department of Transportation constructed a new pedestal for the cannon in 1992. Murphy Rock shows between the trees. Today, the same rock profile is visible from the deck of the H. A. Andersen home. It

appears, from this photo, that the cannon location would have been a little east and across the road from the Andersen home. Photo source unknown. Circa 1930's.

U.S.S. Shark under sail.
Artist Unknown.
Columbia River Maritime
Museum. 1963.197.

Roads and Highways

From its beginning, Arch Cape has been isolated. The natural barriers, Tillamook Headland and Hug Point on the north and the basaltic Arch Cape headland on the south, plus the awesome bulk of Neahkanie, made it impractical to build a road following the coast between Astoria and the Nehalem Bay area. Early settlers used the beach or Native American trails that followed the coast. Beach travel to Arch Cape had to be coordinated with the tides, particularly around the infamous Hug Point where vehicles were sometimes caught by sand and waves.

In 1899, the Oregon State Legislature had ruled that all land between high and low tides in Clatsop County was a public highway. In 1913 this dedication of beach areas as public right-of-way was extended to California. In 1967, the Oregon Beach Bill affirmed this public access to beaches. In 1992, the State Supreme Court said the Oregon Beach Access law still stands.

The first wagon road over Tillamook Head led to the *Elk Creek Hotel* built in 1892 by H. F. Logan. Mr. Logan also organized the Elk Creek Toll Road Company, incorporated October 3, 1890, but the road opened to wagon travel the previous August. About 1901, a sign at the Elk Creek Hotel read: "ELK CREEK TOLL ROAD, Single Horse, Mule or Ass 25 cents; Single Horse & Buggy 50 cents; Double Team 75 cents; Four Horse Team $1.00; Cattle Driven 25 cents; Sheep and Hogs 10 cents; H. F. L. Logan, Pres." (*sic*). The wagon road to Elk Creek country opened the area to homesteaders and settlement.

This old Toll Road from Seaside to Cannon Beach followed a steep Indian trail over the Tillamook headland to Elk Creek, also known as Ecola Creek. The first two or three miles out of Seaside were quite easy until the wagon driver approached the Necanicum River. After fording the river, the often muddy road led through low ravines to Tillamook Head. The narrow road provided few turnouts so the driver stopped approximately every hundred feet. He bellowed loudly and if no answer came, forged ahead. At the end of the journey, the driver with his wagon waited until the tide was just right before crossing near the mouth of Elk Creek for those passengers wanting to reach Cannon Beach. The crossing was dangerous because the tides and river flow at times caused deeper water and different channels than expected. When this happened, it drenched passengers, baggage and supplies. The *Elk Creek Hotel*, located where the *Ecola Creek Lodge* is now at the north end of the Ecola Creek bridge, was the terminus of the Elk Creek Toll Road.

The "Toll Road" evolved from a narrow trail to a road of sorts that early pioneers used traveling from Ecola to Seaside and Astoria for needed supplies. In 1903, the county took over and built a new road following the old route most of the way and constructed a bridge over Elk Creek.

A well-marked route ran from Seaside to Tillamook to carry the U. S. Mail. The Austin House, about a half-mile south of Hug Point, was established in 1891 when the U. S. Post Office Department made Mr. Austin postmaster for Cannon Beach. Mail was delivered between Seaside and Tillamook once-a-week. The carrier walked or rode horseback from Seaside to Cannon Beach the first day. When weather and tide allowed, his route took him around Hug Point and the Arch Cape headland. He negotiated Neakahnie Mountain and went down the coast lowlands to Tillamook. The mail carrier used a buckboard over the route during the summer and delivered supplies as well as mail to beach dwellers. In winter months, however, when trails were crossed on foot, mail deliveries were less frequent. Windfalls blocked the trail for weeks, making it impossible to use a horse or team. High tides forced the carrier overland around Hug Point and Arch Cape. Eventually, the mail reached its destination.

A stage line carried mail between Seaside and the Nehalem Post Office. By 1912, Tillamook County finally had rail service and transferred the mail by rail via Portland instead of using the Seaside-Nehalem stage route. Passengers used the convenient and reliable rail service, so the stage line stopped the run between Seaside and Wheeler. People walked or rode a horse all the way between north coast communities.

Arch Cape remained isolated.

Roads developed slowly because water transportation for freight and passengers was made possible by the vast river system in the area. Early railroads also preceded roads and ran spurs to the great timber areas that harvested virgin stands of fir, cedar and spruce. The Port of Astoria became the hub for commerce and fishing in the Northwest. Passenger service followed. The first passenger train from Portland to Seaside arrived May 16, 1898. The Astoria and Columbia River Railroad Company owned the railroad. Later, in 1907, the Great Northern Railroad acquired the line and became part of the Spokane, Portland, and Seattle Railway Company, commonly known as the S.P. & S.

The automobile and the Sunset Highway were far in the future. The train became the transportation of choice and often its sixteen cars brought 1200 people each day to Seaside during the tourist season. The train usually left Portland with about 200 aboard and between Portland and Seaside it quickly filled to capacity. Two trains ran daily to Seaside. One left Portland at 6:10 a.m., the other at 8:00 a.m. They arrived in Seaside at 10:30 a.m. and 12:30 p.m. respectively, a journey of 118 miles and four and one-half hours duration. An *Oregonian* article dated July 25, 1965 reports: "On week ends the town band of local boys and girls in Seaside would meet the trains and blast off some free music. After everybody had detrained and gathered up their baggage they formed a parade and marched up the main drag to the turn-around and the passengers followed along in the march." The trains leaving Portland 6:20 p.m. every Saturday became known as the "daddy trains" or "daddy specials" for it joined fathers with their vacationing families on Sunday. In 1910, those who traveled from Portland by automobile spent from six to seven hours on dirt or corduroy roads to reach Seaside. The roads, made for horses and wagons, often had lost horse shoes on them with sharp nails, which easily punctured the rubber tires used then and caused further delay. There were no service stations and the driver had to mend the puncture and then pump air into the tire. This was exercise! After a few car trips, people were ready to try the train.

Passenger service declined rapidly in the early 20's after the completion of the Columbia River Highway, which is now known as Highway 30. Rail passenger service continued until 1953, operating the last few years at a loss until it was discontinued. Freight trains serviced the Astoria-Seaside area until the removal of the railroad bridge over Young's Bay in 1982. Since then, Astoria is the end of the rail line.

At the turn of the century Cannon Beach and Arch Cape were isolated. It was not until 1916 that a surfaced road led into Seaside from Astoria. The Arch Cape headland was a monumental barrier for those traveling to the Nehalem-Tillamook area. The Astoria-

Nehalem Highway, about 56 miles in length, was completed in 1914. It went in a southeasterly direction through Jewell and then followed the Nehalem River to the coast. Prior to that time, part of the road was no more than a trail, impassable several months of the year and muddy most of the time. Later, a road beginning at the junction where the former famous Crab Broiler was located on Highway 101 ran inland about fifteen miles. The road then turned south behind Sugarloaf Mountain and Onion Peak to the Nehalem Bay and Tillamook area. This road is now State Highway 53.

In 1919, legislation passed approving the construction of a coast highway from Astoria to California. Construction began on the highway in the late 20's and continued into the 30's along the central and southern Oregon Coast. The highway, originally part of the Roosevelt Coast Military Highway, ran from Astoria to California and was later named the Oregon Coast Highway.

Les Ordway arrived in Cannon Beach in the mid-twenties. For years he owned and ran the Standard Oil gasoline station across the street from where Gary Moon's Richfield Station is today. Les retired in 1978 and the station remained open for another ten years. The site is a parking lot today. According to Les, the road from Cannon Beach to Arch Cape was slow to develop. By 1927, one could drive onto the beach at *The Wavecrest* for the trip around Hug Point down to Arch Cape. The road reached the south side of Hug Point in 1929 and went down to the beach where the present day Hug Point State Park parking lot is located. The beach entrance washed away each winter and cars had considerable difficulty during the summer negotiating the dry sand to the ramp leading up to the highway. The Hug Point beach access was not yet a reliable alternative around Hug Point. In 1935 a rough road reached Arch Cape just before tunnel construction began. Mr. Ordway drove to the tunnel site every day to perform an important duty: he serviced compressors supplying air for drilling tools boring holes for blasting powder.

On February 6, 1936, a contract by the Oregon Highway Department authorized constructing .62 miles of highway roadbed, including 1,227.1 feet of tunnel 36 feet wide and 23 feet high at Arch Cape. Part of the contract included construction of a pile trestle bridge with concrete deck 166 feet in length. The Highway Department set the completion date for December 31, 1936. Due to unforeseen problems and the extra work required, the Highway Department extended completion to February 5, 1938. It wasn't until March of 1940 that all work was finished, which included replacing some of the treated timber and installing the concrete sills, curbs, gutters, and concrete pavement in the tunnel.

The tunnel was an extremely difficult project. Some of the tunnel material was sandstone and some was a much harder basalt rock. Sandstone is less stable than basalt and when exposed to air, sandstone immediately becomes soft and crumbles like dirt. Therefore, sandstone was more difficult to drill and blast than ordinary rock as it necessitated the building of a timber lining to prevent a cave-in. The combination of digging through the soft material and erecting the timber lining was much more difficult than digging through harder rock. When tunneling through basalt rock, the timber lining was not always necessary.

Mr. Charles E. Haddix, former tunnel worker, graduated from Astoria High School in January, 1935. Shortly after graduation he signed on a British tramp steamer for China and returned to the United States on a Canadian vessel. He worked for awhile in a salmon cannery in Mushagak, Alaska, before going to work on the Arch Cape tunnel project in 1936. Here is his story:

"I remember the *Arch Cape Hotel* very well. It was on the ocean side of the north entrance to the tunnel. Orino, Birkemeir & Saramel used the ground floor as a contractor's office and various workmen bunked upstairs. There were two ways to get a truck driving job. One was to know someone who was getting too sick to work and the other was to hang around until the night foreman, who had a hair-trigger temper, fired a man. Mike Oberg and his brother, along with Joel Humphrys, worked the night shift (12 midnight until 8 in the morning). Joel became sick from carbon monoxide poisoning and told me he was quitting, so I was there on the spot. Times were tough and jobs hard to find so health hazards, or ignorance of them, was secondary to employment.

"At the time I worked there, the tunnel was about one-half completed. I worked only on the north side and have no knowledge of anything on the south section. The crews worked around the clock. The blasting crew left shortly before we came to work and left a huge pile of rubble inside the tunnel for us to haul away. A gasoline-powered shovel was used to load the trucks. A large pipe on the west side of the tunnel drew out some of the fumes from the blasting operation and from the gas-powered shovel and trucks. I don't think they could have operated under today's safety regulations.

"I drove an International truck which was very difficult to steer, especially over the broken rocks from the blast. The truck brakes were good and the cab kept out the rain, but I can recall no other comforts by today's standards. Before our shift began, we gathered around a 50-gallon drum fueled with oil, which provided heat and some light. We packed lunch and coffee with us. As soon as the tunnel was clear enough for work, the shovel and trucks began removing the broken rubble to the bridge approaches on both sides of Arch Cape Creek. It was easy dumping rubble on the north side of the creek but it was a challenge to get to the south approach. There, a steep grade led down to Arch Cape Creek which had to be crossed before driving up a steep winding road to the dump site. Severe headaches from the carbon monoxide gasses inside the tunnel caused some men to quit. I managed to last three months. Then, one night I backed into a hole on the fill where I was unloading and as I attempted to pull out, I snapped the left rear axle on my truck. The short-fused foreman was nearby so I happened to be on the receiving end of his wrath that night and lost my job. I tried to get back on in the morning, but it was too easy to get another man so I was gone. With the health hazards as they were on that job, I should have thanked him. But, I had other words in mind at the time.

"The job was hard but fair; work was hard to find in those days. There was no union nor did we try to organize one that I knew of. We took pride in what we did and I was sorry to leave despite all the health hazards, which I assume were the standard at that time. We enjoyed each other's company and the foreman who fired me was probably under considerable pressure himself. I drove to the job site from a cabin on the ocean about five miles north so did not live in the bunk house, and became acquainted only with my own crew (*sic*)."

Mr. E. H. Clymer, Oregon State Highway Department Cost Analyst, reports that the project was delayed for several reasons: heavy rains, mud, inexperienced supervision, improper equipment, and delays in getting timber used for the lining delivered to the job site.

The contract was bid too low, and according to Mr. Clymer, the overall inefficiency resulted in a large loss to the contractors. Here are portions of Mr. Clymer's reports, **exactly** as written by him:

First Report—Summer of 1936

"Rain and mud made the common excavation at the north end of the tunnel very difficult and expensive. The cat and dozer used on common excavation was unable to operate under its own power due to lack of traction and was dragged through with a gas donkey. A 3/4 yard shovel and trucks were also used at the north end portal cut.

"The excavation on the south end of the tunnel, about 20,000 cubic yards was subbed to a sub-contractor who had a cat bulldozer scraper, but due to the difficult location of the cut and the cost of moving in equipment and supplies, the sub-contractor did not earn enough to pay all his bills and these bills were paid by the contractors which increased their cost about $800.

"The tunnel was started June lst, 1936. 288 lineal feet on the north end was timbered. 582 feet of solid rock did not require timbering except to two short sections where the rock was soft and loose. 358 lineal feet on the south end was timbered and due to the tremendous weight and a slight movement of the overburden, the timbers and sills required reinforcing. To prevent movement and additional strain on the timbers the voids behind the lagging were filled with grout consisting of about four parts sand and one part cement which was pumped in under pressure. The timbering on the south end was started about 150 feet back from the point originally planned due to bad conditions of the rock. Additional timbers were required which caused some delay while awaiting delivery. While awaiting delivery a top drift and the sill drifts were driven through which permitted the work to progress and also provided natural ventilation.

"The construction of the tunnel was very slow due to inexperienced supervision and tunnel men and to the lack of proper equipment. The supervision was changed two or three times, and most of the equipment was replaced during the course of the job in an effort to increase efficiency. Four weeks were required to start the tunnel and place the north portal timbers. The progress per work day was about two feet of timbered section and seven feet of rock section, which is very slow.

"The job was bid too low, especially on timber and was not handled efficiently, which resulted in a large loss to the contractors. The loss will continue to increase until the job is completed."

Second Report—January 15, 1937

"The clearing was done with the aid of a gas donkey. All brush (including trees having butt diameters less than 3 inches) encountered in the clearing operations on the north side of the tunnel was used to construct a brush mattress in the marshy area. The stumps in the marshy areas were difficult to shoot.

"A cat and bulldozer were used to move part of the excavation. Some of the material consisted of a soft blue clay, and when working on this, the cat would get stuck repeatedly and could not operate at all during wet weather. Later the gas donkey equipped with a drag bucket was moved in, but when it failed to make much progress, it was hitched to the cat to pull it back up the grade. Later, it became so muddy that a block had to be put on the rear of the cat and another on the hill. With the dead end on the cat this made a three line pull. It was also found necessary to run the haul back line from the donkey line pull. It was also found necessary to run the haul back line from the donkey to a block on the front of the cat to help it down the grade. A shovel and trucks were used to finish the north portal cut. About 20,000 cubic yards on the south end of the project have been moved by R. N. Summit, sub-contractor, but has not been included in this report for the reason that bills incurred by the sub will more than likely have to be borne by the contractors. For a while the drainage in the portal cut was in such a condition as to hinder the movement of materials from the tunnel, but this has been remedied.

"The north portal set was started about June lst, and four weeks were required to install it. After the portal set was in, about two feet of advance per day was made in the timbered section. The advances for the last few periods are: September 11 - October 15, 130 feet; October 15 - November 15, 180 feet; November 15 - January 15, 148 feet. On January 15th the tunnel was in 970 feet on the north side. On the south side the contractor started to excavate by hand a shell large enough to install the timbers, leaving the core for the shovel to take out later. To date only six sets of timbers have been installed, an advance of 24 feet. Due to high tides the contractor has found it almost impossible to get materials and supplies around the beach, and for this reason, it was thought advisable to discontinue work on the south end. The extra expense entailed in this work has increased the cost of tunnel excavation. The contractor's bid on lumber was too low, especially that of cordwood which was bid about one-half the cost of the material delivered on the job. With such an unusually low bid on this item, it is only natural that the contractor take extra precaution that no large overbreak is made. Too much precaution, however, results in lots of hand picking, and extra blasting may be necessary to get the timbers in place.

"Very little planning of the work has been made on this contract. The superintendent at the start of the work made many mistakes in choice of equipment and manner of operation, but since Mr. Saremal dismissed him, the work has been carried on in a more efficient manner. Many changes and additions have been made in the tunnel equipment, which now consists of the following: Two portable air compressors, 2-15 KW light plants, 15 H.P. gas air blower, 80 H.P. diesel exhaust fan, new 1 cu. yd. Lima shovel, 5 drifterrock drills and 6 light trucks. A diesel powered electric generating plant would have been more appropriate for this job. The use of such a piece of equipment would have resulted in a reduction of fuel costs, a more sustained production and with the use of an electric powered shovel would have reduced the amount of exhaust gas in the tunnel. During the last two months the tunnel operations have been fairly well coordinated. Some improvements could have been made if the drilling time had been decreased by the addition of three or four more rock drills. To make this change an additional compressor would have had to be brought in.

"Very little progress has been made in January. Due to the instability of the rock formation on the north end, it was found that it would be advisable to start timbering a distance of about 150 feet back from the point originally planned. As no treated lumber lining can be had until about March 15th, the contractor will either keep his best men on the job driving a small heading through for natural ventilation or close down until the lining lumber is delivered. Due to a disagreement with the McCormick Lumber Company, who had the contract for the amount of treated lumber in the contract, the contractor changed his order to the Crossett-Western Lumber for delivery of Wolmanized treated lining timber."

Third Report - September 15, 1937

"This contract was bid and awarded February 8th, 1936. Work was started February 25th, and up to September 15, 1937, was about 90% complete. The completion date was originally set as of December 31st, 1936, but due to slow progress and delays will not be completed until about December 15, 1937.

"1,145 lineal feet of tunnel has been excavated which leaves about 75 lineal feet still to be excavated. At the present rate of about 12 lineal feet per week, the excavation should be completed in six weeks. After the tunnel is excavated, another six weeks will probably be required to complete grouting, realigning timbers, reinforcing timbers, cleaning up and finishing.

"From the start of the job work has progressed very slowly due to the lack of experienced supervision, tunnel men and proper equipment. The supervision and equipment have been changed from time to time in an effort to increase efficiency, but even at this late date the crew is working in gas fumes due to lack of ventilating system, which decreases efficiency.

"This tunnel has been quite difficult to construct as it was necessary to timber 288 lineal feet on the north and through earth and loose rock before solid rock was encountered that would stand without timbering. Then after digging through 582 lineal feet of solid rock, loose rock and earth were again encountered, which required the timbering of 358 lineal feet on the south end of the tunnel. The earth and loose rock on the south end of the tunnel is very unstable, and the timbering is very difficult which slows up progress. Approximately 75 M-FBM of treated timber more than was originally anticipated will be required to timber the south end of the tunnel as it was necessary to start timbering about 150 lineal feet back from the point originally planned due to unstable condition of the solid rock.

"The pressure is causing some of the timbers and sills to fail in the south end of the tunnel, and reinforcing timbers are being placed where deemed advisable. It will probably require considerable reinforcing to carry the load during the rainy season, but the reinforcing can be installed without too much difficulty.

"The job was bid too low, especially on timbering, and has not been handled efficiently, which has resulted in a large loss to the contractors. The loss will continue to increase until the job is completed."

Fourth Report - September 15, 1939

"(Arch Cape Tunnel—Lining and Paving) This contract was bid and awarded September 1st, 1939; work was started September 11, and the contract was completed March 30, 1940.

"The work consisted of removing 150 lineal feet of temporary timber lining, salvaging the old cedar backfill, enlarging the tunnel bore on a 588-foot section, placing 588 lineal feet of treated timber lining and the laying of concrete sills, curb, gutter and concrete pavement in the tunnel.

"Removal of the temporary lining and packing was easy as the rings could be pulled down after the first few were dismantled.

"About 700 cubic yards of material were excavated in that portion of the tunnel that was enlarged. Up to three feet were slabbed off some sections, and this thin scaling off of the material required shallow holes and light shooting. A 410 cubic foot compressor working from two to four jackhammers was used for two months, and a 105 cubic foot compressor was then used one month. Excavated materials were hand loaded onto trucks and hauled to a small crusher near the North Portal. The total costs of drilling, shooting, hand loading and hauling to the crusher was $8,472 or about $12 per cubic yard.

"Excavated rock from the tunnel was then crushed and used for the rock backfill and the leveling course. This plant, which consisted of a small jaw crusher and rotary screen was standing at the time the contract was bid. Rental of the plant was $5 a day, and the contractor had to put it in shape, repair it and furnish the power. Crushing costs were high, however, due to a very low production.

"Placing of the Wolmanized timber was slow due to an inexperienced crew and only fair supervision. One crew of an average of five men went ahead on one jumbo or carriage erecting the rings and blocking and wedging them into place. A second crew then followed on another jumbo placing the Wolmanized timber lagging and cedar cordwood backfill. Erection of the timber rings progressed very slowly due mainly to the difficulty in getting the necessary bearing surface on the cedar blocking. The walls and roof of the tunnel were very rough with irregular sharp corners jutting out. It was, therefore, necessary after the ring was up, to jack it down, measure the distance from the timber to the wall, then cut the necessary length of cedar block, and then hew out the end to conform to the tunnel surface where it was to be placed so that a minimum of 80% bearing surface could be secured. A crew of five men worked about six hours in getting the ring up and set in, on which about two hours were required to erect the ring and the other four in hewing the cedar blocking and wedging it into place.

"Progress of the cedar cordwood packing was fair, but no proper arrangements were made for a supply. Deliveries of the cedar were, therefore, irregular, and varying prices were paid per cord.

"Concrete aggregates were purchased from a commercial plant at Seaside f.o.b. the tunnel. A 14 cubic foot portable mixer was set up near the north portal, and the concrete was then trucked to the pouring operation. Aggregates were carried from adjacent stockpiles to the mixer with a 20 horse power tractor equipped with a pan that carried about one-half cubic yard of aggregates. Costs were high due to expensive materials and a poor production due to spasmodic operation and a poorly organized crew. A heavy loss was incurred on concrete curb and gutter due to a mistake in the bid of $0.80 per lineal foot which equaled about $11.50 per cubic yard. Form costs on all concrete items were expensive.

"A loss was incurred on this contract due mainly to a low bid; lack of experience in this type of work and consequent minor mistakes in organization of the sequence of work contributed to the small loss. The contractor's bid on this contract was $7,235 below the second bid."

Finley O. McGrew Jr. also worked on the tunnel. He graduated from Oregon State College as a civil engineer on June 3, 1935. The Oregon State Highway Department hired him in May and the college released him a month before graduation, pleased to place him in those depression years since jobs were scarce. After receiving his first monthly paycheck of $90, he married Betty Statelar, also an Oregon State June graduate, on July 3. Mr. McGrew worked in the greater Portland area for the Highway Department until his assignment to the Arch Cape tunnel project in February, 1936.

The trip between Portland and Arch Cape was long, adventurous, and sometimes dangerous, especially in the middle of winter. The route followed what is now Highway 30 through Scappoose, St. Helens, Rainier, Clatskanie, and Astoria. From there the route took Coast Highway 101 to Seaside and then to Cannon Beach.

Betty McGrew, in a letter to her parents February 28, 1936, told of the trip from Portland to an unknown destination. They arrived in Cannon Beach late at night in pouring rain, found a hotel, and aroused the astounded owner out of bed, who gave them a room with a bath. They slept comfortably, then woke at seven the next morning to find themselves looking at the beach. There was hot water, so both bathed and set out on the rocky, unfinished road to nowhere with their kettles and kitchen utensils rattling. The car was stuffed with items they thought they would need at Arch Cape, which bounced all over the car when they drove over the many rough spots. Betty, attempting to keep her head out of the lamp shade, first removed the grater and then a strainer from behind her husband's neck while he struggled to stay on the road. The road was paved only as far as Tolovana Park; the final five or so miles to Arch Cape were on a primitive surface. Finally, the McGrews reached a building where there was smoke coming out of a chimney. It was the right place. It was a cottage transformed into an office and nearby was a row of similar cottages. Mr. Benedict, the project resident engineer, and Ray Cox, a chain man, lived in the end cottage. The first and third were occupied by bewhiskered lumberjacks. The McGrews had the second cottage. Betty describes the cabin as follows:

"It really isn't too bad. We have a kitchen and bedroom. I have a dresser, bright orange and black, and Mrs. Leech gave me a rocking chair. There is a mat on the floor, and the walls and ceilings are unfinished, but the cabin is very clean, which makes me feel more comfortable.

"The stove is the big problem. It is so small it will burn only kindling wood; the oven won't work, and the wood is wet and difficult to burn. It takes Finley about fifteen minutes to build a fire in the morning. I spent all one afternoon trying to build a fire and failed. Finally, Finley did it after work. There is running cold water in a little sink and Mrs. Leech lets me use her toilet off her back porch. The other sad feature is that under the bed are packed our radio, electric clock, iron, waffle iron, toaster and lamp. Ironically, we have no electricity and for light use kerosene lamps.

"You see, we are in this wild country even before the contractor. Finley, Ray Cox and I crawled through the test hole, a small diameter exploratory hole drilled and blasted through before we arrived. Angelo Costanzo worked on the test hole. After about a week, a crew came and began clearing the approach. It seemed a shame to see and hear these great trees crash down. The actual construction work will start next week. Now, Finley, Mr. Cox and Mr. Benedict, all state highway employees, are busy with specifications and construction plans in their office located east of the highway up Webb Avenue on the left side."

The cabins described by Mrs. McGrew are presently owned by Travis Tyrrell. The McGrews lived in the small cabin from February 26, 1936, to August 31, 1936. Later they moved into the lower floor of the Leech house until January 4, 1937, when mortar in the fireplace in that house collapsed and bricks fell in. Then they moved to Cannon Beach for a short time before returning to Arch Cape to a larger living unit. The original four cabins consisted of only a kitchen, a dining area (an extra person for dinner brought his own chair) and the bedroom with a bed, a dresser and a rocking chair. But there was no closet! Mrs. Leech converted what was an open garage into a bedroom so the McGrews returned to Arch Cape until Finley's work was finished April 1, 1938, when a new crew came to install the timber lining.

Early in the McGrews' adventure, Betty writes:

"Today was a bright day. I walked on the beach for the first time. It is a lovely sandy beach with big crags jutting out from shore." Her next letter reads, in part:

"We've had a seventy mile wind which all but picks the cabin off the ground. The bedroom window blew out when Finley came in the door from work. It rained four inches in twenty-four hours and I've never heard it rain as it is right now. Golly, I think we have a cloud burst! The whole lot is just a lake from here to the churning creek."

The McGrews had a baby daughter they called Punkin. She stayed in her crib during the bad weather and her pull toys and red wagon had to wait for a warmer floor and a dry yard.

A December, 1937, letter from Betty to her parents tells about one of their trips from Portland to Arch Cape:

"We left Portland at 3:30 in an awful rainstorm. At Scappoose, twenty miles out, it was snowing which made slow driving. Several cars were in the ditch and out of Clatskanie, we came to a slide that covered the road. As we waited, deciding what to do, we heard this terrific crackling of trees overhead. Finley never made a faster turnabout. Back in Clatskanie we heard that a snow plow was working on the road to Jewell, so we slid and slipped and crawled through the snow over the mountains. A telephone pole was down across the road between Jewell and Astoria. A car slid off the road trying to get around it. There was no one in the car. We waited about forty-five minutes until the snow plow came and Finley helped the driver move the pole. There was no snow between Astoria and Arch Cape and we arrived at 11:30 p.m. to our icy cold cabin—just eight hours later than when we left Portland instead of the five it usually takes. Finley was late to work. He was to be on the transit for the night shift blasting rock."

Betty mentions Mary Ellen and Kenny Cole who ran the Lamphere grocery store. Betty and Mary had attended Corvallis High School together and the McGrews and Coles became good friends while at Arch Cape.

The completion of the road north to Cannon Beach and the road south to the Nehalem Bay area coincided with the tunnel completion. The rock walls and railings along the Neahkanie Mountain section were done under the *Works Progress Administration* (WPA) program and today stand out as one of the most spectacular features of our coast highway where Neahkanie Mountain rises 1,795 feet above sea level.

In 1936, Franklin D. Roosevelt approved a grant of $1,422,730 to build The Wolf Creek Highway between Seaside and Portland, which was opened in 1938. This new route provided two hour auto and bus transportation between the Portland area and the coast. The highway name was changed in 1946 to the "Sunset Highway" and became the shortcut to the sea from the Portland metropolitan area. It is now U. S. Highway 26. The distance to the coast was cut to 78 miles as compared to 136 miles over the Columbia River route. Many improvements to Highway 26 have been made since 1938 and travel time today is usually one and three-quarter hours.

After 1940, Arch Cape finally had easy access from the north, south and east and was no longer isolated. Growth began with gusto following the war years; yet, today Arch Cape remains a relatively quiet and peaceful residential community, a village blessed with the mountains to the east, the ocean and Castle Rock to the west, and the protection of the Cape to the south and Hug Point to the north.

The primitive road around Hug Point was blasted out of sandstone and hard basalt rock about 1910 and made travel between Cannon Beach and Arch Cape easier. Before, a very low tide was necessary to allow travelers to use the beach as a highway. That is a Franklin automobile in the foreground and a Buick in the background. Woodfield postcard photo. Circa 1918. Authors' collection.

Silver Point, circa 1932. Castle rock and the Arch Cape headland are in the distance. Photo is an early post card by Sands. From Eldridge/Coffman album.

Cutting the highway through Humbug Point, circa 1932. Photo is an early post card by Sands. Authors' collection.

Road toward Arch Cape. The culvert carries Asbury Creek across the highway. Circa 1930. Photo source unknown. Authors' collection.

Tunnel construction at the north portal. Oregon Department of Transportation photo. Circa 1937.

Tunnel construction at the south portal. Rail tracks on each side show the method of excavating around the central core and the placing of timbers. Note the man dumping a wheelbarrow over the top of the central core. Oregon Department of Transportation photo. Circa 1937.

Tunnel after excavation completed and ready for the timber lining. Photo labeled "WoodfieldPhoto." Circa 1939. Authors' collection.

Tunnel with the timber lining in place. Photo labeled "Woodfield Photo." Circa 1940. Authors' collection.

Tunnel and bridge complete with roadbed ready for paving. Looks like Maxwell Avenue entrance in the foreground. Oregon Department of Transpotation photo. Circa 1940. Authors' collection.

The end of the road at Arch Cape where cars parked somewhere between Leech and Maxwell Avenue on what is now Gelinsky Boulevard. Three of my aunts are in the picture. Authors' collection.

It was work getting cars through the dry sand and up onto hard ground at Leech Avenue. The Leech house, today the Tyrrell house, is in the background. That is Ralph Forbes at the left—giving encouragement. Authors' collection.

Kent A. Price with the Elk Creek Toll Road sign. Kent Price photo, 1963.

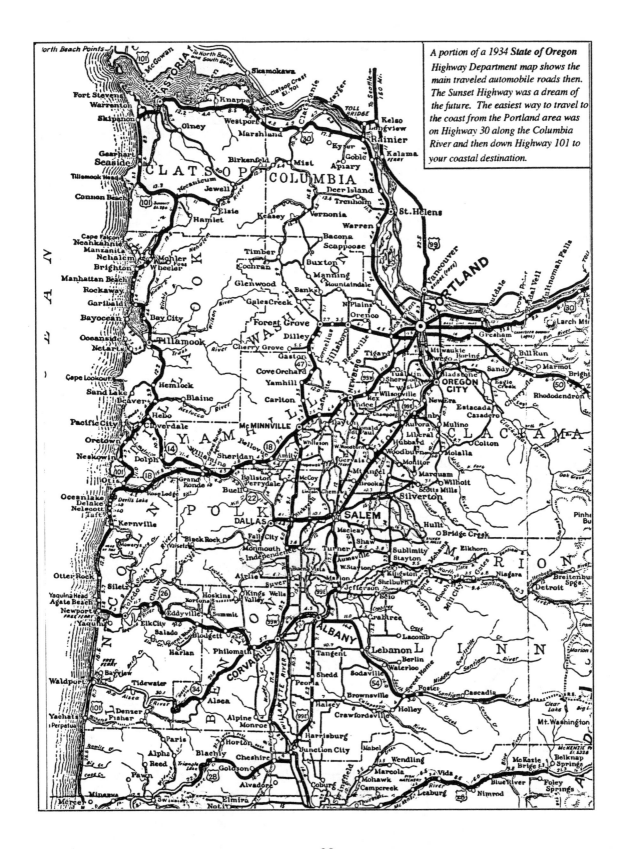

A portion of a 1934 **State of Oregon** Highway Department map shows the main traveled automobile roads then. The Sunset Highway was a dream of the future. The easiest way to travel to the coast from the Portland area was on Highway 30 along the Columbia River and then down Highway 101 to your coastal destination.

Arch Cape Post Office

The post office at Arch Cape has a colorful history, beginning when the mail arrived by ship in Astoria in 1850. The first settlers in the Tillamook area agreed to make the trip to Astoria once a month to pick up the mail. They were to take turns or pay for a substitute to take their turn for them. Often, the substitute was a Native American, who charged only five dollars for the round trip. Mr. Eldridge Trask's house at Tillamook was the first pick-up and delivery station south of Astoria.

In 1887, a twenty-eight mile star mail route from Seaside to Nehalem was established. From 1891 to 1901, the *Austin House*, one-quarter mile south of Hug Point, was the first Cannon Beach Post Office for the Ecola area which included Cannon Beach, Tolovana and Arch Cape. It was here that mail carriers from Nehalem in the south and Seaside in the north met to exchange mail sacks. On May 29, 1891, Mr. James P. Austin, an English immigrant, became postmaster. Mr. Austin named the post office "Cannon Beach," memorializing the elusive cannon from the *Shark*. In 1894, Mr. Austin died of tuberculosis, before the cannon was found, and Mrs. Austin succeeded him as postmistress until 1901, when the post office closed. The rambling *Austin House* served as a hotel, home, general store and post office. The building is gone today, but the site near the beach in north Arch Cape is marked by a Clatsop County historical marker erected in 1961. The house stood on the ocean front west and a short distance north of where the cannon is presently located on Highway 101. The mail was carried by stage, horseback or on foot in all kinds of weather and trail conditions. During the winter, the mail run was over trails; in the summer, they used the beach whenever possible. The heavy mail sacks were locked before the journey and could not be opened except by the postmaster, who had the key. The carrier could not pick up or deliver mail between the post offices. In summer, using a buckboard, supplies and passengers were delivered with the mail from Seaside.

One of the most hazardous parts of the journey was rounding Hug Point. Its name originated from the way its point projects so far into the ocean that it can be walked around only at low tide. At other times travelers used a higher and longer trail or climbed around the point using hand and foot holds, which were made by Native Americans and are still visible today. The holds led to a shallow ledge and from there to other indentations, so the climber literally hugged the cliff. Later, a crude road was blasted through the hard basalt rock and used for rounding the point. The mail deliverers who came to *Austin House* were very familiar with the beach, tides, sand bars and tide pools.

According to a 1987 *Seaside Signal* article, the first mail carrier was John Gerritse, a young Dutch sailor who had jumped ship in Astoria to become an American. He worked on a Clatsop Plains farm and went to school for a year to learn English. The next year he began carrying the mail from Seaside to Tillamook. It was a week-long round trip. John often stopped in Nehalem, where young people danced all night and where, in 1896, he met Mary Edwards, who lived with her family on 160 acres which are now part of Manzanita. Mary and John were married on John's birthday, November 10, 1888. He was 24 years old and she was 16.

After their first baby was born, Mary and their new daughter and two dogs, stayed in a cabin that John built on the Nehalem River. It was while living there alone in the woods that Mary overcame her fear of the dark, the trees, storms, wildcats, bears and living alone. John taught her how to shoot and she practiced, which gave her much confidence—and some wild game as well.

In 1897, after three more children were born, John purchased a farm in Manzanita. He was also renting seven saddle horses to people who wanted to go north to Seaside with the mail carrier. John couldn't find a satisfactory man to carry the mail for him while he farmed, and since Mary was good with horses and begged for the job, he gave her the honor. She took over the route in 1897 and carried the mail from Nehalem to the Austin House until 1901.

The trail over Neahkahnie Mountain was difficult. It was only twenty inches wide in places, and farther on, it led down a very steep cut to Short Sands Beach and over a precipitous trail to Cape Falcon. Once when Mary was riding her horse, Prince, on the narrow Neahkahnie Mountain part of the trail, she had to pass three men on horseback. They were 400 feet above the ocean, but she says she didn't know how to be afraid anymore, although the men were frightened. She loved the adventure. There was one particular part of the trail on Neahkahnie that was especially steep. Her story, told in her own words, is recorded in the 1987 summer and fall issues of *Cumtux,* the Clatsop County Historical Society Quarterly.

Mary says:

At a sharp turn where it started along the rim, I always got off and hiked because the trail was so hard for the horse. I got off on the side opposite the canyon. My weight, as I slipped against the side of the hill, threw Prince off his balance and his hind feet slipped off the trail. He threw himself backwards and lunged to leap back on the trail, but instead, slid down fifty feet, hit a tree and changed ends. The heavy stock saddle broke his fall so he didn't break his back, but one rib was cracked. When he turned, he went around the tree and slid down 150 feet more to the bottom of the canyon facing downward toward the ocean 300 feet below. I knew if he tried to get up where he'd landed on a slanting rock, he would slide head first down into the ocean. The mail tied to the saddle probably saved him from being skinned up too badly.

Mary followed him down and arrived almost as soon as the horse did. She talked to him and soothed him while breaking brush around the area. The main thing was to keep him quiet until a path was cleared for him to turn around and face the upper part of the canyon.

Mary remembers:

When I talked and pulled on the rope, he would respond and try to help get around. Finally, he made a big lunge and got to his feet. It had taken two hours to break the brush with my hands and get him to his feet. We followed the creek up the canyon three hundred feet to where I could get him up onto the trail. By that time he was trembling like a leaf. I hiked all the way to the Cannon Beach Post Office and back home twenty-four miles and did not ride him.

She finishes the story by saying they were three hours late getting to Nehalem and everyone was worried about their safety. It was surprising they were not much later returning home. Prince rested for a few days. The large swelling on his side indicated two broken ribs, but he recovered.

Prince followed Mary everywhere. Once, she was chasing some cattle, and in order to head them off, she jumped off Prince and slid down a steep bank she didn't think her horse could negotiate. When she reached the bottom, Prince was at her side. Another time, he saved her from a falling tree limb. They were standing under a large tree when Prince suddenly jumped to the side and she followed him, although she didn't know why. The limb fell where they had been standing. It could have been fatal. Sometimes he woke her when she overslept on the trail.

One day after a storm, three big waves swept Prince onto the rocks near the arches at Arch Cape. His hoof was caught and his ankle wrenched. John, who was working on the Cape Falcon trail, had to destroy him.

In 1904, the Gerritses moved to Seaside and Mary carried the mail for another eight years. Mary left mail in leather bags hanging on posts. This was known as "Rural Free Delivery," serviced out of Seaside with the address, "Ecola Route, Seaside." She went on horseback in winter and used a team and wagon when weather permitted, fording Elk Creek at low tide. In 1910, the Ecola Post Office was established at Elk Creek and she left the mail there, including mail for Arch Cape, until 1912, when she retired.

For the next two years Arch Cape again had a postmaster. His name was William C. Adams. The book *Clatsop County, Oregon* by Emma Gene Miller, states that Bill Adams, Paul Bartell's brother-in-law, built the *Arch Cape Hotel* in 1905, and apparently ran the post office from that building in 1912 and 1913. Marmaduke Maxwell, who built his Arch Cape home in 1912, purchased the *Arch Cape Hotel* from Mr. Adams in 1914. After that, Arch Cape residents picked up their mail in Tolovana. In 1914, state highway 53 was built from Seaside to Tillamook, making mail delivery easier, except, of course, for Arch Cape. The *Warren Hotel*, situated where *Tolovana Inn* stands today, was an early mail drop for Arch Cape residents. Later, Mary and Duncan Shields had the Tolovana Post Office in their Tolovana grocery store. Janie Brown was postmistress there until Mrs. Shields became postmistress in 1934. Marmaduke Maxwell brought the mail from Tolovana for Arch Cape residents by horseback during those early years. In subsequent years, Eugenia Holderman rode Mr. Maxwell's horse to pick up the Arch Cape mail during her summer vacations.

In 1939, Mr. Ernest White built a structure, known for years as the *Beach House* and now known as the *Inn at Arch Cape*, on the newly constructed Highway 101. It served as his lodging place, a general store and the post office. In those years, his mother, Mrs. Ross White, ran the post office.

Approximately seven years later, the building was enlarged by adding two apartments on the ocean side. Mr. George Hurd moved in and ran the post office for a short while. He was followed by Mrs. Peckover, sister of Mr. Durmire, a local builder. Then Maxine Smith, wife of the shingle mill owner Charles Smith, became postmistress.

In 1953, Ethel LeGault took over the store and post office. She built a new store in 1960 and enlarged it in 1961 to include the post office. To inaugurate the addition, Ethel LeGault celebrated the event with food and door prizes. At closing time, a large crowd sang the Happy Birthday song to Mrs. LeGault and her store and post office. This is the space where the post office and deli/grocery are located today, over thirty years later.

After Ethel LeGault's death in 1971, Ron and Yvonne Rothert purchased the store. That same year, Cliff Harrison, after twenty-five years in the Seaside Post Office, became the officer in charge of the Arch Cape Post Office. Marcia Rothert, Ron and Yvonne's daughter-in-law, was trained by him and worked in the post office Saturdays. When Mr. Harrison went to work at the Cannon Beach Post Office in 1973, the Rotherts applied to the Post Office Department to become a contract station. Their son, George and his wife Marcia, the postal clerk, managed the store and Post Office and the recently acquired gas pumps until 1981. At that time, Ron and Yvonne Rothert sold to Jack and Dorothy Meece. The Meeces ran the store with Dorothy serving as postmistress for the next six and one-half years. They sold the business to Jim Perna and Barbara Bangle and Barbara became postmistress in 1987. In 1990, Steve and Debbie Anderson and Gregory and Carla Mosley bought the business and the post office contract. Christine Baetzle was postmistress followed by Debbie Anderson.

The post office in the deli building on Highway 101 remains the place where Arch Capers trek once a day, whatever the weather, to collect the mail and to greet each other. There are often neighbors visiting over a cup of coffee and the morning newspaper around the large table. Our post office is special in this and in its history, which adds to the flavor of the town.

The Austin House—the first Cannon Beach post office, one-quarter mile south of Hug Point. Mr. James P. Austin was postmaster from 1891 until he died from tuberculosis in 1894. His wife, Lydia, succeeded him as postmistress until 1901, when the post office closed. The rambling Austin House served as a hotel, home, general store and post office. George Shields photo courtesy of the Cannon Beach Historical Society. Circa 1892.

The top photo shows the Arch Cape post office and store from the north in 1942. Note the tall trees on both sides of the highway and the tunnel in the distance. The bottom photo shows the enlarged building when two apartments were added on the ocean side in 1946. "For Sale" signs appear in both photos. Photo sources unknown. Both are post card photos.
Top photo, Coffman/Eldridge album. Bottom photo, Authors' collection.

POST OFFICE AND GROCERY STORE ~ ARCH CAPE, OREGON

Arch Cape Area Geology

T he following material was furnished to me by Dr. James Richmond, retired professor of geology, Los Angeles State University. Dr. Richmond and his wife Gracie were long-time visitors to the northern Oregon coast, first visiting Cannon Beach in 1937. They rented for a number of summers near Lion Rock, just north of Hug Point. The Richmonds purchased their Arch Cape home in 1972 and sold it in 1985, following the death of Gracie. Now Jim resides in Carmel, California, and has been a summer visitor to Arch Cape for years.

An article written by Alan R. Niem published in the ORE BIN, Volume 37 Number 2, February, 1975, describes the Arch Cape-Hug Point geologic history. Permission to reprint information from the publication is granted by the State of Oregon Department of Geology and Mineral Industries.

Many thanks to Dr. Richmond for his guidance and encouragement in the preparation of this material. A glossery of geologic terms appears at the end of this article.

David K. English

Physiographic Features

The Hug Point-Cannon Beach area is part of the Coast Range physiographic province, which extends from the Coquille River and the Klamath Mountains on the south to the Columbia River on the north and is bordered by the Willamette Valley on the east and by the Pacific Ocean on the west. Average elevation of the Coast Range is about 1,500 feet. The 3,000-foot peaks adjacent to Hug Point State Park, Sugarloaf Mountain and Onion Peak, are among the highest in the northern Oregon Coast Range.

The coastline is characterized by steep headlands, sea stacks (small offshore islands), and long narrow beaches. The precipitous headlands, such as Tillamook Head to the north and Arch Cape to the south of Hug Point State Park consist of well-cemented sandstone and are separated by coves which have been eroded in softer sandstone by the pounding waves of countless winter storms. The sea stacks are eroded remnants of resistant basalt sills and dikes.

The inland area just east of Hug Point State Park is a region of forested small rounded hills with lowlands and intervening stream valleys carved into sedimentary rocks. Farther east are prominent steep ridges and rugged mountains composed of basalt.

Bedrock Geology

Hug Point State Park and the surrounding area is underlain by the middle Miocene Astoria Formation and by Miocene Depoe Bay Basalt and Cape Foulweather Basalt.

Astoria Formation

The Astoria Formation in this area is composed of two informal units, the 1,100-foot thick Angora Peak sandstone member named for outcrops in Angora Peak, located about 3 miles southeast of Arch Cape, and the overlying 650-foot thick Silver Point mudstone member named for outcrops at Silver Point.

Angora Peak member: The Angora Peak sandstone member consists of thick layers of laminated and cross-bedded, feldspathic and lithic sandstones interbedded with minor layers of well-laminated, dark-grey, carabonaceous and micaceous siltstones, and channel pebble conglomerates. Local coal beds occur near Angora Peak. The well-indurated sandstones are carbonate cemented, typically orange yellow and iron stained, and at Hug Point State Park form sea cliffs 50 to 100 feet high. The sandstones are medium to very course grained, locally pebbly, and moderately to poorly sorted. They are composed of predominantly subangular and subrounded quartz, plagioclase, potash feldspar, and volcanic rock fragments. Fine-grained fossiliferous shallow-marine sand-stones and siltstones in the upper part of the unit are well laminated, highly carbonaceous, and micaceous. The channel conglomerates and fluvial cross-bedded sandstones contain abundant subrounded, poorly sorted pebbles of quartz, pumice, basalt and andesite, chert, quartzite, and tuff.

Silver Point member: The Silver Point mudstone member, which overlies and may interfinger with the upper part of the Angora Peak sandstones, is composed predominantly of dark, laminated, silty mudstones and very thin-bedded, light-gray, tuffaceous siltstones. The lower part of the Silver Point member is characterized by rhythmically interbedded dark-gray mudstones and light-grey, fine-to-medium-grained, laminated, feldspathic sandstones. Rare channel graded pebble conglomerates also occur. The laminations are produced by a concentration of muscovite, biotite, and dark carbonaceous plant fragments. Sandstones and conglomerates have sharp bottom contacts and gradational upper contacts, are graded, and locally contain contorted laminations, load casts, flute and groove marks, and mudstone rip-ups. The lower part of the Silver Point member is well exposed in the sea cliff at Silver point adjacent to U. S. 101 two miles north of Hug Point.

Deep-maring microfossils occur in the Silver Point mudstone in Ecola State Park. The mudstones contain abundant montmorillonite clay and form extremely unstable hum-mocky slopes. There have been destructive landslides along the coast where winter wave erosion has undercut the support of cliffs composed of this mudstone. At Silver Point, several scarps and landslide terraces contain asphalt slabs of old highway 101. Just south of Silver Point, a 1,200-foot-wide landslide in these mudstones occurred in February, 1974.

Depoe Bay Basalt

The Depoe Bay Basalt, named for exposures at Depoe Bay, Oregon, is a hard, dark-grey, finely crystalline basalt. In the northern Coast Range, it lies with angular unconformity on the underlying Silver Point and Angora Peak members of the Astoria formation. At nearby Sugarloaf Mountain and Onion Peak, it forms more than 2,000 feet of resistant basalt breccias and rarer isolated pillow lavas and pillow breccias. The breccias consist of poorly sorted, angular fragments of dark aphanitic basalt and basaltic glass in a matrix of dark-yellow-brown palagonite and basaltic glass (sideromelane and tachylyte). The brecciated lavas were extruded on the ocean floor and formed by fragmentation of hot molten lava flows coming in contact with the cold sea water.

Numerous Depoe Bay Basalt sills, dikes, and irregular intrusions associated with the extrusive Depoe Bay breccias penetrate the underlying Astoria Formation. Some sills are thick (up to 600 feet) and form wave-resistant headlands, such as Tillamook Head near Seaside and Neahkahnie Mountain, four miles south of Arch Cape. These large sills generally dip gently to the southeast and are commonly in fault contact with the surrounding Astoria Formation. The sills range from finely crystalline basalt to diabase and are characterized by well-developed, nearly vertical columnar jointing. The dikes are finely crystalline to aphanitic basalt and are also columnar jointed. They are generally thinner than the sills and irregular in shape. Small sills and dikes are abundant in Hug Point State Park. Thin, reddish baked zones occur where the hot lava came in contact with the surrounding host rock.

Cape Foulweather Basalt

The Cape Fowlweather Basalt was named for exposures at Cape Foulweather north of Newport, Oregon. The unit overlies the Depoe Bay Basalt and the Astoria Formation in the Oregon Coast Range. It is characterized by large, scattered, yellow phenocrysts of plagioclase in a groundmass of aphanitic to finely crystalling, dark-grey basalt. Cape Foulweather submarine breccias overlying Silver Point mudstones form Haystack Rock near Cannon Beach. A Cape Foulweather Basalt sill is exposed near Silver Point. The Depoe Bay and Cape Foulweather Basalts are middle Miocene in age (14 to 16 million years old based on potassium-argon dating).

Unconsolidated Deposits

Marine terrace deposits occur in small coves between headlands. They are 25 to 40 feet thick and are composed of thin layers of well-sorted, reddish, iron-stained beach sands, lenses of rounded basalt gravels, layers of peat and carbonized tree limbs, irregular gray, thin ancient soil horizons, and thin ash beds. The deposits are soft and unconsolidated and can be excavated easily. The anatomy of a marine terrace deposit (30 feet thick) is well exposed along the beach near the parking lot at Hug Point State Park.

Beach sands are laminated, well sorted, and fine grained. Subangular to subrounded quartz and feldspar are the dominant mineral constituents. In the winter, several feet of the beach sands are removed by strong storm waves to form offshore bars, thus exposing the underlying well-rounded basalt gravels on the upper parts of the beach zone.

Landslides are common along the coastal sea cliffs, particularly in the Silver Point mudstones and Angora Peak sandstones and in marine terrace deposits between Hug Point and Arch Cape. Landslide terrane is hummocky and poorly drained. Cliff exposures of landslides along the beach consist of chaotic mixtures of gray, sticky, plastic muds, with tree limbs and blocks of basalt, and sandstone. Recent movement on landslides is recognizable by cracks in the pavement of the highway and by trees tilted in many directions.

Geologic History

The rocks in the Hug Point-Cannon Beach area were deposited during the Miocene Epoch (approximately 13 to 35 million years ago). During and since the Pliocene Epoch (3 to 13 million years ago), the rocks of the Coast Range have been gently uplifted, faulted, folded, and eroded. The strata are unconformably overlain, in places, by a thin veneer of Pleistocene marine terrace deposits, Holocene dune and beach sands, and stream alluviam (gravel, silt, and sand).

Miocene Epoch

During the middle Miocene, much of western Oregon was uplifted above sea level. Along the western margin of the uplifted area, however, local subsidence produced a shallow marine embayment from the Hug Point-Cannon Beach area to Astoria. Great quantities of sand, mud, and gravel were transported westward from the early Cascade Mountains and eastern Oregon, Washington, and Idaho via an "ancestral Columbia River." These sediments were deposited in the Hug Point-Cannon Beach area in the form of a large delta, much like the Mississippi or Niger delta today. The delta contained a distributary river system and intervening coal-forming marshes and swamps. Along the delta front, strong wave-energy reworked the sands in the form of shallow-marine bars, beaches, and spits and into a broad sheet of shallow-marine, fine-grained sands with shells of mollusks and other marine animals. These lithified sediments form the Angora Peak sandstones, the main cliff-forming unit in Hug Point State Park.

The embayment continued to subside, and, in time, the shallow-marine sands of the Angora Peak member were superseded by deep-marine muds of the Silver Point member. The graded sandstones in the Silver Point member probably were deposited by turbidity or density currents of muddy water which formed as a result of submarine slumping or sliding of muds and sands from the delta front into a deeper basin. The graded bedding formed where the coarser and heavier grains suspended in the current settled out first and were followed by the finer grains. The mudstones and thin siltstones represent the clays and silts that settled very slowly by pelagic sedimentation on the sub-marine part of the delta. Uplift and erosion produced an unconformable surface on the Astoria Formation. This was followed by further subsidence and inundation by the sea.

During the latter part of the middle Miocene, great volumes of basalt breccias (the Depoe Bay Basalt) were erupted on the deep-sea floor from a north-south trending series of submarine volcanic centers. Eroded remnents of the volcanic rocks now form the two highest peaks in the Hug Point-Cannon Beach area—Sugar Loaf Mountain and Onion Peak. This submarine volcanism was contemporaneous with eruption on land of the Columbia River Basalt of eastern Oregon and Washington.

The submarine lava flows along the coast were fed by many basalt dikes. Some dikes and sills intruded and locally deformed thick piles of semi-conslolidated Astoria Formation strata. In certain places, forceful intrusion of hot magma into these water-saturated sediments formed dikes of pepperite composed of angular blocks of altered basalt, sandstone, and mudstone. Great volumes of steam were generated as a result of this interaction and may have helped displace and deform the semi-cohesive sediments in the contorted form seen on the beach just north of Hug Point. Steam blasting incorporated angular pieces of the host sedimentary rock into the dike. A north-trending pepperite dike occurs approximately 600 feet north of Hug Point.

Pliocene Epoch (3 to 13 million years ago)

During the Pliocene, the Coast Range was uplifted. No marine Pliocene strata are recognized in the Hug Point-Cannon Beach area, but thick strata occur in the nearby offshore area. During this time of mountain building, a large north-south syncline with its axis trending across Onion Peak and Sugarloaf Mountain and a smaller adjacent anticline were formed. The sedimentary strata and breccia were also displaced several hundred feet by high-angle faults, one set trending east-west and the other north-south. Some smaller faults are visible in the sea cliffs at Hug Point State Park where adjacent layers of Angora Peak sandstone have been broken and displaced. An anticline and an adjacent syncline in Angora Peak sandstones with east-west trending axes are readily observable in Hug Point State Park. These small folds may have formed during the Pliocene, or earlier at the time of the middle Miocene intrusions. The syncline near Austin Point has a width at beach level of about 600 feet and the anticline has a width of 1,000 feet. The strata were tilted from 23 to 44 degrees to form these folds.

Pleistocene (11,000 to 3 million years ago) and Holocene Epochs

Erosion became the dominant geologic process after the main uplift and deformation of the Coast Range in the Pliocene Epoch. Stream and sheet erosion excavated valleys in the softer Angora Peak sandstones and Silver Point mudstones, leaving the harder, resistant Depoe Bay Basalt sills and dikes as elongated narrow ridges and the volcanic breccias as high, rugged mountains.

Sea level fluctuated several times during the Pleistocene owing to development of continental glaciers and their subsequent melting. In addition, continued uplift of the Coast Range may have influenced the relative sea level. As a result, wave-cut benches representing former stands of the sea lie 40 to 100 feet above present sea level along this part of the Oregon Coast. In Hug Point State Park, wave erosion planed off the flat surfaces that now form the tops of the sea cliffs. Beach sands and gravels were deposited locally between headlands to form flat marine terraces.

Since the Pleistocene, waves have been carving a new wave-cut bench below the surface of the water and have been eroding away parts of the less resistant rocks to form stacks, caves, notches, cliffs, and narrow sand beaches, leaving the more reisitant headlands, such as Hug Point.

Hiking Field Trips Along the Beach

A short, interesting hike along the beach and sea cliffs beginning at the Hug Point State Park parking lot is available. Points of interest along this hike are shown on the enlarged geologic map of the Hug Point area:

(A) Austin Point A small headland appears approximately 600 feet south of the parking lot. A thick, dark dike of Depoe Bay Basalt intrudes yellow, cross-bedded, coarse-grained Angora Peak sandstones. The sandstones dip 40 degrees southwest and form Austin Point (passable at low and slack tides).

(B) Small headland approximately 780 feet south of Austin Point There is a sill of Depoe Bay Asphalt 10 feet thick in Angora Peak sandstones. The sill has well-developed, columnar joints that formed perpendicular to the cooling surface. The baked zone is only a few inches thick. Between Austin Point and this headland is the axis of a westward-dipping syncline. At this location, one limb of the syncline is dipping northward and the other limb can be seen in the southward-dipping beds of Austin Point.

On the south side of the small headland is a good example of cross-bedding involving pebbly sandstone with very thin mudstone interbeds. Grading along the cross-beds probably represents deposition in large submarine sand waves at the mouth of an ancient river channel. The orientations of the cross-beds indicate that the river currents flowed from east to west. Abundant pebbles of quartz, quartzite, pumice, and chert, basalt, and andesite suggest that the material was eroded from the ancient Cascade Mountains and rocks of eastern Oregon and Idaho and brought here possibly via an "ancestral Columbia River." Some fragmented fossil plant debris, including carbonized logs up to eight inches long, can be found in these channel deposits. The homes south along the beach are built on a flat Pleistocene marine terrace

(C) Eroded cliff of Pleistocene marine terrace deposits approximately 200 feet south of Hug Point parking lot The deposits are composed of soft, iron-stained, easily crumbled or pulverized beach sands, carbonized tree limbs, and thin, reddish, clayey ancient soil horizons. This terrace deposit fills an old cave cut into the Angora Peak sandstones. Winter storm waves now undercut the soft terrace deposits, resulting in many landslides. Several live trees are tilted in a variety of directions where landsliding has been recently active. In winter the beach consists of basalt gravels and piles of logs.

(D) Small sandstone headland approximately 400 feet north of parking lot

(passable during low or slack tide) Laminated, coarse-grained Angora Peak sandstones, cut by a thick Depoe Bay Basalt dike with well-developed columnar jointing, are partly contorted, but the overall dip is to the north, representing the limb of the anticline whose axis passes approximately through the parking lot. The sandstone contains many small calcareous and pyrite-filled nodules. The southwest side of the headland has been infilled with blocks of alluvium. The abrasional action of beach sand and the hydraulic compressive force of waves have created a deep, narrow sea cave in a crack between the basalt dike and the sandstone.

(E) Waterfall and sea caves 550 feet north of parking lot The waterfall is in the northward dipping Angora Peak sandstone. Ocean waves have undercut the sandstone faster than the downcutting of Fall Creek, resulting in a waterfall here. The pinnacle of Angora Peak sandstone is a resistant erosional remnant. A fault between the pinnacle and Fall Creek is a possible reason for the location of Fall Creek.

(F) Hug Point Large deep sea caves and sea notches are carved into Angora Peak sandstones by storm waves. South of Hug Point, blocks and layers of sandstones are verticle or overturned. Note the abrupt vertical break between the contorted strata and the layers of cross-bedded sandstone 20 feet east of where the old stagecoach road rises above the beach. This break is a high-angle, north-south trending fault; the layers on the west have been moved upward relative to the contorted layers on the east. A narrow sea cave has formed along this fault where the strata were broken and fragmented and thus were easier for waves to excavate.
    Follow the old stagecoach road around Hug Point (passable during low and slack tides). Note that the pebbly cross-bedded Angora Peak sandstones that form Hug Point dip 15 degrees northeastward. The prints of many wagon wheels cut deep ruts in the old roadbed.

(G) Sea cliff 70 feet high approximately 200 feet northeast of Hug Point There are verticle standing beds of Angora Peak sandstones in a contorted zone 50 to 100 feet wide. Differential erosion has cut a bowl-shaped depression into many of the vertical layers. The sandstones are mostly fine grained but contain some local conglomerate channels and pebbly zones. Two thin basalt dikes cut through the deformed sandstones.

(H) Sea Cliff 1,000 feet north of Hug Point A pepperite dike at the base of the cliff consists of angular blocks of fine-grained laminated Angora Peak sandstones and altered greenish to dark-grey basalt in a sand matrix. The dike trends north-south, is approximately 15 feet wide, and is partly covered by beach sand. Associated with the dike are vertical beds of very fine-grained, Angora Peak sandstones which are a continuation of the contorted zone 200 feet northeast of Hug Point. The pepperite dike probably formed as a result of steam blasting and quenching of hot molten basalt magma in contact with water-saturated, semi-consolidated Angora Peak sands soon after their deposition. The forceful intrusion of the magma displaced and folded the strata into a vertical position. Microfaults that formed in the mobilized semi-consolidated sands can be seen in the sea cliff.
    Note the hummocky landslide area to the north of this sea cliff. The ocean is undercutting the toe of the slide, setting the scene for continuous landslide movement in this area.

Road Log From Silver Point to Arch Cape on U.S. 101

The stops in this 4-mile road log are shown on the geologic map of the Arch Cape-Cannon Beach area and include two short hikes to the beach.

Stop 1 Follow U.S, 101 north from the Hug Point parking lot for two miles to Silver Point. Pull off the road at southernmost viewpoint.

Sea stacks at Silver Point, west of the first parking lot, are wave-eroded remnants of a once more-extensive basalt sill. To the north is the steep cliff of Tillamook Head, a 600-foot thick basalt sill. Haystack Rock in the foreground is composed of Cape Foulweather Basalt pillow lavas and breccias unconformably overlying Silver Point mudstones. Hug Point can be seen to the south. The large roadcut on the east side of U.S. 101 exposes the Silver Point mudstone member of the Astoria Formation. Approxmately 200 feet above this exposure are the overlying Depoe Bay submarine basalt breccias that form the high hills above the roadcut. Recent landslide debris in the center of the roadcut illustrates a common engineering geology problem in these mudstones.

The sea cliff directly below the viewpoint parking lot is a large landslide block composed of interbedded fine-grained graded sandstones and silty mudstones typical of the Silver Point member. A trail over the slumped pavement of old U.S. Highway 101 provides access to the beach.

Proceed south 0.1 mile on U.S. 101.

(0.1) In the spring of 1972, a section of U.S. 101 two-tenths of a mile in length dropped three to six inches as the result of a landslide in the Silver Point mudstones. In February 1974, after heavy rains had saturated the mudstones and winter storm waves had undercut support of the toe of the slide, there was extensive renewed movement. U.S. 101 dropped 25 to 35 feet vertically and moved 100 feet toward the sea. The slide covered an area of 1.25 square miles and destroyed this section of U.S. 101 and several homes. The headscarp of the slide is a quarter of a mile above the road. In order to stabilize the landslide, highway engineers terraced the slope near the top of the slide to remove excess weight, developed a drainage system to remove surface and ground water, and re-aligned the highway. The road now curves around the slide.

(0.5) In roadcuts on both sides of U.S. 101, a basalt dike is exposed which intruded and deformed blocks of Angora Peak sandstones.

(0.7) **Stop 2** Humbug Point. (Arcadia State Park) Pull off on the gravel road at the day-use area. Follow the trail to the beach. The small headland 100 feet to the north (Humbug Point) is held up by a 20 to 30 foot thick basalt dike surrounded by a chaotic mass of sedimentary blocks of fine-grained, well-laminated Angora Peak sandstone in a pebble sandstone matrix. The force of the intrusion probably deformed and broke these semicohesive strata because this sedimentary breccia zone parrallels the trend of the dike. Some small pyrite nodules and crystals can be found between the sedimentary breccia fragments.

(2.0) Continue south on U.S. 101 at the intersection with the Hug Point State Park road.

(2.3) The north limb of the syncline of Angora Peak sandstones is in the deep roadcut on both sides of the road. The beds dip 45 degrees to the south.

(2.5) The south limb of the syncline of Angora Peak sandstones is dipping 35 degrees northward. A thin basalt sill parallels the bedding.

(2.7) **Stop 3** Pull off on the left. The Cannon Beach historical marker tells about the shipwreck of the U. S. Naval schooner *Shark*, in 1846, from which cannons washed ashore fastened to a section of the deck.

(3.5) You are entering Arch Cape. Arch Cape is built on flat Quaternary marine terrace gravels and sands.

(3.6) **Stop 4** Take the paved road at the south end of Arch Cape just before entering the tunnel toward the ocean for one-tenth of a mile. Walk south about 800 feet to the headlands that forms Arch Cape and cross Arch Cape Creek. Arch Cape is a large intrusion of Miocene Depoe Bay Basalt that forms a southeast-trending ridge one mile long and 400 feet high. Very well developed fan-like columnar jointing and huge incorporated blocks of Angora Peak sandstone occur on the seaward face of Arch Cape and passable only at low tide. The highway tunnel just south of the town of Arch Cape is bored through this basalt mass. There are two arches eroded through the basalt at sea level about 300 feet south of the stream and around the tip of the cape: therefore, the name Arch Cape.

GEOLOGY GLOSSERY

ANDESITE — A dark colored fine-grained extrusive rock that often contains phenocrysts of plagroclase and pyroxine in a ground mass of the same minerals.

APHANITIC BASALT — A dark rock of such close texture that its separate grains are invisible to the naked eye.

BASALT — A grey to black dense to fine-grained rock suggestive of the intrusion or extrusion of magma or the activity of volcanoes or formed by solidification of molten magma, composed chiefly of calcic plagioclase and pyroxene.

BIOTITE — Generally black or dark green form of mica forming a constituent of crystalline rocks and consisting of a silicate of iron, magnesium, potassium, and aluminum.

BRECCIAS — A rock consisting of sharp coarse-grained fragments embedded in a fine-grain matrix (as in sand or clay).

CARBONACEOUS — Containing carbon or coal; also a period of the Paleozoic Era.

CHERT — Rock resembling flint.

DIABASE — An intrusive rock as contrast to extrusive basalt, conspicuous by plainly visible crystals of plagioclase and pyroxene.

FELDSPAR — Any of a group of crystalline minerals that consist of aluminum silicates with either potassium, sodium, calcium, or barium. They are constituent of nearly all crystalline rocks.

HOLOCENE — Most recent epoch following the Pleistocene Glacial Era.

HUMMOCKY — Rounded knolls and hillocks.

INDURATED — Hardened.

LITHIC — Relating to or made of stone.

MICACEOUS — Any of the various colored or transparent mineral silicates crystallizing in monoclinic forms that readily separate into very thin leaves.

MIOCENE EPOCH — 13 to 35 million years ago, preceeding the Pliocene Epoch.

MONTMORILLONONITE — A group of expanding lattice clay minerals swelling on wetting and shrinking on drying. Complicated chemistry.

MUDSTONE — Hardened shale produced by the consolidation of mud.

MUSCOVITE — A mineral that is colorless to pale brown potassium mica.

PELAGIC — Relating to, or living or occurring in the open sea.

PEPPERITE — Dark color tuff containing various minerals, crystals, and fragments of rock.

PHENOCRYSTS — A rock with large crystals prominently embedded in a fine-grained ground mass.

PHYSIOGRAPHY — Study of the description and origin of land forms.

PLAGIOCLASE — A mineral that at high temperatures forms a complete solid solution and is a common rock-forming mineral having calcium or sodium in its composition.

PLEISTOCENE — 11,000 to 3 million years ago - the Glacial or earlier epoch of the Quaternary Period.

PLIOCENE EPOCH — 3 to 13 million years ago-the earliest epoch of the Tertiary Period and immediately preceeding the Pleistocene Epoch.

QUARTZITE — A hard but unmetamorphosed sandstone compacted by pressure solution of quartz grains.

QUATENARY — The most recent Period which includes the Holocene (recent) and Pleistocene (glacial) Epochs. The period includes four episodes of continental glaciation.

SCARP — A line of cliffs produced by faulting or erosion.

SIDEROMELANE — Basaltic glass commonly found as chilled margins of dikes, sills, or flows.

SILTSTONES — A rock whose composition is between sandstone and shale and of which at least two-thirds is material of silt size between 1/256 to 1/16 mm.

TACHYLYTE — Black glossy basalt. (same as sideromelane)

TUFF — A general term for all consolidated pyroclastic rocks; that is, rocks formed by volcanic explosion or aerial expulsion from a volcanic vent. Consolidation is the gradual reduction in volume and increase in density of a soil mass in response to increased load or effective compressive stress. Tuff has this history. Mt. St. Helen's pyroclastics are still ash, not old enough to have experienced compression of 50%.

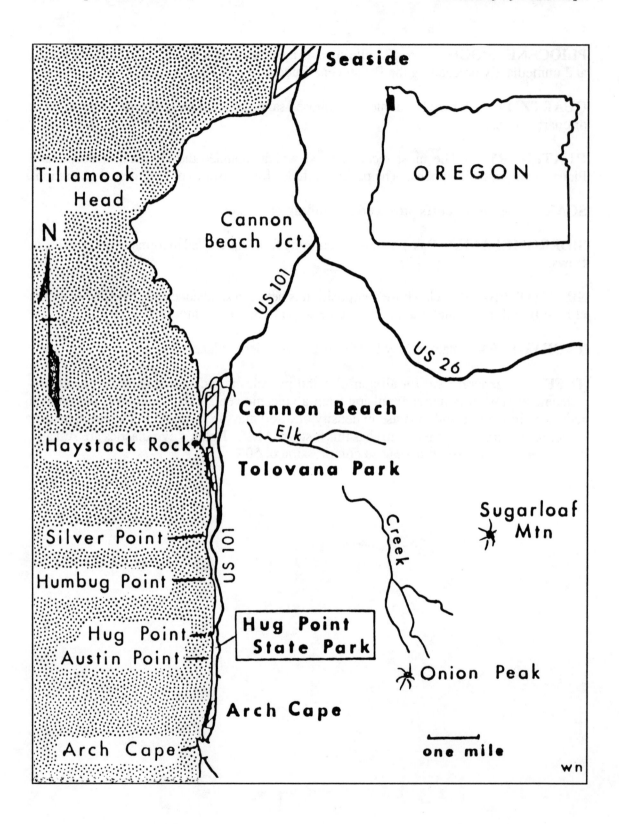

Seaside

OREGON

Tillamook
Head

N

Cannon
Beach Jct.

US 101

US 26

Cannon Beach

Elk

Haystack Rock

Tolovana Park

Creek

Sugarloaf
Mtn

Silver Point

Humbug Point

US 101

Hug Point
State Park

Hug Point

Austin Point

Onion Peak

Arch Cape

one mile

Arch Cape

wn

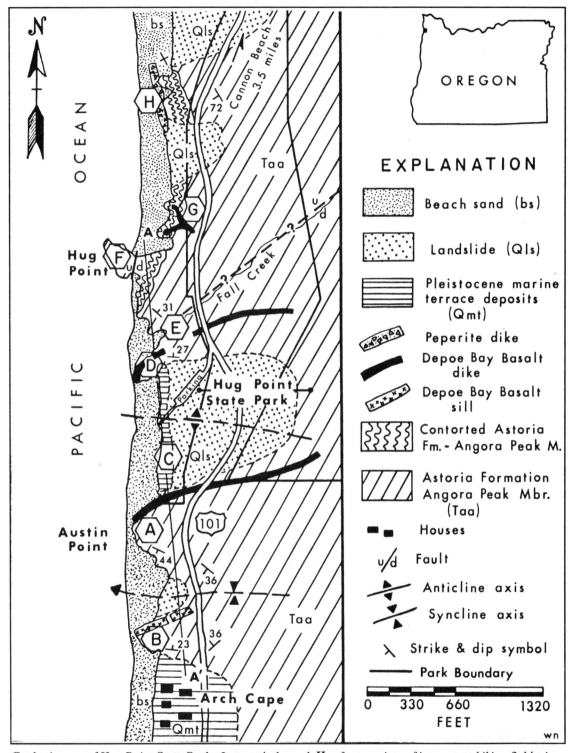

OREGON

EXPLANATION

Beach sand (bs)

Landslide (Qls)

Pleistocene marine terrace deposits (Qmt)

Peperite dike

Depoe Bay Basalt dike

Depoe Bay Basalt sill

Contorted Astoria Fm. – Angora Peak M.

Astoria Formation Angora Peak Mbr. (Taa)

Houses

u/d   Fault

Anticline axis

Syncline axis

Strike & dip symbol

Park Boundary

0   330   660   1320
FEET

wn

Geologic map of Hug Point State Park. Letters A through H refer to points of interest on hiking field trip described in text.

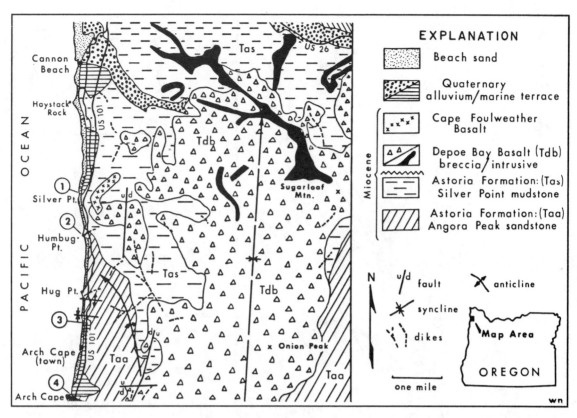

Geologic map of the Arch Cape-Cannon Beach area. Numbers *1* through *4* refer to stops on highway field trip described in text.

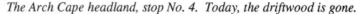

The Arch Cape headland, stop No. 4. Today, the driftwood is gone.

Sea cave with dark basalt dike on left and light-colored Angora Peak sandstone on right. A thin basalt dike also cuts diagonally through the sandstone on right. David English photo.

At its mouth, Fall Creek plunges over a waterfall onto the beach between sea caves on left and the pinnacle with a thin vegetative cap. David English photo.

Coastal stagecoach road blasted into the sea cliff at Hug Point. David English photo.

South entrance to the Hug Point stagecoach road. David English photo.

St. Peter the Fisherman Church

Arch Cape's St. Peter the Fisherman Church stands at a slight elevation east of Highway 101 behind a split rail fence. The graying cedar siding exterior resembles many of the homes in the area, and the weathered shingles on its roof give it a rural and rustic appearance. Over the front door, a carving of St. Peter in a fishing boat with its pile of nets blends with the seascape and its immediate surroundings. This church is the result of the dreams, prayers, hard work, and financial gifts of local Catholics in the 1960's who desired a place to worship for themselves and Arch Cape visitors. Since its completion, St. Peter's has also served as a community center for Arch Cape. It is a place for classes, health checks, potlucks, business meetings, programs, and large celebrations.

The basic church building was completed in 1965 after years of effort and planning spearheaded by Mrs. Ethel LeGualt, who came to Arch Cape in 1953 and became the postmistress and owner of the Arch Cape Grocery. The idea began to take shape in her store in 1963 with a conversation between Mrs. LeGualt and Mr. Maurie Clark, a local resident and philanthropist. They consulted with Father Nicholas Deis, who was at that time the pastor of our Lady of Victory Church in Seaside. These three "go-getters" saw no reason to hesitate and proceeded to make their dream for a mission church in Arch Cape a reality. Mrs. LeGualt collected $8,000 for the project and Maurie Clark offered to underwrite the balance.

They engaged a lawyer to hold donations in escrow for the Diocese, and to find out who owned potential land sites which were for sale. Mr. Ernest White donated land in memory of his wife, but the site was considered too far off the road. Arch Cape residents Howard Vollum and Dr. Leo Meinberg, with many other contributors, purchased and donated property on the highway instead.

Father Deis, who had just finished overseeing the building of a convent, sought parishioners from the Cannon Beach, Arch Cape, and Seaside areas to work on the new construction. They hired two lead carpenters and imported two amateur carpenters from the Jesuit Novitiate in Sheridan, Oregon. Although not a member of St. Peter's, Mr. Floyd Scott recruited the local work force, with the assistance of Berkeley Snow. Also, Mr. Scott asked weekenders to bring their hammers when they came to town. Approximately twenty men worked for three months to assemble the basic structure. Father Deis helped whenever his schedule permitted.

It is not possible to list all the donors to this church because so many gave their time and whatever money or goods they could afford. Perhaps only fifty percent are known by name at this time. In this chapter a few are mentioned regarding specific items, but many others helped during that summer of 1965 and later. Two lists were mailed to members: one asked for cash, which was sent to the chancery; the other requested needed items. Getting St. Peter's built took a lot of "sweat and tears." As Reverend Henley from the Chancery said, "The sweat came from the men and boys who had not worked that hard before and the tears from those trying to pay the bills."

Services and materials came from many sources. Mr. Wilbur Markham donated the surveying. Mr. Walter Church, a local architect, designed and contributed the drawings. Crown Zellerbach donated the logs and Neidermeyer Martin Lumber Company sawed the timbers as a gift to the project. Lumber and plywood were purchased and Oregon Brass gave the hardware. The Sisters in Seaside made the wooden boat and carving of St. Peter that is above the door, as well as The Stations of the Cross inside the building. Larry Ward, a floor covering specialist and brother-in-law of Ethel LaGault, supplied the floor tile for the church hall and donated his time to surface the floor. A packing plant in Astoria loaned its crane and operator for positioning the trusses. Dick Grulick did all the wiring and hung the light fixtures. Ferris Ferrington completed the cabinet work in the kitchen and the Ed Polaske family furnished the kitchen stove. Parishioners and other local citizens contributed everything from the land to all the furnishings needed for a complete sanctuary: vestments, books, altar cards, candlestick holders, and chalices. Jim Hannen, a Cannon Beach artist, created three stained glass windows which he made as memorials given by parishioners. He installed the last one in 1990.

Mr. and Mrs. Brady of Manzanita donated a Hammond organ that later began to blow fuses. Maurie Clark offered to purchase a replacement in 1988. Inarose Zuelke, occasional organist at St. Peter's, volunteered to find a new organ. She located a fine Italian instrument in Portland for $7,000, but Inarose didn't want to offer more than $4,000 of Mr. Clark's money. She explained how much it was needed and why, and the seller said "**SOLD**" for $4,000. "You do deliver," Inarose asked. "Absolutely," he replied. Inarose then asked, "Have you ever heard of Arch Cape?" He turned white but kept his promise and did deliver the organ.

The church bell came from the old St. Mary's Hospital in Astoria, a gift from The Sisters of Providence. Second collections paid for the bell tower. A Seaside parishioner (name unknown) built the brass tabernacle, which other parishioners polished and lacquered. Two water color paintings by Jule Kullberg, artist and former Arch Cape resident, hang in the Parish Hall. Bridget Snow gave one in memory of her husband, Berkeley; Lucille Houston donated the other in memory of Monsignor Smith. It was gifts such as these that enriched the St. Peter's project. Community members worked hard with many devoted Catholics to complete the project. Maurie Clark met the payroll for carpenters, roofers, and glazers; he also paid workmen's compensation and insurance for the volunteers.

During construction, Father Deis' sense of humor kept things moving smoothly. Although comically moaning all the while, he put aside personal considerations and worked enthusiastically to help in many ways. He facilitated orders through the Diocese and arranged for the work to proceed. In addition, he communicated with and encouraged the parishioners. His energy seemed miraculous. His letters to the Chancery Office or to Maurie Clark were often typed between midnight and four in the morning, since by day he kept busy with Our Lady of Victory parish in Seaside as well as with the Arch Cape project. The Chancery commented that both his handwriting and typing were getting harder to read, but the humor contained in the letters compensated for any eyestrain incurred.

The church is simple, designed to fit the liturgical changes taking place at that time. Architects planned the Nave to be small for easy maintenance in winter and yet expandable for summer crowds. The Nave is 36 feet by 64 feet and seats 70 people; the Parish Hall, which opens into it, is 36 feet by 74 feet, providing seating for an additional 130 worshipers. Outside the Nave is a twelve foot vestibule with a small ante room dedicated in 1976 to Ethel LeGault. Inside the Sanctuary are a sen wood altar, life-size statues of Our Lady and St. Joseph, and a hand-carved crucifix from Italy. Mrs. Gertrude Derrah of Surf Pines fashioned the holy water font; and Jay Stewart, from Cannon Beach, made and donated a baptismal font, a later addition. In 1986, Mr. Tom Hughes, an Arch Cape artist and woodworker commissioned by Maurie Clark, completely remodeled the altar. He also installed new benches, shelving, carpet and candle holders in 1986. In 1988, he made a frame for the baptismal font.

The estimate for building expenses was $40,000. This figure included the concrete floor, which was $3,500; the heating plant, $1,835; and, with donated help, $1,900 for the sanctuary. Other costs were for building materials, drainage field, septic tank, grading, gravel, clearing, benches and carpentry. Mr. Clark said that costs exceeded the estimate, but they carried no debts and proceeded on donations.

The first Mass and a simple blessing occurred November 14, 1965, with Father Deis as Celebrant. On December 19, 1965, Archbishop Howard formally dedicated St. Peter the Fisherman Church at Arch Cape. After viewing the ocean from the front door, the Archbishop told the parishioners he expected they would spend a long time in Purgatory because they were enjoying Heaven on earth now.

The first priest assigned to St. Peter the Fisherman Church was Monsignor Charles Smith, retired from the Reno Diocese and more recently from a chaplaincy in the Navy at Tongue Point. He resided in Arch Cape while serving as pastor of this mission church from 1965 to 1974, when ill health forced him to move east to be with his family until his death in 1977. He is remembered fondly, as is his dog McDuff, usually called Duffy, who walked on the beach with him as he read his breviary and lay at his feet when his master paused.

After Monsignor Smith left, the Jesuit Order from Portland cared for the Arch Cape Mission, supplying priests until 1976. In that year Father Gerald Quintal from the House of Studies in Portland took over care of the Arch Cape church until 1978, when he became a pastor in Salem. Since then, Jesuits from Jesuit High School in Portland have been providing priests for Mass Saturday evenings and Sunday mornings.

The year after St. Peter's was finished, Father Deis retired and Father Maurice Grammond became pastor of the Seaside Church and the Arch Cape Mission.

In 1973, Maurie Clark purchased a duplex next to the church for use as a rectory and a retreat house for parish priests on one side and a caretaker's apartment on the other. Owning the duplex gave the church a square piece of property measuring 400 feet on each side. Angelo and Lucille Costanzo moved from Mill Road into this duplex to maintain the church, the grounds, and the apartment for priests. Angelo died in 1986 and Lucille moved to Vancouver, Washington. Sister Bernadette Ann Sohler then came as resident helper to serve the church and visiting clergy. Gardeners from Coaster Properties keep up the grounds, and janitors from Seaside clean the church. The area behind the church plot is used as a picnic site and will be donated to the church. The woods behind it are home for bear, coyote, and elk.

Sometime in the midst of the hurly-burly of building in 1965, Father Deis, Maurie Clark and Mark Gill, contributors to the church, were drinking "a tall one" and talking about a name for the new edifice. Mark Gill favored "St. Mark" and Father Deis suggested something " . . . by the Sea". Maurie disagreed with them, saying too many churches already had those names, so they commissioned him to choose one by himself. After much discussion with his wife and research in the phone book, he came up with the name St. Peter the Fisherman, a name both uncommon and appropriate.

After Maurie chose the name, Ethel LeGualt found a dusty religious picture in a book store and purchased it to donate to the church. She took the picture to be reframed and the framer discovered that behind the top print was one of St. Peter the Fisherman! This was confirmation enough. Maurie and Ethel hung that picture in the vestibule in the new frame— and the name was adopted.

Today, St. Peter the Fisherman Church is a landmark for this community and is a natural focus for the life and activity in this small community. Many people benefit from its existence in Arch Cape and are thankful for the spirit and generosity of those who worked so hard and gave so much to make it all possible.

St.Peter the Fisherman Church sits in rural Arch Cape east of Highway 101. The bell tower shows at the northeast corner of the church and the rectory and retreat house for parish priests along with caretaker's quarters is immediately east of the church. Photo source unknown.

Many willing hands helped during construction. Photo source unknown.

Kelps in Clatsop County
by
James W. Markham, Ph. D.

Kelps are the largest and most conspicuous seaweeds on this coast. Kelps are a kind of seaweed, and seaweeds are a kind of algae.

ALGAE

Algae are a very large and diverse group of organisms, occurring in all habitats, including fresh water, seawater, hot springs, snow, and deserts. They range in size from microscopic phytoplankton to giant kelps over 100 feet long. The only things all algae have in common is that they are all plants and they have reproduction unlike that of other plants. Botanists have divided the Plant Kindom into 24 Divisions. Algae comprise 9 of all of these Divisions. Flowering plants, from pansies to palm trees, are all in one Division, which indicates how much more diverse algae are. Most algae grow in water. Those that grow in fresh water are called freshwater algae. Those that grow in the ocean are called marine algae or seaweeds.

SEAWEEDS

Most seaweeds fall into one of three major Divisions, which are distinguished by several characteristics. The most obvious characteristic distinguishing Divisions of seaweeds is pigmentation, which gives them distinctive colors. The three groups are the Green Algae (Chlorophyta), the Red Algae (Rhodophyta) and the Brown Algae (Phaeophyta). Divisions are divided into Classes, which are divided into Orders, which are divided into Families, which contain various Genera (singular = Genus), which contain one or more Species. An individual alga is designated by a Genus and species name (for instance, *Nereocystis luetkeana*). Some seaweeds have common English names, but most only have Latin botanical names. Sometimes the same common name has been applied to several different species of algae and some species have several different common names. Some widespread algae have different common names in several languages. This can be very confusing. In order to avoid confusion it is usually better to use the Latin names of plants, because each name is unique to only one species and is the same no matter what language one is speaking.

There are also two marine flowering plants on this coast, the sea grasses. These are the surf grass (*Phyllospadix*), which has long narrow, cord-like, dark green leaves and grows on rocks exposed to surf; and the eel grass (*Zostera*), which has long, flattened, bright green leaves and grows on sandy or muddy bottoms in sheltered bays. These are true flowering plants and not algae. They have inconspicuous flowers and an internal anatomy like other flowering plants. All the rest of the marine plants on this coast are algae.

SEAWEED DISTRIBUTION

Different seaweeds have different requirements for their habitat, which limit where they can grow. Large scale geographic distribution of seaweeds is controlled primarily by temperature. The seaweeds found on the Oregon Coast are only those which can tolerate fairly cold ocean water. Most of them could not survive if the sea water in summer exceeded a certain temperature, but this critical temperature is different for each species. Local distribution of these cold-water seaweeds is controlled by their tolerance or requirements for other factors. The most important of these are exposure to surf; exposure to drying during low tide; and light. Another factor which controls the distribution of some local seaweeds is burial under sand. [See *Laminaria sinclairii*]

Surf

Some seaweeds grow only where they are pounded by surf. An example is the kelp *Postelsia palmaeformis*, the sea palm. Some other seaweeds cannot tolerate surf at all and grow only in sheltered bays.

Drying

Some seaweeds grow in the intertidal zone, that portion of the shore which is exposed and falls dry during low tide. Others are restricted to the subtidal zone, that portion of the nearshore ocean bottom which is never exposed by low tides. Seaweeds which can tolerate more drying can grow higher up in the intertidal zone, where they are exposed for longer periods by low tides. The highest kelp on these shores is usually *Hedophyllum sessile*. At the other extreme, two kelps, *Nereocystis luetkeana* and *Macrocystis integrifolia,* are restricted to the subtidal zone.

Light

Requirements and tolerance for light are very important in controlling the vertical distribution of seaweeds. Seaweeds are plants and plants need light to survive and grow. Some cannot tolerate high light. Some seaweeds need more light and some are adapted to grow in very low light. Anything growing at the upper limit of the intertidal zone will normally be exposed to full intensity sunlight for fairly long periods of time during low tides. At the other extreme, organisms confined to the subtidal zone are never exposed to full sunlight.

Algae which cannot tolerate high light can also grow higher in the intertidal zone by growing on shaded sites. These may be underneath larger algae—the underbrush of the algal forest—or under an overhanging rock, or perhaps in the deepest part of a tidepool which holds water when the tide goes out. An extreme example of an alga which grows very high in the intertidal zone but tolerates very low light, is found in the caves at Hug Point. On the walls of the caves, so high it is often not submerged in sea water for days at a time, is a reddish fur, which is the red alga *Adouinella purpurea*. This alga tolerates extremely low light, long periods of drying, and even, at times, dripping fresh water. The same plant can grow in more light and more submergence. In these cases it grows much larger than in the caves.

KELPS

There are several Orders in the Brown Algae. The Order of the most complex and largest algae is the Laminariales. The members of the Laminariales are called **kelps**. A typical kelp plant has three parts: **holdfast, stipe and blade (or frond)**. These correspond roughly to the roots, stems and leaves of higher plants, but do not have the same structures or functions. Kelp plants are attached by holdfasts, which consist of finger-like appendages called haptera, which adhere to the surface. These are not quite the same as roots, because roots anchor the plant and also take up water and soil nutrients for the plant. Holdfasts only attach the plant. They do not need to take up water, etc. for the plant because the entire kelp can get all the water and nutrients it needs when it is submerged at high tide. Above the holdfast is the stipe, like a stem or a tree trunk. The stipes of some kelps are stiff enough to hold the plant upright when is is out of the water. Unlike stems, kelp stipes do not transport water up from the base because the entire plant is bathed in water. At the top of the stipe is the blade, also called frond or lamina. There may be one or several blades, depending on the species. They are usually thin and flat and may be branched or simple. Blades correspond to leaves in shape and position, but the function of higher plant leaves to gather light to make food for the plant is performed in kelps by the entire plant. The primary growing part of a kelp plant is not at the tip as is the case with a tree, but rather in the region between the stipe and blade, called the transition zone. Thus a blade grows at its base and sometimes may be eroded away at its tip, if surf is heavy for instance. This erosion does not affect the growth of the plant because the growing part is protected. Some perennial kelps shed their blades at the end of a season and then grow new blades the next season. Since the growth area is at the base of the blade, this is no problem.

The kelps on the shore represent one phase of the kelp life cycle. At certain times of year, the blades have reproductive areas called sori (singular = sorus) which produce swimming spores. These microspopic spores are released when the kelp is submerged and swim to the bottom. There they settle down and develop into miscroscopic male or female plants, the other phase of the kelp life cycle. The male plants produce swimming sperm which swim to eggs produced by female plants. These sperm fertilize the eggs and the result of this union grows into the large kelp plant visible on the shore.

Clatsop County Kelps

Habitat:
　　　All the kelps listed here have been collected at the sites listed in Clatsop County. When Arch Cape is listed, this refers to the rocky area around the Cape, not the sandy beach, which lacks suitable attachment for kelps. Those kelps which grow in the intertidal zone may be seen attached to rocks at low tide. Those restricted to the subtidal zone can only be seen by non-divers when they wash up in the drift on the beach after being detached from the bottom. All the kelps listed here have been found in the drift at some time on the Arch Cape beach.

Classification:

There are three Families of Laminariales or kelps on the Clatsop County Coast. These families are separated on the basis of elaborations and variations on the basic body plan. In all, 9 genera and 11 species of kelps have been found in Clatsop County.

Laminariaceae

This family has the kelps with the simplest structure, representing the typical kelp body. There are 3 genera and 4 species in Clatsop County.

Laminaria setchellii

Plant consists of a single rigid stipe, ca. 1" in diameter and 20" long, arising from a holdfast consisting of many coarse, branched haptera. The single blade is smooth and flat, 5" to 9" wide, deeply divided, almost to its base, into many uniform segments, in a palm-like manner. The whole plant is up to 50" long, perennial from the stipe, with the blade shed and renewed every year.

Habitat: On rocks in the lower intertidal and upper subtidal zone.

Sites: Indian Point, Ecola Point, Chapman Point, Haystack Rock, Jockey Cap, Hug Point, Arch Cape, Gull Rock.

Laminaria sinclairii

Plant consists of many stipes arising from the holdfast. Holdfast is an extensive system of coarse branched haptera. Stipes are very narrow, flexible and cord-like, ca 1/4" in diameter and 12" long. Blades are flat, smooth and narrow, usually less than 2" wide and up to 3 ft. long. Blades are shed every year, then renewed.

Habitat: Lower intertidal zone, on rocks which are buried under sand in summer. In years when the sand is high, the entire plants are buried. In other years, only the holdfasts and parts of the stipes are buried. This plant does not grow in places which are never buried under sand. It is one of very few algae that can withstand sand burial and sand scouring.

Sites: Indian Point, Ecola Point, Chapman Point, Haystack Rock, Jockey Cap, Lion Rock, Hug Point, Arch Cape, Gull Rock.

Hedophyllum sessile

Plant is a broad, irregular blade, 12" long and about 30" broad, sometimes deeply divided, with haptera arising directly from the blade, with no stipe. This plant has the basic *Laminaria* plan, lacking one important element, the stipe.

Habitat: On rock in the middle intertidal zone. This kelp is found higher on the shore than any others.

Sites: Indian Point, Ecola Point, Chapman Point, Haystack Rock, Jockey Cap, Lion Rock, Hug Point, Gull Rock.

Costaria costata

Plant consists of a single stipe, somewhat flattened, about 1" wide and 6" to 10" long,

and arising from a holdfast of branched haptera, with a blade up to 24" long and 12" wide. This kelp is easily distinguished from others because the blade has five prominent ribs extending through its whole length, each projecting on one side only and alternating, with three ribs on one side and two on the other side. The portion of the blade between the ribs is puckered, causing one book to call this the "seersucker kelp."
Habitat: On rocks in the lower intertidal to upper subtidal zone.
Sites: One specimen has been found at Ecola Point.

Alariaceae

This family has plants showing the basic kelp body plan, but with the addition of lateral blades arising from near the transition zone between the stipe and the main blade, or from the stipe itself. The main blade has a prominent midrib. Sori are borne on the lateral blades, which are called sporophylls, There are 2 genera and 3 species in this family in Clatsop County.

Alaria marginata

Mature plant consists of a single stipe, 1" to 3" tall, arising from a mass of wide-spreading haptera. Main blade is broad and as long as 100" or greater, with a conspicuous midrib. Many flat, smooth lateral blades arise at the upper end of the stipe near the transition zone.
Habitat: On rocks in the lower intertidal zone, exposed to considerable surf.
Sites: Tillamook Head, Indian Point, Bald Point, Ecola Point, Chapman Point, Haystack Rock, Jockey Cap, Hug Point, Arch Cape, Gull Rock.

Alaria nana

Mature plant consists of a stipe 2" to 3" long, arising from a holdfast of branched haptera, and a relatively broad blade, up to 30" long when intact, with a conspicious midrib. Many (20-50) lateral blades arise from the stipe, just below the transition zone. This plant has a relatively longer and stouter stipe than *Alaria marginata*, but the plant as a whole is smaller. In areas exposed to much surf, the main blade is often eroded back to its base, leaving only the stipe with its lateral blades.
Habitat: On rocks in the middle intertidal zone only in areas exposed to the full force of surf.
Sites: Indian Point, Bald Point.

Egregia menziesii (Feather Boa Kelp)

Mature plants are up to 30 feet long, with a branched stipe arising from a sturdy compact holdfast. The stipe is cylindrical in its lower portions, up to 1/2" in diameter, and flattened higher up, becoming 4" to 6" wide, with its rough surface covered by many blunt projections. From each edge of the stipe, many flattened blades, 1/2" to 3/4" wide, and many small air bladders or floats arise. The kelp is often called the Feather Boa Kelp because of its appearance.
Habitat: On rocks in the middle intertidal to upper subtidal zone in areas exposed to considerable surf.

<u>Sites:</u> In Clatsop County this species has only been found in the drift on the beach. It probably grows on Castle Rock and the outer sides of Haystack Rock and similar sites.

Lessoniaceae

This kelp family includes the largest plants in the ocean, as well as some of the most complex kelps. The stipes are branched. The branching is produced by splits which originate in the transition zone, then progress toward the end of the blade, as well as down the stipe. There are 4 genera, each with one species, in this family in Clatsop County.

Lessoniopsis littoralis

Plants are up to 80" tall with a very sturdy holdfast up to 6" wide at its base. The stipe is woody and rigid, like a small tree trunk, in its lower portions, and repeatedly and regularly branched in its upper portions, resulting in very many stipes, with long, narrow blades, 1/4" to 3/4" wide and up to 30" long. A narrow midrib runs the length of each blade.
<u>Habitat:</u> On rocks in the lowermost intertidal zone in areas exposed to the full force of the surf.
<u>Sites:</u> Indian Point, Bald Point, Ecola Point, Chapman Point, Haystack Rock, Jockey Cap, Hug Point, Arch Cape, Gull Rock.

Macrocystis integrifolia

This is the smaller northern relative of the giant kelp of California (*Macrocystis pyrifera*), the largest kelp in the world. Holdfast is flattened and branched, with numerous branched haptera arising from the margins. Multiple stipes arise from the holdfast. Stipes are slender, 1/2" in diameter and from 20 to 60 feet long, depending on where they grow. Leaf-like blades arise at intervals along the stipe. At the point of attachment of each blade to the stipe is a round, gas-filled float. Above the float, each blade is flat and wrinkled, broad at the base and gradually tapering to a pointed tip. Hundreds of blades with basal floats may be borne on each stipe. The floats support the plant so that the upper portions float in the water, and allow the whole plant to drift long distances when it becomes detached from the bottom.
<u>Habitat:</u> On rocks in the lowest intertidal and upper subtidal zone in areas protected from heavy surf, such as inlets and bays, but only in areas with full ocean salinity, i.e. not diluted by any fresh water. There appear to be no such sites in Clatsop County, and the plants found here have probably drifted a considerable distance.
<u>Sites:</u> Found as drift on the beach at Arch Cape.

Nereocystis luetkeana (**Bull Kelp**)

This kelp is one of the largest kelps in the world, and the largest which grows in Clatsop County. From a massive holdfast, up to 15" broad, composed of many branched haptera, a long stipe arises which is solid in its lower third and then gradually larger in diameter and hollow in the upper two thirds. The stipe may be up to 80 feet long in some cases. The hollow stipe terminates at its upper end in a single, hollow, spherical float, 4" to 6" in diameter. From the top of the float, 2 clusters of flat, smooth, branched blades arise, which are 4" to 6" wide and up to 14 feet long. This kelp, the largest and most conspicuous on our beaches, has often been called "Bull Kelp" because it resembles a bull whip. Some of those washed up on the beach may be densely covered with smaller algae, expecially red algae, growing on them as epiphytes. This is a very interesting and remarkable plant. Although it is the largest kelp in local waters, it is an annual plant. All this tremendous length is attained in a few months of rapid growth, which in June may be as much as 6" per day. Young plants usually begin to grow about April and reach their maximum length by about September. The plants grow only in the subtidal zone and are held upright in the water by the hollow float. The plants usually grow until they reach the surface of the water, so those bull kelps which grow in deeper water will grow longer. In late fall and winter the holdfast loosens its attachment to the bottom and the plant drifts away, eventually winding up on a beach.

Habitat: Restricted to solid surfaces—bedrock, boulders, etc—in the subtidal zone, growing as deep as 60 feet. This kelp forms offshore kelp beds which can be seen from the shore because the floats float at the surface and the fronds stream out near the surface.

Sites: Found in drift on all Clatsop County beaches, especially in fall and winter.

Postelsia palmaeformis (Sea Palm)

This kelp resembles a small palm tree, 6" to 12" tall. A thick hollow, cylindrical stipe arises from a holdfast composed of numerous short, stout, finger-like projections. At the top of the stipe is a group of blades, as many as 100. The blades are 1/2" to 1" wide and up to 10" long. The flat blades are covered on both sides with longitudinal grooves. The upright stipe with blades hanging down looks very much like a palm tree.

Habitat: This kelp grows only in the middle to lower intertidal zone on rocks which are exposed to the most severe battering from surf. All the sites in Clatsop County which are exposed to enough surf for *Postelsia* are inaccessible on foot. This kelp is often found in the drift on the beach at Arch Cape and it seems likely that it grows on the west side of Castle Rock.

Sites: Found in drift on beaches, especially at Arch Cape.

For Further Reading

A—Books

Abbott, Isabella A. & Hollenberg, George J. (1976). *Marine Algae of California.* Stanford: Stanford University Press.

> This is the most comprehensive guide to Pacific seaweeds, including all species, not just the common ones. Although this book is for California, it works very well as an Oregon guide because there are very few seaweeds in Oregon which do not also occur in California. Excellent line drawings make identification much easier.

Bold, Harold C. & Wynne, Michael C. (1985). *Introduction to the Algae : Structure and Reproduction. 2nd ed.* Englewood Cliffs : Prentice-Hall.

> Excellent general text on the biology of algae.

Dawson, E. Yale. (1956) *How to know the seaweeds.* Dubuque : Wm. C. Brown Publishers.

> Picture key to identify seaweeds. This is for both Atlantic and Pacific Coasts and includes only the most common seaweeds, but it works well for identifying these.

Dawson, E. Yale. (1966). *Marine Botany: An Introduction.* New York : Holt, Rinehart & Winston.

> A general introductory text to learn about seaweeds in general.

Lüning, Klaus. (1990). *Seaweeds: Their Environment, Biogeography and Ecophysiology.* New York : John Wiley.

> Excellent modern discussion of the biology of seaweeds, with the best explanation of the effects of light on seaweeds.

Scagel, Robert F. (1967). *Guide to Common Seaweeds of British Columbia.* Victoria : British Columbia Provincial Museum.

> The common seaweeds of British Columbia are mostly the same as the common seaweeds of Oregon. This book has good drawings which aid in identification.

Waaland, J. Robert (1977). *Common Seaweeds of the Pacific Coast.* Seattle : Pacific Search Press.

> This is mostly about Washington and British Columbia, since there are many more suitable habitats for seaweeds there, but common seaweeds of Oregon will be found in this book. Drawings and excellent color photographs help identification.

B—Articles in Scientific Journals

Markham, J. W. (1968). "Studies on the haptera of *Laminaria sinclairii* (Harvey) Farlow, Anderson et Eaton." *Syesis* 1:125-131.

> Fragments of *Laminaria sinclairii* can produce outgrowths which grow into entire plants, which provides an alternative form of reproduction. No other kelp does this.

Markham, J. W. (1969). "Vertical distribution of epiphytes on the stipe of *Nereocystis luetkeana* (Mertens) Postels and Ruprecht." *Syesis* 2:227-240.

> Describes which algae grow on *Nereocystis*, at which height, and at what season of the year, at Friday Harbor, Washington.

Markham, J. W. & Newroth, P. R. (1972). "Observations on the ecology of *Gymnogongrus linearis* and related species." *International Seaweed Symposium Proceedings* 7:127-130.

> *Gymnogongrus linearis* grows only on rocks which are buried under sand in summer. The ecology of this red alga was studied at several sites in British Columbia and at Arch Cape, near the Cape.

Markham, J. W. (1973). "Distribution and taxonomy of *Laminaria sinclairii* and *L. longipes.*" *Phycologia* 11:147-157.

> *Laminari sinclairii* occurs from British Columbia to Southern California. A very similar kelp, *Laminaria longipes,* occurs from Southeast Alaska through the Aleutian Islands to the Kurile Islands [now Russian, once Japanese] in the Western Pacific. It was thought these two species might actually be the same species just growing in different places. Extensive field and laboratory studies, including reciprocal transplants between Alaska and Oregon, confirm that these two plants have several differences and are indeed two distinct species.

Markham, J. W. (1973). "Observations on the ecology of *Laminaria sinclairii* on three northern Oregon beaches." *Journal of Phycology* 9:336-341.

> A detailed study, with comparison photos between summer and winter, of how *Laminaria sinclairii* is buried under sand in summer, then exposed again in winter, and the ecological adaptations that allow this plant to survive this.

Markham, J. W. & Celestino, J. L. (1976). "Intertidal marine plants of Clatsop County, Oregon." *Syesis* 9:253-266.

> The most complete list of all seaweeds found in Clatsop County, 164 species, with details of exactly where and when tney were found, up to 1976. This paper represents the first record for the State of Oregon for 15 species of algae.

The Arch Cape Fire Department

The origin of the Arch Cape Fire Department was the result of action by the Cannon Beach Commercial Club in 1947. Kent H. Price, the Commercial Club President, appointed a committee of himself, Bud Campbell, and James Hicks (a retired Portland Fire Captain) to form such a district. A petition was filed in March of 1947 with the County Court to form a Fire District. The County Commissioners held the required public meetings during the month of April, and on May 14th, an election was ordered to elect five directors for the new district. Those elected were Frank Cox, Leonard Mansur, Charles Nish, William Silva and Harvey Willis. The district extended from Ecola State Park to the Arch Cape tunnel. In later years, it was extended to include Cove Beach.

The district purchased a surplus amphibious duck (a WW 2 landing craft) for $500 in 1947, outfitted it, painted it, and manned it for surf rescue work in the Cannon Beach-Arch Cape area. It had mobility but became a burden, and in two years, was exchanged for a rescue truck to use with swimmers. The truck allowed for quicker response in an emergency and was much easier and less expensive to maintain.

The volunteer Cannon Beach Fire Department was well-trained, had good equipment, and a dedicated chief, Delno McCoy, who had the ARCO station in Cannon Beach. The department was run on a shoestring budget, and Delno McCoy's shoestring at that.

Arch Cape enjoyed a spurt of growth in the 50's and 60's and had many new homes occupied by full-time residents. Fire protection for Arch Cape was furnished by the Cannon Beach Fire Department, which was over five miles away. This resulted in an undesirably long response time for Arch Cape emergencies.

In 1965 fire insurance rates for Arch Cape doubled because fire fighting equipment was too distant for quick initial response. The directors of the Cannon Beach Fire Protection District offered to place a fire truck in Arch Cape. First, the Arch Cape residents needed to find space to keep it secure, dry, and ready for quick response.

Much credit for bringing good fire protection to Arch Cape must go to the early leaders of the community who pushed for the creation of the Arch Cape Community Club in 1966. The first president, Mr. Walter Weibenson, was succeeded by Mr. Floyd Scott, in 1967. Under the leadership of Mr. Weibenson and Mr. Scott, and with help from Walter Church, Berkeley Snow, Elmer Ramsey, Lowell Hawkins, and Gale DeLashmitt, the Arch Cape Community Club decided to build a fire house as a club project. Over $2,500 was collected from local property owners. The convincing argument was that reduced fire insurance rates would return the cost within a few years.

Col. Maurice Simmonds, an Arch Cape resident and Secretary-Treasurer of the Cannon Beach Fire District, negotiated with the directors of the F. Theo. Dichter estate for land, which was then purchased by the Arch Cape Community Club. The county deeded an additional portion and also vacated that part of Walsh Avenue alongside the new station. This completed the building site owned by the club. The construction of the new fire house could now officially get under way. Many Arch Cape residents and others were involved with making the new fire house a reality:

Wilber A. Markham surveyed the property and gave approximately $100 worth of building lumber.

Walter Church designed the building and prepared the working drawings.

Ethel LeGault solicited gifts and kept track of funds designated for the new fire house.

Vic Shults conceived the idea of using fill rock from the bed of Arch Cape Creek. Charles D. Smith, his son-in-law, owned the adjacent Bear Creek Shingle Company and gave use of a heavy-duty bulldozer to scoop the gravel from the creek onto the Shults' yard for storage. Ray Gourley, an employee, operated the dozer without pay.

Charles and Maxine Smith gave all the shingles needed for the fire hall roof.

Clatsop County donated fifty feet of culvert, and Cannon Beach Lumber furnished the balance of the building material at cost.

Dick Greulich took off a week from his job and did all of the electrical work.

Mr. Jess Barton, District Property Agent for the State Highway Department, came from Salem to help clear up title to the property. The county commissioners, particularly Jim Scarborough, cooperated with help at the county level.

George Cole, Deputy District Attorney for Clatsop County, was most helpful in giving his time in aiding with the vacating of Walsh Avenue.

Lowel Hawkins contributed hours and hours coordinating all these donations of time, skills and materials. He supervised the construction and was called a "one-man-gang." The project would have been much more difficult without his devoted service. Bill North served as Hawkins' right hand man.

Hawkins and North, with the assistance of many willing volunteers, finished the building and dedicated it on July 1, 1966. The Arch Cape Community Club deeded the building and land to the Cannon Beach Rural Fire Protection District.

Fire Chief Delno McCoy sent a fire truck with additional equipment to complete the package. The first volunteer fire crew, all of whom had assisted on the station construction, consisted of John Hughes, Captain; Maurice Simmonds; Harold Schaeffer, Engineer; Elmer Vick; Ron Vick; and Travis Tyrrell. Training sessions were held each Wednesday at 7:00 p.m. with Chief McCoy. He was a very thorough teacher, so that by the end of summer, the crew was fire-ready. As predicted, fire insurance rates dropped.

There were several major fires after the Arch Cape Fire Station was activated in 1966. While not classified as a major fire, the first fire call was taken quite seriously, as were all fire calls. Captain John Hughes received a call from Cannon Beach indicating that there was a fire in a log house on Shingle Mill Road. The Arch Cape Crew responded with alacrity and hooked up to the nearest fire hydrant on Shingle Mill Road. The truck and most of the crew continued up the road, laying out hose to the only log cabin in the vicinity. Colonel Maurice Simmonds, with great presence of mind, stayed at the hydrant with a chemical extinguisher. He noted a monkey puzzle tree directly across the road from the hydrant. The fire truck was barely out of sight when a woman came out of the house behind the monkey puzzle tree waving her arms and shouting, "The fire is in here." Simmonds, with great haste, dashed into the house with the extinguisher and put out the fire. Damage was minimal except for the well-doused roast in the oven.

At three in the morning July 12, 1967, a fire totally destroyed the Arch Cape Shingle Mill, owned by Charles Smith. Firemen with two trucks from the Cannon Beach Department and the truck from the Arch Cape Fire Station responded to the call and stayed until 7:30 a.m. They kept the fire contained to the mill and put out spot fires to protect nearby homes and the surrounding forest. Water from the Arch Cape system and from the mill pond were used. They saved the office and a supply of shingles. The mill was not rebuilt.

In 1968 the Arch Cape crew responded to a call from neighbors that June Murphy's house on Beach Street was afire. June was not in residence at the time, so the fire was well advanced before the call came. The truck and most of the crew stopped at the fire and started pumping. Two men laid hose manually to the nearest hydrant at Beach Street and Markham Avenue, keeping the truck supplied with water. A truck from Cannon Beach soon arrived and started pumping, but little of the house was saved. Neighbors assisted by keeping nearby buildings wet with a hose connected to a private fire hydrant on Cannon Street immediately west of the fire. June Murphy rebuilt her home on the same site.

The Arch Cape home of Eugene L. Welling suffered approximately $13,000 in damage as a result of bedding getting too close to a baseboard heater in a bedroom where four people were asleep. Smoke and fire damage were severe, but the nine people in the home escaped without injury. The fire occurred April 25, 1969 at 2:30 a.m. Fourteen firemen and two vehicles responded from Cannon Beach and one rig came from the Arch Cape Station.

In 1977 Ed Wunderlich, who at that time owned the Viking Motel in Tolovana Park, was the lieutenant assigned to train Arch Cape fire fighters. Mike Graham joined the crew of seven which included Al Nelson, Jack Foster, Ed Elberson, George Rothert, John Tyrrell, and Bill David. The apparatus assigned to the Arch Cape station was Engine 77, a 1947 Mack, 750 gallon-per-minute pumper, which replaced the 500 gallon-per-minute Ford pumper. The Mack truck was extremely hard to drive. The steering wheel was gigantic and difficult to turn and the transmission gears were stiff and elusive. The batteries were weak and unpredictable. On numerous occasions the truck would be in the garage—dead. The rare Arch Cape calls and the tight maintenance budget in Cannon Beach meant little help trickled down to the smaller community; however, the pump on the old Mack, when provided with a proper transmission pump gear, was able to pump sufficient water from under the bridge.

In those days the Arch Cape engine responded to calls from Silver Point to Falcon Cove. The only Cannon Beach calls responded to were second alarm structure fires, which were infrequent. In 1977 there were two fire and ten medical calls in Arch Cape. The fires were minor, and since Mike Graham was not yet an Emergency Medical Technician, the Arch Cape Station did not respond to medical calls.

It was different in 1978, however. In the afternoon of June 18, the Arch Cape Fire Department responded to a structure fire in Falcon Cove. Someone had set an old shed on fire and Al Nelson, the only fire fighter to show up at the station, drove Engine 77 south and singlehandedly fought the fire until back up units from Cannon Beach arrived.

The next call came November 23. In a cabin on Highway 101 between Arcadia and Hug Point State Park where two young men attempted to start a fire in the fireplace with wet wood. Unfortunatley, they used a can of gasoline. The can exploded and set the house afire and severely burned one of the men. The two scrambled to their car to search for a telephone in the Tolovana Park area to call the fire department. At that time, each fireman had only a Plectron, a radio device kept at his bedside to alert the crew for an emergency. If the firemen were at work or away from home, they did not hear the call. Since the siren in Arch Cape had no power source, it did not work either. Consequently, Cannon Beach units put out that fire. Around six that same evening, it rekindled. This time, Mike Graham heard the call and raced to the fire station. He met Bill David there and both piled into Engine 77, but the truck would not start. Dead batteries! They grabbed their gear, jumped into their own cars, and raced to the fire where they met Cannon Beach units. The value of the building and contents were estimated to be $21,000 and it was a total loss.

One of the most spectacular and heartbreaking fires in 1978 occurred December 18, at 8:49 in the morning. That morning the temperamental truck with the battery problem did start, and it was a good thing. Dr. Filmer Carter's house off the intersection of Cannon Street and Ocean View Avenue was ablaze. Cold weather and icy roads added to the problem. Jack Foster, Bill David, and Mike Graham rode the truck to the Carter house, but the fire already had a head start. Flames lapped out of the garage door and the ground floor windows and they fought the fire to no avail. The walls had no fire stops and were covered by one-quarter inch paneling. The men struggled to keep surrounding structures cool. It took nearly twenty minutes for back-up help to arrive from Cannon Beach over the icy roads. This lack of manpower hurt even though there was a full Arch Cape crew on site. It was estimated the fire had been burning for about forty-five minutes before being noticed by neighbors. The exact cause of the fire is unknown; however, a floor mounted L.P. (liquefied petroleum) gas furnace with the thermostat off is believed to have malfunctioned. The loss was estimated at $25,600 and the house was totally destroyed. These 1978 fires were serious losses to this rural community.

There were no major fires in 1979. It was a quiet year with only two fire calls and eight medical calls.

Major changes began to occur in 1980. The citizens within the Cannon Beach Rural Fire Protection District voted to increase its tax base. For the first time in the history of Arch Cape, ample money was available to upgrade old equipment. Cannon Beach received a new pumper, and in the process, sold the old Arch Cape 1947 Mack truck to the Wolf Creek Fire District. Arch Cape received a 1963 Ford pumper from Cannon Beach and developed new operating procedures. Portable pagers, which are portable receivers worn on the belt, replaced the primitive Plectrons. Response time dropped dramatically.

Arch Cape became more involved with fire fighting in Cannon Beach. The new Engine 77 responded to all structure fires in Cannon Beach. This had several important results. It merged the two stations into a more unified operation than in the past. The Cannon Beach Fire Department had more calls than the Arch Cape Station, therefore giving the Arch Cape crew valuable hands-on fire fighting experience. The Arch Cape fire crew responded to eight fires and fifteen medical calls in 1980.

The Cannon Beach Fire Station had a great reputation with its Emergency Medical Response Team. The department had eight state certified Emergency Medical Technicians in the early 1980's, but Arch Cape had no EMT's until Mike Graham became certified in 1983. The EMT course takes 104 hours to complete, and at that time, applicants had to pass both written and practical examinations.

The call-out summary for 1981 included twelve fires and sixteen medical calls. There were nine fires and ten medical calls in 1982 and Mike Graham replaced Ed Wunderlich as the Arch Cape lieutenant. In 1983 there were fourteen fires and nine medical calls, and in 1984 there were ten fire calls and seven medical calls. The only significant Arch Cape call came at 5:30 a.m., January 7, when a VW Rabbit burned while parked at the Coleman residence on Carnahan Street. The Arch Cape crew smothered the fire, which had totally involved the car upon their arrival.

January 26, 1985, saw another VW fire. A Portland couple operating a VW van had just come through the tunnel north bound when their engine compartment caught fire. They pulled over on Highway 101 and Beach Street, near the fire station. Response time was extremely quick, but flames completely enveloped the van when the crew arrived. The crew knocked down the fire quickly, but the $12,800 van was a total loss. There were fifteen fire and fourteen medical calls in 1985.

The Arch Cape Station handled eleven fire and twelve medical calls in 1986, including two major fires. There was a car fire at Tide and Columbia Streets in Falcon Cove June 1, at 8:17 a.m. The car, valued at $4,000, was a total loss, despite an eleven minute response time to the far south end of Falcon Cove. Then on August 29 at 11:21 a.m., a structure fire from an electrical problem caused $6,000 damage to the Schmiege residence at 1470 Pacific Street in Arch Cape.

The Arch Cape station responded to thirteen fire and ten medical calls in 1987. One call involved a car fire at Hug Point September 12 at 2:45 a.m. The car had been burning for some time before the crew arrived on the scene. Loss on the vehicle was $3,000, and the cause was of electrical origin.

1988 was a busy year. The Arch Cape Station responded to twenty-one fires and twenty-one medical calls. Significant fires included an April 13 fire at 11:26 p.m. at the Bob Turk residence at Silver Point with a loss of $95,000. A spark from a chainsaw ignited a nearby can of gasoline in a combination garage-living area in the home. There was a truck fire near the Arch Cape Sewage Treatment Plant at 3:15 p.m. July 15 with a loss of $1,000.

Twenty-four medical calls and twenty-four fire calls made 1989 the most active year so far for the Arch Cape fire crew. A two-fatality motor vehicle accident occured near the grocery store on September 17 of that year. The Jaws of Life tool was required to cut into the vehicle to remove the victims. On September 22, a house fire at 2325 Carnahan Street caused $10,000 damage and it was suspected that a hot charcoal briquette from a barbecue dropped on the deck next to the house.

The Arch Cape Station responded to twenty-five fire calls and fifteen medical calls in 1990. A truck fire June 22nd at the Arch Cape Deli caused minor damage. On December 19th, a chimney fire caused considerable damage to the chimney and fireplace of the George Cerelli home.

In September, 1991, the Cannon Beach Station took delivery of a new 1,500 gallon-per-minute pump truck equipped with a combination fifty-five foot water tower/rescue ladder. The truck, built by *Beck Fire Apparatus* of Cloverdale, California, cost $271,000 and greatly expands the department's ability to provide quality protection within the district. Brian McDonough retired from the Arch Cape Station. Doug Shadbolt, a state forestry fire fighter and long-time Cannon Beach resident, joined the Arch Cape crew. Doug constructed a new home in the Arch Cape area.

There were no major fires in 1992. It was a quiet year with eleven medical calls and fifteen fire calls. Jack Foster retired in 1992 after seventeen years on the department.

In summary, the Arch Cape Fire Department has averaged 29 calls per year for the past 12 years. Three major arson fires, (April 29, May 31 and October 9th), concerned the

Cannon Beach Station in 1991.

Arch Cape's fire station renovation began in the summer of 1984 and was completed in early 1985. The total project cost of $65,000 was spread over two budget years and came from the Cannon Beach Rural Fire Protection District, of which Arch Cape is a member. Property taxes for the district, which extend from Cannon Beach to Falcon Cove, paid for the expansion and renovation. As a result, the local residents paid a fraction of what it would have cost had the community been incorporated. The renovation saw the creation of a 720 square foot meeting room which was the original bay of the 1966 garage. A double bay of 2,184 square feet was constructed to the south. A 1963 Ford pumper and a 1953 Dodge mini-pumper are currently parked there. The district purchased a new pumper in 1991 which operates out of the Cannon Beach Station. The addition of an emergency response vehicle in Arch Cape is planned for the near future.

The Cannon Beach firehouse has a 1979 Seagrave 1,500 gallon-per-minute pumper; a 1991 Beck 1,500 gallon-per-minute pumper with a 55 foot ladder and water tower; a 1968 Western States 750 gallon-per-minute pumper; a 1965 ladder truck; a 1978 G.M.C. rescue truck and a Zodiac surf boat.

The 1988 crew consisted of Ken Campbell, Jack Foster, Ray Hill, Tom Hughes, Brian McDonough, Al Nelson, Dick Pearson, and Lieutenant Mike Graham. Jeff Hull joined the department and Mike Graham was made Fire Marshall of the Cannon Beach Fire District in 1989.

There are 255 dwellings in Arch Cape with an approximate permanent population of 120. The eight Arch Cape Station volunteers and residents are proud of the fire house and the equipment stored within. Equipment other than the two pump trucks include an oxygen bottle, a basic life support medical equipment box and a medical suction unit. There are many amenities that did not come from the taxpayer, but were donated or obtained at cost. Larry Ward, who has an Arch Cape home at the intersection of Ocean Road and Pacific Street, secured and installed the thick red carpet that once graced the executive offices of the Portland Trail Blazers basketball team. The room boasts a 19-inch color television set and a living room couch.

In the kitchen, there is a stove, refrigerator, custom wooden cabinets, and a stainless steel sink. On the opposite wall, there is a pale yellow counter with wooden trim. There is a bathroom with a shower and, in the new garage, an indoor basketball hoop and weight lifting apparatus to keep the crew in shape

All this began in 1965 when a few dedicated and far-sighted Arch Cape residents realized the need for better fire protection. Could they possibly have dreamed that the Fire House they created would grow to such size or that the expanded facility would house such a variety of equipment?

The Arch Cape crew works with the Cannon Beach crew responding to emergencies other than fire and medical calls. Both work in conjunction with the Coast Guard and law enforcement agencies on drownings, on hikers trapped by incoming tides, and on stranded cliff and rock climbers.

(The top photograph on the following page shows the first volunteer Arch Cape fire crew. Ron Vick, the young man on the left was 14 years of age when he joined the crew. Since one needed to be 16, Ron was made a honorary member until he reached age 16.)

The first Arch Cape fire crew. From left to right: Ron Vick, Elmer Vick, Maurice Simmons, John Hughes, Travis Tyrrell and Harold Schaffer. July, 1966. Photo Source unknown. The 1993 crew from left to right: Al Nelson, Doug Shadbolt, Mike Graham, Tom Hughes, Ken Campbell, Dick Pearson, Ray Hill , and not shown, Ron Schiffman. June, 1993. David English photo.

The Arch Cape Sewer System

In April of 1966, the Oregon State Sanitary Authority notified the Clatsop County Planning Commission that soil conditions in several areas of Clatsop County, including the entire Arch Cape area, were unsatisfactory for disposal of waste through septic tanks. The Sanitary Authority recommended that Clatsop County issue no building permits for new construction in the community of Arch Cape. After this directive, the county authorities refused virtually all such requests for new building permits. This area had very little top soil and a deep layer of impervious clay. This meant that any septic tank wastes deposited in this soil had little chance of being properly distributed and quickly found their way into one of the many local streams, swamps or roadside ditches.

Because of these conditions in Arch Cape, the Oregon State Sanitary Authority strongly recommended that its citizens formulate a program to correct existing and future public health problems. A Sanitary District or Service District needed to be formed as soon as possible. In order to do this in an efficient manner, the County Commissioners directed that an engineering study be conducted, with assistance from a federal grant, to investigate a sewage disposal and treatment system to serve the Arch Cape district. The engineering firm of Cornell, Howland, Hayes and Merryfield, from Portland, made this study. Their report recommended establishing a disposal system that would serve all existing dwellings, places of business, and vacant lots on permanent roads in the community, as well as establishing a treatment plant with pump station and stabilization pond located near Arch Cape Creek. The document also contained detailed engineering and cost data for the system it proposed.

Approximately one hundred Arch Cape property owners met on August 9, 1968, in the meeting hall of St. Peter the Fisherman Church to listen to sanitary engineers from the county and state. Among matters discussed was the urgent need for sewage facilities; the current rules, regulations and administrative policies with respect to sewage disposal; and policy enforcement for both present and future use. Also discussed were alternative methods of collection and treatment; anticipated costs of facilities, methods of financing; and alternative government programs through which construction and management of such facilities might be affected.

After much discussion, a committee was selected to formulate a specific proposal for the establishment of a government agency to deal with the sanitation problem: Alfred Harsch was chairman; William Bond, Angelo Costanzo, Floyd Scott, Betty Snow, and Walter Wiebenson served on the Arch Cape Property Owners' Committee and were also the members of the Community Club's Health and Sanitation Survey Group. It was suggested that an engineer, a lawyer, and a doctor should be members of the committee. Richard A. Greulich, an engineer, and Elmer Ramsey, a lawyer, became committee members. Dr. Leo J. Meienberg, while not a member of the committee, agreed to serve as consultant to the committee and to assist in medical matters. All three of these professionals were Arch Cape property owners.

At an election held November 5, 1968, the voters of this area rejected the proposal for creation of the Arch Cape Sanitary District by a 40-40 vote.

Two years later, the Arch Cape Community Club's 1970 Progress Report again stated the need to establish a sewer system within this area. Although this continued to be of paramount importance, there were not enough permanent residents willing and able to serve on a board which must assume full responsibility for planning, bonding and administering a sewer district. Because of this, a petition before the County Commissioners to form a Sanitary District was withdrawn. Subsequently, at the request of the commissioners, the board of the Arch Cape Community Club made a personal check of all registered voters within the area and reported that 78 of the approximately 88 registered voters were in favor of a County Service District to develop and administer a local sewer system. At that time, a new committee was appointed by the board: Lowell Hawkins was chairman; Ray Doherty, Angelo Costanzo, Dwight Lester and Elmer Ramsey were other committee members. With the approval of the membership, the board had the responsibility of working with the commissioners toward the solution of the sewer problems.

On March 20, 1970, the Community Club forwarded a letter to the County Commissioners stating that a canvas of the residents indicated that a large percentage preferred a County Service District over a Sanitary District. Acting on this information, the county commissioners published a notice of a public hearing on September 30 to establish a County Service District and to set its boundaries. The members of the Arch Cape Sewer Clarification Committee and several residents attended the September 30 meeting and the series of meetings which followed. These meetings secured an agreeable boundary for the district. The original engineering study was refined for better definition of present and future needs for improvement of the effluent disposal process.

A special election was held on March 2, 1971, with thirty-four votes for and twenty-four votes against forming a County Service District.

There was no sewer system progress in 1972. The county still would not issue any new building permits in the Arch Cape area until the entire sewer project was determined. The Community Club was waiting for a report by the county commissioners, who were waiting, along with other counties, for funds before they could initiate any action. It was becoming more difficult to deal at the county level on this and other matters since the Federal Department of Environmental Quality had begun to exercise its authority.

In 1973, the voters of Arch Cape approved the sale of bonds for the Arch Cape sewer by a 55 to 23 margin. Construction was scheduled to begin in 1974. The county commissioners formed a Citizens' Advisory Committee of Arch Cape residents to approve the financial plan of the project and to act as a liaison between members of the community and the county. Lowell Hawkins, Gertrude Hill, George Rothert, and Dorothy Price were committee members.

It took eight years of work by committee members to plan and secure financing before the Arch Cape Service District became a reality and commenced operation in March, 1976. Those on the committee at that time were Chairman Travis Tyrrell, M. R. Simmonds, Gertrude Hill, George Rothert, and Kent Price.

Future plans include replacing or rebuilding the current effluent discharge system by 1994. Studies will be completed for this plan in 1992 with costs determined and a financing method recommended. Of continuing interest is correcting, as much as is financially practical, the inflow of surface water into the system. Sections of the sewer are viewed by closed-circuit television to find the source of water and to determine an individual leak-at-a-time repair.

Current policy for sewer hook-ups requires the installation of sewers and manholes designed to meet the system's needs at the developers' sole cost. This work is inspected and supervised by engineers employed by the district with these costs paid for by the developers. Connection fees are paid to the district in addition to construction costs. The fees are $2,000 for a single-family residence and higher for businesses and other uses.

Brian McDonough, board chairman, announced at the Arch Cape Community Club meeting May 18, 1990, that in 1993 Arch Cape must purchase the land it is now leasing for purification and the access strip leading to this land or develop a new solution for sewage disposal. The district lease will not be renewed at that time. Now, the treated effluent is pumped to the leased flat site and sprayed there when necessary between May 1 to October 30th. The district must come up with a plan soon to dispose of treated sewage effluent. Arch Cape Creek, which runs through the community and down onto the beach, does not have the flow to dispose of the effluent during the summer.

The 1992 Arch Cape Service District board (same board for both the water and sewer systems) engaged Curran-McLeod, Inc., Consulting Engineers, to do a Utilities Systems Capacity Analysis. The engineers conclude, in part: (1) the plant has the capacity for about 60 more homes; (2) The steel components of the plant are constantly under corrosive attack in the coastal environment. Time and salt air take their toll and some of the steel is ready for replacement. Most notable are the headworks components and aeration basin feed launders; and (3) The existing effluent utilization program is rapidly drawing to a close and immediate attention is necessary to avoid major legal entanglements.

The report recommends: (1) To apply significant funding resources to Infiltration/Inflow controls. Systematic reduction of infiltration/inflow will extend the life of treatment facilities and provide expanded capacity. Infiltration and inflow is water entering the system through pipe leaks, surface water flowing into the system and homeowners allowing water to enter the system from down spouts and ground drain systems; (2) To begin to set aside funds from fees and charges to assure that plant expansion will be achievable when population growth dictates; and (3) To undertake the determination of an effluent use plan which will permit uninterrupted operation of the waste facilities.

Our waste water system is under pressure. Major upgrades will have to be undertaken to meet future regulatory standards and additional spending is envisaged to bring the system into compliance.

PROJECT EXPENDITURES (original construction)

Sewage Treatment Plant	$ 577,550	The original
Interceptor Sewers & Pump Stations	517,500	assessment for an
Collection Sewers & Service Connections	357,250	average fifty by
Interim Financing	70,000	one hundred foot
TOTAL	$1,522,300	lot was $934.55.

PROJECT INCOME

Project Grant	$ 767,000
FHA Grant	190,000
Assessments	338,000
Warrants & General Obligation Bonds	227,300
TOTAL	$1,522,300

Arch Cape Water Systems

Perhaps the first Arch Cape water systems were the abundant springs and creeks in the the area, for early maps show many of them winding down from the hills to the ocean. The first land grant settlers established themselves near creeks in the 1890's: Joseph Walsh built near Arch Cape Creek; Bell, Astbury and Clark Carnahan built near Asbury Creek; and S. P. Adair and James P. Austin, near Fall Creek just south of Hug Point. The preceding names came from a map prepared by the Surveyor General's Office, Portland, Oregon, dated February 1, 1895. Bell and Astbury's first names are not noted on the map. The "Astbury" name appears on later maps as "Asbury." The earliest sizable structure between Hug Point and Arch Cape Creek was the Arch Cape Hotel, which Bill Adams constructed in 1905. Marmaduke Maxwell purchased the hotel, which was next to his home in 1914 and sold it to Marie English in 1929. The hotel had a commode, tub and wash basin on the second floor; a toilet facility on the first floor and water in the kitchen where the hot water tank was located. Could the water supply to this structure have been the first Arch Cape water system?

Early settlers hauled water from Arch Cape Creek by way of a path that went through the Walsh property. A deep pool under the present highway bridge was the source; galvanized water pails on wooden yokes were a common sight.

Workers found a spring due east of Marmaduke Maxwell's barn when they were building the Arch Cape Hotel. The spring supplied water to the hotel and to Mr. Maxwell's house. At times, the spring ran dry or the water would be just a trickle. That is why Mr. Maxwell kept a large rain barrel filled on his back porch. Also, an old tub with a dripping faucet was in the back yard of the hotel. The old Maxwell house, built in 1912, is still standing at the end of Maxwell Avenue. The home is now owned by the decendants of Dr. Frank and Betty Maddison and Clinton and Jessie Reynolds, who purchased the property in 1948.

With help from her brother, Mrs. Elizabeth Archer built a cabin in 1921 where her granddaughter, Gwen Carney, now has a house on the corner of Cannon Street and Ocean View. Mrs. Archer and her children carried water from the same source that supplied Mr. Maxwell and the hotel.

In 1933, Wilbur and Mamie Markham built a structure at the end of Marshall Street on property they purchased from Dow Walker. Dow Walker owned most of the property in that area then. The Markhams had running water that came from a spring east of the present store and post office. Only two homes were on the system in 1936—the Markhams' and the Walkers'. Later, this system furnished water to the old post office and store that Ernest White built. That is the structure just north of the present store and post office, for years referred to as The Arch Cape Beach House, and presently, The Inn at Arch Cape. Mr. White purchased the water system from Dow Walker and expanded the water supply to furnish water to new homes built in the area at that time.

There were three water systems in the 1940's serving residences between Hug Point and Arch Cape Creek:

The South Arch Cape System

Angelo and Lucille Costanzo moved to Arch Cape in the mid-thirties when Angelo was hired to supervise the blasting of the tunnel. Angelo developed a water system that came from Arch Cape Creek. Ernest White decided he had no further need for his water system, so he deeded it to Angelo and Lucille. In 1945, Angelo, Lucille and their son Robert formed a partnership to furnish water to 46 residences between Arch Cape Creek and the Kent Price Park subdivision. Angelo found a spring in the hills south of Arch Cape Creek, where he built an open holding pond fed by the spring. He also installed a four inch transite main (a trade name for asbestos-cement pipe) along Cannon Street and Pacific Avenue to Kent Price Park to serve the growing community better. Dr. John Countryman cleaned the holding area weekly, making certain that dead animals did not contaminate the water, as chemicals were not used at that time. For his services, Dr. Countryman received free water.

Theo Dichter, along with his sons Ted, Ralph and Jack, purchased the Arch Cape Water System on July 1, 1954. The Dichters hired Angelo as manager. The system served 54 residences at a cost of $20 per customer per year. The Dichters, with Angelo's help, installed a 20,000 gallon wooden water tank near the site of the open holding tank in 1956. In 1962, they placed another 30,000 gallon wooden tank alongside the first tank to provide needed storage capacity and they purchased a chlorinator at that time. The two tanks are still on site, partially collapsed and difficult to locate because of the brush and growth surrounding them.

The Kent Price System

In 1944, Mr. Kent Price Sr. purchased the quarter section now known as Kent Price Park from Mr. Jack Shanks. He was particularly interested and charmed by the large trees, grounds, and natural beauty near and around Arch Cape and always wanted to own property in the area. Mr. Shanks had a water system serving his place and several other homes in the area. It was a gravity system consisting of a cedar tank mounted on four huge logs situated at the highest point in the area. Water came from Shark Creek, a tributary of Asbury Creek east of the highway. Mr. Price found an ideal spot between heavy rocks on Shark Creek, where he installed a reservoir dam, and the Shanks' tank on the logs was abandoned.

The present Kent Price water system was installed about 1954. The Price system furnished water to residents between Columbia Avenue and Maple Street in Arch Cape. It took a carload of pipe and at that time was the most costly and complete development by one individual in Clatsop County.

At the request of home owners, the pipe later extended to the northerly line of the Arch Cape subdivision, which is the corner of Carnahan Street and Larch Street.

The Cannon View Park System

The beginning of the Cannon View Park water system in north Arch Cape can be traced to May 10, 1898, when Lydia A. Austin received a United States patent for a Reservation of Water Rights from springs. This is the same Austin family who had a dwelling, a truck farm, a store and a public lodging facility located at the north end of what is now Cannon View Park. It was here that the first Cannon Beach post office was located in 1898. Mr. Austin was postmaster.

Rudolph and Carolina Kissling purchased the Austin property and the water rights on September 22, 1925. They operated the small hotel along with several guest houses until 1944.

In 1944, Mel Goodin purchased the area and called it Western Shoreways. He removed the timber, leveled ridges and filled in creek beds after placing drain pipes to the beach to channel the creek water. He developed about 25 beach front home sites and about the same number of ocean view back lots. The area became known as "The Flats."

By 1967, Western Shoreways consisted of 30 homes trying to exist on a one 1 1/2 inch water line punched under Highway 101 by Cannon Beach handyman Joe Betz. Mel Goodin had hauled three ten-foot diameter 800 gallon redwood stave wine tanks from a California winery in 1950 for water storage. Time had taken its toll. The tanks had deteriorated and so had the tank covers. Many water leaks in the rusting iron pipes appeared which were difficult to repair, and it was impossible to keep bugs, birds and animals out of the system.

This old Cannon View Park distribution system, with its rusting pipes and deteriorating iron fittings, was a constant problem for early residents. Hardly a week went by without calling on Harold Schaeffer at the Texaco station or Mack McLaughlin, a retired plumber living on Webb Avenue, for help to solve some problem. Mack had a gold mine of old fittings, valves, and parts. Jack Foster, Superintendent of the Dichter Water System, was always ready to help and Bob McEwan was never far away with his back hoe. The Kent Price transite system was new so parts were not compatible with the older Cannon View Park system.

The spring water source east and up the hill across the highway was crystal clear and abundant, but the storage and supply system was in trouble. Water samples were not meeting the Oregon State Board of Health requirements; in addition, the Public Utilities Commission pointed out there was no fire hydrant and, as reserve water for fire protection was unavailable, fire insurance rates were high. The state issued *Western Shoreways* an ultimatum to resolve these pressing problems. This prompted Mel Goodin to call a meeting of the home owners to negotiate selling the system.

In 1968, the home owners purchased the water system with all of its rights, easements, roads and improvements for one dollar. A community committee formed Cannon View Park, Inc., a non-profit corporation. To meet Oregon State Board of Health requirements, community members repaired, cleaned, sanitized and covered the three old wood stave tanks. A four-foot cedar tree blew down in 1970 next to the water source, and instead of spring water, the system had surface water. The board engaged Angelo Costanzo, the local water system specialist, to rebuild the spring supply system in such a way that water was never exposed to daylight. He installed a four-foot wide section of concrete culvert, bell end up, to collect incoming spring water. An outlet led to the three holding tanks. All animal life, including insects, was kept out of the new spring concrete culvert collecting tank. A rubber gasket between the concrete culvert section and the metal lid sealed the collecting tank. Later, padlocks were installed on the metal tank covers to keep out the curious. The results were so effective that chlorination was not required.

After the availability of potable water was ensured, the community started a fire protection project. Fire underwriters required a minimum 30,000 gallon storage tank with a 6-inch supply to a hydrant located within 1,000 feet from insured homes. A 75,000 gallon concrete tank replaced the three wine tanks in 1977 and a six-inch plastic water main fed the centrally located hydrant. Jim Grasseth prepared the tank site and access road and John Kroo constructed the concrete tank. Residents Bob Preir, Paul Nelson, Alan Nelson and Gordon Hauck dug ditches and laid the pipe by hand because the steep grade prohibited using power equipment. Bob Preir and his crew dug the ditch for the 6-inch P.V.C. (plastic) pipeline from the tank to Highway 101; Ivan Tinkess, from the Portland Raleigh Water District, and Bob McEwan from Gearhart, bored under the highway. The community-financed project, sponsored by Cannon View Park, Inc., sold 8 percent notes to homeowners. The community contributed much of the labor. Income from water sales and hook-up charges to new home builders retired the notes. The distribution system, completely rebuilt using P.V.C. pipe, cast iron and brass fittings now meets all state and federal requirements.

The first Board of Directors for Cannon View Park, Inc. was Dr. Leo Meinberg, president; Walter Wiebenson, secretary/treasurer; Thomas Moore, legal advisor; and Gordon Hauck, engineering consultant. The 1993 Board members include Gordon Hauck, president; John Brosnan, vice president; Elmer Simpson, secretary/treasurer; Alan Nelson, water master and fire marshall, and Dick Petrone, Thomas Moore, and Alfred Illge. Cannon View Park, Inc. has funds set aside to add a 70,000 gallon tank for added storage and for fire protection. The board is in the design stage now and is applying for the necessary permits for the new tank.

Considerable growth and development occurred in the Arch Cape area in the 50's and early 60's. In April of 1966, the Oregon State Sanitary Authority requested no future building permits be issued until sanitary conditions in the Arch Cape area were improved. The early 70's were transition years for Arch Cape. Growth came to a standstill until sanitation problems could be resolved at a cost the community could afford.

Beginning in 1973, both the Price and Dichter systems had problems with bad water. Trouble with turbidity followed heavy rains and both systems consistently had bad reports from the Health Department.

Construction of the sewer system began in 1974 and caused considerable turmoil in 1975 with the Dichter Water System between Leech and Maxwell Avenues. Ditchdiggers inadvertantly broke water pipes in the ditch digging and pipe laying process. Fifteen area residents became ill when broken water lines became contaminated. Tests showed Arch Cape water at the time was unusually full of bacteria and contained no chlorine. The chlorine distribution center for the water system was subject to failure without notice. At that time, the Health Department advised south Arch Cape residents to boil all drinking water.

The Kent Price System ran a line south on Pacific Avenue from Columbia Avenue to Marshall Avenue to connect with the Dichter System to assist in emergencies. Those who maintained the Dichter and Price Systems worked hard to deliver pure water. They found this task impossible until provided with a properly covered holding facility, which included filtering and chlorinating systems that met the tough new federal clean water standards. Both the Dichter and Price families could have been wiped out financially had there been any legal action and they felt jeopardized. Therefore, they sold both systems at a reasonable price to the Arch Cape Community, which allowed for a water district to be formed under Clatsop County authority.

A petition was filed by the Arch Cape Community Club September 15, 1976, to form an Arch Cape Water Service District with Travis Tyrrell as chairman. Committee members were M. R. Simmonds, Gertrude Hill, George Rothert and Kent Price. The A.C.W.S.D. purchased the Kent Price and Dichter Brothers' Systems on a contract basis, with payments to be made to them out of a fund from a $200 assessment to each water district homeowner.

The South Arch Cape Dichter System and the Kent Price System became one district but continued operating as two systems for quite awhile. The Dichter System still drew water from the stream which fed two tanks located up the hill south of Webb Avenue. The supply did not last in the summer, so water had to be pumped from Arch Cape Creek. It was harder to maintain the Dichter System because of the location of the tanks, so temporarily, that system would occasionally depend on the Kent Price System to supply its needs.

In 1976 Jack Foster retired from the dental sales business and took over the water system operations from Mr. Constanzo. Foster began his commitment to the service district as a Community Education Training Act trainee. The Arch Cape Service District secured funding in May of 1977 from the CETA program and was now able to employ two trainees, Jack Foster and Mike Graham. Rex Camp had been running the waste water plant since it went on line in 1975. He was on loan from the Clatsop County Road Department. Starting in 1978, Jack and Mike ran the systems and Rex Camp returned to the county. Jack and Mike worked 70 percent of the time for the sewer system and 30 percent for the water system; that split has been modified over time due to the changing nature of the job. Today, equal time is allowed for both important tasks.

Mike Graham left the Service District in January of 1980 and was replaced by Marv Mathre, a Seaside man who had an extensive background in waste water treatment operations. He and Jack ran the systems until Marv retired in 1983. Ray Hill was hired to replace Marv. Jack retired in 1986 and Mike Graham returned to work for the District.

Much happened in the 80's. In 1984, a $275,000 ten-year bond issue financed a new water tank. That money not only provided for the purchase of land, but also a 250,000 gallon redwood stave water storage tank, a 72,000 gallon-per-day charcoal filter and chlorination system, as well as various smaller items. These improvements were necessary to comply with the Environmental Protection Agency requirements in force at the time. The system more than met the stringent requirements then. The project was designed by Handforth & Larson, Inc. of Manzanita, who was also responsible for construction supervision and contract compliance.

Mike Graham and Ray Hill learned by trial and error the portions of polymers and chlorine necessary to meet output quality standards. The quality of raw input water as to turbidity and suspended solids has a great effect on the output; as the input changes, the necessary mix of chemicals also alter, but not always in the same proportion. Mike Graham and Ray Hill worked with Water Tech personnel from Vancouver, Washington, who furnished and installed the filter and chlorination system.

The new tank was in service for less than two months when it ruptured and collapsed. Two men were working on a perimeter fence for the project on the east side of the tank when it burst. Fortunately, they were out of the line of fire when the hoops began breaking, but the noise, they said, was as if someone were firing a high-powered rifle right by their ears. Investigation of the cause of the failure revealed that the contractor had used a spacing between the hoops at the lower third of the tank that was not narrow enough for the tank capacity.

Many acrimonious discussions at board meetings had occurred during the early decision making regarding the tank. Should it be redwood, concrete, or steel? Because of cost considerations, engineers at Handforth & Larson, Inc. prevailed and built the redwood tank. After its collapse, the discussion renewed vigorously. Finally, it was decided that replacing the lost tank with concrete or steel would mean the District could face substantial legal bills, a large delay in reconstruction and difficulty collecting damages from the tank contractor. The contractor, therefore, rebuilt the tank at no cost to the district and it is working well.

Pure water costs money. The Water Board proposed and charged a new rate structure for water service that defined single and multi-family usage. The board found the old fixed-fee billing method unacceptable and introduced the idea of installing water meters and charging for actual consumption. Residents approved the plan in 1986. The water district installed water meters in 1987 and 1988 for all Arch Cape residents. Each connection cost the homeowner $120 for the meter, meter box, labor, and for miscellaneous pipe fittings. The district charged $120 for second meters and eventually established separate water and sewer accounts. Some locations required larger meters and those accounts paid a proportionately higher fee.

To determine a rate structure that would insure the financial stability of the District, Mike Graham and Ray Hill, water and sewer plant operators, made a detailed study of metered usage for several months before actual billing began. The rate structure provided a reasonable degree of equity between the vacation home user and the permanent residents and has two parts. A basic charge of $11 per month which included the first 5,000 gallons of usage in the month and a usage charge of ten cents for each one hundred gallons or fraction thereof over the basic 5,000 gallons. Billing is done on a quarterly basis, but the 5,000 gallons is *monthly* and is *not* cumulative for the billing period.

Ray and Mike found substantial leakage on the customer side of many meters and when found would disconnect the service. They notified the homeowner and turned on the water when the homeowner resolved the problem. Water consumption decreased dramatically after leaks were located and fixed and after meters were installed. Water usage, as indicated by the system flow meter, decreased on the average of 22,000 gallons per day.

The district serves 218 customers of which 75 are full-time residents. The lots in Castle Rock Estates are all sold and future developments will put pressure on our system. Our present plant can grow to about 320 customers before a second filter plant is needed. The building and piping were designed with this in mind, so a filter costing $100,000 to $125,000 would double the water supply capacity. This plant expansion would be necessary to handle the additional water main capacity, which would be required to supply adequate water pressure for fire protection and for home use. Replacing the water main from the plant to the highway is already in the district's five year plan. Other work not tied to growth includes finishing the "looping" of the system, completed in 1992.

The looping system is an eight inch water line that runs north and south on the east side of Highway 101 from Maple Street to Mill Road. A water line crossing at Maple Street, Ocean Road, Markham Avenue and Mill Road ties this main transmission line into the existing line west of the highway. This "loop" makes it possible to work on sections of line without shutting water off to major parts of the town and assures adequate water circulation in the distribution system. Seven hundred feet of six inch PVC line was installed up East Mill Road which replaced leak-prone asbestos cement pipe.

An Arch Cape Advisory Board makes policy recommendations to the Clatsop County Board of Commissioners, which is the governing body for the Water District. The 1991-92 board members were: Pat Noonan, Chair; Dick Pearson, Vice Chair; Robert Green, Jack Meece, Ken Campbell, Gordon Hauke and Robert McCullough.

Mike Graham and Ray Hill, our water and waste water technicians, work hard improving and maintaining our water and waste water systems.

On September 20, 1954, Mr. Kent Price Sr. was granted a permit (No. 22996) to appropriate the public waters of the State of Oregon. The permit allowed the Kent Price water system to draw 0.50 cubic feet per second from Shark Creek, approximately 320,000 gallons per day. Later, since the system served only about thirty homes, the state reduced the water right to 0.05 cubic feet per second, allowing only 32,313 gallons per day. Today, the Arch Cape water system source, with about 250 homes, is still allowed to draw only 32,313 gallons a day from Shark Creek.

The Arch Cape water system was stressed in 1992. The very dry year and the demand for water exceeded the system's water rights (32,313 gallons per day) from the water source, Shark Creek. Every year, usage in August and through the Labor Day weekend exceeds what the system is legally allowed to draw from Shark Creek, so the excess water used comes from the system's 250,000 gallon storage tank. According to the 1992 Advisory Board report, the water system needs an increased water source, an increased storage capacity and added filtering capabilities. See page 93 for updated information on the water and sewer systems.

Cannon View Park September, 1949. Ackroyd Photo. Courtesy Gordon Hauck

Kent Price Sr. with the family dog, Sally, standing by a pile of pipe for the Kent Price water system. Sally's Alley, between Donlan and Columbia Avenue, was named after Sally. Circa 1954. Kent Price Collection.

The 250,000 gallon redwood storage tank next to the Shark Creek impoundment dam and the filter station, both installed in 1984, supplies treated water to Arch Cape homes. David English photo.

The water tank on Shanks Avenue that furnished water to the area before Kent Price Sr. purchased the property. Circa 1951. Kent Price collection.

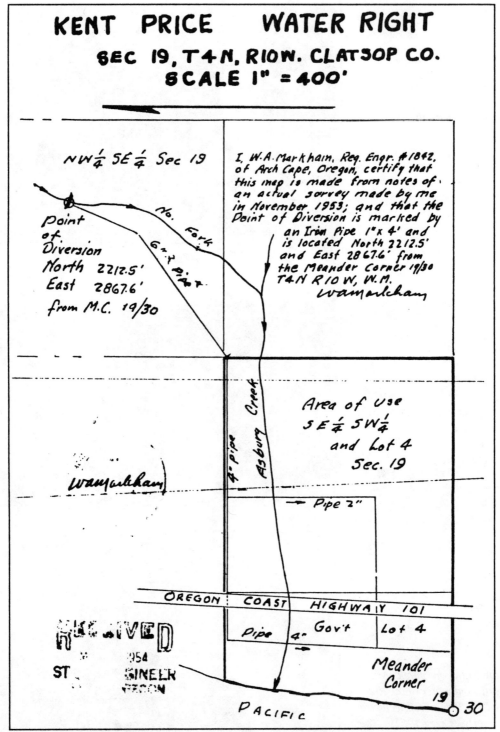

KENT PRICE   WATER RIGHT
SEC 19, T4N, R10W. CLATSOP CO.
SCALE 1" = 400'

NW¼ SE¼ Sec 19

Point of Diversion North 2212.5' East 2867.6' from M.C. 19/30

No. Fork

6" Pipe

I, W.A. Markham, Reg. Engr. #1842, of Arch Cape, Oregon, certify that this map is made from notes of an actual survey made by me in November 1953; and that the Point of Diversion is marked by an Iron Pipe 1" x 4' and is located North 2212.5' and East 2867.6' from the Meander Corner 19/30 T4N R10W, W.M.

W.A. Markham

4" Pipe

Asbury Creek

Area of use SE¼ SW¼ and Lot 4 Sec. 19

Pipe 2"

Oregon Coast Highway 101

Pipe 4"   Gov't   Lot 4

Meander Corner

19   30

Pacific

RECEIVED 1954 ST. ENGINEER OREGON

The Kent Price Water Right map prepared by W. A. Markham in 1954. This map has been reduced. Do not use the scale shown at the top of the map. Courtesy Kent Price.

Recent Water and Sewer Advisory Board History
By Dick Pearson, Vice Chair
June 1, 1993

During the summer of 1991, the Water and Sewer Advisory Boards became concerned that our systems were reaching the limits of their capacities. After soliciting proposals from several engineering firms, Curran-McLeod, Consulting Engineers were retained to analyze the systems. They began their work early in 1992.

By May, Curran-McLeod had advised the Board that we were withdrawing more water from Shark Creek, our water source, than our water rights allowed. Our peak usage was 75,000 gallons a day. Our water rights allowed us to withdraw 32,300 gallons a day.

The Board recommended and the County Commissioners approved a moratorium on new water hook ups until new sources of water could be found to supplement the water supply. This occurred in early August.

The summer of 1992 was unusually hot and dry and Shark Creek, below our impoundment dam, literally ran dry that August.

At this point, the Oregon Department of Water Resources took over the operation of the water district from the district board, which is the County Commissioners. Strict water restrictions were put into effect in order to reduce our daily water needs to 32,300 gallons per day. This was successful.

The Advisory Board went to work to try to acquire more water. Water rights held on a tributary of Arch Cape Creek was considered, but due to the uncertainty of that water source and the cost of transmitting the water to the treatment plant, the effort was shifted to an attempt to acquire additional water rights on Shark Creek and on Asbury Creek. Strict water restrictions are now in place for the summer of 1993; however, if additional water rights are granted on Shark Creek in the very near future, these water restrictions will not be necessary. The District is also investigating digging a well. Three potential sites have been recommended by Paul See, a local geologist.

During the time that the crisis with the water system was going on, the local advisory board, with the blessing of the County Commissioners, was investigating the formation of a local service district governed by a board of locally elected residents. The vote on the district formation is June 29, 1993. At that same time, a board will also be voted upon so that they will be ready to go to work if the district is formed.

The Curran-McLeod studies also show that after there are 50 more sewer connections, we will have reached the capacity of that system as well. Currently, efforts are underway to acquire a site for our effluent. The lease on the site now used expires in September, 1994. Future plans for plant improvements are also an immediate task for the new district board, if it is formed.

On June 29, Arch Cape registered voters approved local control for the sewer and water boards. Sewer Board elected members and their votes are: Dick Pearson, 114; Bill Owens, 91; John Zommers, 89; Bob Green, 67 and Frank Dorscheimer, 64. Water board members elected and their votes are: Dick Pearson, 105; John Zommers, 98; Bill Owens, 96; Frank Dorscheimer, 70 and Pat Noonan, 68. Source, *Daily Astorian*, June 30, 1993.

Sally's Alley
By Jan Tarr with help from Dorothy Horn

One of the ways you can tell who is on the beach is by identifying the dog that is accompanying its owner. Arch Cape dogs are individuals that are easily recognized by their physical characteristics and remembered fondly for their idiosyncrasies. There are dogs of all colors and sizes and personalities here and they live a long and happy life in this town. Most love the water and enjoy chasing sea gulls, balls and frisbies. Some jog almost every dawn with their owners; others prefer to run with them at low tide; and still others would rather run by themselves. Often, they tag along to help pick up the daily mail and wait patiently at the Post Office entrance for their owners to make the return trip home. Their presence seems to shadow their owners' heels even after they are gone—an after image that never fades.

One dog's name will be remembered even by those who never laid eyes on her. Sally belonged to Kent Price, Sr. and his family. Sally's accustomed path to the beach, between Donlon and Columbia Avenues, now named Sally's Alley, has become a favorite access for homeowners living on both sides of Pacific Street from Shanks Avenue on the north to Marshall Avenue on the South.

Over the years, however, erosion and use deteriorated the slope to the beach. In 1987, at the instigation of Mrs. Dorothy Horn, thirty-one property owners contributed $5,021.50 to its rehabilitation. This money was spent on a concrete walk, a cedar railing, a gravel walk, a brick retaining wall, an overflow catch-basin and a thirty-foot covered culvert to redirect water from the walkway.

Acting on a suggestion by Marian Rall's son, attorney Marty Rall, who donated hours to the project, Mrs. Horn acquired a title search and copies of Arch Cape surveys to distinguish between county and private land. Mr. Thomas Sweeney, well-versed in real estate law, met with the committee and advised them. With Dick Pearson as treasurer of the group and Dorothy Horn as everything else, the job was done and the neighbors enjoyed several potluck dinners at Mrs. Horn's home in the process.

After a report from Randy Trevillion, County Roadmaster, the Clatsop County Commissioners approved county work in 1988 on a culvert under Pacific Street at the junction of Sally's Alley to prevent flood damage. The Sally's Alley project participants paid for the pipe.

For this attractive and useful addition to Arch Cape and for the community's cooperation, we give thanks in Sally's name.

Dorothy Horn at the beach end of Sally's Alley. All of the exposed rock tells us it is wintertime. Dorothy Horn Photo.

The Arch Cape Shingle Mill

C huck and Maxine Smith moved to Arch Cape in 1946 and shortly afterwards purchased the Arch Cape Grocery store from Mr. Schyler "Doc" Collingwood. The same
building, which is north of the present store, contained the post office where Mrs.
Ross White was the postmistress. Today, that original structure is used as a motel and people
refer to it as *The Inn at Arch Cape.* In 1946 the Smiths formed a partnership with Vic Shults
to build a shingle mill. They thought Arch Cape was a perfect location: Arch Cape Creek
supplied ample water, and the surrounding territory provided the raw material, since stands
of cedar trees covered the area at that time.

The Smiths and Shults bought property from Anna C. Taylor and later built the mill
near the site of the present sewage treatment plant. To add to this acquisition of land, George
Van Vleet leased land to them that provided space for the mill pond and log deck. The Van
Vleet timberlands produced an abundant supply of cedar and were the main source of supply
throughout most of the time the mill operated. Also, a large amount of cedar came from the
Crown Zellerbach holdings in Clatsop and Tillamook Counties and some came from local
land owners harvesting their cedar, which was a valuable crop even in those days.

During construction, Chuck Smith and Vic Shults built two bunk houses for
employees. Later, mill hands occupied the bunk houses for five or six years. Water from the
creek filled the mill pond and provided a route for cedar logs to chug up the chain to a platform
where men cut them into bolts for the sawyers. Sawyers faced two occupational hazards. The
high speed of revolution of the saws they worked with took its toll of fingers and thumbs.
Another occupational hazard was the high level of noise which caused severe hearing
damage.

After the mill was completed and operating in the fall of 1948, Mr. Smith withdrew
from the partnership of the Arch Cape Shingle Company and in 1949 sold the store to Ernest
White, son of the postmistress. Chuck and Maxine Smith then moved to the Willamette
Valley, but in 1953 moved back to Arch Cape to manufacture hip and ridge shingles from
shingles they purchased from the Arch Cape Shingle Company.

The mill burned at night September 3, 1954, and destroyed everything except the
shingle mill office and a storage shed stacked almost full of bundled shingles. Workers, with
help from volunteer firemen and local residents, saved some machinery, and Mr. Shults
immediately constructed a larger mill on the same property and soon had production on
schedule. In the early years of the operation as a two-machine mill, it ran two shifts and
employed 16 people per day. The mill was powered with a diesel engine driving a shaft from
which belts went to the saws and other machines. In later years, running at capacity with three
machines and three shifts, the mill employed 40 people. Employees lived all over Clatsop
and Tillamook Counties, but most lived in Cannon Beach and Seaside, and some in Arch
Cape.

In 1958, the Smiths moved to Svenson, Oregon, where they bought a shingle mill and
operated it as The Bear Creek Shingle Company. In January 1962, they moved back to Arch
Cape and bought the Arch Cape Shingle Company from Mr. E. V. Shults, who wished to retire
and pursue his hobby and avocation as a rock hound. His lapidary, known as Far West Rocks,
Inc., was at the corner of Beach Street and Mill Avenue. He had a large inventory and his

many boxes of rocks from all over the world were a popular attraction during the tourist season. He operated in this location from 1962 until 1972. Mr. Shults died in July 1975 at Wheeler, and Mrs. Shults died in May 1979 at Seaside. Raymond Hill purchased the Shults property in 1980.

The Smiths changed the name of the Arch Cape Shingle Company to Bear Creek Shingle Company and operated the mill until it burned down again July 12, 1967. The timber supply had declined in the whole area so they decided not to rebuild. Mr. and Mrs. C. G. Gredvig purchased the mill site property from the Smiths.

The shingle mill; the Van Vleet logging operation; Angelo Costanzo's logging of the Arch Cape Creek area; the Arch Cape Cabins owned by Albert and Nellie Leech; the Arch Cape Hotel; the store and post office; the Beach House motel and the Texaco station across from the store were the early commercial enterprises in South Arch Cape. About 1947, Isis Laboratories, a cosmetic firm owned by Rex Pomfret, moved from Portland to a building in Arch Cape on the highway just north of Ocean Road. The firm manufactured and shipped by mail eighteen cosmetic products. The shingle mill had an enormous impact on this area, since it was a viable operation that involved many people for more than twenty years.

The shingle mill crew. Circa late 40's or early 50's. Those logs were cut on the hillside behind the St. Peter the Fisherman Church and were so large that they were illegal to haul by truck on the highway so were hauled at night to the mill site. Photo, Elmer Vick collection.

Burned down shingle mill. Note the large straight-grained cedar log on the head rig. Photo source unknown.

This unusual aerial photograph shows the Mill Road area as it looked in 1960. The shingle mill was a large operation for this area and employed 40 men at one time. Note the large mill pond where cedar logs were floated to a ramp leading up to the head rig where the shingle processing began. A thin strip of Highway 101 can be seen at the top of the picture. Mr. Lee's home is at the right of the west intersection and Mr. Shults' home and rock shop is at the top left of this photograph, across from Mr. Lee's home. Today, the Mersereau home shows south of Mill road, on Third Street, which crosses Mill Road just a little west of the mill. If you look carefully, you can see the swinging bridge, recently rebuilt, which is the entry point for hikers when leaving Arch Cape to follow the Oregon Coast Trail when traveling south. Today, many homes line Mill Road. The Arch Cape Service District sewer treatment plant, which began operations in 1976, occupies the old mill site.

This photograph was made by Western Ways, Inc., Aerial Photographic Specialists, Corvallis, Oregon. Permission to use this photo could not be granted for the company is no longer in existence. Photo source, Christine and Reginald Ehler.

The Akeson Connection
Memories, by Nancy Akeson

Merle and I are not newcomers to this area nor are we old-timers—just folks up Arch Cape Creek, perhaps better known as up Mill Road, with a home on the creek side about half way up before the road ends.

Lady Luck introduced us, along with our children Stephen, Susan, and Santha, to Arch Cape in 1959 where we were guests in one of the Leech cabins. We had just returned from Liberia, West Africa, where Merle developed village schools. We spent all our spare time there on the beach and in the warm waters of Equatorial Africa. The entire family fell in love with the strong Arch Cape waves, the chilling water, the isolated beach, and the beautiful singing sands all along the high tide mark that met the driftwood. One could get out of the wind and relax, it seemed, forever. The Arch Cape beach since then is referred to by the family as "our beach."

Cambodia was the family home in 1960-62 for another job with schools. Upon returning, Merle took a position at San Francisco State University where he taught education classes. Merle had strong ties on the coast because his parents had owned two lots in Tolovana since 1927. We had relatives in the Portland area and we both made a vow to find property on the Northern Oregon coast.

But, before the search could begin, the children insisted that we stop for a picnic on "our beach." Frank Lee came by to say hello and Merle asked if any property was for sale in the area. Frank replied that there were two "widow cabins" up Mill Road on the creek. We were told that many couples bought cabins at the beach so husbands could be weekend fishermen. Reluctant wives accompanied them but for the most part only "tolerated" the situation. Following both husbands' deaths, the ladies were eager to sell the cabins and shake the sand from their feet; consequently, the term "widow" cabin. We walked up the road, found the cabins, and twenty minutes later decided to buy *Snug Harbor*, the name of one of the cabins. This spontaneous decision in the summer of 1962 became the delight of our lives.

Merle was a teacher and had three months off every summer. My job gave me a month's leave. Merle's teaching responsibilities were varied. He prepared graduate students for teaching in secondary schools in California. In addition, as a result of his anthropology background, he prepared Peace Corps teachers to serve in cross-cultural settings. In later years, he taught regular classroom teachers about the needs of Special Education children. My position as a Home Counselor with the *Blind Babies Foundation* kept me tied closer to San Francisco. I had a large geographical area and a case load of about 50 families who were parents of preschool (birth to six years) blind children. I loved my work, but always begrudged Merle his three months' summer vacation when compared to my one month. The last school bell each year signaled the Akeson family to head for *Snug Harbor*. Merle and the kids remained all summer and I returned to my San Francisco job when my month's vacation expired.

Snug Harbor was a tiny two room cabin built with loving care by someone with an eye for detail and precision. A loft above the kitchen held a double bed. The 10 by 19 foot kitchen housed a double bed, single bed, wood box, refrigerator, hot water heater, sink, two chests of drawers, suspended chain for hanging clothes, drop leaf table and a marvelous old wood stove. I wish I had a count of how many blackberry and huckleberry cobblers came out of that old stove. And, don't forget that blackberry jam cooked on the hot wood stove was usually done in the middle of August. I still miss our table covering method. We carefully piled lots of newspapers on the table top. It was easy to wrap up the refuse in the top layer of the newspaper as the preparation for the meal progressed. Then, with an always clean and tidy paper on top, one could set the table and be ready for the next meal.

The living room, with a sofa bed and a few pieces of furniture, completed the cabin. The east wall, carefully constructed from stone, had a big fireplace. The fireplace smoked so we made the chimney taller so it would draw more efficiently. My father and brother helped us replace the tile floor, but the rest of the cabin was fully furnished and ready for our occupancy.

No trip to the beach was complete without the string bag used to collect driftwood and bark washed ashore by the sea. We made periodic trips to Cove Beach where the wave action made wonderful bark deposits. We abandoned the wood stove in 1984. I find I still hate to pass by a good piece of bark spotted on the beach. The shingle mill operated at this time and much scrap wood was available for our wood stove.

There are numerous memories associated with those early summer vacations when the children were small and the area less populated. The shingle mill operated full time, often two and three shifts per day. Thundering trucks hauling loads of huge cedar logs to the mill caused our little cabin to vibrate so severely that pictures on the walls sometimes crashed to the floor and china rattled and shook. During flood stages, the creek ran bank full and debris from the mill roared past with tremendous speed, emptying at the mouth of Arch Cape Creek. With help from the ocean waves, the flotsam was spread upon the beach northward for a mile or so for local residents to gather. Cedar scraps from the mill split easily, as the grain of the wood was usually fine and straight, and therefore, were great for starting fires in the wood stove or fireplace. Today, one would prize such an easy source for kindling.

A trip to the mill always included a visit with Iva DeLashmitt, who lived across the creek from the mill. Iva was a wonderful neighbor since she always accepted the "catch of the day" for her cats. One year, just as we were ready to leave the beach and head south, our eldest son, Steve, decided he had to surf fish one more time. I agreed, since I assumed he would catch zero. I should have known better. To my dismay, he arrived much later than we had agreed upon with a catch of 65 surf fish. Bless Iva, she was willing to put them in her freezer.

We were fortunate to live on a road with "permanent" neighbors as well as "weekenders." Our neighbors helped us become part of the Arch Cape community. Iva and Gayle Delashmitt were at the end of the road. Next came Mr. McLoughlin, known as "Mac the pea man," as he grew a magnificent garden and specialized in peas, cherished by all who lived in the area. Mac's wife died before we purchased *Snug Harbor*. We always enjoyed the company of Mac and his grandson, Randy, who often played with our kids. A walk up Mill road still shows Mac's resting seat nailed to a spruce tree on the south side of the road just west of Beck's log cabin.

Lucille and Angelo Costanzo became family to us. They kept an eye on our cabin when we were away. Angelo Costanzo was responsible for the water supply in the early days. The kids loved to walk up the trail to the "water works" with Angelo and wait in eager anticipation for the bears to accost them. Unfortunately, from their standpoint, this never happened to them personally. They never tired of hearing Angelo tell about finding himself between a mother bear and her cub. His dash for the water shack with his Clorox bottles separated him from the mother bear and he waited there until the mother bear and her cub moved away.

Pete and Isabelle Szambelan, also newcomers to Arch Cape, bought the cabin next door to us. The Becks lived just west of us and Mr. Vic Shults, former owner of the Arch Cape Shingle Mill, had his rock shop at the intersection that leads to Highway 101. Ray Hill, who helps care for our water and sewer systems, lives there today.

Frank Lee, who lived across the road from the rock shop, had a special talent for making bird houses. We salvaged his last remaining "condominium" birdhouse before the bulldozer took it out of the field adjoining his house. It now sits on a stump at *Snug Harbor*. It is the work of an artisan. Handmade shakes cover the roof, which sports four ridges and valleys with flashing all in place. Each side has three or four individual compartments with private entries. We store the condo in the garage during the winter.

Arch Cape Creek was a glorious play area for the children on gentle days. The children made rafts and floated them seaward to the large natural pool just under the bridge about fifty yards east of the mouth of the creek—a child's paradise. There were times when our two-year-old son, Scott, had to be tied to one tree and Koaya, our Liberian monkey, to another to keep them both out of the creek.

Wild animals were constant neighbors. Skunk, raccoon, elk, deer, and bear all enjoyed the flat land bordering both sides of the creek and the hill rising south toward the Arch Cape headland. Hiking throughout the territory was another memory, especially when we searched for the elusive lake above the falls the kids insisted we could find, but never did. The kids also spent many an interesting hour in the rock shop owned by Mr. Shults on the corner of Mill Road and Beach Avenue. He had a large inventory and was nationally known for his lapidary skills.

Our older teenagers' first jobs were at the Whaler Restaurant in Cannon Beach and our youngest son, Scott, learned how to work with his first and favorite boss, Angelo Costanzo. Angelo needed an agile weeder and all-purpose "gofer" and Scott had free time, lots of energy and loved hearing Angelo tell stories. Angelo taught Scott invaluable yard maintenance skills as he mowed, raked and cared for many lawns in the Arch Cape area. One day Angelo taught Scott how to kill weeds on the slope in front of the church by using a small flame thrower. Unfortunately for Angelo's work pants, Scott turned to admire a fancy car and managed to ignite Angelo's pants at the same time. Angelo's wife, Lucille, insisted that it was a blessing. She had been trying to get rid of those particular pants for a long time. I like to think the flame thrower experience at age 12 had something to do with Scott's current career as a fire fighter. Scott also helped Angelo scrub the inside of the wooden holding tanks for the water system. Working with Angelo was a wonderful apprenticeship for a young boy. Scott never succeeded in winning a game of "Indian arm wrestling" with Angelo, but he never ceased to try.

Ethel LeGault, the owner of the store and post office for many years, made our whole family feel that we were a part of Arch Cape. Ethel is high on our list of our many and precious early Arch Cape memories. Our first ritual each June was to announce our arrival to Ethel, pay our post office box rental fee and establish our Arch Cape roots for the summer. We had no phone for many years and Ethel was our connection to the outside world.

When Merle's work took us to Africa and Afghanistan again, relatives used the cabin and kept it ready for our return. Finally, in 1974, we stopped our wandering, and *Snug Harbor* and Arch Cape have become a focal point for the Akeson clan. The kids continue their summer cycle, which now includes two granddaughters, Claire and Ann, who love the creek and can't wait to go to "their beach."

Al and Shirley Kalkhoven (Nehalem Bay Woodworks) helped us remodel the cabin in 1984. With Merle's half-time retirement in 1985, we have been able to extend our three months' schedule to six months and are residents in Arch Cape for half the year.

We've seen many changes since we purchased *Snug Harbor* in 1962 and know more changes will come in the future. We are grateful to Lady Luck for introducing us to this special part of our lives.

Susan holds the family pet, a Liberian monkey named Koaya, and Scott holds its tail while playing on the Arch Cape Beach in 1963. Akeson photo.

Snug Harbor as seen from the creek side before the 1984 addition was done by Shirley and Al Kalkhoven. Circa 1962. Akeson photo.

Merle and Nancy beside the condo birdhouse constructed by Frank Lee and rescued by the Akesons. A bulldozer clearing the lot next to Frank Lee's home was about to destroy it. David English photo. 1993.

Snug Harbor from Mill Road. David English Photo. 1993.

The Archer, Crawford, Ellis, Carney Connection
Memories by Gwen Carney

Elizabeth Ann (Grey) Crawford Archer — 1881-1971

About the turn of the century a Minnesota farm girl came out west to view the mighty Pacific Ocean. In a day when proper women wore skirts down to their ankles, gloves and hats, young Elizabeth Grey found these clothes far too confining for the activities she planned for this vacation. She purchased men's pants, hiking boots, a gun and holster, a rifle, and with her cousin, Claude Ellis, set out to explore the Pacific Coast beaches. They started at some point in Washington, then hiked the Oregon Coast and continued down along the California seashore for some distance. At the conclusion of the journey, Claude returned to Portland and Elizabeth to her home in Minnesota. On her return, she announced to family and friends that she had seen the most beautiful beach on the whole Pacific Ocean, Arch Cape, and one day she would own property there.

In 1908, Elizabeth married John Julian Krawczak and moved into a new home in St. Paul, Minnesota. The next year George John was born, followed by a daughter, Mildred Rose in 1911, and another son, Walter Harold in 1913. For reasons never explained, this marriage did not last.

In 1918, Elizabeth Gray Krawczak packed what she could, gathered the children and left her husband. She moved to Portland, Oregon. That same summer, she brought her children to the Arch Cape area and camped beside Arch Cape Creek. The first part of the trip was by boat, the *Georgiana*, from Portland to Astoria and cost fifty-cents a person. From Astoria to Seaside they rode in a jitney bus, much of the way on cord wood roads. They traveled from Seaside to Cannon Beach in a horse-drawn buckboard and then walked the seven miles to Arch Cape. Adding to the logistics of the trip, there were the summer's provisions to be packed in from a Cannon Beach store (Cannon Beach Mercantile Co., now Osborns, or the Coles Grocery). These provisions: one slab of bacon, ten pounds of beans, ten pounds of flour, one pound of coffee, a bag of salt, baking soda, five pounds of sugar, five pounds of lard, two cans of milk, five pounds of raisins, nutmeg and a five-pound tin of Karo syrup were carried to Arch Cape. Walter, being the youngest, carried the smallest parcel, the tin of syrup, and often complained how the wire handle dug into his hand. He did this quietly to Mildred as Elizabeth did not tolerate complaints. Other supplies carried were tin pie plates, a graniteware multi-purpose pan, one frying pan, candles and a Colt revolver.

Elizabeth settled her children, ages six, eight and nine, into a camp near Arch Cape Creek. Housing in camp, depending on the location, was a tarpaulin fashioned into a tent or simply a roof with corners tied to conveniently located trees. Dry grass covered with a blanket became a bed, with two more blankets for warmth. At night, they were lulled to sleep by the sound of the sea. Elizabeth returned to Portland where she obtained work as a store detective, first for Eastern Outfitting Company and later for Lipman Wolf and Company. She returned to Arch Cape weekends to be with her children.

Fish, razor clams and crabs were plentiful. Occasionally, they gathered rock oysters from rocks near the arches. They were difficult to find and harvest. A hammer and a screwdriver were used to break up the sandstone between oysters. This took time and patience, but the delicate flavor of the tiny mollusks made it worthwhile.

After 1922 they traveled by train from Portland to Seaside, for one dollar, and by buckboard to Ecola (Cannon Beach). It was a seven mile hike from Ecola to Arch Cape and this had to be timed so one could pass both Silver and Hug Points at low tide.

Both Joe Walsh and Marmaduke Maxwell had cows and sold milk by the pail to the Krawczak children. Eggs cost ten cents a dozen and milk was ten cents a pail. Fresh vegetables, including potatoes, could be purchased from Mr. Maxwell, who had a large garden. Up the hill above the old water reservoir stood the Simmons' place with the apple orchard. Those apples were available to anyone willing to harvest them, but the uncared-for and brush covered trees produced wormy and small fruit. Millie said they salvaged what they could from each apple for sauce because they were free and the taste was great. The Simmonses had deserted their house by the time Elizabeth and Millie arrived in Arch Cape. Mr. Simmons was ill for some time and was on heavy medication. According to Millie, many empty medical bottles of various sizes and shapes were tossed behind his cabin. Millie and Wally scavenged some of the bottles, but Elizabeth made them throw them away because she was afraid they might carry some harmful germs.

In the area south of Leech Avenue were three deserted primitive cabins. The children preferred the tarpaulin tent by the creek, but when it rained, they moved into one of the cabins. One cabin had an old rusted wood stove, but it was adequate for cooking. No one seemed to know who built these shelters and they were used on a first come basis.

Mildred told of her experience with Wally in early summer of 1921 when they were joined along the creek with about 25 Boy Scouts. Sometime after dark, a flash flood developed. She and Walter grabbed the cabin with the stove, leaving the two stoveless cabins for the Boy Scouts. The cabins had openings for windows and doors; none was in place. No one drowned, but the water from the creek almost reached Leech Avenue and tin cups, plates, and camping equipment sailed away with the swift rising current.

The area north of Leech Avenue was a meadow with mounds of mussel shells. The Maxwell and Walsh cows grazed in this meadow right up to the sea shells. There is a story told by Marmaduke Maxwell to Bert Patton who told Mildred and Walter that Indians would take their canoes out to Castle Rock and harvest the large mussels. These mounds of shells were the remains of those harvests. Because of this story, Mildred and Walter spent hours poking through the mound of shells looking for arrow heads. They found a few beads but no arrow heads.

After the summer of 1919, George had time for only occasional visits to the beach. He was a large boy for his age and found work in Portland to supplement the family income.

In 1920 Elizabeth and Wally, age seven, Millie, age eight and George, eleven, took the train to Wheeler via Tillamook, a ferry across the Nehalem River, then hiked into Manzanita and on over Neakahnie Mountain to Arch Cape.

A landmark on the Neakahnie trail was the swinging bridge. Mildred describes her first crossing on the swinging bridge. It traversed a sea chasm near the present location of the large parking lot and beautiful rock walls near the top of Neahkahnie Mountain on Highway 101. This bridge was two planks wide with cables for hand rails that were randomly connected to the lower cables holding the planks. Mildred was half way across when the wind caught the bridge and the hand cables pulled her high enough so her feet could not touch the plank walkway. As she stretched her toes out toward the planks below, her eyes caught the white water breaking over the rocks hundreds of feet below. At the same time, Elizabeth was on the other side yelling at her to "keep moving and don't look down." Elizabeth expected obedience regardless of the circumstances. Mildred said, "I was absolutely terrified, not of falling to the rocks below but for the spanking from Elizabeth should I fall." As quickly as the wind picked up, it died down. Her feet made contact with the planks and she scrambled the rest of the way across the bridge.

On several occasions, the family visited the agate caves at Short Sands Beach. On the north side of the cove are three sea caves that can be reached only during a two-foot minus tide. In the 20's there was an abundance of smooth white stones on the floors of these caves. Even on a low tide, it is necessary to climb over large moss and kelp covered rocks to reach the caves. It was still a slippery and dangerous hike when Pat, Juliann and Margaret Carney made this same trek in 1981.

In 1919, Elizabeth purchased a lot on the southwest corner of Cannon Street and Ocean View Avenue from Joe Walsh for $50. Because the nearest water was piped only as far as Mr. Maxwell's house, the family continued to camp summers by Arch Cape Creek until the late summer of 1921. At that time, Elizabeth's brother, Mark Grey, came down from Seattle and helped her build a one room cabin with both a front and a back porch. Lumber and supplies for building the cabin were hauled from Cannon Beach by wagon. Now Mildred, who was ten years old and Walter, who was eight, spent summers there. Elizabeth and George, now twelve, joined them when they could get away from work. The family carried water, using buckets, from Mr. Maxwell's spigot located near his barn.

As the children made friends in Portland and in Arch Cape, they became aware that people had difficulty pronouncing their last name, Krawczak (Kruff´-check). To overcome this they adopted their present name, Crawford. In the late 30's both George and Walter had their last names legally changed to Crawford. Elizabeth married Raymond Archer in 1926. Two years later, in 1928, Edward Roy Archer was born and the summer cabin at Arch Cape was becoming too small. The back porch was enclosed and converted into a kitchen with the addition of a large porch on the south side of the cabin. Then a garage was built on the east side of the house. There were few people in the area and little concern with the fact that this garage was not on Elizabeth's property, but was built on a dedicated street adjourning her property. The garage, however, was never used to store a car. It contained wall to wall beds to receive the overflow of house guests. Two other buildings on or near the property were the privy and the woodshed.

A number of the early residents in Arch Cape remained single. The Crawford-Archer family had varying degrees of contact with some of these neighbors, and stories regarding them have been passed down to the present generation. One of them was Marmaduke Maxwell.

Marmaduke Maxwell, an unforgettable bachelor, moved to Arch Cape in 1912. His eyes alone struck a person as being remarkable. Blue, kind looking and crinkled at the corners is the way Mildred described them. He wore a pair of leather pants so stiff they stood by themselves when removed and propped in the corner. He kept his money in a draw string leather pouch. When the children purchased whole milk rich in cream for a dime a bucket or vegetables from him, they watched his ritual of opening the pouch and selecting the correct coins for their change. This they recounted, not because Mr. Maxwell was dishonest, but they knew they would have to account to Elizabeth for every cent they spent.

The Crawford children were awed by Mr. Maxwell and watched from a distance his daily dip in the ocean. Each day he walked out to the shallow surf in his robe with his thermometer and checked the temperature of the ocean. If it was cold water, he dove through a wave or two and returned to his house. A warmer thermometer reading meant he remained in the water for a longer time. He kept daily records of the weather and ocean temperatures.

Marmaduke Maxwell was the only person the children knew who swam out to Castle Rock which is about a mile off shore. This feat was told by Bert Patton many times. Millie, Wally and Elizabeth believed Mr. Maxwell actually did this. The story seems probable because Mr. Maxwell was a strong swimmer. In Bert's retelling of the story, he always said that "even though Maxwell was a strong swimmer, the swim was more difficult than he had anticipated and that he never tried it again." The cold water temperatures, the cross currents around the rock and the pull of the tides: Are all ingredients for a difficult, but not an impossible swim.

The children were fascinated by Mr. Maxwell when he rode his horse named Lil or hitched her to his buggy when going to Cannon Beach for supplies and the mail. He owned several horses over the years for they didn't seem to take the ocean dampness very well.

Len Menrow was a single man who came to Arch Cape for a relatively short period of time. Perhaps he was a drifter. He lived with Marmaduke Maxwell and was an able carpenter. Elizabeth hired him to build the cabinets in her kitchen before he moved on.

Marmaduke Maxwell moved to Arch Cape in 1912 and Bert Patton purchased his property in Cannon View Park with a partially completed log cabin in 1921. The cabin was a little north and east from Elizabeth's property. In the ten or so years prior to Mr. Maxwell's death in 1931, they became good friends. Bert worked as a blacksmith in logging camps and was not a full-time Arch Cape resident. They both looked after each other and Mr. Maxwell watched over Bert's property, especially during the early construction period while Bert finished his log cabin. Bert continued recording daily records of the weather and ocean temperatures after Mr. Maxwell died.

Bert Patton was a warm and caring person and the Crawford children looked upon him as a father figure. My mother, Mildred, often recalled the time she, her brother Walter, and their dog Spot waded out to the second rock off the Arch Cape headland to fish over the tide. They had no access to tide tables. As the tide rose, they huddled together on the topmost pinnacle of the rock with Spot held between them. The white water broke around their feet. Then they spotted Bert ambling up the beach. He was pacing back and forth and it was only their sight of him that kept them glued to the rock until the low tide came that evening. Neither of the children could swim and their lower limbs were numb with cold. Bert was still there as he always was for so many of his friends and neighbors, especially when children were involved. During the depression, Bert's home was open to families who were out of work or had no resources for food and shelter.

In the late 20's, Louis C. "Smitty" Smith moved to Arch Cape. He built a small cabin on an island in Arch Cape Creek at the end of Webb (Mill) Avenue. Smitty was a hunter and a loner. He was also single and lived with his dog, Tippy. People in Arch Cape joked about

Smitty's having the most fertile ground around. He was always shooting wild animals, and after meat had been shared with other residents, the carcasses were buried in various spots on the small island. No one in the family can recall when Smitty left the area or what became of him.

Another personality who left an impression on Arch Cape was Sam Webb. Sam lived in Astoria, but was involved in the land company that promoted and sold lots in Arch Cape as well as being a dealer in other real estate developments. He was a handsome man with dark curly hair, but was described by Elizabeth, as "slick as oil." He wooed a number of widows between Astoria and Arch Cape. He left his relationships richer, but he remained single. This was the sad experience of a widow friend of Elizabeth's. Sam's life was cut short on a trip to California when a tree fell across the vehicle in which he was a passenger. Elizabeth could not wait to tell her friend that "Sam was killed dead." In her typical Libby style, she said, "You reap what you sow."

The single women that settled in Arch Cape were not the robust pioneer type one would expect in an undeveloped area. Miss Eva Benson was petite and her brown eyes seemed almost too big for her face. She had a tendency to flutter and twitter, reminding one of a small nervous bird. This impression, as well as her stature, belied the fact that she was a capable woman. Eva Benson was a piano teacher in Portland until arthritis crippled her hands. In later life she went to library school and before her retirement was head of the catalog department of the Multnomah County Library. She had a gentleman friend, a druggist from Portland, whose name was Mr. Foster. He visited Miss Benson and pitched a tent on the ocean side of the property. They swam every day. Miss Benson wore a cap with her long wool bathing suit with a skirt that came to her knees. She waded while Mr. Foster dove through the waves and swam in the ocean. She often invited Millie and Wally to dinner with Mr. Foster and frequently served eggplant. Later, they all roasted marshmallows in the fireplace on sticks Eva had sharpened. She drove a black Model T Ford and was a willing chauffeur, but in later years was one of Arch Cape's worst drivers. Everyone who experienced riding with Miss Benson told of often ending up in a ditch or almost colliding with another vehicle. This car was a symbol of her independence and she did not want to part with it even though she recognized that she could no longer drive. For years, after she stopped driving, the car sat on blocks in her garage.

Miss Benson was estranged from her brother most of her adult life, but when he was old and ill, he looked her up and she took care of him until he died. He was somewhat of a tyrant and was fussy about food and visitors. Miss Benson chatted with friends on her back porch as her brother didn't like guests in the house. She died of cancer in the Wheeler Hospital and her ashes were scattered in the ocean along the Arch Cape beach.

The 30's were years of change. Elizabeth's marriage to Ray Archer failed and jobs were scarce. George and Walter finally found employment working on the tunnel in Arch Cape. Because there was a need for eating facilities for tunnel workers, Elizabeth, with eight year old Eddie, moved to her Arch Cape cabin to cook for them. She made arrangements with a store in Cannon Beach to deliver groceries to her twice a week. She also extracted a promise from Smitty to provide her with fresh meat and for clams and crabs, when available. In no time, she had ten men from different shifts and had as many customers as she could handle. She served two meals a day and packed lunches. It was a blessing that Elizabeth was born with above average endurance. Her venture allowed for no holiday vacations and water for cooking and washing was hauled from Mr. Maxwell's spigot by his barn.

Walter shared some of his experiences with us when he worked on the tunnel. One evening about dusk when he was getting off work, he decided to walk home by way of the beach. He'd worked that day and was very tired. Down the path he saw someone he didn't recognize picking salmon berries. He knew most of the people in the area by sight, so he squinted his eyes to focus on this figure only to realize it was not a person but a bear standing upright. Beyond the standing bear were two cub bears. The mother bear saw Walter at the same time and charged on all fours. Walter took a shortcut over a rock pile from the tunnel excavation, ran through the creek with his boots on, made a bee-line through the salal to the cabin and collapsed across Elizabeth's back porch. As a child, I would pry for more details. "Did the bear stop chasing you at the bottom of the rock pile or did she stop at the creek?" I asked. Walter's answer was always the same: "I don't know. I never looked back." Walter also told me he saved his wages from his tunnel job to buy Aunt Aggie her wedding and engagement rings.

The family started a population explosion in 1934. Mildred married Donald D. Ellis; that same year George married Eva. In 1935, I was the first child born to Don and Mildred. My brother, Ronald Bruce, followed in the spring of 1939. Walter married his high school sweetheart, Agnes B. Baron, June 12, 1937. Seven years later Walter Harold Crawford II was born.

Elizabeth continued to live at the beach after the tunnel was completed. Her one problem was education for Eddie. The nearest school was in Cannon Beach, but no Arch Cape school bus was available at that time. It was a seven mile hike at low tide from Arch Cape to Cannon Beach. Elizabeth's solution to the problem was simple. She did not enroll him in school. Instead, she asked Mildred to take Eddie to Portland to live with her family so he could begin his formal education. Not always separated, the family traveled to the beach on weekends to visit Elizabeth, and the cabin became overcrowded with the growing family. Elizabeth used the building intended for the car as an unheated bedroom for guests. In the main room of the cabin, she used curtains on wires around each bed to give a semblance of privacy. When the cabin and garage were full, my brother and I slept on straw-filled ticks on the floor. Children have little concern for the hardness of a floor. I can still recall the sweet smell of the fresh cut straw in my tick.

It was also in the late 30's that electric lines came to Ocean View Avenue. Elizabeth welcomed the new development and had her cabin wired on the north and west sides. We had a two-circuit fuse box located next to the kitchen sink. We placed a copper penny next to the family drinking cup to slip behind the fuse if it blew. One of the first electric appliances in the house was an ornate toaster. It toasted bread only on one side. When bread reached the desired level of browness, one had to flip down the side of the toaster and turn the bread to brown on the other side. Elizabeth could not delegate authority. While she was stoking the stove, boiling the coffee and stirring the mush, the toast burned. Not one to waste burned bread, she scraped the charred part of the bread into the kitchen sink reminding everyone, "Never waste—never want." The standard joke in our family was not how dark do you want your toast but how thin do you want it.

On December 7, 1941, World War II changed all our lives. Elizabeth moved back to

Portland to take a job in the shipyards, and trips to the beach cabin became less frequent because of gas rationing. Tires and cars were hard to come by, for so much was going to the war effort. Sugar and shoes were rationed and women waited in long lines when nylons were available. George was drafted into the army and Eva followed him and obtained a job packing parachutes. About once a month the family could save up enough gas ration coupons to take one car to the beach. It was a four-hour drive from Portland to Arch Cape then, as the Sunset Highway didn't exist. We traveled a route through Hillsboro and Forest Grove to the Wolf Creek Highway. A mile east of the summit of the coast range, we would begin to see cars pulled over with overheated radiators or flat tires. Everyone carried tire patch kits and a familiar childhood experience was watching someone remove the tube from a tire, submerging it in the nearest water to identify the hole, then cleaning and drying it and carefully applying the patch. By the end of the war, Walter joked, "My tire tubes had patches on top of patches." Once overheated radiators and flat tire problems were corrected, drivers could not exceed thirty-five miles per hour. The new speed limit imposed was designed to conserve gasoline. Of course, impatient drivers raced past us going forty-five or fifty miles per hour, and car tires threw gravel that bounced off our windshields from the partially graveled narrow road.

The most memorable part of each trip was the miles of hairpin turns driving from the Cannon Beach Junction into Cannon Beach. No matter how car sick I was, the first sight of the ocean sent shivers up my spine. To me, there would be the same rush of emotion one feels when the American flag passes by or the euphoria of returning home after a long absence.

During World War II, an air attack or an invasion by the Japanese along the Pacific Coast was considered a possibility. Even after Fort Stevens was fired upon by a Japanese submarine, there was no mass hysteria; but the effects of the Civil Defense Program were felt in Arch Cape. An air siren was mounted on the gas station across from the post office and store and was tested at unannounced times. At night, the local air raid warden walked around the neighborhood and checked the houses for total darkness. All beach homes were required to have blackout curtains on all windows that let light out toward the west. Cars driven without blackout covers on the lights were subject to a stiff fine.

The coast guard took over one of the rental cottages on Leech Avenue to house men and dogs who patrolled the shoreline from Cove Beach to Hug Point, weather and tides permitting. They carried radios and were to report anything suspicious. Most of the men were young and homesick from being stuck in isolated Arch Cape.

On several occasions, we watched navy planes as their pilots practiced dive bombing skills on Castle Rock. The bomb seemed to produce a white dust that rose in the air after impact. Elizabeth had her own opinion as to what was happening one mile off shore. 'The military is terrorizing innocent birds by bombing the rock with my hard-to-get flour,' she thought. When Elizabeth heard the planes off shore, she clenched her fists, set her jaw and spit out a string of oaths that would cause a logger to blush.

The time came when Elizabeth's cabin could not contain the growing family and their friends. Walter and Aggie purchased four lots on Cannon Street just south of Elizabeth's cabin. Bert Patton helped them build a modern beach house—one with inside plumbing—on one of the lots. The Amy family owns that house today, but the name **Old Timer** is still on the front of the house. George Crawford purchased a lot north and east of Elizabeth's cabin and began building a home with his second wife, Doris, and son Tim. Milly and Don Ellis purchased property with a little cabin that was bordered by Arch Cape Creek on the south, and on the west by the beach and ocean. In 1953, Edward married Roseanna Brook and by 1959 had three daughters, Paula, Linda and Sandra. Since the three oldest children had their own cabins, Elizabeth gave her cabin to Ed and Rose Archer. The Ellis cabin near the creek had one bedroom and became inadequate in the years following my marriage to George Carney and my brother's marriage to Elfriede Baer. By 1973 there were four Carney children: Patrick, Kathleen, Elizabeth Juliann and Margaret; and two Ellis children, Christopher and Alexander. In 1978 Don and Milly began construction of their new beach front house at 1398 Pacific Street.

Maintence on Elizabeth's cabin became a burden. Shingles peeled off the roof in the winter storms, and dry rot and wood boring ants destroyed the structural strength of the building. Ownership of the cabin changed hands several times but always stayed in the family and eventually was given to me. In spite of a strong maintenance program, we were losing Elizabeth's cabin to dry rot and the carpenter ants. In the spring of 1979, with mixed feelings, we made arrangements with the Cannon Beach Volunteer Fire Department to burn the cabin to the ground as a training exercise.

That same summer we watched Bob Cerelli begin construction of our new house at 107 Ocean View Avenue. The new home was not a cabin, but years of habit resulted in our calling the new house **The Cabin**.

Between 1970 and 1989 Elizabeth, her children and their spouses (with the exception of Roseanna, Eddie's wife) have died and most have been interred at the American Legion Cemetery in Nehalem, Oregon. Elizabeth lived to age ninety, having outlived one son, Walter. I have to smile at the arrangement of graves in the family plot. It was no secret in our family that Elizabeth did not hold her son-in-law, Don, in high regard. Don was short and sensitive about his stature. When Elizabeth came to visit, the first loud words out of her mouth were always, "Where is Shortie?" In later years, Milly often threatened to bury Don next to Elizabeth. They were probably both pleased that Elizabeth Archer lies at one end of the family plot and Don Ellis is next to Mildred at the other end.

Almost a century has passed since Elizabeth made her first trip to the Pacific Northwest. She not only fulfilled her dream of owning property at the most beautiful beach on the mighty Pacific Ocean, but instilled in her children, grandchildren and great grandchildren an abiding affection for this spot along the north Oregon coast called Arch Cape.

Elizabeth Krawczak on a hike to Manzanita. A thin strip of Nehalem Bay in front of mist-covered hills appears in the background. Circa 1919.

From left to right: George; Bill, the son of cousin Claud Ellis; Walter, Elizabeth's friend Violet Hanson and Mildred at the Arch Cape Creek camp site, Circa 1918.

Mildred, Gwen and Elizabeth Archer in the summer of 1946 on the south side of Elizabeth's cabin and in front of the back porch.

The Ellis cabin north of Arch Cape Creek. Photo taken in 1980 shortly before the cabin was burned to make way for five home sites. This cabin sat east of the present Steve Petrucci home.

Grandma Archer with George and Wally on Leech Avenue (then Walsh Avenue) in 1923.

			June 1,	19 55

M

Arch Cape Water Co.
THE THEO. DICHTER CO.   WARRENTON, OREGON

To   Elizabeth Archer,   13067 S. E. Sherman, Portland, Oregon   Dr.

Terms _____

Gibson's Billheads Nº 10.

June	1	Water rent 6/1/55 to 6/1/56	20	00	
		Make check payable to The Theo. Dichter Co.			
		Water rent payable in advance.			
		THE THEO. DICHTER CO. WARRENTON, ORE			

Elizabeth Archer's 1955 water bill from the Arch Cape Water Company, $20.00. It was the same in 1952.

Elizabeth Archer at the wheel of her Chevrolet with Edward on her lap and with two friends. Circa 1929.

Elizabeth, Aggie (Walter's wife) and Millie at the north portal of the unfinished Arch Cape tunnel. 1941.

Mildred, Elizabeth and Walter at Falls Creek, just south of Hug Point. Circa 1923. Photos from Gwen Carney collection.

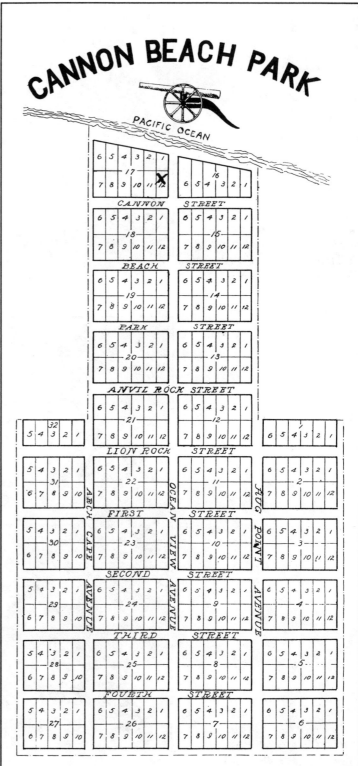

This is the 1919 plat map Elizabeth used when purchasing her Arch Cape lot near the west end of Ocean View Avenue—lot 12, the one marked with a X. That is the same lot where the present **Cabin** is today. Today, Hug Point Avenue is Markham Avenue and Arch Cape Avenue is Maxwell Avenue.

The text on the following page appeared at the bottom of the plat map.

Continued from previous page. Text copied exactly as shown on the plat map.

INFORMATION

Finest seaside resort on the North Pacific Coast. Situated in Clatsop County, State of Oregon, between "Hug Point" on the north and "Arch Cape" on the south. It is sheltered from the objectionable winds, particularly the cold winds from the north, so noticeable at some resorts.

The broad Pacific Ocean is here in view with a speck of a sail or the dark smoke from some passing steamer, while the mild zephyrs waft shoreward the health-bearing ozone to the visitor or resident. Down the mountain rush the cool, sparkling waters of Arch Cape Creek.

Adjacent to the property is a broad stretch beach of smooth sand which has the singular property of giving forth musical sounds, when tread by enamored lovers and is known as the "Singing Sands."

Here sixty years ago, a wreck of the sailing vessel "Shark" came ashore with several cannon —hence the name "Cannon Beach."

Near by is Necarnie mountains where it is reported some treasures are buried by one Pacific Captain Kid. Many people have tried to find the hidden wealth, but being unable to interpret the mystic characters that are supposed to lead to the spot where the treasure is hidden.

The sea has worn a tunnel, forming an arch, through the cape, called Arch Cape.

Some unfortunate ship wrecked on the beach here one hundred years ago, left a vast quantity of beeswax buried in the sands. Considerable dispute has arisen between scientists whether this was real beeswax or a mineral product.

From another wreck, many moons past, a rescued sailor was nursed back to life and strength through the efforts of a dusky maiden, a Tillamook princess. They married and became the ancestors of Chief Cuhsby, the red-haired Indian seen by Captains Lewis and Clark at Fort Clatsop.

Here are to be found fresh air, salt and fresh pure water, fine scenery, places with historic and legendary lore, beach drives, mountain climbing, retreats in scented pine forests, fishing, hunting and boating. All that any one can wish in favor of health and pleasure is here.

The survey of the Astoria & Columbia River Railroad runs across the Park.

Lots fifty by one hundred feet.

Call on or address,

(Here we are, seventy years later, and are told now not to get exposed by ozone. The above ad mentions "singing sands," which all Arch Cape beach lovers recognize. So, what is new? The same descriptions often appear in real estate ads today.)

The Balfour Connection
Memories—by David Astle, Nephew

Although my mother's family had been vacationing in Cannon Beach since the 1910's and 20's, my first trip there occurred in the summer of 1946. We stayed at a cottage called *Cuddle Doon* near the old Ecola Hotel. That was the first time I had seen autos on the beach and it was a thrill to ride down the sand to Hug Point. Up until then, our coastal vacations—usually my aunt, uncle and I—were at Seaside and it usually involved a train trip back to Portland, which made leaving the coast one of the best parts of the vacation.

Train trips to Seaside continued through the war years and probably into the early 50's. All my rides, at least three, were made from Seaside to Portland, probably in 1943-45. One thing I remember for sure—we were in Seaside when the first A-bomb was dropped. My uncle, Dave Balfour and aunt Ethel took me to Seaside where we stayed a week or two and then returned on the train at the end of the vacation.

In 1948 we started staying at the Glocca Morra resort on the beach just north of Hug Point. A Mr. and Mrs. Lee were managing Glocca Morra for Clyde Ruegg in those years. I'm not sure if this is the Arch Cape Frank Lee, but they were a very nice couple.

Of course, as kids, we walked the beach to Arch Cape and beyond in those days, including scaling the north side of Hug Point on one memorable summer afternoon (and wondering if we would live to tell about it).

In late 1956 my aunt and uncle, Dave and Ethel Balfour, purchased a vacant lot (now 1680 West Pacific—between Jim and Gertrude Hills' home and David Johnson's, the second house south of where Jack Foster formerly lived.) I have a copy of Ethel Balfour's letter to me dated December 6, 1956, in which she writes about finding a suitable oceanfront lot at Arch Cape in Kent Price Park. It appears they got it for the outrageous price of $3,000 from a widow by the name of Mrs. Doris Ferris. The transaction was handled by Kent A. Price. Al Gambell, an architect friend of theirs, designed their home and it was constructed during the late spring and summer of 1957.

Ethel LeGault and I were good friends. She built her new store in 1960 and enlarged it to accommodate the post office in 1961. She catered to my interest in postage stamps and saved for me plate blocks of all the latest commemorative issues.

Ethel Balfour was a Catholic and very desirous of having a church constructed at Arch Cape. Monsignor Willis L. Whalen and I spent some days there staining and varnishing the interior walls just after the construction of St. Peter the Fisherman Church was completed.

Ethel Balfour died in September, 1960. My uncle, two years later, married my father's other sister, Margaret. Dave Balfour (a Portland stockbroker since 1932 when he, Ethel and others started their own firm) retired fully in the early 70's. Dave and Margaret lived at the Arch Cape home full-time until Margaret's death in July, 1979. Dave then resided at a nursing home in Portland until his death in 1984. The Balfours were well acquainted with Bridget and Berkeley Snow, Ella and Floyd "Scotty" Scott, Gertrude and Jim Hill, Gracie and Jim Richmond, the Gills, Colemans, Fosters plus many others. I inherited the Arch Cape house from Dave Balfour and expect it will remain in the family for many years to come.

One summer when my father was visiting Arch Cape, Uncle Dave mentioned that Scotty now lived there and would enjoy seeing my father again. Dad said "My God, he must be awfully old by now!" (Floyd Scott had been Dad's insurance agent when we lived in Longview in the 30's, and I believe Scotty was once mayor of Longview part of that time). At any rate, Dad was very pleased to see that Scotty hadn't aged much at all and had retained all of his faculties. Of course, Scotty's daily walks on the beach, with dog and walking stick, were a good opportunity to stop and visit with one of the nicest fellows you would ever meet.

The Tom 'n' Larry tradition in Seaside seems to be fading, but it was surely the place to buy candy in the 40's and 50's. We'd wait for candy in the long line leading to the sales counter during the war and pray that the cut-off (because of sugar rationing) would come behind and not in front of us.

One nice summer day, my friends and I succeeded in damming Asbury Creek, creating a large reservoir that caused some of the large logs to float. Many children were attracted to the reservoir and came with automobile tire inner tubes and other floating devices. Dorothy Price lived in the first house north of Asbury Creek and was amazed at what we had done and she mentioned that event to me for many years afterwards. It was also a surprise to the couple who were dozing and sunbathing on the south bank of the creek and awoke to find themselves on the north side of our diverted creek. When we released the water, auto traffic on the beach had to wait a few minutes while the flood subsided.

Harold and Florence Schaeffer were special friends of ours. Harold did routine maintenance and mechanical work on both my uncle's car and my car. My wife Kathy and I spent our first post-honeymoon vacation at Arch Cape in October, 1964, where we had one week of fantastic coastal autumn weather. We had just purchased new ten-speed bikes and enjoyed riding them extensively that week. Harold and Florence were our guests for dinner on the evening of October 21, 1964. I quote from my diary: *"Schaeffers arrived at 6:30 for dinner. We talked 'til 7:30, then ate a fine dinner. Played Canasta afterward. Harold and I beat Florence and Kathy. Harold told us the fantastic story of his life."*

Unfortunately, I did not record, nor do I remember much about the story, except that he had done a lot of amazing things and was on his own at a very early age. If you can arrange to have Kathy or me transported back to that evening via hypnosis, then we possibly could provide some interesting details about the Schaeffers.

I spent many hours visiting with Harold at the service station over the years. He gave us two of his boat models. I also enjoyed his outdoor train tracks and supporting structures he built after he quit the service station business and moved to a duplex next to the station. Harold was one of the nicest, most helpful and sincerest persons I have ever had the pleasure of knowing. He was always cheerful, as was his wife, Florence. We missed them greatly when they were no longer part of the Arch Cape scene.

One rather unimportant, but nevertheless vivid, recollection in October, 1964, was seeing the sun shine on the big orange "76" sign on Harold's service station when driving into Arch Cape one evening just before sunset. It was a Union station for a long time before it became a Texaco station.

My two biggest disappointments in the years I have spent visiting the Oregon Coast were: the landslide at Ecola that destroyed some of my favorite parts of the park, and the termination of passenger train service between Portland and Seaside. Lamb chops never tasted as good as they did in the dining car of that train.

The Beck Connection
By Doris Beck

I am Doris Beck, daughter of Leo and Viola Beck. My folks first visited Arch Cape in 1929 from Portland by way of Hug Point and camped in the caves south of Hug Point or near Arch Cape Creek. Our cabin, built in 1935 by my dad and his brother when I was about six months old, stood about 150 yards east of the intersection of Mill Road and Beach Street. They did it in their two week vacation time, and without the benefit of power tools. Mill Road, named Webb Avenue in the early days, ran east and west. The cabin, surrounded by huge spruce trees, still stands between the road and Arch Cape Creek. Today, the cabin has a tendency to tilt a little. A huge rotting stump under the house creates an unstable foundation. My parents originally owned property where the highway is today and also the property between the highway and where the Fire Station is located. The Oregon State Highway Commission purchased the land because it was part of the highway right-of-way when the tunnel and the trestle bridge were constructed.

My parents purchased our present property from Mrs. Anna C. Taylor after selling the other land to the Highway Department. I don't know how many lots were included in the sale from Mrs. Taylor. Later, in 1945, they bought the lots across the street, also from Mrs. Taylor, who at that time owned most of the property up Webb Avenue. As I remember, someone lived in a small building on our lot. It looked like a wood shed, and later, that's what we used it for. It had a makeshift kitchen, a bed and some old furniture. We have pictures of that old shack before tearing it down some years later to make room for the new cabin.

Dad worked as an accountant in Portland for Centennial Flour Mills, which later became Crown Mills. The trip to Arch Cape from Portland was always a traumatic ordeal for me and my brother, Jim, when we were small. We drove through Banks, Forest Grove, Jewell and on down the infamous winding road with many sharp curves to Cannon Beach. That drive made us very car sick by the time we reached Arch Cape, especially those riding in the back seat. Usually, we left early Saturday morning for the two and one-half hour trip to the beach every month of the year, except in the winter when roads were impassable.

No one else that I remember lived on Mill Road at that time except for the house where the hermit named Smitty lived. At least, we always thought he was a hermit, so that is what we called him. I remember he grew a beard. My brother and I often visited him. I especially remember one visit that really scared us. He came from behind his house where he was dressing a deer he had just killed. Blood dripped from his beard. He said he eats the liver raw and told us that this was the best way to eat it. I was only six years old then!

Our water, including drinking water, came from Arch Cape Creek. We never worried about the purity or that animals used it, too. I can't recall that any of us became sick drinking creek water. It was a great trout stream when I was young. There was always a fishing hole directly behind the woodshed where we caught rainbow trout and many bullheads. The fishing for me was recreational for I am not fond of fish. Jack salmon and steelhead migrated up Arch Cape Creek to spawn.

There was no electricity yet in Arch Cape. For light, we used kerosene lamps most of the time, but also had Coleman lanterns which produced a much brighter light. I remember pumping them with gusto before using and replacing the delicate mantles. The Coleman lanterns, though much brighter than the kerosene lamp, were noisy for they "hissed" from the compressed air that made them work.

Electricity arrived in Arch Cape in 1940, about the time the tunnel opened to traffic. We couldn't come down as often as we wanted during the war because gasoline was rationed. My uncle installed wiring in our cabin, perhaps in the late 40's or early 50's. I am sure it was done after the war. He ran the wiring above the ceiling in the attic crawl space where possible, but the wiring to wall-mounted switches and outlet boxes was exposed where it came down the walls from the ceiling.

My dad laid his own water pipes and connected them to a line coming from a tank up the hill about two hundred yards east of the north tunnel entrance. That line furnished water to those that lived up Mill Road, known as Webb Avenue. He ran a water line all the way down to the Stills' place. The Stills were from Astoria and owned a home where the monkey tree now grows several lots east of Beach Street on the south side of Mill Road. The Stills were Finnish and had a sauna. Since my dad was Finnish, he liked to use the sauna, too. They built a wood fire to heat rocks, threw water on the hot rocks to generate the moist heat, and then jumped into the creek to cool off.

My parents, along with the dog, took my brother and me to the water tank site and then up the stage coach trail. We enjoyed these hikes, for a well-defined horse trail and wagon road began just north of the tunnel entrance and up past the water tank. It is an easy grade to walk and is still visible today. The trail was spectacular. We hiked it two or three times each summer, but it was too muddy for winter enjoyment. Today, I still enjoy hiking the trail. Even though much growth gradually closed over some sections, it is still passable. Many animal tracks, mostly elk, are visible. The animals help keep the trail open.

The Oregon Coast Trail, maintained by the Park Department, intercepts the old road in places. The original route used over the Arch Cape headland by mail carriers and for those travelers between Astoria and the Tillamook Bay area doesn't appear to have been completed. Perhaps the planners intended that the trail and road meet the one coming from Wheeler in the early days. The old route, however, is part of the Oregon Coast Trail today. As children, we came to the end of the trail when we hiked with our parents. Also, our family explorations took us through the tunnel many times just for recreation.

Webb Avenue, today named Mill Road, was a one-way dirt road. Flowers grew between the ruts, and tree branches covered the road and gave the sensation of driving through a tunnel. It was the route from Highway 101, east, to the few homes there. The magnificent forest across the road from us was home for cougar, deer, elk and bear. At times, we could hear the cougars screaming.

The Mill Road area was logged in the late 40's. The loggers were the ones who put in the present road bed to get equipment in and the logs out. Sometimes loaded log trucks came down the road with just one log per truck because the logs were so huge. Our dog, a field spaniel named Bouncer, would be out there watching those trucks go by. The drivers would honk their horns at him but he wouldn't move, so, they would go around him. We also had a cat named Figaro, who shared the territory with Bouncer. Logs were dumped into the creek and floated down during high water when the creek was bank high. Log jams were frequent up and down the creek and were very destructive, causing much erosion. Logs and logging debris jammed water flow behind the bridge piers, and at times, caused concern that the pressure might damage the bridge timber and pile foundation. The high water in the winter brought logs down the creek on occasion and sometimes banged into our bank.

The Arch Cape Service District sewer system was constructed in 1974. The main line traveled down Mill Road, and gravel pulled from the ditch in front of our house indicates the creek at one time flowed where the road is today. Early maps show that Arch Cape Creek did considerable meandering in the flat area on its way to the ocean. Perhaps the loggers straightened out the creek bed when the road was punched into the area.

We had a storm in the early 80's that did considerable damage to much of the Short Sands State Park area. That same storm blew out our door, ripping it right out of its frame. We've had many problems with Arch Cape Creek flowing by our place. I wish my dad were alive so he could see what was done to protect the creek bank next to the cabin. In 1983, we poured concrete on the stream bank above and below our property. We used 80,000 pounds of concrete. One can't possibly imagine the trauma obtaining the numerous permits necessary from many different government agencies. Also, scheduling concrete trucks nearly became a disaster. In prior years, my dad bulldozed gravel from the stream bed up on the bank. It still is a continual battle to keep the creek from coming into our property and house. I found pictures that show where dad constructed a wall out of ship lap to keep the creek from washing the bank away.

The land on our property is soft and the cabin shakes when elk run through our yard. When log trucks passed by, our place shook and rattled so severely that stove pipes fell apart. We put them back together before starting the fire and finally had to fasten the pipes with sheet metal screws to keep them in place.

Everything in this cabin is original, but dry rot had taken over and the cabin was being chewed apart by termites and carpenter ants. The foundation was settling, too. The future of this memorable and fun-filled place was questionable. In 1991, the dry rot was repaired and new foundation timbers, windows and siding gave new life to the structure.

At times, we found many interesting things along the stage coach trail, and, as kids, did not appreciate the value of those items. A building along the trail, probably used by workers building the stage coach line, still stood when my brother and I explored the old trail. We found old high button shoes, bottles, pans, dishes, and all kinds of old things. Some of the items we found are in our cabin. I have a piece of a dish and a ring with a section of chain used to tether horses and the mules that packed supplies into the area. We heard that the Arch Cape Creek originated from a lake, so we searched for it but never found a lake. We did find a 100 by 100 foot area covered with deer and elk bones. I often wonder about this and why those bones were all in one area.

There is a suspension bridge over Arch Cape Creek off Mill Road down 3rd Avenue used by those who cared for the old water system. I believe the bridge was first put in by Mr. Costanzo because he took care of the water system for a long time and had to have access to the tanks. The bridge over Arch Cape Creek is now maintained by the Park Department because it is part of The Oregon Coast Trail. John Mersereau's home is close to the creek and the bridge. For years, John, as a volunteer, raised salmon and steelhead for the Oregon State Fisheries Department in holding pens he built and maintained. Arch Cape Creek water flowed through those pens, and according to John, a few silver salmon and steelhead still migrate up Arch Cape Creek.

I've found the second tank to the left and up the trail after crossing the suspension bridge. It is hard to find because it is surrounded by a heavy stand of new alder growth. These holding tanks were subject to animal pollution and had to be cleaned and serviced often. Mr. Merle Akeson and I found the chlorination shed and hundreds of plastic bottles scattered about that formerly contained clorox bleach. At one time, several bridges installed by loggers crossed the creek when the area was logged, but since then, all but one have been washed out by high water. The one left is the bridge previously mentioned, maintained by the Park Department.

Cougar hunters, with their dogs, used the stage coach trail at night. We heard the dogs and saw the lights moving at night through the brush and trees. Oh, how those dogs could howl.

My dad and I fished off the rocks at the mouth of Arch Cape Creek for sea perch and flounder. We fished with kelp worms and tore barnacles off the rocks to find them. They are hard to find now. We climbed over the rocks above the high tide mark and then waited six hours until the tide went out to get off the rocks. I had my own fishing pole and one time Dad left me on one side of a rock to fish while he fished the other side. The high tide completely surrounded me. I could not see him nor could he see me, but he felt I was trustworthy so didn't worry.

The Coast Guard patrolled the beaches with dogs during the war. Once, I waved at them and they thought I was stranded. The dogs tried to get to me, but couldn't because of the high tide. My mother came down. The coastguardsman mentioned to her that there was a little child stranded on a rock. She explained to him that I was her daughter and I was fishing for sea perch with my father. Dad was also a great crabber. They were plentiful and very large in those days. He tied them to his belt and they fought all the way home.

Navy planes used Castle Rock as a target for bomb practice exercises during the war. Blimps from Tillamook flew along the coast; later I learned they patrolled for enemy submarines.

My brother Jim, who is four years younger than I, was a great companion when we were at Arch Cape exploring the territory, playing on the beach, visiting Smitty, and doing what kids like to do. I suspect the beach was our favorite playground: it was a place to pitch a tent, build a fortress, dig holes, swim in the ocean using inner tubes to float over the waves; and of course, we had the great Arch Cape Creek to enjoy.

We found many items washed in by the tide, especially near the mouth of Arch Cape Creek. My brother was much better at finding treasures, yet I have a Japanese clog I found which hangs on our cabin wall as a reminder of those carefree childhood days at Arch Cape. We were pals, for no other children were around. But at home, we were at each other while growing up about the same as other brothers and sisters.

My brother is now a stockbroker. He and his wife, Barbara, have three sons, two grandsons, a granddaughter and live in Tigard. I was employed by Tektronix, Inc. for thirty years, half of that time as a Manufacturing Engineer. Since 1987, I've worked for Precision Interconnect Corp., a wholly owned subsidiary of AMP, Inc., in Tualatin. I am a Process Engineer developing processes for manufacturing medical, computer and test and measurement cables such as those used in oscilloscopes. Our firm is one of the world's leading ultrasound cable manufacturers.

I have many early-day memories and realize how fortunate my brother and I were to have parents with the vision to find Arch Cape, for it was isolated, primitive and demanding in many ways. Roads were slow in coming, and when they did arrive in the mid-thirties, I was just a baby. I grew up to see many changes. The tunnel and highway, electricity, telephones, water and sewer systems all stimulated growth to the area and changed the landscape forever. I've loved Arch Cape all of my life and hope the area continues to be a quiet residential place where families can grow and enjoy a part of what I've learned to appreciate.

The original Arch Cape Creek Falls before loggers blasted away the top half of the rock formation. Doris Beck Photo.

Louis C. "Smitty" Smith's cabin on the hill above the present waste water facility up Mill Road. Doris Beck and her brother are at the front door. Circa 1941. Doris Beck Photo.

Louis C. Smith with his dog Tippy January 1, 1935. Eldridge/Coffman photo.

The Ray Brown Connection
As told to David K. English

Ray Brown is not an Arch Cape resident. He grew up in Tolovana and presently lives in Cove Beach but he has an Arch Cape Post Office box number. He helped build the road into Arch Cape, he drove log trucks through Arch Cape for years on the road he helped construct and has flown his white airplane with light blue horizontal accent stripes down this coast for years. His humor is legendary and his warm sparkling eyes capture one's attention when in his company.

Today, Ray's Cove Beach home is easy to find for a wooden propeller mounted above his garage door shows the way. His home, both inside and outside, is immaculate. One only needs to see his firewood pile to understand his attention to detail and neatness. It is straight as an arrow, uniform in height and not one stick out of line, truly a work of art. Here is his story: (sic)

"My mother died when I was born. I stayed with different aunts and uncles for short periods of time. None of my uncles were married and it was a difficult situation for them to care for a young child. When I was age five, I entered an orphanage where I stayed until I was seven. My aunts and uncles paid five dollars a month for my keep. I hated the home. There were about one hundred children. One section of the orphanage was set aside for the girls and another part set aside for the boys. The treatment was O.K. but I just didn't like it. We marched to school from the orphanage. One time me and another kid stole some carrots out of a garden along the route to and from the school. We were caught, and for supper that night we ate nothing but carrots. I earned five cents a week for making four beds every day. Then, on Saturday, I often sat in a chair in the matron's office, sometimes for a long time before I received my week's pay. That precious nickel purchased lots of candy in those days, which was a special treat after eating orphanage food all week. The nickel earned each Saturday and the candy it purchased are the only good memories I remember from back then.

"My uncle Henry married and he and his wife took me in. I lived with them until age fourteen. Then, one of my aunts took a job through an employment agency to be a chambermaid at the Warren Hotel in Tolovana, near Cannon Beach. I was fourteen then and my aunt asked Mrs. Edra Warren if she could bring her nephew down to work. Mrs. Warren said 'yes' and I began a new life doing chores.

"The Warren Hotel was built in 1910 by Mr. Mark Warren. It had sixteen rooms and only one bathroom. If the water was turned on downstairs, then there would be no water upstairs. He also purchased seven small one-room loggers' crew shacks from Crown Zellerbach which cost him twenty dollars each. He moved them to the hotel site. They had a water basin and the bedroom was curtained off for privacy. There were windows with curtains—no glass—but no one complained. Guests ate meals at the hotel. No road led to the Warren Hotel until about 1912. Most guests took the train to Seaside, then rode a stage, a Chalmers or a Cadillac, to Cannon Beach and then drove down the beach to the hotel. Later on, when roads came to the area, Mr. Warren set aside space for an auto camp, where he pitched tents on wooden floors and charged one dollar a night for their use.

"Chores then were much different from today's chores. I was paid $35 per month plus room and board. I began at five in the morning building the fire for the cook, then milked four cows, cranked the cream separator (it made lots of noise and I worried that it bothered people, but it didn't), then fed the chickens and built the fire in the lobby fireplace for the guests. Then, it was breakfast time so I rang the gong to let guests know it was ready. Daytime was busy, too. Back logs for the fireplace fire were three feet in diameter, and just barely fit through the doors leading to the fireplace. Using the old Republic truck, with no cab, brakes or license, I gathered wood from the beach to feed the ten-foot fireplace in the hotel lobby. When tides were right, I dug clams and raked crabs for the cook. He had to have mussels every day no matter what the weather was like. Clams and crabs were abundant then. It was my responsibility to help cook and process the crabs and clean the clams. I ate meals in the kitchen and slept on a cot in a garage. The dishwasher also slept there.

"The Warrens also had a team of horses which I cared for. Mark Warren pulled cars stuck in soft sand or mired in a tide pool to high ground. He did this for his guests and for others, for many inexperienced beach drivers drove on the beach then.

"Chicken dinners served on Sundays at the Warren Hotel were five-course meals, relished by guests and local residents. They were gourmet dinners and cost only one dollar then. We began preparing for those dinners Friday night when Mrs. Warren and I went to the chicken coop where we picked out ten to twelve fryers and then put them in a gunny sack. I learned that you can only catch chickens at night. I chopped off their heads Saturday morning. Ever see a chicken with their head cut off? Boy, they go. I picked the feathers off and then the cook took over.

"I lived with the Warrens for sixteen years, from age 14 until age 30. I worked at various jobs away from them at times but considered the Warren Hotel complex my home. The Warrens had no children and treated me like I was a family member. I have many memories of those wonderful years with them.

"As I mentioned earlier, I milked cows. Well, I remember one time when this guy brought his fancy new car to the hotel. The cow seen her reflection in the side of the car and attacked it with her short horns. Boy, was he mad.

"The Warrens had a bull named Emperor. I would stake him out every day. When I came home, he'd come right up to me. I'd jump on his back and ride him past the people eating in the hotel. If he was good, I'd let him sniff each cow. If not good, I'd jerk his nose ring and lead him right by.

"One year, we had a pet seal named Bill. He ate smashed potatoes and often made a mess on the back porch. I took Bill swimming in the ocean once a day. He stayed so close to me that I could feel his whiskers on my neck. One time a bunch of people were in a circle around him. They poked sticks at him. He saw me and bellowed and I picked him up and took him home. Boy, were they surprised.

"Once a goat got into the kitchen and started leaking. Mrs. Warren put a tin can under her. A guest popped in just at the right time and said, 'What a smart goat.'

"Sometimes Mrs. Warren drove to Cannon Beach in their 1924 Chevrolet and then on the road to Seaside to buy groceries. A twenty-dollar bill filled the car with groceries, including the chicken feed.

"About 1933, I began driving a Mack dump truck, with the huge bulldog hood ornament above the radiator (a trucker's status symbol in those days), during the highway construction north of the tunnel and in the Asbury Creek area. I moved to Portland in 1934 and drove fuel tanker trucks for years but returned to the coast often on weekends where I always had a place to stay with the Warrens. I drove a single axle Federal truck without side curtains to protect me from wind and rain. One had to pick a place to stop miles ahead of time for the trailer was not equipped with brakes. We used the truck foot brake, the transmission gears and the Johnson bar to slow down the truck and keep it under control. The Johnson bar was our name for the hand brake. When I started driving fuel trucks, I made fifty cents per hour and didn't get paid for loading, unloading, changing tires or anything other than my actual driving time. Then the Teamsters Union took over and we made ninety cents per hour plus getting paid for the other stuff. Also, side curtains were installed along with a hand operated windshield wiper. Later on, my Peterbuilt truck (called a tractor by the trucking industry) pulled two fuel trailers and was equipped with power steering and power brakes, plus other modern features such as power windshield wipers, rear-view mirrors and a comfortable adjustable driver's seat.

"This is a different part of my life. I began flying lessons at Swan Island Airport in 1937. It took me seven or eight hours of instruction to learn to fly solo. I bought my first airplane in 1938, an old American Eagle, and only paid $175 for it. I learned to do all of my own airplane maintenance. The bi-winged plane had a V-8 OX5 ninety horsepower water cooled engine and had no brakes. The OX5 engine is legendary and I still belong to the exclusive organization of those who flew planes with that power plant. I often flew my plane to the coast and landed on the hard sand beach in front of Cannon Beach and in front of the Warren Hotel, where I took friends for sight-seeing tours up and down the coast. I sold my American Eagle in late 1940.

"I joined the service in 1941, hoping to become an air force pilot but was told that I was too old. I went to England with a maintenance squadron servicing B-24's and B-17's. I was stationed near London where I heard the air raid warning sirens and the following bomb and rocket raids made by the German air force.

"I ran across this picture of the Sellwood bridge over the Willamette River in the *Oregonian* and it reminds me of the time I flew under the cuckoo's nest. It was not a dull evening. It started in 1945 when I was in the Portland Veterans Hospital. I became acquainted with a truck driver in the bed next to me. We got to talking about trucks and airplanes. He was telling me how good he could drive and I told him how good I could fly.

"I told my roommate that I had an airplane out at the Beaverton airstrip. So, we decided to apply for a pass for the afternoon that was good until seven that evening. The first thing the truck driver wanted to do was to drive down to 2nd and Stark Street. I didn't know what for but as soon as I stopped, he ran over to the liquor store and came out with a fifth. That's not what I had in mind. We took off for Beaverton and cranked up the Student Prince, a plane made in Portland by Cox Aviation. Only five or six were made. I think he had a nip or two, but not me then. I can't remember. Maybe later I had a little.

"We had a good flight around Troutdale and then took a big circle around Oregon City. I flew down the river, past a sea plane base where they had a couple of small planes moored, flying rather low. They didn't like my fly-by and turned in my numbers. The C.A.A. caught up with me two weeks later and gave me a lecture.

"We were flying down the river and came to the Sellwood bridge and were too low to go over the bridge so flew under the bridge. We then flew up and past the windows at the vets hospital and some of the veterans said they had seen us go by. We parked the airplane and headed for some food. My friend being the best truck driver (and me being the best airplane driver) wanted to drive my car. We were headed for Chinatown when at 6th and Couch Street, he hit two young fellows in a car which forgot who had the right-of-way. It made no difference because I told the kids—'you fix your car and I will fix mine'—no police report. We made it to our Chinese food and then headed back for the hospital. My friend weaved back too far and ended flat on the sidewalk. 'Well', I said, 'I am going anyhow.' I did help him up before I took off but I don't think he stayed on his feet. He showed up late that night. He did O.K. for he got his hospital discharge the next day. I'm not sure about the cuckoo's nest being up under the bridge. It may have been in the cockpit.

"In 1952 I went to Yakima, Washington, and took lessons to learn how to fly crop dusting airplanes. The cost was $500, and if you passed the course, you were assigned to a job and the $500 was deducted from you earnings. I, along with a number of others from Washington state, flew our old open-cockpit Stearman crop duster planes to New Brunswick, Canada. It took about five days then to reach our destination, for we only flew about 100 miles per hour.

"I never had a forced landing and I never crashed. I did turn over once on take off after hitting a gopher hole. There was little damage to the airplane but oil came out of the instrument panel and covered my goggles so I couldn't see. The Stearman was a great air force training plane. For crop dusting, the plane was equipped with a more powerful engine that made the plane appear to be nose heavy. The extra horsepower was needed to carry the spray material and to have control when flying low to the ground. I flew to New Brunswick for five summers spraying and helped spray the whole province to eradicate the spruce bug worm. There were eighty spray planes from all over the United States and Canada on that project.

"Most of the trips flying our spray planes to New Brunswick were routine. One time, I flew with a fellow named H. Hughes. I told him, 'You do the navigating. I will follow you.' We had trouble all of the way there. We stopped at Ogdon, Utah, in the morning and took off for Cheyenne, Wyoming, following a snow storm. I'd look at my compass and it didn't look right and I was getting cold, for there was snow in the air. I looked ahead and there was a huge body of water, Salt Lake. We had made a complete circle—my partner's navigation wasn't too good and we ran back into the same snow storm. I pulled up aside of him and signaled, 'Lets go back,' so we returned, gassed the planes and went to bed.

"The next morning was beautiful and we figured we would have no problems. I flew what I thought a straight course. My partner was way up to my right. We could see each other all of the time and I wondered why we weren't getting somewhere. Finally, we closed in and I could tell he was lost. He left me and landed on the highway. He stopped a tourist and asked which way to Cheyenne and the lady said, 'about sixty miles that way.' He had the airplane parked on the highway with the motor ticking away at the early hour of six in the morning. He was ready to take off when a car came from one direction and another from the other direction. I could see they were wondering what an airplane was doing on the highway. Meanwhile, Hughes barreled down the highway with both cars blocking his way. He had lots of power and no load and really gave those guys a buzz job. All the time I was up in the air waiting and looking. We had trouble all the way to New Brunswick that year."

"My wife Margie and I built the home I live in today. In retirement I enjoy my many friends. I especially enjoy my white plane with blue horizontal stripes as I often fly with a good friend who is also a skilled pilot, not too high above the breakers from Seaside to Short Sands Beach. You will see me when the sun shines.

Wave, when I go by."

Mark Warren's Republic truck used by Ray Brown to haul back logs for the hotel fireplace. The tent house for the hired help and the light plant show in the background. Circa 1924.

The American Eagle OX5 purchased for $175 by Ray after he took flying lessons at Swan Island Airport in 1937. Ray often landed on the sands of Cannon Beach and Tolovana park where he took friends for scenic tours of the area. The OX5 90 horsepower water-cooled engine is legendary and Ray belongs to the exclusive organization of pilots who flew planes powered with the OX5.

Ray Brown stands beside his Stearman crop dusting airplane. He flew the plane to New Brunswick, Canada, for five summers, spraying to eradicate the spruce bug worm. The Stearman, a well-known air force training plane, was equipped with a larger engine that made the planes look nose heavy. Note the spray bar underneath the lower wing. Circa 1953.

Ray hauled logs up and down the coast past Arch Cape for years. This Kenworth truck driven by Ray hauled logs off of Mt. Hood. 1958.

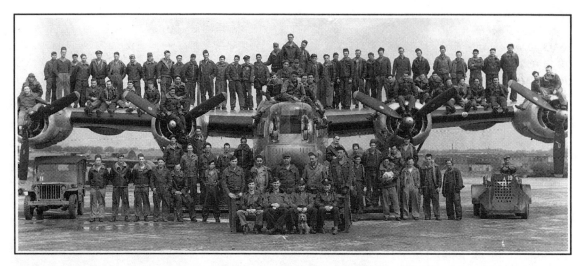

Ray joined an Air Force maintenance squadron in 1942 servicing B-17 and B-24's. He is the second man from the left sitting on the wing. Circa 1953. **Bottom photograph.** *Ray has been involved with airplanes all of his adult life. For the past 20 years his white Luscomb airplane with blue trim has been parked at the Seaside Airport. The Luscomb was the first all-metal small aircraft manufactured. Ray's plane is almost 50 years old and in excellent condition. It has been a familiar sight cruising up and down the north coast. Ray still flies. 1992. Photos, Ray Brown Collection.*

The Conway/Brown Connection
Material gathered from family diaries
Compiled by David English

John F. Conway and Lorna Brown Conway, aunt and uncle to Shirley and Larry (Bud) Brown, first came to Arch Cape in 1927. They constructed a home on property located three ocean lots north of Leech Avenue, named their home the *Great House* and called the area *Pelican Point*. Perhaps the massive Arch Cape headland inspired the name and maybe brown pelicans were Arch Cape summer residents in those days just as they are today. The Conways built a second structure in the early 30's on property east of the *Great House* and named it the *Wee House*.

The *Great House* was a two-story shingled dwelling with green trim. A large living-dining room, kitchen, bedroom and an open front porch filled the main level. A back porch with a bathroom added early in the 30's modernized the home. John and Lorna replaced the original wood cook stove with a noisy oil burning stove in the 40's, and in the 50's they purchased an electric stove. Built-in coolers for food predated the refrigerator. Candles, kerosene and Coleman lamps provided light and the old candle sconces and lamp brackets are still in place. A steep stairway led to the two upstairs bedrooms. Built-in cupboards and window seats utilized every bit of space and all windows had brass hardware and latches. John Conway and Lorna's father, George Arthur Brown, built the house with occasional help from friends, neighbors and family. The dominant feature of the main floor was the huge stone fireplace with a hanging canvas swing facing the hearth. The fireplace, rebuilt in the 40's by Paul Bartells, is the focal point of the living area and remains a classic example of his skill. The front porch was enclosed with glass in the late 50's.

George Arthur Brown had three children: Lorna, who married John Conway in 1927; McDannell, who married Gretchen Brown (maiden name also Brown) and with her had two children, Linda and Robert; and Laurence (Larry), who married Mildred McClung, also had two children, Shirley and Laurence Jr., also known as Larry or Bud.

George landscaped the grounds with many camellias and hydrangeas to surround the driftwood tables and stools. He built a curved concrete and stone pathway to a driftwood bench overlooking the ocean, and a plank walkway over drift and logs which led to the sandy Arch Cape beach. George died in 1937.

The *Wee House*, also shingled and with green trim, was originally designed to be a garage. Instead, John used rough boards in the interior to create a living-dining room, a tiny kitchen and a bathroom on the main level. The attic loft provided sleeping space; a fireplace and a wood cook stove provided heat. The rustic cabin became very popular with a number of families who returned summer after summer for many years.

The Conways never fully retired to Arch Cape from Portland where Mr. Conway practiced law, but Mr. and Mrs. Conway, it appears, spent almost every weekend and summer vacation at the *Great House*. Only bad weather or serious problems kept them away.

John began a diary in June, 1937, which ended in 1968 with his death. His writing is informative, full of names, and is an exciting journal of what Arch Cape life was like in the 30's, 40's, 50's, and 60's. It is obvious John worked most of the time building, repairing, and remodeling the *Great House* and the *Wee House*. He found time between work sessions to play a great many horseshoe matches, organize and plan huge neighborhood feeds and picnics, and host other gatherings involving guests and neighbors. The Conways knew how to have a good time and how to entertain guests.

As I read the three descriptive journals filled with names, events, and the fun people experienced at Arch Cape, it became apparent to me those years were banner years for folks fortunate enough to have lived here at that time. Central heat meant a fire place or a wood cook stove. The comfort station was "way outside." No community water system existed. Electricity for lighting, for appliances and television was in the distant future. Other creature comforts such as telephones, gas-powered chain saws and lawn mowers did not come until the early 50's.

The Conway saga spans four decades: the 30's, a developing and a building time; the 40's, war years with rationing; and the 50's and 60's, for the enjoyment of those exciting activities they found at *Pelican Point*. Of course, I don't want to imply that good times were not part of the plan during the first two decades. The pages of the log relate that fun and games were always part of daily activities.

The entries in the 30's center around John (aka Barnacle Bill) and Lorna (aka Baby Doll) Conway, who, with help from relatives and friends, worked on the *Great House* and the *Wee House*. Many entries tell about the nine-foot misery whip (a hand-pulled cross-cut saw) used for cutting firewood for the kitchen stove and the huge fireplace. Often, after only four or five cuts, painful blisters appeared and excused the victim from that very important chore—for awhile! With the power saws we enjoy today, we can make ten cuts or more in the time it took to do one cut then. In those days, many logs for fire wood were available on the beach and all hands gathered bark chunks and wood for the fireplace. This never-ending activity inspired the name *Rustlewood*, which gradually replaced the name *Great House* for the beach home at *Pelican Point*.

John and Lorna always had building projects. They added gables, installed ceilings, replaced coils in the stove, propped up the foundations, fought carpenter ants and termites, and did cabinet work. They "made love" to the commodes, showers, and basins when they needed attention. John worked on improving the water system, fixed hinges, oiled door hardware, mowed (massaging, as John claims) the yard, and cut the ever growing "pucker brush" around the territory. But, they still had time to be superstars when it came to friends and guests.

The following from John's journal describes the mood of the time:

> Projects to the right
> > Projects to the left
> The next time it is mentioned
> > I am heading to the west.
> Gin and whiskey, beer and wine,
> > You can shingle any time.
> Arch Cape weekends are always fine,
> > Scene and company quite sublime.

At the time this was written, the Pelican Point Carpenters Union No. 1 held a sit-down strike that did not end until friends arrived with a carton of Whitehorse.

Many entries in the Conway log tell about the crabs guests caught and the clams they dug. Some often bagged a dozen or two with their clam guns (a common name for a clam shovel). In those days they seemed as easy to get at Arch Cape as they were at Bird Rock or in Seaside. To dig sixty or more clams was not unusual. Once the clams were dug, someone had to clean them for the evening "fry" and for "chowder makes." Clams and crabs were regular fare for Arch Capers when the tides were right.

The sun room at *Rustlewood* became the place of choice for card games, chess matches, and partying. The same room also provided sleeping space for the overflow of guests and friends one gathers at Arch Cape. Many of these brought steaks, hams, beef roasts, seasonal fruits, vegetables—and spirits. It is apparent to me that partying was the "in" thing at this time. If not partying, guests engaged themselves in board games; others occupied themselves in more vigorous activities. Swimming in the brine, throwing horseshoes, and hiking attracted the athletic ones. Beachcombing for glass balls and picking berries drew the dreamers. Crabbing and digging for clams was popular with shell fish aficionados. Whatever the activity, guests found their favorite thing to do.

My aunts, Elsie and Marie English, owned the *Singing Sands Hotel,* several hundred feet north of the Conways. For some reason they stayed for a time at the Conway house along with their sister Irene, from Rochester, Minnesota. Perhaps *Singing Sands* was filled with workers on the tunnel, which was under construction then. Here is my aunts' message, August 13, 1937:

> *The end of the road and it's night*
> *A frail new moon gives us light*
> *Straight to the Conways we go*
> *The house we all know*
> *Where the latch key is always in sight.*

That same night after the three English girls had retired, John Conway arrived with a friend after a six hundred mile drive. Here is his entry:

> *John and Don Turnbull arrived in the V-8. The three English sisters had retired and refused to admit us until after prolonged persuasion. Thereupon, we entered in due and ancient form after Marie inspected us with her flashlight. After a quiet night we breakfasted on French toast, coffee, bacon, eggs, jam, all of which was inspired by the night cap Marie and Irene had after being rudely awakened and annoyed the night before. Thereafter, Don and John tore into the carpenter work upstairs in the hostesses' bedroom and worked until six p.m., completing the south side, front, and gable, with time out for a delightful lunch from the three English sisters. That evening we had an exquisite dinner with Marjorie Holderman, Grace Pajunen and the three English sisters.*

The Holderman's home was just two lots north and the Pajunen home was directly across the road east of *Rustlewood.* Another entry, typical of many dealing with food, drink, games, and good company reads as follows:

After tossing off a couple of scotch and sodas, we take on some Royal Chinook, fried to the Queen's taste on the pancake grill. Thereupon, in due course, my partner and I sit east and west and Lorna and her partner sit north and south for a couple rubbers of contract. The east and west came through, winning 297 to 1,110, with much enthusiasm for the early morning clamming expedition. P.S.—won last year too!

Many entries tell of guests' and residents' walking into the tunnel construction between 1936 and 1940. First, they could walk 500 feet, then 700 feet, and finally were able to walk all the way through, a total of 1,277 feet. That had to be an exciting event to experience.

And then there are countless entries about "going in the brine," which all seemed to enjoy, except John Conway who did not like cold water, no matter what the month or the time of day, it made no difference. Once in a while some one would get into oil that had been dumped by a passing ship.

John and Lorna visited Bert Patton's newly-built log cabin on August 6, 1939. In November of that year, the Conway family served their first roast turkey at *Rustlewood*.

Mr. Maurice R. Simmonds, otherwise known as First Lieutenant, Quartermaster Corps, Reserve, arrived on the Arch Cape scene early. There are many entries about and by him when he visited the Conways.

(Writer's note) In 1957, Maurice "Simmy" Simmonds and his wife, Eleanor, purchased Mabel Lensrud's home on Pacific Avenue, the place that has the guest cottage four lots north of Ocean Road. There is a new home now on the ocean side but the guest house still stands.

The following entry by Simmy, dated April 18, 1938, says it all:

When your work's done and you want some fun
Away from all your troubles and cares
Just slip in your car and give it the gun
And head for Arch Cape and salt air

Even though outside it may rain and storm
Conway's Rustlewood fireplace is cozy and warm
You can snuggle up close on the hammock that swings
Turn on the Victrola and let everyone sing

Although it rained Sunday—we didn't care
For we knew that on Monday it would be fair
We went to bed and turned off the light
And in the morning found I prophesied right.

Roads were primitive in the 30's. There was no Sunset Highway, no freeway, and travel over some roads, at times, could be treacherous. The Oregon State Department of Highways map in the *Roads and Highways* section of this book shows the route in 1934 from Portland via St. Helens, Vernonia, Mist, Jewell, Elsie, Necanicum Junction, Cannon Beach Junction and Cannon Beach to *Pelican Point*. It was 95.4 miles and took three hours and twenty minutes from house to house. Today it is an easy one and three quarter hour drive from Portland over the Sunset Highway to the beach.

The plumbing and sink were completed in the *Wee House* and the stove was installed and connected to the new chimney in 1941. John lit fires in the stove and fireplaces for the first time, and according to John, "both draw like the Tacoma Narrows." The whole event gave an excuse for preparing the first *Wee House* dinner served at 8 p.m. on July 19, 1941.

Paul Bartells, called an artist by John, installed the chimney in the *Wee House* and a year later replaced the original huge stone fireplace and chimney in *Rustlewood*. It is still in use today, which attests to Paul's skill.

An article in the June 6, 1954, *Oregonian* labels Paul Bartells as the **Bricklayer Extraordinary.**

There has been a lot of brick stacked up through the years along the Cannon Beach coast from Arch Cape to Ecola Park, and most of it laid by one man, Paul Bartells. He has been building Cannon Beach fireplaces now for the past 45 years.

In 1909, Bartells built a stone fireplace for Emil Gelinsky at Arch Cape. The Gelinsky home was two lots north of the Conway home. Rocks for the project were hauled up from the beach and beach sand was used in the mortar mix. Although Paul wouldn't use this type of construction today, he is quick to admit that the Arch Cape fireplace served its purpose. As a matter of fact, it was still in use in 1954 when this article was written.

In striking contrast to the steady trend toward brick in beach construction today, Bartells points out, brick wasn't popular in the coastal area after the turn of the century. Most beach fireplaces then were built of stone. Brick had to be shipped into Seaside and then carted by wagon along the precarious road to Cannon Beach. Few early-day builders elected to shoulder either the expense or trouble involved in brick construction under those conditions.

The 40's were a continuation of the 30's for John and Lorna Conway. Remodeling and repairing, participating in beach activities, and enjoying neighbors and guests was a way of life at Arch Cape. However, two major events changed it. The tunnel was officially opened August 3, 1941, which brought more people and traffic to Arch Cape; and the bombing of Pearl Harbor on December 7, 1941, brought war. The hostilities touched all of America and the small community of Arch Cape did not escape its grasp. Many entries from the Conway diaries explain the changes Arch Cape residents and visitors experienced.

Trips to the beach had to be carefully planned, for gasoline rationing began December 1, 1942. The United States Army patrolled the Arch Cape beach shortly after the war began. A number of *Pelican Point* crabbers swarmed out on the beach about 5:30 a.m. August 10, 1942, and were chased back by the army. No one was to be on the beach in the dark so there were no crabs to eat. The Cannon Beach Bakery closed for the duration November 4, 1942. The United States Coast Guard took over the Cannon Beach Hotel on January 2, 1943 and replaced army personnel who had been patrolling the Arch Cape beach. The Coast Guard was active in the area morning and night all through the war. Mr. and Mrs. Albert Leech leased a cabin just south of *Rustlewood* to the Coast Guard for the duration of the war. Two months later, dogs moved in and began patrol duty with their Coast Guard masters. John mentions patrolling the beach with Coastguardsmen Henderson and Frank.

Scrap iron was gathered in the Arch Cape area to help in the war effort. It was hauled to the Tolovana Store and Post Office, which served as a collection place. Duncan Shields and his wife Mary owned and ran the store and post office then.

Blimps from Tillamook on submarine patrol were a common sight throughout the war along with navy planes on training missions from bases along the Oregon and Washington coast. Castle Rock was an often-used target for improving dive bombing skills. The bombs were practice bombs and seemed to have a small bag of "flour" that made a small white puff on impact. There was more oil on the beach and hikers at times came in with "submarine oil," as it was called, on the soles of their shoes.

Activities never stopped at *Rustlewood* during the war years. More effort was focused on gathering food supplies of all kinds, for many things such as canned fruits and vegetables were rationed. Many entries in the Conway log refer to gathering huckleberries and blackberries, digging clams, raking for crabs and growing victory gardens. These projects were shared with neighbors and guests. Recently, the young couple living in the *Wee House*, Jason and Tari Merson, cleared an area out of a jungle of salal and blackberries just north of the house for their garden. It is outlined by a cedar rail fence in excellent condition except that the posts are a bit suspect at ground level. It appears this may have been the site of the Conway victory garden, as it had to be fenced to keep the deer and elk away. Many Arch Cape residents planted victory gardens during the war years.

Remodeling and repairing continued. Shingles were purchased in 1943 for $4.80 per square. (This writer paid $60 a square 40 years later.) Flat tires caused by the local rough roads were common, as tires were another rationed necessity and were driven until they fell apart.

Many entries in the 40's mention food. Roast beef and pork were special treats along with the available chicken, clams, crab, homemade breads, cake, pies and salads. Fried chicken was popular as it could be purchased from local outlets. One noticeable "necessity" in short supply was liquor. When it was part of the scene, residents relished it on special occasions.

Here is a light breakfast menu from the diary, May 12, 1945, for a Lieutenant Olsen who was on leave from Australia: fruit, toast, coffee cake, doughnuts, baked beans, bacon, eggs, pilchards and coffee. (Pilchards! Ugh. That's an oily fish like a very large sardine. One wonders how they were prepared.) For dinner, they served roast turkey.

The war ended August 14, 1945. The Conways were at *Shady Rest,* their Portland home, where the neighbors rallied around beginning at 5 p.m. and continued far into the night celebrating the end of hostilities. Gasoline rationing ended along with the rationing of food items. Then came the signing of the peace parchment on the USS Missouri in Tokyo Bay. Four bottles of clam nectar, etc. helped celebrate this event at *Pelican Point.*

The war years were now history and *Pelican Point* in Arch Cape began to hum again. Horseshoes returned, ladies sunned themselves in the season's approved styles and the hardy went surf bathing. All were out at 5:30 a.m. the day after Labor Day for clamming at Gearhart and returned with six dozen clams for a great fry that evening and for chowder later.

Glass floats were easy to find during storms for anyone willing to brave the elements. Those and other treasures found on the beach brought great recognition and status to the finder. Persistent searchers who found floats used sneaky methods to hide their finds for future recovery. Here is what John records in his log November 12, 1945, during a wild storm when waves were crashing over Queen Vic, the locals' name for Castle Rock:

I found two treasures south of Arch Cape and buried same in brush five paces in a certain direction from a certain snag, thence to the left one pace in a certain direction, and will recover later.

The following verse by Doris Keeler, friend of John and Lorna, written August 12, 1946 tells what she liked best at Arch Cape.

Doug and Millers stayed at Leech's
Friday Hal and Doris came
To add to Arch Cape's widening fame
Singing Sands exhibited art
Water colors did their part
Nut bread sandwiches and tea
Made a salon by the sea
John and Lorna came at eve
When the tide began to heave
George and Betty Griffins, too
Came to join the motley crew
With their lovely daughter Joan
Came far from the telephone
Sunday night the big buffet
Made the people want to stay
On through Christmas, Easter, too
Summer, autumn, winter through
Leeches' guests are of the best
Not a one can be a pest
George who runs the paper mill
No one can call him a pill
Art who runs the old S.P.
And his spouse, fair Dorothee
And their lovely daughter Jackie
Likes the Beach, I swear, by crackie
Arch Cape weekends are a treat
East and west, they can't be beat.

The 40's were memorable times for Arch Cape residents: Electric service and plumbing became a reality; the Cannon Beach Bakery re-opened in 1947; more cars got stuck in the sand by inexperienced drivers; sand filled the Arch Cape beaches, and clams came back to our area.

There was a problem in the late 40's regarding a property line disagreement involving Gelinsky, Morrison and the Conways. Morrison, in May of 1947, told Emil Gelinsky he was partly on the wrong lot and filed a lawsuit requiring him to move his property line. Emil, in August, was still stewing about the lawsuit over his property. On January 22, 1948, the case between Morrison and Gelinsky was settled while John and Lorna Conway were on their way to the Astoria courthouse to be witnesses for Emil Gelinsky, who was allowed to keep his house and chic sale (outhouse) where it was. Morrison got the lot between Gelinsky's and the Conways' property. It was set up several feet over Conway's line though, so, according to John, "they would have to see about that feature."

Late that afternoon, Mrs. Holderman, her daughter Eugenia, Eugenia's husband Clay Dooley and Walter and Emil Gelinsky met at *Pelican Point* to "partake of some libations" while discussing the day's court activities. John later notified Morrison by letter and demanded he move his house off that part of John's lot by August 11. All was eventually resolved. Perhaps the 20-foot width of the westward end of Maxwell Avenue is an outcome of that disagreement. Present day plat maps show Maxwell Avenue to be 20 feet wide west of Cannon Street and 30 feet wide east of Cannon Street. The problem didn't end there. Fence lines were still a sticky issue until the county surveyor located corners. The property owners, the Conways, Morrisons and Gelinskys made adjustments late in 1948.

According to John, June 26, 1948, was an interesting day at *Rustlewood*:

The Turnbulls arrive with fresh picked strawberries and raspberries. Ted Huff trims us at horseshoes. About 11:30 p.m., Linda 'Polecat' Brown and Shirley Brown undertake to open a can of rotten fish. The can had a large gas swell, so when they opened it in the kitchen, it caused immediate evacuation of the property. Baby Doll wakes up with a bang from the big hanging couch in front of the fireplace and hits the floor with both feet and gets the tongue wagging fast and loud. Shirley and Polecat had found several cans on the beach and were a bit too curious about the contents. The writer, John Conway, had previously retired and got a good strong whiff up the stairs. Never a dull moment, and after strawberry shortcake for dinner.

This must have been a very active summer for Shirley Brown. She and her friends ushered in the Fourth of July with an aerial bomb serenade that shook up the local elders who had retired for the night, July 3rd.

Other bits of local news in brief follows:

Major Maurice and Eleanor Simmonds arrived on August 11, 1948, from Korea for a few days.

The big news in 1948 had to be the opening of the Sunset Highway on October 4, which made the 85 mile trip from the Conways' Portland home to *Pelican Point* much easier and faster.

About this time Portland architect Sidney Hayslip and his wife, friends of the Conways, tried to purchase the Maxwell house from the Corneliesons. They offered them

$3,500. Instead, the house was sold to the Maddison and Reynolds families from Tacoma, who were friends of the English girls, for $5,000.

On the afternoon of June 30, 1949, the Conways' long time friend and good neighbor, Nellie Leech, passed away at Good Samaritan Hospital in Portland. She hadn't been well for some time. Lorna and Aunt Kate had seen her the previous Tuesday and missed her presence at the beach very much.

The August 21, 1949, entry tells about what may have been the first *Pelican Point* drowning:

Sam Rice, of Portland, age 55, had gone into the surf at low tide with Bill Markham of Arch Cape about one-half mile north of Rustlewood. The crab hole and outgoing tide were a bad combination. Sam Rice drowned. The lifeguard from Cannon Beach and a Dr. Baird from the University of Oregon, who happened to be present, couldn't save him. Sam left his wife and two children.

The next day everybody at the house, including John, went for a dip in the surf with Dr. Countryman and his son, Dr. George Countryman. Lorna, who stood on shore, hollered about not going out too far.

There was a serious brush and forest fire on Sugar Mountain back of Cannon Beach September 26, 1949. The east wind blew large clouds of smoke and ashes over Cannon Beach, Tolovana Park and out to sea. The fire department alerted the town, as it was 80 degrees at ground level and humidity was low. Lorna and John had driven down to protect their homes from hot ashes. Local fire fighters, with help from the Navy, brought the fire under control in three days. The local market and bakery donated food for the fire fighters.

The 40's end with this little ditty from the log:

> *Here's to Arch Cape by the sea*
> *It is the place for you and me*
> *Where we love to see our friends so dear*
> *And drink their whiskey and also their beer.*

The 50's began at *Rustlewood* with a twenty-three degree temperature January 1st with snow on the ground and icicles hanging from the eaves. The kitchen oil stove burned all night long to provide heat. The next day was cold, also. John emptied the fire extinguishers on the back porch, poured kerosene into the toilet bowls, drained the water lines, and prepared and checked *Rustlewood* for winter.

A very definite pattern emerged in the 50's regarding time spent at *Pelican Point*. According to John's log, the Conways traveled to the coast almost every weekend except in the winter. They closed *Rustlewood* and the *Wee House* toward the end of October and opened again the following spring. Weather permitting, they did celebrate many Thanksgiving, Christmas and New Year holidays at *Pelican Point* with friends and neighbors. That meant considerable work getting *Rustlewood* back in working order and then "winterizing" again before returning to *Shady Rest*. John often mentions the harsh Arch Cape environment in respect to moving parts, such as door and window hardware, and the need to replace and repair everything on and around the two structures constantly.

Rarely did John and Lorna leave Portland without something in their vehicle needed for *Rustlewood* or for the *Wee House*. They did extensive remodeling on the *Wee House* during this decade. Also, it had been over twenty years since *Rustlewood* was built, and even though John kept a strong maintenance program, weather and time took their toll. Frank Lee, the Arch Cape handyman, helped often and worked with John for years on many projects. Numerous entries in the log demonstrate the many changes John and Lorna made in *Rustlewood* and the *Wee House*. Here are examples from the log illustrating why the Arch Cape community appreciated Frank Lee:

The motor on the kitchen stove is out of order so we switch to wood for cooking. Frank Lee removed the motor so I could take it to Portland for repairs. We fixed the wash basin in the Wee House, as it froze up since New Year's. Frank had me disconnect chrome fittings on the supply pipes and drain the system. Plumbing always needed attention, especially the moving parts in toilet tanks. Frank installed new brass double guides imported from Kass Hardware Company, Philadelphia, on both tanks and it stopped the tanks from leaking.

Cedar rounds from the shingle mill replaced the front porch on the Wee House. Frank Lee fixed the ridge on the Wee House with aluminum ridge flashing and some shingling. He helped install the ceiling beam to support the upper level and finished that area into a bedroom.

A new range for the Wee House arrived via Nehalem Valley Motor Freight and was left near the front door step. The brick masons who were working on the house were away and Frank Lee was asleep, as he works the night shift at the shingle mill. Later, Frank and John moved the stove in place and connected it to the hot water tank and ran wires for the burner and the igniter on the burner. It took a lot of manipulating before we finally got it working properly by seven p.m. I got out the jug and discussed public affairs with Frank for about an hour in front of the fireplace.

A wash basin gasket didn't make it through the winter and squirted water around until Frank Lee, then living in Albert Leech's place, brought over a wrench to fix the problem.

Frank Lee, now handling Albert Leech's rental cabins since Albert took sick in January, installed a 165 foot one-inch water line to the Wee House and Rustlewood from the new main line on Cannon Street. It was a good deal because we have more pressure.

It is apparent, based on John's log, that Frank Lee's know-how was indispensable to the community. He repaired and cared for many homes in the area just as if they were his own. (Even after John's death in 1968, Lorna hired Frank to keep things going around *Rustlewood* and the *Wee House* as long as his health allowed him to do so.)

Maintenance work still was an important part of John's activities, but it became more methodic and efficient in the 50's. The chain saw and the Whirlwind power mower, his pride and joy, made two necessary and important tasks much easier. Early in the 50's, he brought the new mower down one weekend to give the "hay field," as he called the territory around *Rustlewood*, a good mowing. Eugenia came over and lured him to her place to cut her grass for a couple of good shots of bourbon. The Whirlwind also cut the Huff yard, and in appreciation, the Huffs invited Lorna and John to dinner that evening.

Carpenter ants and termites are a constant worry for beach dwellers. In 1953, John had a battle getting rid of termites in both the *Wee House* and in *Rustlewood,* where they were found over the door and inside the door casings from the kitchen to the dining room. This meant removing the casing and replacing damaged material. In the *Wee House*, a four by four foot section of the kitchen floor where the refrigerator sat was badly damaged. An old stump under the house floor was rotten and started the deterioration. Replacing the sub-flooring plus the top material and linoleum solved the problem.

Social activities continued during the 50's, perhaps at a faster pace than the previous two decades, as more full-time residents lived in Arch Cape and more vacation homes were built. Many property owners lived in Portland and Seattle and the improved roads to Arch Cape made travel much easier than before. On May 23, 1953, John drove over the new Cannon Beach by-pass, missing the town altogether.

Here are more selected entries from the 50's involving some of the many Arch Cape activities:

Elsie English came over and gave Lorna and the ladies at our place a pep talk about glass balls. I drive them to Hug Point and the girls swarm all over the territory combing the beach on the way home. No balls, but a wave sneaked up on Aunt Phoebe Hayslip and dunked her girdle. Albert Leech, with his daughter Elsie and family, call in the afternoon and we try a hot toddy or so. Uncle Sid provides crab cocktails. They all came down today to bring Albert back. Albert and his grandson, David Wood, came over later for dinner and a card game.

The family arrives after fried crab legs for dinner at the Crab Broiler to find the "cheerful" camellia in bloom near the house. Brought a new motor for the oil burning kitchen stove, cost seven dollars, and had it installed and going by seven p.m. the same evening. Rough surf and much rain. Played cards in evening. Had rib roast beef with rhubarb pie from the garden—good.

Lorna lost one of her red boots with a shoe inside. She suspects the big black neighborhood mutt who chases sticks. Lorna swarms over to the English "Termite Trap" and finds her boot and shoe there along with the big black mutt. Now she feels much better.

Clammed in morning. Had tournament, horseshoes. End of tournament, Huff 12, John 17, Uncle Ted blew up again. He lost a game, 21-0. Dinner great: homemade baked beans, brown bread, ham, salad and Betty Crocker Huff cake and coffee for dessert for all the lads and lassies. Fireworks by Wee House guest Harvey Sethman at 9:30 p.m.

Much surf bathing. Water 57 degrees. Usual horseshoes, card playing, clamming, sunbathing, ham dinners, and a new card game—Ship, Captain and Crew. Uncle Ted found a jug on the beach and had dyspepsia for two days (indigestion). The next day he suffers mal de mer.

Lorna takes first prize in Seaside flower show for most novel arrangement and second prize for living room bouquet.

It was a bright and sunny day with gardening in the morning and horseshoes in the afternoon. Barry Hayslip, Uncle Sid and Aunt Phoebe's son, blows up because he doesn't throw enough ringers. Uncle Sid arrives at 4:30 p.m. and reports a sunny day in Portland, also. He arrives just in time for horseshoes with his new horseshoe pitching shoes. But, Uncle Syd is a bit out of practice and we adjourn for the happy hour about six p.m. as a prelude to roast leg of lamb and frozen Hale peaches. We played Ship, Captain and Crew after we see a very unusual sunset in high color with first quarter moon and stars.

The Conways and Barry "Slug" Hayslip arrive in the rain, the first heavy measurable rain for a record twenty-seven day dry spell in Oregon. Frank Lee says it is a million dollar rain and should put out the Tillamook area forest fires. Good dinner of center cut of pig meat with homemade fancy stuffed marshmallow sweet potatoes and rhubarb pie.

These two entries in the 50's report the loss of two long-time Arch Cape residents:

Albert Leech died June 27, 1951, in Good Samaritan Hospital about eight p.m. We saw him that day and he knew us, but he was having a bad time. Very sad situation. Ted Huff and I were among the pall bearers for the funeral, eleven a.m. June 30th.

On February 15, 1953, our old and good friend, Dr. John Countryman, died about 4:30 a.m. at the Wheeler Hospital from a heart attack. The neighbors felt very sad.

John Conway records this bit of nostalgia August 31, 1957:

The old beachcomber, John Conway, retires early. However, he arises again 11:15 p.m. to take a peek at turning off the light in the Tillamook Lighthouse, which was done at 12:01 a.m. sharp. The Simmonds and Lorna and I watch from the meadow in a clear, stormy night, with the big dipper out in full view and a few clouds on the ocean horizon. Very sad, like losing an old friend of many years.
A sixteen foot high whistling buoy with a blinker light on it was installed Thursday, August 29th, 1957, about a half mile at sea west of the old lighthouse to replace the old light which had been there about 75 years. But, it doesn't have the atmosphere of the old light and can't be seen nearly as far away, as the old light was 133 feet above the sea.

Somehow, John lost his "Dead End" sign he placed at the entrance of what is now *Gelinsky Boulevard.* He located it on the sign post leaving Highway 101 entering Maxwell

Avenue when he was inspecting the English sisters' new home under construction. Who would do that? With the help of a crowbar, he removed the sign and placed it where it belonged.

The 60's begin at *Pelican Point* for the Conways in February, a month with strong winds and heavy seas. Frieda Billings and Genevieve Smith were swamped and nearly drowned at the end of Leech Avenue when a huge wave roared in and pulled them seaward. Many logs rolled into the meadows and all paths to the beach were blocked. Leech Avenue and the Travis Tyrrell yard were cluttered with debris and logs, but no damage was done to homes or fences. Mother Nature did help some, though, for much firewood was close for anyone to cut.

Rustlewood and the *Wee House* were now over thirty years old and major repairs and remodeling began in 1960. John built a woodshed. The Arch Cape Shingle mill delivered twelve squares of No. 1 shingles to re-roof Rustlewood at $10.75 per square in September, 1961. He also enclosed the front porch with windows in 1962, which added much more room to *Rustlewood*. Frank Lee removed the oil-burning kitchen stove and hot water tank and installed an electric stove and hot water tank. He also installed electric baseboard heaters.

The Conways' long time and very good friend, Ted Huff, died September 2, 1961. One couldn't count the number of horseshoe matches Ted and John played at *Pelican Point*.

Just before Labor Day in 1962, Frank Lee had three men working with him to replace all outside walls on the Huff house with plywood, building paper and shingles. Also, they replaced new bottom plates and floor joists on the foundation. According to John, it was a good job and cost the Huffs $850. Jack and Dorothy Birkby purchased the Huff house in 1965 and did extensive remodeling. They sold to K. C. and Margaret Short in 1992.

In 1963, Frank Lee did repairs on the water system and installed new 12-inch foundation blocks under the *Wee House*

The sewer lines, septic tank and drain field were cleaned and repaired in 1965. This task seemed to be endless for John and Frank Lee. Plumbing systems were vulnerable in the harsh Arch Cape climate.

John and Frank Lee began shingling the south side of *Rustlewood* in 1965. The shingles came from the Bear Creek Shingle Company in Arch Cape. The total job cost $114.30. Frank also painted the kitchen and shower. He was age 75 then but still did respectable work. In 1967, John makes this observation:

Frank Lee calls and gets his check for $34 labor for paint job, floor tile job, and basin job in wash room of Rustlewood for seventeen hours labor. Twenty dollars would be about enough for such work. But Frank, age 76, is not as fast as he was a few years ago.

Upgraded roads and better automobiles allowed the Conways to spend more time at *Pelican Point* during winter months. Electric heat and improved plumbing systems made it much easier to open and close *Rustlewood*. Social activities continued, though at a slower pace.

Roast beef seemed to be the preferred meat now instead of the often-prepared grilled hamburger served in the 50's. Steaks were favorites too. Some varmint took an uncooked steak John left sitting by the broiler. It was probably a hungry raccoon. On the way to and from Pelican Point they enjoyed Dungeness crab leg dinners at the *Crab Broiler,* located at the Cannon Beach junction.

In the early 50's, John acquired a breech-loading cannon manufactured by Winchester Repeating Arms Company that fired 10-gauge shotgun shells. John and Lorna always raised our country's flag on a pole at the dune line. It was a must to lower the flag at sundown and with total reverence for what that great symbol means. The cannon was successfully detonated many times for flag ceremonies at sunrise and sunset and many guests' entries in the log attest to this cherished tradition. The cannon was also loaded and fired for special occasions and holidays. John enjoyed waking his sleeping guests early in the morning, especially after a long evening that stretched into the "wee" hours. In fact, the thunder of the 10-gauge shells during the flag raising ceremony woke everyone in the neighborhood. In August of 1963, he brought down and mounted on a plank a new 12-gauge cannon, made in France, that he purchased in Detroit, Michigan. He bought blank shells at Oregon Marine Supply in Astoria for nine cents each. Both cannons were fired many times in the 60's during the flag raising and lowering ceremonies, for heralding arrivals and departures of *Pelican Point* guests, and as salutes celebrating the Fourth of July and other holidays. He fired the new cannon for the first time at three in the afternoon for Robin Church's birthday party.

There were a number of other items in the 60's from John's log worth mentioning. Alder firewood sold for $18 a cord. In 1992 it cost $85 to $90 a cord.

Gas could be purchased from the "Arch Cape Super Service Station," as John called it, run by Harold and Florence Schaeffer. Harold was a genius at fixing gas-powered lawn mowers; at supplying fan belts, generators, carburetors, and gas line filters; at repairing flat tires; plus fixing other mechanical problems in the Arch Cape area.

The Harrison Bakery at Seaside became a favorite stop for doughnuts, haystack bread, blackberry pies and other tempting goodies to those passing through on the way to *Pelican Point.*

The Astoria Bridge was dedicated August 27, 1966. It shortened the time for those living in Washington to reach the Oregon Coast. The toll then for a car was $1.50—and still is. Previously, travelers from the north had taken the ferry from Megler on the Washington side to Astoria on the Oregon side. The ferry capacity was limited and during the vacation rush, people often had to wait for a second ferry, which delayed their travel several hours.

John often mentions Barney Buff, their dog, and their daily walks to the creek for many years. Barney Buff died December 28, 1967, at age 17. John and Lorna acquired a new dog, Tuffy, a golden cocker on March 31, 1968.

The Conway saga ends September, 1968, when John died. Lorna continued to enjoy *Rustlewood* until her death in 1983. Today, Shirley and Larry Brown, niece and nephew of John and Lorna, own and maintain the property. They recently re-roofed *Rustlewood* and did major repairs and remodeling on both houses. The Conways were true Arch Cape "beach bums." They loved every precious moment when at *Pelican Point.* They loved their neighbors, friends and guests who were lucky indeed to be part of the Arch Cape scene for those four decades. This story is possible because John Conway kept a log spanning 35 years. His writing is informative, factual, and at times downright humorous. Thank you, John.

John and Lorna Conway, Circa 1940.
The couple that made things happen in Arch Cape
for three and one-half decades.
Harry Teller Photograph.

The Conway house in 1931. Today the house looks exactly as it did then except for the enclosed porch, which was done in 1962. The Pajunen house shows in the left background and one of the Leech cabins shows to the right. Photo, Eldridge/Coffman album.

Mrs. George Arthur Brown, Lorna's mother, is in the center and Lorna Brown, about age eleven, is second from the right. This photo shows Hug Point just before the rock was blasted away to make a road around Hug Point. Circa 1907. Photo, Shirley Brown collection.

Shirley Brown is on the left with Donna and Betty Pajunen, who were her very best friends while growing up in Arch Cape. The Pajunen house was directly west of the Conway house across Gelinsky Boulevard in Arch Cape. 1934. Photo, Eldridge/Coffman album.

John and Lorna are sitting on the back steps of the Gelinsky-Holderman home with their dog Barney Buff. Note the water pipe and the two work areas on the porch. Circa 1966.

There they are, lined up at the Holderman's bar rail. From left to right: Bert Patton, Dr. E. E. Pajunen, Nell Makie Mott, Mabel Coffman, Grace Pajunen, Marge Gelinsky Holderman, Emil Gelinsky and Mrs. Aletha Eldridge. October 1, 1939. Photos, Shirley Brown Collection.

Robert Brown, 5 and Linda Brown, 8, grandchildren of George Arthur Brown and the children of McDannell and Gretchen Brown, also niece and nephew of John and Lorna Conway. That is Helen Coffman Bampton, Mable Coffman's daughter and the granddaughter of Aletha Eldridge in the background. 1935. Photo, Coffman/Eldridge album.

Shirley Brown, 8, and her brother, Larry (Bud) Brown, 3, grandchildren of George Arthur Brown and children of Laurence and Mildred Brown, and also niece of Lorna and John Conway on the Arch Cape beach. That is Betty Ann Pajunen, Shirley's Arch Cape friend and neighbor, upper left. Today, Shirley and Larry own the Conway/Brown home. Circa 1933. Photo, Shirley Brown collection.

Lorna Conway sold crabs for ten cents each or three for twenty-five cents in 1924. Photo, Shirley Brown collection.

Angelo Costanzo
As told by his wife, Lucille

My husband Angelo was born in Italy in 1895. He left home at the age of ten by box-car from a rail yard near his home in Santa Famia. He said he never had enough food, and he felt if he left, the rest of the family would have more. His trip ended at a rail siding near a dock on the coast of France. He was dirty, hungry, and his body was covered with lice. He walked to the dock where he heard a man talking in a dialect he understood. He ran to the man and asked him if he knew where he could get something to eat. Angelo was all alone in a strange land and he was freezing in the winter cold. The man looked him up and down and all he could see was a dirty little boy that needed help. The man asked him to come with him to his house and he would give him something to eat. When they got there, the man said to his wife, "Look, Ma, we got a boy."

The wife looked at Angelo and saw how dirty his clothes were and how badly he needed a bath. She prepared a tub for him and told him to get undressed and take a bath. Afterwards, she gave him some clothes that were his size. Unknown to Angelo, they had a son about his age and size who died six months before. Angelo's clothes, which were practically crawling by themselves, were burned, and then the wife fixed Angelo something to eat.

Angelo explored up and down the docks and admired the many ships loading and unloading cargo while living with his new-found family. One morning, he asked the owner of a ship if he could go aboard, and the man invited him to go ahead and look around. He liked this young boy and asked Angelo if he would work for him. He put him to work washing dishes and when the ship left France, he became a cabin boy. Angelo spent two years going from France to St. Johns near Montreal. They wouldn't let him off the ship because he wouldn't tell anyone where he lived. He said his mother and father were dead, and he had no papers to prove his identity. One day he asked the captain if he could go ashore in Canada to buy some new clothes. It was obvious to the captain that the boy had outgrown what he was wearing. The captain said, "Here, I'll give you the greater part of what you have earned." So Angelo left the ship in Montreal, wandered around until he became disoriented and couldn't find his way back to the ship. He still could not speak much French. When he went into stores to buy something, he pretended he could not speak. He pointed to things he needed, whether it was bread, clothes, or anything else.

The ship sailed without Angelo so he boarded a train in Montreal that headed west. He remembered he had some relatives in Portland, so he purchased a ticket to Portland without being questioned at that time. However, when the train almost reached Spokane, the train crew found out he carried no identification documents and were going to ship him back to Montreal. The conductor asked, "Do you have anyone we can contact?" Angelo told him he had uncles in Portland and gave him their last name. His uncles were well known contractors in the Portland area. He was sent on to Portland and his two uncles posted bond for him. This was so he would not be a burden to the United States.

Well, he didn't stay long with his uncles either. The wife of one of his uncles was miserly and tight. Angelo loved his uncle but not his uncle's wife. She would lock the bread box and everything else at night. When you are about twelve or so and a boy, you are hungry all the time. She also had one of Angelo's cousins living with them whom Angelo loved very much. His cousin told me how hard they both worked and how terrible it was to work all day and then not have enough to eat. Anyway, he moved away from his uncle's home and sold papers for two years in Portland. He had a stand in front of the *Imperial Hotel*, which is on Broadway, one of Portland's busiest streets, and it provided a good living for him.

Angelo worked for a very wealthy man by the name of Healy. Mr. Healy wanted Angelo to work for him when he was building Healy Heights in Portland. He wanted to teach him what he knew about the building business.

It was said by some that if you gave Angelo a pick and a shovel and told him to make a straight ditch across country from here to New York, you would find it would never be out of line. He worked for his uncle and that is what his uncle did for a living. They dug. They dug basements for commercial buildings and for homes. They did the University Medical School in Portland. Angelo was the supervisor on that huge job which was all done with men using picks and shovels.

One day, while in a store in Portland, Angelo met a man who was a railroad contractor who hired workers to build new rail lines. Angelo asked him if he needed a water boy. The man said he did, and that if he wanted the job, he should come back in the morning. Angelo was 14 or 15 at this time and became a runner or "go-fer" for the workers. He gained valuable experience working on many of the tunnels between Portland and Spokane. He also learned about blasting powder while working in the tunnels.

Angelo heard that help was needed in the mines out of Salt Lake City. He decided to give it a try and with a can of sardines and a loaf of bread, started up the mountains toward the mines. He was hired and soon became a foreman.

World War I began while Angelo was in Utah so he enlisted in the Army. He was about 22 at the time and was sent to the *Presidio* in San Francisco for several months of training. He loved San Francisco. One day, it was rumored that their company was to be sent overseas. As they were lined up preparing to leave, Angelo asked permission to speak. He told his captain he was not a United States citizen and would be sent back to Italy and put in the Italian Army. He said he didn't want to be in the Italian Army, that he loved America and wanted to be in the United States army. The captain then asked that anyone else not having citizenship papers to step forward. Over half of the men took that step forward and he marched them all down to headquarters and swore them in as citizens of the United States. That was the best thing that ever happened to Angelo. He thought he had Heaven on earth and treasured that piece of paper all his life. I think he would have died had he ever lost that precious document. He ended up in France and was there until the war ended. When he returned from France, he was sent to Fort Douglas in Utah to be mustered out of the army.

We were married in 1919 in Farmington, Utah. Angelo worked in the mines as a foreman and received a fair salary. He worked in a shaft two thousand feet below the surface where water flowed constantly. One night, when Angelo came home, I opened the door and saw a friend of his lying on the ground. I said, "That is enough." I'd lived in that town long enough to see what the mine did to the men. Men 30 and 40 years old looked old enough to have sons their own age. I couldn't stand to see this happen to Angelo. It wasn't that they didn't have everything possible to work with, it was what the working environment did to the men. Managers were always searching for new materials and better methods to operate the very productive mine.

I wrote to Angelo's uncle in Portland, a contractor, and asked if there was work available there. He sent him enough money to get to Portland and I stayed behind for several months before I was able to follow him.

Angelo had an idea no one had tried before. He wanted to build a super service station with a garage and some little shops. He found the spot he wanted which was near the Ross Island bridge in Portland. But, after it was finished and ready to operate, it was decided that the Ross Island access to the bridge was to be closed completely until the bridge across the Island was finished. There we were with $80,000 worth of inventory and fixtures and couldn't sell one gallon of gas a day. So what could one do? We went broke. Thank goodness, Angelo could mentally handle this catastrophic set back. I had a harder time as it darn near drove me crazy after working so hard on a dream only to lose it all through no fault of ours. He had borrowed enough money from his uncle to build the place. Angelo's attorney advised him to give the business to his uncle. At the time, it didn't set well with the uncle. He couldn't understand how a nephew could do such a thing. Eventually, the uncle tripled the amount of what we had borrowed from him, but that of course, didn't make any difference to the uncle at the time. He still couldn't accept what the nephew did to him. We couldn't help it. It was the product of the time and of the place.

Angelo's uncle was a contractor and well known in the Portland area. There were seven children in that family. If you were to walk around the University of Portland today, you would find the name *Costanzo* on the sidewalks and the year they were put in. Our grandson Mark had attended the university and came home one day and told us about it and asked us if that Costanzo was related to us. I told him about the Costanzo Contracting Company.

Angelo was a very knowledgeable man with a keen mind and if he could have had an education, I'm sure, would have been a good engineer. His uncles sent him to the Catholic School at age 13 when he first came to Portland. The nun in charge of his class had a six year old girl tutor him and attempt to teach him. Here is this tall boy, much older than the girl, who had been on his own and had to fend for himself for years. Perhaps they used the wrong tactics on strong-willed Angelo. I really don't know what happened, but he wouldn't stay in school. One day he picked up his teacher nun, who was a little bitty thing, and shoved her out the school room window. Father Balestra was in charge and was also Italian. He said, "Angelo, Angelo, you are Angel with horns." Years later when Father Balestra saw Angelo, he remembered the "angel with horns." Anyway, that was the end of Angelo's schooling. People that can't read or write are handicapped, for no matter how you talk to them, they refuse to discuss their problem. He could take a long list of numbers and add them as fast as anyone. He could write and read a little. He did keep his own books and the time his men worked. He was self-educated and wasn't afraid to tackle anything, no matter how imposing or difficult it might seem at the time.

Angelo had not given up his dream of owning a super service station. He watched a man who had a piece of property in front of where we lived. He had built a service station there and Angelo would watch the progress every morning for he wanted a station so badly. We had begun building a home on the corner opposite a service station. We were going to have a home and a little store. We had paid the contractor a down payment and building began. The man that owned the service station wanted part of our property so he bought it from us. We had paid $600 for it and we sold it for $2,600. Now we had money for a service station, but it wasn't enough. We found another Italian as a partner. Our station was a success and we eventually sold it for considerably more than we paid for it. We used our house in Laurelhurst as part of the down payment when building the next super service station. Then the Depression came and we lost everything, including our home.

The depression years, 1930 to 1936, were pretty tough. One of Angelo's uncles used horses because he had no faith in trucks. Angelo wanted him to buy a couple of trucks so they could do clean-up and hauling jobs. The older Mr. Costanzo had purchased what is now known as Dunaway Park in Portland, which at that time, was a huge hole. He used this hole to dump all kinds of debris like bricks, concrete, tin cans and debris hauled away from old buildings. The city wouldn't allow dumping garbage that was smelly. Anyway, somebody bought Dunaway Park. I really don't know the details of it, but it now belongs to the city of Portland. Today, it is used as a park.

We later bought a little farm in Bethany, just north of the Sunset Highway on West Union Road, which cost us $25 per month for mortgage payments. The depression was still with us and it was very difficult to find work. Angelo didn't have previous employers to ask for work because he had been on his own for a long time. Anyway, we had our wonderful little farm to keep us busy but still had no work to bring in any income. Finally, Angelo did get a job with Multnomah County, where a building was under construction along Skyline Boulevard. Men would work two weeks on and six weeks off so many men would have some income rather than a few with full-time jobs. Angelo's boss found out that he knew how to handle blasting powder, so then he worked two weeks on and two weeks off. The county tried hard to find jobs for veterans. When he wasn't working for anyone else, Angelo walked to the Portland Veterans' office to see if work was available. They finally found a job for him working on the Bonneville Dam so we moved to Cascade Locks, Oregon. There he met Mr. Orino, the contractor who had the Arch Cape tunnel project. Angelo was a laborer at the time but Mr. Orino soon learned of his skill and experience with tunnel work and blasting powder. There was a depot at Bonneville where they contracted to build a rock wall. Angelo built that wall and it was said that a person couldn't put a sliver between those rocks. This was a rock wall with no mortar.

Angelo moved to Arch Cape to work on the tunnel in August, 1936, and was the supervisor for the tunnel. He did the blasting and it was his responsibility to see that the job was done and the hole completed. He worked for Mr. Orino, who was one of three contractors that were project partners. They later became involved with six companies, but when the tunnel was bored, Mr. Orino's portion of the contract was completed.

There were many obstacles on the tunnel job. At times, water was a serious problem, with underground springs going swoosh all over the place, sometimes washing out days of completed work in minutes. One time the creek flooded suddenly and covered all the cars in the parking lot under the bridge. These kinds of problems kept Angelo in that hole most of the three-shift day. He left the tunnel only to go home for a few hours of sleep. There were other terrible experiences. Angelo smashed into a deer one night on his way home and crushed the front of the car. It made me almost crazy with worry because he was never home.

I lived in Cannon Beach while Angelo worked on the tunnel in 1936. Our children went to school there. Robert was 15 and attended Seaside High School; Lawrence was 13; and Paula, 5. Lawrence, with five classmates, was a member of the first Cannon Beach graduating class. Anne Sieverts was teacher and principal of the one-room school serving Cannon Beach at that time. I didn't get down to see them work very often because I was busy with our children and involved in many social activities. I loved Cannon Beach, for it was a lovely community with many friendly people. We moved back to Portland and Angelo continued working in construction going from tunnel to tunnel to tunnel.

World War ll came along. Angelo worked at the shipyard building Liberty ships and soon became a supervisor. My husband advised me to apply for a union card and to tell them that I was a shipwright. He said that would be a nice, clean job and I would be installing furniture. That would be a dandy job, I thought. Well, I ended up in the middle of the winter in a dirty tent sorting out nuts and bolts that were swept off the streets of the shipyard. That didn't last forever and I became a tool checker in the electrical department. We worked there for four years.

My two sons were in the service and we were blessed that they both came home. They now live in California. I have one daughter, Paula, who is my pride and joy, and lives in Vancouver, Washington.

My son, Lawrence, delivered papers in Tolovana Park when we lived in Cannon Beach. He knew a little old lady there, Mrs. Anna Taylor, and when we moved to Portland, he found out the same lady lived a couple blocks from us. She said she had 80 acres in the Mill Road area. Lawrence said he would like to buy a lot down there. Mrs. Taylor told him she had many lots and when he got around to it, he could buy one. She offered us the whole parcel for $10,000. We took her up on it. She said we could pay her after we sold a lot and there would be no interest on the agreement. We logged all the large trees off the property in one and one-half years and paid her the $10,000 owed. We didn't have a dime when we started this project. The property was logged after 1946 and was south of Arch Cape Creek. The timber was mostly spruce and hemlock and was sold to a Warrenton mill. Angelo did not do any logging for the shingle mill.

Angelo was removing some large stumps near Arch Cape Creek with blasting powder when a fellow challenged him and wagered a bottle of whiskey that he would blow them all over the territory. Angelo said they would not and said he would take that bet. He lifted those stump out hardly scattering anything. Again, Angelo proved his skill working with explosives.

Today, Arch Cape Creek runs rather straight from the old shingle mill site to the ocean. Earlier, the creek meandered several times across the present road, and Angelo, with his Caterpillar dozer, drove down the creek bed to straighten the channel. He nearly lost his machine once, and when the water was soaking his pants, he decided he had better do something quick or sink out of sight. He barely escaped, but he is responsible for the present course of the creek. Angelo also worked on the Mill Creek road so logging trucks could deliver logs to the shingle mill. The road, at that time, was very unstable and would shake severely as loaded logging trucks delivered their cargo of cedar logs to the mill.

Angelo worked at the shingle mill for awhile as a clean-up man. I was the one who went for help when the fire broke out, but it was too late. The mill burned two times and was not rebuilt after the second fire.

We had a logging operation in the Wilson River area near Tillamook from 1952 until 1954. Unfortunately, we were involved with a dishonest man, and again, lost everything. We moved back to Portland, and later purchased a home where we lived until we moved permanently to Arch Cape in 1956. We had kept a home in Arch Cape and were contacted and asked if we would come down and take care of the water system properties. Angelo's agreement was not in writing and all of these plans changed with the death of the system's owner.

Authors' note:

Angelo left his mark in Arch Cape. For years he was available to help one solve or work out a problem. He was "Mr. Waterworks." Another section of this publication outlines the history and development of the Arch Cape Water system. Angelo was a vital part of this development, especially in the early years when he worked so hard and diligently to provide all residents with pure clean water piped through a system he developed and cared for. He had no prints or maps of his system but knew the location of every riser, tee, connection, and fitting in the entire area for it was logged in his head, and he could without error, locate a problem or tell a resident where to dig or locate a pipe or a connection when a problem surfaced.

Angelo and Lucille moved to the duplex behind St. Peter the Fisherman Church in 1976. They took care of the church until Angelo died November 15, 1983, and then Lucille moved to Vancouver in August of 1985, where she presently lives.

Angelo, 82 years old and Lucille, age 75,
Circa 1981. Paula Sommers photo.

"Eldcoff"
The Aletha Eldridge/Mabel Coffman Connection
By Barbara Bampton Miller, Great Granddaughter/Granddaughter

Although my first visit to Arch Cape was in May, 1941, when I was eight weeks old, the story of *Eldcoff* at Arch Cape really began in June, 1927. Ads appeared in the newspapers to sell lots at Arch Cape, an addition to Cannon Beach, for $1 down and $1 per week for $99 total. This was a Sam H. Webb promotion where his ads claim: "You can't go wrong at this price. Any lot in Cannon Beach is worth more than $99. We desire to place a few of these sites into the hands of individual owners. We know the price will do it." (See a copy of the ad at the end of this story.)

Apparently, my great grandmother, Althea Eldridge, decided to purchase a lot at Arch Cape. In 1929 she held "open house" at her cottage, located two houses south of the Leech/Wood home. Ten years later, construction began on the house and the cottage became the garage. The cabin name *Eldcoff* is a combination of the Eldridge and Coffman names. Althea enjoyed thirteen years at Arch Cape, possibly living part of the year at Arch Cape and part of the year in Portland.

During Aletha's years at Arch Cape, her daughter, Mabel Coffman and granddaughter, Helen Coffman, visited many times. Pictures in our family album show many good times on picnics and outings with friends and neighbors, in particular with Elsie and Marie English. Aletha saw the passing of the "hugging days" around Hug Point with the completion of a rough road to Arch Cape in the early and mid-thirties. She was present at the Ecola State Park dedication in 1937. In 1939 she saw the Arch Cape Tunnel punched through as part of the Oregon Coast highway system.

Aletha passed away in 1941 at the age of 71. Her daughter, Mabel Coffman, inherited the home and lived there alone for approximately five years. I remember one story she told me of how there were Japanese submarines in the ocean in front of Arch Cape. One night she heard a large crash and was sure she was being invaded by the Japanese. In fact, a large mirror fell off the wall and crashed to the floor. Mabel also told of collecting the glass Japanese fish net floats that washed up on the beach. I still have some of them.

As I mentioned previously, my first visit to Arch Cape was in the spring of 1941 when my mother, Helen Coffman Bampton, returned to Arch Cape with her husband and infant daughter. I also spent my first Christmas at Arch Cape. Although I was quite young during my subsequent visits to Arch Cape, I have flashes of memory: the abundance of bleached driftwood around the property; the paths to neighbors and to the beach through much greenery; the slugs in the garden; the big "rocks" in the roaring ocean; the curving roads; the ride through the tunnel in my parents' car. I can feel myself wading in Arch Cape Creek. I can still recall when Elsie and Marie English held me on their laps for pictures. I remember sitting on the sand as the waves rolled over my feet, scaring me at first, but delighting my sister Roberta immediately.

Perhaps it was Mabel's ongoing throat problems requiring treatment that prompted Mabel to sell *Eldcoff* and move back to Portland. She sold the property in 1945 or 1946. Mabel passed away in 1965 at the age of 78 in New York City. She relocated from Portland,

Oregon, to New Jersey in 1956 when her daughter Helen and family were transferred there from Shelton, Washington. Helen passed away in 1980 at the age of 68.

When I returned to visit Arch Cape in October, 1992, after almost fifty years, I found it as beautiful, if not more beautiful, than I remembered. Arch Cape sparked my love of the ocean and I am sure that is why I live on the ocean today, although it is the Atlantic Ocean instead of the Pacific Ocean. The ocean water off Hampton Beach, New Hampshire, is as cold as that off Arch Cape, Oregon.

*Aletha Eldridge's **Eldcoff** cabin in 1929. That is my great grandmother, Aletha, standing near the chair. The structure was planned to be a garage for a home to be constructed at a later date. See the photo below. Eldridge/Coffman photo.*

*Aletha standing in front of **Eldcoff** in 1941. The original cabin became a garage and the roof was removed to make a sun deck. Eldridge/Coffman photo.*

Four generations at Arch Cape May, 1941. Left to right are Aletha Wells Eldridge, Helen Coffman Bampton holding Barbara Bampton Miller and Mabel Wells Coffman. Eldridge/Coffman/ Bampton photo.

Barge washed ashore September 13, 1936 just north of the arches. My great grandmother and my mother are on the deck. Eldridge/Coffman photo.

July 4, 1937 gathering at Arch Cape. Note the abundance of drift wood. Automobiles could drive from Cannon Beach around Hug Point or drive down the primitive road to Arch Cape and then down Leech Avenue to the beach. Eldridge/Coffman photo.

RSDAY, JUNE 30, 1927

$1.00 DOWN $1.00 WEEK

ARCH CAPE

Addition to Beautiful

Cannon Beach

We will sell to the first fifty buyers the choice of these beautifully wooded beach lots for only $99.00 total, and on the very attractive terms of $1.00 down and $1.00 per week. These are large sites and are worth from $350 to $1000 each, at the present market price. Do not confuse this tract with other holdings far back from the beach. CANNON BEACH PARK fronts on the beach, it is high and dry, and very accessible, lots are level and well timbered.

The Coast highway will intersect this tract, crossing the property five blocks from the beach near the center of the tract.

Remember—all lots are the same price during this sale—$99.00—that's all—and $1.00 cash and $1.00 per week to the first 50 buyers.

Mail us $1.00 today—we will make you a selection, then upon your first visit to the property you may select any unsold lot should you prefer another location.

Or, better still, come into our office, make your own selection, and you have the same privilege of making a different selection when you visit the property. Even though our lots are selling at $500 when you get to the property your price is $99.00 today.

We desire to place a few of these sites into the hands of individual owners. We know this price will do it.

You can't go wrong at this price. Any lot in Cannon Beach is worth more than $99.00. Mail coupon today.

HEALTH   PLEASURE

Arch Cape Addition offers you an opportunity to secure a site for a summer home at a very low cost, and at the most remarkable terms at which you ever heard of such property selling. A place at the beach for your family, for you, to take a vacation, or your week-ends, will see your wife and kiddies grow healthier and stronger; the rejuvenation the salt air will give you, yourself, will fill you with new zest for your work, will add years to your life. You always have wanted a place of your own at the beach. You won't have a chance again to buy so cheap, or at terms of $1 down, $1 a week. Fifty lots at $99.00 each won't last long.

Arch Cape Addition is located admirably for a pleasure resort. It fronts on the beautiful bay formed by Arch Cape. It has the wonderful and beautiful Cannon Beach, the delightful motor way. Arch Cape Addition lies with a gentle slope down to the beach. It is under the shadow of the beautiful Neah-Kah-Nie mountain, and looks out upon majestic Arch Cape. Swimming, boating, fishing, hiking, mountain climbing, hunting or merely enjoying the pleasures and beauties of a wonderful beach, all are offered you by owning a lot in Arch Cape Addition. In 60 days 300 lots in Cannon Beach Park, adjoining, have been sold. These 50 won't last long. Do not delay.

*Sam Webb's newspaper ad, probably from the **Oregonian**, advertising Arch Cape lots for sale in 1929. The ad continues on the next page.*

The English Connection
Recollections by David English

The English Connection began in 1905 when Bill Adams built the *Arch Cape Hotel*. It was the first commercial Arch Cape enterprise to accommodate coast travelers between Astoria and Tillamook. The *Arch Cape Hotel* was a magnificent place, isolated and primitive, for roads to the area did not arrive until the mid 30's. Only a few structures existed between Hug Point and Arch Cape Creek at the time. In 1919, the hotel had rooms for ten guests at a rate of $2 per day or $12 per week, if one chose the American Plan, a plan whereby guests are charged a fixed sum for room and meals combined.

In 1912, Mr. Marmaduke Maxwell, a native of Devon, England, purchased the lot just south of the *Arch Cape Hotel* and built a home that year, which still stands at the west end of Maxwell Avenue. In 1914, he purchased the hotel from Mr. Adams, the original builder. Previously, Mr. Maxwell had a sheep ranch in north central Oregon near Shaniko.

No roads connected the Arch Cape area to Cannon Beach and Seaside until 1933. The beach was the easiest way to travel much of the way between Astoria and Tillamook. In our area, travelers worked the low tides around or over Hug Point and on down the wet sand to the magnificent Arch Cape area.

Elsie and Marie English, both school teachers, found Arch Cape in 1922 and liked what they saw. They stayed at the *Arch Cape Hotel* part of the summers of 1922 and 1923 and rented the entire hotel from June 15 to September 1 for the next five years. On August 17, 1922, Marie purchased her first Arch Cape property, a parcel of land several lots north of the hotel: Lot 1, Block 17, Cannon Beach Park. James Finlayson, Trustee for Cannon Beach Park, sold the property to her for $350. The 1922 Tax Statement valued the property at $70. Taxes paid that year were $2.67 and in 1923, $2.62.

Part of a June 14, 1927, letter from Marmaduke Maxwell to Aunt Elsie reads as follows: "I think that $50 a month is reasonable, as it is way below prices at Cannon Beach." Imagine getting five or six rooms plus a kitchen, dining area, a huge living room, and all the spectacular surroundings—for fifty dollars a month.

The living room, the focal point of the Arch Cape Hotel, featured a grand piano and a fireplace made from native rock built by Paul Bartells, brother-in-law of Bill Adams. A huge wood box sat next to the fireplace. Guests filled the box daily with drift and huge Douglas fir bark chunks gathered from the beach. Seldom would one need to cut wood for the fireplace because an abundance of the right size pieces was always available on the beach. The rustic room was about thirty feet deep and twenty-five feet wide with vertical grain fir flooring. I've been told that the rock fireplace was not part of the original construction but was added later. Early pictures show a round pipe-like chimney on the south side of the hotel where the rock chimney appears on later photographs. Heat came from a huge pot-belly stove before the fireplace was built.

Wide windows allowed a view of Castle Rock and the mouth of Arch Cape Creek flowing at the base of the steep basaltic Arch Cape headland. Huge rock formations stretched westward from the Cape toward Castle Rock. Comfortable upholstered chairs invited guests to sit and observe this panoramic view. Straight back chairs surrounded a game table. A wind-up phonograph with a supply of needles and records stood in one corner for use by anyone willing to crank the handle. It was a made-to-order room for enjoying company, playing games, reading, or just relaxing.

The dining room, which also faced the ocean, was almost as large as the living room and had the same rustic appearance. The enormous dining table, perhaps sixteen or eighteen feet in length and about four feet wide, could seat twenty for meals. I especially remember the red and white checkered table cloth always in place for meals. Between meals, residents used the table as a surface for sewing projects, repair work, and for craft activities, making the huge table the center of in-house activities, especially when the weather was bad.

The one bedroom on the lower level was vacant most of the time. Some early guests reported they heard sounds and noises coming from the room. After that, my aunts assigned only "new" guests to that room. They soon learned of the resident ghost, and they, too, began to hear those night noises and asked for another bed location. Eventually, the room became more a storeroom than a bedroom. My grandmother, Jennie English, didn't believe in ghosts and volunteered to sleep in the haunted room. For her, it had the added convenience of a small bathroom next to the bedroom, so she would not need to compete with others for the lone facility upstairs.

The kitchen occupied part of the east side of the structure and measured about twenty feet by twelve feet, including the walk-in pantry. A large Monarch wood stove with coils feeding a monstrous storage tank furnished hot water for the kitchen and bathrooms. Counters with a sink and cupboards for china covered the walls. Pots and pans hung everywhere. Next to the stove, a wood box occupied valuable floor space and demanded much more effort keeping it filled than did the fireplace wood box. Drift from the beach wasn't acceptable because salt accumulations would eat through hot water coils and stove parts. The Swedish fiddle (cross-cut saw) became the tool of necessity to cut logs around the property or to cut "clean" logs available on the beach. Kitchen wood had to be almost dry and cut to length and split to the proper size. The stove and hot water tank were a bonus during cool times of the year, but during hot weather, the kitchen became a sauna. A window above the sink allowed the prevailing southwest wind to pass through the kitchen and out the back door on the east wall. Water pipes led to an outside shower east of the kitchen so surf bathers could flush salt and sand away. Hot water to the shower was available only when the kitchen stove was burning.

The porch, extending about twelve feet westward and along the full width of the structure, completed the first level of the *Arch Cape Hotel*. It had a shed roof beginning just below second story windows which provided protection from sun and storm and allowed space for outdoor furniture. Large boxes along the wall stored wood, and all guests carried something back for the fireplace when they returned from the beach.

The second floor had five bedrooms on the west side; on the east side was a bedroom, a large bathroom and a storage room. The bathroom had a wash basin, a bathtub with claw-shaped legs, and a flush toilet—social amenities then for a "civilized" society. Towel racks made from driftwood covered all available wall space.

The storage room was large and included a secret hiding place made of wall panels with no handles. For my amazement and astonishment my aunts would stand back, say **abracadabra**, and **presto**, the panel opened. I thought my aunts had magical powers. Actually, Aunt Elsie pulled at the joint between two panels to open and then close the panels without leaving tell-tale fingerprints. My aunts used this space to store all linens, bedding and other items in metal containers at the end of summer for winter storage. These metal buckets, about a third the size of an oil drum, formerly contained lard that hotel and restaurants used and were the only way my aunts had to keep mice from nesting in the bedding over the winter. My aunts also stored canned and dry food items in these metal containers for use the following season. They were perfect for storage, for they had tight lids and the interiors had a varnish or a similar type finish that did not rust.

In the early days, the *Arch Cape Hotel* closed from September to the following June. My aunts gave away all perishable food or took it back to Seattle, feeling the hotel was "secured" until the next season. It was a difficult challenge to outwit the mice, the rats, and the dampness always associated with the coast.

In 1929 my aunt Marie agreed to purchase the hotel and some of the surrounding property from Mr. Maxwell. Imagine these terms just before the Great Depression: $1,500 for the hotel and surrounding property to be paid $60 or more a quarter in United States' gold coin at 5% interest per year. Mr. Maxwell died at age 87 in 1931, and the note was assigned to his heir, Catherine Burd, who lived in England, and had an August 9, 1932, due date.

Marie asked for an extension on the note without success. At the time, school districts paid teachers with warrants redeemable in the future, instead of paying by check that had immediate cash value. Somehow, Marie managed to make the payments and paid the note in full. The Satisfaction of the Debt signed by Burd December 29, 1932, gave Marie clear title to the property.

I have many letters Mr. Maxwell wrote to my aunts. Most of them deal with rental terms, storm damage, tide tables, and beach driving conditions with strong opinion when to come and when not to come to the beach. Other advice included purchasing maintenance items in Tacoma or Seattle, as they were not easily available in the Arch Cape area.

The following quotation from one of his letters gave this advice to Marie shortly after he sold the hotel to her: "By the way, you ought to change the name to something more appropriate to your profession, something not quite so common. It is up to you all to hunt up or invent, I should say, compose something descriptive as well as striking." The fine and dry sand between the driftwood and the wet high tide mark had a musical tone when one ran or walked on the beach. Elsie and Marie named their newly purchased hotel *Singing Sands*.

Here is a copy of an advertising flyer my aunts prepared: (sic)

"SINGING SANDS" invites you to spend a week or more at Arch Cape, Cannon Beach, Oregon.

AMUSEMENTS—swimming in the surf; crabbing at sunrise; clam digging; walks along the shore at morning, in mist, and at sunset; visits to Bird Rock on a minus tide or to Hug Point when the surf is high; exploring wave-made caves and arches; hikes in the virgin forest to the falls; bicycling on the hard sand; sun baths; bridge.

RATES—Ten to fifteen dollars a week, two dollars by the day. Please give approximate time of your visit as the guest rooms are limited to six. June 15th to August 20th."

It also provided this advice:

"To anyone planning to spend a few days at Singing Sands—

HOW TO GET THERE—Arch Cape is 240 miles from Seattle. Seattle-Tacoma-Longview-Rainier-Astoria-Seaside-Cannon Beach-Arch Cape. Bring covering for your car, for garages are not always available at Singing Sands. You may prefer to leave your car at the garage at Cannon Beach and for one dollar have the stage bring you to Arch Cape.

WHAT TO BRING WITH YOU—Bring comfortable clothes, a few warm ones, for it will take a little time to become accustomed to the ocean air. There will be no dress-up occasions. Bring old shoes, and extra ones. The salt water and sand are hard on shoes and hose. A heavy coat is desirable on the beach at night. Close-fitting hats and caps are useful.

You will like your sojourn at the ocean and will be glad that you made the effort to come."

Another advertisement touting *Singing Sands*

SINGING SANDS

CANNON BEACH, OREGON

Elsie English

•

Open - - - June 15th to August 15th

Rates - - - $12.50 per week - $2.50 per day

My aunts packed the Buick touring car to the brim each June when school dismissed for summer vacation. At that time, it was an eight hour trip from Seattle to Arch Cape. Travel plans had to accommodate the tides. Everyone drove from Cannon Beach to *Singing Sands* on the sand and around or over Hug Point during a tide low enough to negotiate that dangerous obstacle. The final trauma was getting the heavily laden automobiles through the dry sand and rocks up to Leech Avenue. Driftwood, shovels, planks, gunnysacks, and many hands pushing helped reach firm ground for the final few yards down Gelinsky Boulevard to the rear of *Singing Sands*. At times, tide and weather conditions would not allow driving around Hug Point or over the narrow Hug Point road. High tides forced those going to Arch Cape to remain in Cannon Beach until the next low tide, ten or twelve hours in the future.

Most guests were educators, but others came, too. Soon, new patrons filled the rooms and many returned to Singing Sands summer after summer. Guests helped in some way with the many daily chores. They washed dishes, cleaned and swept floors, gathered wood, peeled vegetables, helped with the laundry, washed the coal oil lantern chimneys, and repaired anything broken or malfunctioning. Something always needed fixing. Rust and salt air caused problems with door and window hardware, hinges and plumbing. All moving parts constantly begged for oil.

Clams and crabs were plentiful from the beaches and tide pools around the rocks. Blackberries, huckleberries and wild strawberries were easy to find. Trout fishing was available in Arch Cape Creek, where anglers could find many quiet sections of water between the mouth of the creek and the hills eastward. Cole's Grocery and the Cannon Beach Mercantile Co. (now Osburn's) delivered in the summer to Arch Cape on Wednesdays and Saturdays.

Aunt Elsie was a genius in the kitchen. Her clam and crab feeds were legendary, and she organized the clam and crabbing expeditions that provided the shellfish. From then on, Aunt Elsie ran the show. She supervised the entire process outdoors. Using ocean water, Elsie delegated one of the gang to cook the crabs in a huge metal pot on a beach fire exactly twenty minutes in a full rolling boil. The crabs, lined up like soldiers in formation on a driftwood log or plank to cool and dry, were the responsibility of another. If not guarded, gulls and crows would steal the catch. When cool, the aunts and guests processed the crabs immediately.

The clam cleaning took the appearance of a factory production line. The first person removed the clam meat from the shell and pulled off the slimy stuff; the next cut the tip of the neck and slit open both channels; the third cleaned the boot; and the fourth did the washing and final cleaning. Elsie was at the end of the line for the final inspection. She made the cleaning task fun and gave all the helpers a sense of appreciation for this great ocean delicacy.

The early 30's were difficult years for everyone, but my aunts still managed to get to Arch Cape. In 1933, the highway department punched through a rough road to Arch Cape. In 1936 a major event occurred that changed the tranquility of Arch Cape forever. The Oregon State Highway Department issued a contract for .62 miles of highway, which included 1227 feet of tunnel 36 feet wide and 23 feet high through the Arch Cape headland. The department also constructed a pile trestle bridge with concrete deck 166 feet in length over Arch Cape Creek. When the bridge was completed in 1941, it was no longer necessary to struggle around Hug Point, and it was much easier to get needed supplies and food items.

Irene English, elder sister of Elsie and Marie, came to Arch Cape in 1938 after a long and illustrious career in nursing. She first worked for the Northern Pacific Railroad in hospitals in Glendive and Glasgow, Montana, then joined the Mayo Clinic. She became head of the nurses' training school and later head of nurses for the five hospitals that were part of the Mayo complex. In 1939, Irene married Dr. John Countryman, a retired country doctor and master surgeon from Grafton, North Dakota. They moved to Arch Cape and lived in the old *Singing Sands* hotel for a year during 1939 and 1940 while their home was under construction, one lot north of the hotel.

Dr. Countryman used a room he named *The Bailiwick* on the lower level of their new home as an office and a space to meet and discuss medical problems with local residents. A closet filled with medications, bandages and equipment allowed Dr. Countrymen to handle most emergencies. Even though he was retired, he never turned anyone away who needed consultation or assistance, nor did he charge anyone for his help and advice. Dr. Countryman died February 15, 1953.

I cleaned the supply closet in 1965 and found all sorts of bandage material, sutures of all sizes, enough medication to open a small drug store, and a great variety of medical instruments. His black medical bag was supplied and ready for emergencies. It was given to his grandson, Dr. Leonard Cobb from Seattle, the co-founder of the Medic-One (911) program. Dr. Cobb and his wife, Else, have a home in Cove Beach.

The fourth family member, Mabel English Lensrud, oldest of the English siblings, and her husband, Hoken Lensrud, moved to Arch Cape from Seattle, Washington, in l945. Mabel was a librarian and Hoken, a tailor and a violinist. Mabel graduated from the University of Washington Library School after rearing her family. Hoken was born in Sweden and arrived in the United States as a teenager. Mabel was an avid gardener and Hoken worked in their planting areas with Mabel and hauled many loads of seaweed from the beach for fertilizer. He played his violin almost every evening. Hoken died in l955 and Mabel sold the Arch Cape home to Colonel and Mrs. Maurice Simmonds and moved to Astoria in 1956. She was 70 years old when she became the catalog librarian for the Astoria library. Everyone was so proud of her getting that job at her age. She had a skill and a talent for her profession that few possess at any age. She worked at the library for several years before retiring to the Bayview Manor in Seattle where she passed away in 1978.

Many important events occurred in the early 50's. Elsie and Marie retired from teaching. In 1951, they built a temporary home on the lot behind the Maddison-Reynolds home, which they named *High Tide*. In 1954, construction contractors tore down the old *Singing Sands* "termite trap" and the new *Singing Sands* rose in its place in 1955. Then, Elsie and Marie moved from *High Tide* to the new structure. Sam English, my father and brother of Elsie, Marie, Irene and Mabel, moved to Arch Cape with his wife, Mildred, in August of 1960. They came from Anchorage, Alaska, where my father worked for a wholesale grocery firm. They moved into *High Tide*. All five family members lived in Clatsop County—four in Arch Cape and one in Astoria.

The 50's and early 60's were banner years for the English family. They were close-knit, sharing, and always willing to go that extra step to help one another with what talents each possessed. Evenings were social gatherings involving neighbors playing card and board games and perhaps sharing someone's pastry delight prepared that day. The same group filled the days, rain or shine, with outdoor activities such as picnics, beach breakfasts and other gatherings shared with friends and relatives. The garden and book club gave members the opportunity to share and solve garden problems and to present book reviews. The Arch Cape residents had no dull moments during this era.

Elsie and Marie were responsible for many permanent residents' buying property and building homes in Arch Cape in the early 40's and 50's. These folks learned about this isolated bit of paradise while guests at the old *Singing Sands* hotel in the 30's and 40's.

Former hotel guests Jule Kullberg, Orlena Harsch, Frida Billings, Jessie Fair and Mary Walsh were educators. Jule and Orlena owned a home two houses south from the last road turning left off Leech Avenue. Frida and Jessie built the home where Bridget Snow now lives. Mary Walsh had a small cabin off Maxwell Avenue and east of the path between Maxwell Avenue and Leech Avenue. In 1984, Coryell and Marilynn Berry, with Bill and Mitzie Walsh, constructed a new home on the same site. Marilynn and Bill are niece and nephew to Mary Walsh.

Floyd (Scotty) and Ella Scott, long-time friends and guests of my aunts, built a house in 1955 at the end of Maxwell Avenue. The home now belongs to their daughter, Marnie, and her husband, Dr. Melvin Beemer.

In 1945 Clinton and Jessie Reynolds, in partnership with Dr. Frank and Betty Maddison, purchased the Marmaduke Maxwell home from Dora and Lil Cornelison. Both families were former *Singing Sands* hotel guests. Dora and Lil purchased the home from Marmaduke Maxwell. Mrs. Reynolds suffered a stroke in 1969 and Mr. Reynolds sold his interest in the property to the Maddisons. Now, the home is back in joint Maddison-Reynolds ownership. This is one of the oldest occupied homes in Arch Cape, built in 1912 by Marmaduke Maxwell.

Ralph and Lucy Forbes, also former hotel visitors, purchased the home presently owned by the Sinai family. Ralph's daughter, Barbara, and husband, Jim Shaw, now own the home immediately north of the Sinai home.

I believe there was never a more thorough and caring support group than the early south end Arch Cape residents in the 40's, 50's and early 60's. Yet, nothing is forever. Time and age will catch up with all of us. Marie had a massive heart attack and died in 1966 at age 76. My father, Sam English, had a stroke and other complications and died in 1967 at age 75. Dad's wife, Mildred, returned to her home state, Minnesota, to be with her family. Aunt Irene moved into Singing Sands with Elsie, and I took over the Countryman home. Elsie had a severe stroke and died in 1970 at age 82, and Aunt Irene died at age 92 in 1979. At this date, 1992, all the "old guard" early timers have passed away except Orlena Harsch, who lives in Seattle, and Betty Maddison, who lives in Tacoma.

My wife Alma and I had resident guests for years after acquiring Aunt Irene's home. Susie and Henry were swallows and each year in early summer constructed a mud and grass home in the front porch above the door trim. They were master builders as they had little foundation for their eventual nest. I placed a "potty shelf" for them. Susie and Henry were friends for years, never afraid of us, and a joy for us to watch as their families developed.

Carpenter ants are ugly antagonists for Arch Cape home owners. Stumps, downed trees and old beach logs were home to those persistent home destroyers who managed to find comfort and lodging in most beach homes. It was a constant battle to outwit them. The south wall above the fireplace in Aunt Irene's home was being eaten to the point where pyramids of sawdust covered the stone fireplace mantle every day. I pulled the ceiling trim, drilled quarter inch holes on six inch centers, and squirted strong poison into the wall section being destroyed by the ants and solved the problem. Other efforts around the home—foundation spraying, removing growth close to the house and getting rid of dead wood around the home resolved the "ant" problem for me. It was a war and I won.

Scotty, our neighbor, had problems. He had beams supporting his flat roof house, and when reading at night and all was quiet, he could hear noises in the ceiling. Ants were chewing his ceiling beams. Dr. Maddison, Scotty and I had a visit and compared notes regarding ant eradication. When Dr. Maddison learned that Scotty "heard" ants chewing at night, he suggested using his stethoscope to pin-point exactly where the varmints were active. With a step ladder and Dr. Maddison's skill with his stethoscope, the problem areas were found. Then, Dr. Maddison brought out a large syringe with a section of medical tubing on the end; this was used to pump poison into holes drilled where busy ants were most active. This method of eradication worked.

Then there are the moles who can devastate a beautiful yard overnight. They are super diggers and never give up. Brian McDonough sticks a burning highway flare in a mole runway and smoke appears all over his lawn. Walter Cauble puts a piece of a highway flare in a tin can, places it in a mole runway, and then lights it with a propane torch. Jim Shaw has the most effective device. He removes the muffler from his gas powered mower and attaches a section of flexible electrical conduit which is run down a mole runway. With vengeance, he fires up the mower and carbon monoxide gets the little pests. I placed poison peanuts in mole runways with mild success. And then, I had a funnel with two feet of one-quarter inch hose attached to it so I could thread the hose into the runway. Then, a mixture from the garage and tool shed poured down the funnel seemed to do the best job for me. Perhaps, the little varmints just moved next door.

In 1971, Walter and Virginia Cauble moved into *High Tide* to help Aunt Irene and to care for her property. Walter worked for the Tolovana Inn and for the Gearhart-By-The-Sea Resort Condominium Complex as Maintenance Supervisor. Virginia took care of the house and prepared Aunt Irene's meals. They made a great team, for Walter kept the growth cut, the lawns mowed, and repairs made. Virgie, as we all called her, cared for the flowers and roses. Her "green thumb" provided cut flowers all year around. Aunt Irene died in 1979 and Walter and Virgie stayed on to care for the property. After eighteen years, Walter and Virgie retired to Aurora, Oregon. I will always appreciate the love and care they gave my Aunt Irene. Walter died May 28, 1993, from cancer. Last year he brought me two four-foot Sitka spruce trees which we planted just inside the dune line—now called *Cauble* spruce.

Ann Lensrud, grand niece of our aunties, now owns *Singing Sands* and *High and Low Tide*. I sold the Countryman home in 1984 to Kyle and Stephanie Corwin of Vancouver, Washington. My wife and I built a new home on the two lots north of the Countryman home where we now divide our time between Seattle and Arch Cape.

I was probably the most fortunate boy in the whole world between age five and twelve because the Arch Cape *Singing Sands* hotel was my home most of every summer from 1926 until 1933. I had for my private playground the beach with all its drift and sand, Arch Cape Creek, the meadow where Marmaduke Maxwell had his barn and kept his horse and cows, the surrounding timberlands and the old hotel. From morning to dusk, this magical background brought me new experiences and adventures daily.

Arch Cape Creek was the most exciting play area for me because I had my private yacht made from cedar poles decked with planks salvaged from the beach. It was moored in the deep pool next to the hill on the south of the creek. Sometimes, after a heavy summer rain, the raft floated out to sea and later washed ashore on the beach. I'd build a new one with the readily available drift and continue my explorations of Arch Cape Creek.

I had a dog named *Tippy* who was my constant companion. He was a mixed breed, not very big, and was distinctive because of his white paws and white-tipped tail. What other name could he have but *Tippy*? He wasn't my dog but belonged to a man named Louis C "Smitty" Smith. The aunties called him a hermit and a woodsman. He lived in the woods in a cabin above the present site of the Arch Cape sewer system treatment facility. I remember Smitty as a tall, slim man with a kind disposition. He was a hunter and pretty much lived off the land, for game was plentiful then. He traded meat, clams, and crabs to others for staples. Each summer was a reunion for Tippy and me. A photo appeared in the August 27, 1932, *Oregonian* with the following caption:

Louis C. Smith and Henry Hartzell, both of Arch Cape, helped by Tippy, their small but valiant terrier, trailed a big cougar all day and night. The next day they treed him five times and finally bagged him when they cornered him in a cave at the headwaters of Elk Creek. The big cat measured eight feet six inches from nose to tail. He had been in this vicinity for years and one hind claw was lost in a trap three years ago.

I had chores to do when at the beach and I never hesitated doing them. In fact, I enjoyed it. My major responsibilities were to keep the wood boxes filled, the kindling cut, and the lamp chimneys washed daily. I washed them with soap and warm water and wiped them dry until they sparkled. I trimmed the lamp wicks and poured kerosene into the lamp base when necessary. I responded to these tasks with gusto and always managed to schedule them when they would not interfere with my other beach activities.

My only paying job was pulling dandelions from the huge grassy areas around *Singing Sands*. My recollection tells me that more weeds covered the lawn surface than grass. I still have the pulling tool that I used then. Aunt Elsie paid me ten cents per bucket and those earnings came in handy when visiting Cannon Beach to swim in the salt water natatorium or to roller skate where the Coaster Theatre Playhouse now stands.

Marmaduke Maxwell taught me so much. I learned how to recognize the local trees: cedar, fir, hemlock, alder, maple, and spruce, and the ones to gather for kindling and for firewood. He taught me how to use a hatchet and how to cut kindling needed daily for the fireplace and the cook stove. His cutting tools were always razor sharp. He used a treadle powered grinding wheel with a huge round white stone. It had a water reservoir above the stone that dripped a constant stream of water as he sharpened his tools. I enjoyed watching him, and when I did, I was responsible to keep the reservoir filled. That experience lives with me today. My pocket knife and cutting tools are always sharp.

The most impressionable memory I have of Marmaduke Maxwell was his patience. He taught me how to make two traps, one for catching chipmunks and one for catching rats:

the "good creatures" and the "bad creatures."

The first trap was a figure four trap and simple to construct. It resembled the figure "4" that made the tripping mechanism and held up one end of a box. When tripped, the box fell and captured the chipmunk. When the trap caught a chipmunk, we transferred it to an enclosed pen to study and feed it before turning it loose. Mr. Maxwell explained that wild creatures should not be kept from their natural environment.

The second trap was lethal and was certain to reduce the rat population in the area. A five gallon square can with the top removed was the basis of the trap. A stiff wire threaded through the top of the can about a third of the way from one edge and also through a wood strip provided a tripping mechanism. The wood strip extended from the edge of the can to the wire and out beyond the wire about three inches. The end of the wood strip was baited with cheese. The rat walked out onto the wood strip after the cheese and then tipped into the can and fell into about two inches of kerosene and drowned. Very successful!

Mr. Maxwell also taught me how to make kite frames with cedar and string. These were traditional four-sided kites with a bowed cross member tied with a string. Newspaper and flour paste provided the surface that worked fine unless one had a crash or ran into moisture. The kite tail came from colorful strips of rags knotted together to provide stability. Kite making and flying gave me many hours of fun and joy for years. Many years later my brother-in-law, Bob Street, helped me construct a huge model that we covered with plastic from a dry cleaner's garment bag. Once high in the air, the kite became invisible—all one could see was the long colorful tail flowing in the wind. The following day was a blustery and rainy day, but we successfully flew our creation until a sudden gust caused our kite to crash into the surf. Today, I own several colorful modern store creations that do all kinds of tricky things, provided one knows which strings to pull.

Grandma English came to Singing Sands every summer when I was there. Never idle, her fingers wove strips of wool from old garments into hooked rugs—and they were beautiful rugs. Her frame for the rugs was often on the porch of Singing Sands, where she obviously gained inspiration and energy from the view and the fresh air blowing in from the sea. She always wore a shawl and rarely left her work station when she was busy on a project. It seemed she just had to get that extra row finished. However, she would always stop to visit with me. As could be expected, her guidance and advice really did not sink in until many years later. Grandma English died December 9, 1942 at age 86. I was in a Japanese prison camp then and did not learn of her death until I returned home in November of 1945.

I managed to get to Arch Cape several times during my high school years in the late 30's. Then WW2 came, and after five and one-half years of service, I resumed my love affair with the beach. I married Alma in 1947 and we came down often on weekends, holidays, and summers, whenever our professions would give us time, until our retirement in 1985.

The 50's and 60's were very active years for us since weekend trips to the beach were very common all year long. In the 50's, West Coast Airlines flew DC-3's from Seattle via Moon Island Airport in Hoquiam, Washington, to Astoria and back. The schedule was perfect. The flight left Seattle at 8 a.m. Saturday from Boeing Field and returned to Seattle leaving Astoria Sunday evening at 7. The cost at that time for a round trip was $9 to $11 per person. That gave us a very long weekend at the beach. My aunt Elsie met us at the airport in her new Ford Fairlane and allowed me to drive to *Singing Sands* where we unloaded and prepared for the weekend activities. There were many weekends, and those wonderful trips became routine.

After getting unpacked and settled, I drove Aunt Elsie south for her weekly shopping trip to two very special places. We stopped at the Tillamook Cheese plant in Mohler, between Nehelem and Wheeler. In those days, the Tillamook Cheese Company had many small satellite factories in the area stretching from Mohler south throughout the Tillamook Bay area. Aunt Elsie had a mission. She purchased cheese, cottage cheese, cream and milk. I will never forget her cheese-purchasing ritual. The cheesemaker took us to the aging room where, using his sharp knife, he shaved samples of aging cheddar for her to taste from huge cheese rounds. It was a thin shaving to bring out the flavor. Finally, Auntie selected what she wanted and the man cut off a large wedge, took it to a vat of molten wax, dipped it to seal in the flavor, and then wrapped it in cheesecloth. Today, all cheesemaking for the Tillamook Cheese Company is done in Tillamook.

Then we stopped for Gustin chickens and eggs on the way home, usually purchasing two fryers and a stewing hen, plus several dozen eggs. It took me awhile to figure out what Aunt Elsie meant by "Gustin" chickens. I knew about Rhode Island Reds, White Leghorns, Plymouth Rocks but never heard of a Gustin chicken. Later on, Auntie introduced me to Mr. and Mrs. Gustin, who lived a short way off the Manzanita-Nehalem highway.

Aunt Elsie ruled the kitchen and prepared all meals with unusual variety, flavor, flair and was full of surprises. They were always a gourmet's delight. One of her most popular and memorable meals had dumplings floating in a huge cast iron pot filled with Gustin chicken stock. She made popovers for lunch on occasion, a favorite of mine, and it was often served with a fruit salad. Aunt Marie, with help from Aunt Elsie at times, took charge of the yard. Aunt Irene lived next door and became involved in everything, especially organizing social gatherings. Card and scrabble games, beach picnics, evening bonfires, birthday parties and luncheons involving neighbors were daily activities.

The many dinners shared with the aunties at the Crab Broiler in the 50's and 60's bring fond memories. The Dungeness crab legs served with a baked potato, vegetables and cold slaw was my favorite meal. The serving was generous and the price low. It was difficult to pass the Crab Broiler, located on the east side of the highway near the Cannon Beach junction, if one drove by during the lunch or the dinner hour and not stop to eat.

In the 50's and 60's Alma and I always returned to Seattle "bushed." It took us awhile to figure why. The three aunties planned our activities. While two were resting, the third one had us hopping. Then another took over the second shift and finally a third one came on the scene while the others rested. We mowed lawns, cut brush, visited neighbors, dug clams, repaired this and that, shopped and were always doing something other than resting. We were busy and scheduled almost all the time by those three organizers.

The early 70's were memorable years. To start, they were unusually productive salmon fishing years. I moored my boat at Hammond during summer vacations and caught many fish in the ocean over the Columbia River bar and behind the south jetty at the entrance of the river. I caught my largest fish, a thirty-three pound Chinook, behind the South Jetty. The limit then was three fish and a number of times I'd come home early in the day with my limit when fishing alone. Changes were occurring as the fabulous 80's approached. El Niño, a phenomenon that produces abnormally warm waters along the northern United States coastline, reduced fish stock in the early 80's. Also, commercial fishing pressures helped curtail sport fishing. Fishing time was drastically reduced and the limit was cut to two salmon per day.

We adopted a new family member in 1975. Rufus, our golden retriever, came into our lives and became a first-class beachcomber. He especially loved Arch Cape Creek, just as his master did when he was a young boy. Rufus died September 30, 1991.

Today, in retirement, Alma and I spend about half of our time at our Arch Cape beach home; the rest of the time in our Seattle home. Here is a quotation from Bridget Snow that I like: *To be in Arch Cape is about as close to heaven as one can get.* I agree.

This is what Arch Cape looked like in the early 1930's. The Arch Cape Hotel and Mr. Marmaduke Maxwell's house in in the center of the photograph. George Arthur Brown's house (now owned by Shirley and Larry Brown) is north a few lots and the Henshaw home, now owned by Travis Tyrrell shows on the right. Note the heavy timber down to the shoreline and the massive line of drift at the high tide mark. Maxwell Avenue would be just to the right of the hotel and Leech Avenue just to the right of the Henshaw house. Photo, authors' collection.

This is the Arch Cape Hotel shortly after construction in 1905. Note the hand-placed rock wall on both sides of the steps and the mass of rock on the beach. There is a plank walk over the rock leading to the sand somewhere to the west. The sign reads ARCH CAPE HOTEL, MEALS SERVED AT ALL HOURS.

Photos, authors' collection.

*The Arch Cape Hotel was purchased by Marie English in 1929 and named **Singing Sands**. Mr. Maxwell's home and the hotel show behind the driftwood in this 1939 photo.*

Aunt Marie, Irene and Elsie with my grandmother, Jennie, behind the Singing Sands Hotel. Circa 1937.

Singing Sands Hotel guests. The sign is still intact today. Aunt Marie and Elsie are in the forground with my grandmother. Circa 1937. Photos, authors' collection.

Here I am rafting with Tippy in my favorite playground, Arch Cape Creek.

Tippy gets a bath.

My aunt, Mabel Lensrud, in 1961 with Library friends Marge Sorenson, lower left and back row from left to right, Donna Syvanen, Eleanor Davis and Pat Fisher at the Astoria Library. Could be Mabel 's retirement gathering or for a friend's birthday. 1961.

My cousin John sat me on a modern barber's chair and cut my hair. Mr. Maxwell's barn shows in the background. Circa 1930. Photos, authors' collection.

Here is some serious fishing on Arch Cape Creek. I am on the left and my brother Sam is on the right. Note the log and plank bridge over the creek. Circa 1927.

My sister Irene, brother Sam, myself and my sister Liz, circa 1931. Photos , author's collection.

The author stands at the left with the knobby knees and bow legs. His brother, Sam, is to his right. The next boy is Buck Miller. His sister Grace has her arm around Ella Scott. Marnie Beemer is sitting on the log with folded hands. Jean Miller is standing on the log, also with folded hands. The others are unknown. The picture is taken near the arches. Circa 1927. Photo, Marney Beemer collection.

The caption of this <u>Oregonian</u> article, circa, 1930, shows what Smitty did best. He was a hunter. Article from Gwen Carney collection.

HUGE COUGAR TRAILED TO CAVE AND KILLED

CANNON BEACH, Or., Aug. 27.-(Special.)-Louis C. Smith and Henry Hartzell, both of Arch cape, assisted by Tippy, their small but valiant terrier, trailed a big cougar all day and night. The next day they treed him five times and finally bagged him when they cornered him in a cave at the headwaters of Elk creek. The big cat measured eight feet six inches from nose to tail. He had been in this vicinity for years and one hind claw was lost in a trap three years ago.

These were my favorite beach activities. Salmon fishing in the Columbia River and in the ocean behind the south jetty was one of my exciting pastimes. This salmon weighed 33 pounds and the one on the rack 20 pounds. I moored my boat at Hammond and often was back at Arch Cape by 9:30 with my limit of three

fish. Clamming also was easy and productive. These were dug on a sandbar just north of Castle Rock. Cutting firewood, fishing and clamming was easy until the 80's. Then El Niño and fishing regulations drastically reduced fishing and the clams disappeared and so did the wood. My most enjoyable and long-lasting beach activity is walking the Arch Cape sands searching for treasures and meeting friends.

David English photos, Circa 70's and 80's.

Four Generations in Arch Cape

The Cerelli family is unique in our town. Perhaps they are the only four generation family that live in Arch Cape full time. There is George, his mother Alba (also known as Peggy); his son Bob and Bob's son Vito and daughter Micah; and daughter Janis and her daughter Brigid

After George retired from the wholesale meat business in San Francisco, he and his wife, Florence, moved to Arch Cape to be near their family. Their son, Bob, a local home builder, lives in Arch Cape. Bob is in partnership with John Mersereau and they call their company the Merserelli Builders. George and Florence's daughter, Janis Cerilli, is a local area teacher.

Some in the area refer to George as the operator of the Arch Cape Taxi Company. He willingly offers rides to those walking to the store, those caught in rain storms or to anyone who needs to go shopping. His friendly greeting of "What do you say?" gets one's attention. George is presently the chairperson of our Design Review Board and is a past president of our Arch Cape-Falcon Cove Beach Community Club.

Bob's Oregon Coast roots began when he was five years old. His aunt, Lena Adams, who lived in Cannon Beach, invited Bob, his sister Janis; and their two cousins, Steve and Linda Tognoli, to stay with her for a number of summers. They left San Francisco the day school dismissed and returned just before school started in September. Bob had many jobs during those summers. Paul Swigart rented horses and Bob guided groups for one and one-half hour beach rides, for which he was paid fifty cents. He drove a stage coach pulled by burros and piloted a stern-wheel boat up and down Elk Creek entertaining tourists. He never saved any earnings. After work he met with his friends at Swigart's hamburger bar, a popular hang-out for kids in those days, and spent his earnings.

Bob moved to Oregon in 1969 to attend the University of Oregon, where he majored in architecture. After two years his love for the coast and surfing won out. He married Sandy Senseney in Arch Cape in 1977. In 1979 they began building their Arch Cape home on the corner of Cannon Street and Maxwell Avenue. They have two children: Vito, age 7 and Micah, age 5. Both attend the Fire Mountain School in Cove Beach.

Last summer Bob took Vince Morrison out around Castle Rock. He has made this trip a number of times, both in the winter and summer. Viewing the beach from that distance and finding your landmark ashore is a thrill.

When son Vito was four years old, Sandy and other mothers in the area formed an "at home preschool." The mothers took turns on a weekly basis sharing teaching responsibilities in their homes. Classes began at 9 o'clock and continued until 11:30 or 12:00 noon. They had various projects: story telling, reading, art, music and learned how to socialize and work together. The following mothers and their children became part of the "in home school": Sandy Cerelli, with her son Vito; and Deb Mersereau, with her daughter, Ashley; are from Arch Cape. Wendy Crosta, with her son, Trevor; Jude Dooley, with her son, Noah; Katherine Mersereau, with her daughter, Annie; Barbara Temple-Ayers, with her daughter, Zoe: all from Manzanita. Perhaps this is where Vito's love for art and drawing began. Today, Sandy often volunteers as a teachers' aid at the Fire Mountain School.

Almost daily, you will see Bob and Sandy with the children on the beach playing ball, bicycling, walking, playing in the surf or just sitting enjoying the sand and the beach. If the waves are right, Bob will be kayaking or board sailing. Both Sandy and Bob will tell you Arch Cape is the world's best playground for children.

The Gardner, Smith and Priddy Connection
by Fay Priddy

As far back as I can remember there has been the beach house. As a child, it seemed to me the house had always belonged to my immediate family, Mother and Dad, Marcia and me, but that is not accurate. In the very beginning, the beach lot was purchased for ten dollars in June of 1912 by my great-aunt Effie Olive Smith Gardner, and the house was built the same year with supplies freighted from Seaside. It was a two-story house with a long, rectangular living-room/dining room facing the ocean, a large kitchen, and an outside uncovered porch in back. A stairway open to the living room led to two front bedrooms and one back bedroom upstairs.

My great-aunt, known by the family as "Aunt Attie," was a sister of George Smith, who was my grandfather. George and Rebecca Keays Smith had three children—Mabel Gordon Smith Kingsbury, Fred Gardner Smith and Gordon Keays Smith, my father. Around 1902, Aunt Attie had opened a business college in Vancouver, Washington, later moving to Portland and locating first in the Marquam Building and then the Fieldham Building. Many prominent Portland men and women were graduates of this institution. In 1911 she built a multi-level four bedroom house in Portland Heights, which she later shared with her older sister, Amanda June (Jennie June) Smith Proebstal. Jennie June was an artist and had a studio in downtown Portland. She taught art and worked in charcoal, watercolors and oil.

The great-aunts were childless but enjoyed the company of their niece Mabel and nephews Fred and Gordon and lovingly embraced their children—Jean and Dick, sons of Mabel and Lee Kingsbury; Virginia, daughter of Fred and Etta Smith; and Marcia and Fay Gordon (me), daughters of Gordon and Fay Smith.

Access to Arch Cape was difficult in the early days. It was a seven mile hike from Ecola (now Cannon Beach) to Arch Cape and certain rocky points were passable only at low tide. Aunt Attie often invited beach hikers for lunch or for a cup of coffee. There were fewer than a dozen summer homes between Hug Point and Arch Cape. Few property owners stayed year-round.

In the 1860's, John Hobson had sighted, but had not recovered, a cannon believed to be lost from the schooner Shark when it was wrecked crossing the Columbia River bar on September 10, 1846. It was almost buried in a sandy creek south of Hug Point and thereafter the early pioneers called this area "Cannon Beach." Family photographs from 1912 are labeled "Cannon Beach" in india ink on the negative and clearly show our family beach house, Castle Rock, Arch Cape Creek, or the arches in the background. "Arch Cape" was the cape itself, so named because of the large natural double arch formed by the rocks through which one could walk to Falcon Cove when the tide was out. The cannon was rediscovered in 1898 in front of the Austin house and placed on blocks nearby. The children always enjoyed having their pictures taken astride the cannon.

On October 6, 1928, Jennie June died in Portland and Attie, in great sorrow at the loss of her sister, collapsed and died a week later. Aunt Attie left her estate to be divided among her niece and nephews. In the final settlement, my father received the beach house, which was his favorite of the properties.

In the next few years, our family made the five-hour trek from Portland to spend most of the summer on the warm Arch Cape sand and the heady air. What is now Highway 101, stretching from Canada to Mexico, stopped well south and north of our summer home. Dad attempted to time our departure from Portland to coincide with low tide as the last leg of our journey involved driving from the highway onto the beach to reach the house.

We usually left in the middle of the night. Marcia and I curled up on the living room floor and tried to sleep through our excitement until it was time to crawl into the already-packed car to begin the trip to the coast. I usually slept until awakened by the swaying of the car on the curvey highway from Cannon Beach to Hug Point. At this point, we did not have to drive on the road cut into the outer edge of Hug Point, but could access the beach on a road immediately south from there, where Hug Point State Park is today. Sometimes we arrived before low tide and waited in the car for the ocean to recede. Often it was still dark, but some arrivals coincided with the early morning sun. My sister and I strained eagerly from our perches on the back seat to catch our first glimpse of the ocean as we came around the final curves.

Marcia and I spent these summers in total freedom. We jammed apples and crackers into our pockets and roamed the beach. Sometimes we rolled with pleasure in the cold surf playing "seals." We played in Arch Cape Creek, whose contours changed from year to year and often emerged from the winter storms with deep pools in which we swam or poled rafts. Seldom would another person appear except when children of friends arrived, left by their parents taking long vacations to California. The big house was often full during the summer.

In retrospect, this couldn't have been much fun for my mother, who was expected to feed and account for up to seven children for several weeks at a time. The household was still very primitive with no electricity or inside plumbing. We children didn't miss these conveniences, but with my dad back in Portland during the week, most of the extra work fell on Mother. I never heard her complain, as she loved the beach as much as we did.

Some supplies were purchased in huge cartons to last the summer—canned goods, sugar, flour, apples, soap, toilet paper, etc. Preservable staples left at the end of summer were stored under the eaves in a secret hideaway behind lift out wall panels in the back bedroom. They were rescued, dusty and slightly rusted, the following year. We received weekly deliveries of baked goods, dairy and other perishable groceries transported in a boxy milk-wagon type truck from Cannon Beach. Marcia remembers a single delivery that included twenty quarts of milk. We called our house "The Grocery Man's Delight."

Cooking was done on a wood stove which, along with the huge living-room fireplace, provided heat on chilly mornings and evenings. There was always plenty of driftwood from the beach to fuel both fireboxes.

Our meals then were simple, but now could be called gourmet fare. We raked crab for delicious feeds and dug razor clams that were cut up and made into chowder or delicately sauted. Clams and crabs were plentiful and easily gathered. The first dish I learned to cook was clam chowder—New England kind, of course. We often enjoyed fresh-baked wild blackberry pie. Mother always said the best baking she ever did was in the wood cook stove's big oven.

We bathed in the ocean or in water carried in buckets from Arch Cape Creek which was one- quarter mile away. We heated it on the wood stove and then poured the water into large oval metal tubs that we placed on the kitchen floor. One year—it must have been after the Tillamook burn in 1933—the ocean seemed unusually warm. We bathed in it and emerged covered with soot that had washed down to the ocean and on our beach. We really had to scrub to wash off the grime.

Dad shingled the house and added dormers across the front bedrooms in the summer of 1933. That same year, on September 2nd before returning to Portland, we walked up the new Highway 101 to Hug Point where the highway crew had just finished grading.

Sometime later Dad boasted that we had the first indoor toilet in the neighborhood. True or not, I was grateful I no longer needed to wind my way barefooted to the outhouse. With my flashlight in hand, I tried to avoid stepping on slugs or their sticky trails. Dad built the new bathroom in the summer of 1936 on the landing half-way up the stairs to the bedrooms. That same year he painted the kitchen and put in a new stove and sink. He also repaired the back porch and added a water faucet to replace the water buckets formerly carried from the creek. Oh, joy!

After the Wolf Creek Highway (changed to "Sunset" Highway in 1946) was opened and the tunnel completed in 1940, travel between Portland and the coastal towns increased. Nothing was the same—outhouses and kerosene lamps were out; plumbing and electricity were in.

Dad and Mother divorced in 1936 and Marcia and I no longer spent long summers at the beach. Dad married Ella Anderson in 1941 and they planned his retirement and a permanent move to Arch Cape. In 1937, he built an apartment over a garage at the back of the lot and in 1946 he tore down the original house preparatory to replacing it with a more modern one. He also converted the garage into another apartment and built a workshop and garage on a second adjoining back lot. Dad and Ella had started to move into the new house when Ella died suddenly of a stroke.

Dad moved to the beach alone and later met Genevieve Waples, who was visiting friends in Arch Cape. They were married in 1948 and subsequently moved into the new house. Dad died in 1968 and Genevieve died ten years later.

The property is still in my family, now owned by my daughter, Jan Priddy, Gordon's granddaughter, and Gary Anderson, who moved here from Seattle in 1979. In 1984, Jan and Gary extensively remodeled Gordon's house. They now live in the third version of the beach house with their sons Alan and Ian, the fifth generation of my family at Arch Cape.

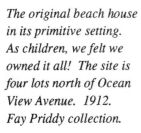

The original beach house in its primitive setting. As children, we felt we owned it all! The site is four lots north of Ocean View Avenue. 1912. Fay Priddy collection.

Back row: Dick Kingsbury, Horace Jackson (my grandfather), Rosa Jackson (my grandmother), Fay Jackson Smith (my mother) holding me; front row: Jean Kingsbury, Aunt Attie, Marcia (my sister), and Aunt Jennie June. 1926. Photo by Gordon Keays Smith.

Fay Gordon Smith, David Porter, Marcia Smith (shading eyes) on the cannon at its original location in 1929. Photos, Fay Priddy collection.

Fay Smith holding Fay Gordon; and Gordon Smith with Marcia in 1929.

Gary holding Alan, and Jan holding Ian with Castle Rock in the background in 1983

184

The Jan Priddy/Gary Anderson home after extensive remodeling in 1985. This is the third home on the same lot since Aunt Attie's first beach house constructed in 1912.

From top to bottom—Alan, Ian, Gary and Jan in 1992.

Gordon and Genevieve Smith in 1948.

My children, Jan and Neil Priddy in 1985. Photos, Jan Priddy Collection.

The Gelinsky, Holderman, Dooley Connection
Memories by Eugenia Dooley

My Arch Cape years began in 1907, at age three months, with my parents, Arthur Benson Holderman and Margaret Holderman. My maternal grandparents, Albert and Elizabeth Gelinsky, and my mother Margaret visited the Northern Oregon Coast shortly after the turn of the century and liked the Arch Cape area. It was primitive, isolated, sparsely populated and was surrounded by huge trees, ocean waves and craggy rocks. My grandmother especially fell in love with Arch Cape and purchased two lots on the beach front just north of the Cape.

Imagine, with the inconveniences in those days, when my grandmother, my mother, and my uncle Emil traveled to Arch Cape for the summer bringing a young baby. It was no small task. We took the train from Portland to Seaside where we spent the night. The next day a stagecoach transported us from Seaside to Elk Creek, where we planned to stay in the hotel under construction on the south side of Elk Creek. There, we were to wait for a tide low enough so the stage could drive around Hug Point for a planned trip to Arch Cape. The road over Hug Point did not exist then, so the only way to reach Arch Cape was by beach. Walking, of course, was the means of travel for many. Rocky points along the beach, high tides, and heavy seas that washed away the sand made travel hazardous. Trails through the forest over the many headlands also were dangerous, for winds blew trees down along the way. Those hearty souls who loved this part of Oregon expected and endured the hardships.

My uncle, Emil Gelinsky told me the following story: "We arrived in Seaside by train from Portland and took the stage from Seaside to Elk Creek, later named Ecola and now named Cannon Beach. My uncle, with the stage driver John Gerritse, crossed at the mouth of Elk Creek and drove to the Log Cabin Hotel that was under construction, located where the Conference Center is today, and found we couldn't stay there. Of course, they had to take care of the horses, so my uncle put me down behind a log where my mother could find me while he looked for a place for us to stay that night. It was getting dark and the tide was coming in so they were unable to get to Arch Cape that night. The driver found a place for my mother to sleep and for a pillow, he gave her a sack of oats. My uncle, at that time, searched for me. Grandmother was frantic because my uncle had forgotten behind which log he had placed me. I cried and was soon reunited with mother for a happy reunion." This was in August, 1907.

A wood floor and foundation put down the first year provided space for a large tent. Lumber was at a premium in those days and cost one cent a pound delivered from Seaside by horse and wagon to Arch Cape. A year later we built our cottage on the wood flooring where the tent had been and added a porch across the entire west side of the new structure. A kitchen and dining room were added later. We often spent evenings on the porch and ate most of our meals there, too.

There were no stores in Cannon Beach in those days, so supplies came from Portland to last the whole summer and were hauled by wagon from Seaside to Arch Cape. Mother's order included dried food, canned milk, flour, sugar, raisins and anything else that kept without refrigeration over the summer.

Our family owned a meat packing company in Portland known as the *Gelinsky/Holderman Meat Company*. My father joined the business with the Gelinskys after he married my mother in 1904. They later called the meat company *The National Market.* The market supplied meat and fish to steamboats traveling up and down the Columbia and Willamette Rivers as well as to area restaurants.

The family spent summers at Arch Cape after 1907 and Father, after checking tide tables, often put a roast on the train about 8 o'clock in the morning. It would be in Seaside by noon. The stage carried it to Arch Cape, via Ecola, so the roast arrived that same afternoon. (That had to be the predecessor of UPS.) The meat, after arriving in Arch Cape, was immediately placed in the oven to roast and then kept on top of the stove and reheated every day. A large roast would last a week. Bacon, salt pork and smoked ham, shipped from the packing plant, kept us in meat. If a little mold accumulated on the outside, it was wiped off. Grandmother took clean cloths saturated with vinegar and wiped the bacon and hams before hanging them behind the stove to dry.

After several summers, we brought six to eight live chickens from Portland to supply us with eggs. They were turned loose and stayed around the place for they were gentle and tame. We built a small shed behind the house for them to roost at night. The chickens, placed in a box, rode in the baggage car from Portland and then to Arch Cape at the back of the stage. They were well-traveled chickens and spent many summers with us at Arch Cape. I recall one very large black hen, a Menorka breed, with a huge feathered topknot. I have never seen another like her. Our dog, a Boston terrier named Queen, kept the skunks away from the chickens and, at times, became very smelly.

I was about three and my brother Gilderoy six months old when our maid, Bessie, came to Arch Cape from Portland to care for us during the summer. She watched us and played with us on the beach. Bessie did this for several years and then married. By that time we were old enough to care for ourselves.

The men of the family came down weekends unless they were too busy at the market. My father, Uncle Emil and Uncle Walter and families visited weekends or while they were on vacations. Many friends came from Portland to visit during our summers at Arch Cape. In those days, travelers walked from Seaside to Tillamook. They stopped by to visit up and down the line.

John Gerritse, who drove the stage from Seaside to Cannon Beach for years, brought passengers to Arch Cape and then on to Wheeler on horseback. My mother told this story of a passenger named Mrs. Wheeler on her way to Wheeler to attend the wedding of her son. I believe she was connected with the sawmill at Wheeler for whom the town of Wheeler is named. Mrs. Wheeler had a memorable time with Mr. Gerritse. He kept a flask of liquor beneath the front seat of the stage and every so often would have a little nip. I presumed he was pretty well organized by the time he arrived in Arch Cape. This frightened Mrs. Wheeler. She was so pleased when she arrived here after surviving the trip. Mrs. Wheeler looked bedraggled having dressed in all her finery for the wedding. Her hat sported ostrich plumes that were in sad shape. The hat was hung behind the kitchen stove to dry and after dinner, Mrs. Wheeler spent the night. The next morning, she shared breakfast with us and when Grandmother asked her for fifty cents for room and board, she thought that was an exorbitant price. She finally parted with her fifty cents and traveled on horseback over the trail to Wheeler. Years later she visited Mrs. Aletha Eldridge in Arch Cape and I met her, but I never referred to the time when she stayed at our home.

The Cannon Beach stage drove to Joseph Walsh's barn from the beach up a driveway just south of his barn, on the site where the Conway-Brown house stands today. This allowed horseback riders and the stage coach to leave the beach and deliver passengers and mail to the Arch Cape area. Passengers and riders often stayed at the *Arch Cape Hotel*. They stabled their horses in the Walsh barn until it was safe to negotiate Hug Point for the return trip to Cannon Beach.

Mr. Walsh, an early resident of Arch Cape and supposedly a remittance man, came to this country on his yacht. His family owned silk mills in London. He homesteaded just north of Arch Cape Creek in 1893 and built a home and barn in a clearing a short distance from the creek. The house had a cedar shake roof and cedar siding and included a living room, a kitchen and two bedrooms. His large barn was located north of the house. At one time, he owned the greater part of Seaside and Elk Creek, now Cannon Beach. Eventually, through gambling, he lost all the land he owned.

Joe Walsh had a small herd of cattle which roamed everywhere and kept growth down, for they often fed in the surrounding brush. At one time, Joe had a big Durham bull. The cattle would often go out on the beach and lie there to rest. We children joined them and most of the cows allowed us to lie down beside them. After awhile they would get up and go to the water's edge and drink sea water before returning to the meadows to graze. Since there were no salt blocks for them, they probably drank the sea water for the minerals.

To my knowledge, Mr. Walsh never worked, but he did have to take care of his cattle. Ample grazing in the Arch Cape area was always available. During the summer months the meadows provided enough forage to feed the cattle; during the winter, hay and alfalfa for the cattle and horses came in bales shipped from Eastern Oregon. On occasion Len Gerritse, son of John Gerritse, butchered and dressed an animal and then his father hauled the beef to town by wagon where Mr. Walsh sold the beef.

Joe Walsh, a man of slight stature, wore a vest with a gold chain that went from one pocket to the other and was anchored by a gold watch at one end of the chain. He always carried a bull whip for his protection, though I doubt he had the strength to use it. After Joe Walsh lost everything to gambling, he moved to a house near Asbury Creek, almost a mile north from his previous location and lived there for the rest of his life. A small creek ran through his property and was the source of his water. Today, the same creek flows down Sally's Alley.

There were times during the summer evenings when my mother, my grandmother, Gilderoy and I walked up the beach to visit Mr. Walsh. It was a special treat for us to hear music from the old cylindrical records he played for us on his Victrola. The dog on the Victrola advertisement looked just like the black and white fox terrier Mr. Walsh owned.

In 1923 or 1924 Mr. Walsh suffered a stroke. Len Gerritse and his wife Dolores, who lived in Cannon Beach, cared for him until his death. He is buried in Seaside. I was sixteen or seventeen then.

I've always loved horses and as a child, a broom became my horse. I enjoyed exploring on the beach while riding my broom. A sheep called Bo Peep arrived on the beach to play with us. Bo Peep belonged to Bill and Marie Adams, owners of the *Arch Cape Hotel*. Bo Peep had a habit of scratching her back beneath our dinner table when we ate outside. We chased her away, but she always returned and became a real pest. One time, when I was about five years old and on the beach with my "broom horse," Bo Peep visited me. While I was playing with her, she suddenly butted me down on the sand. My parents were watching and thought how cute Bo Peep and I were playing together. She butted me down on the sand so many times that I began to cry and became hysterical. Bo Peep took advantage of me so Father rescued me and my "horse."

My grandmother drank sea water strained through fine linen for she believed sea water was loaded with vitamins. That was long before vitamins cluttered drug store and super market shelves. If we had spinach from the garden for dinner, she would ask me to drink the spinach water because it was good for the blood. I had to be the healthiest kid enjoying the Oregon Coast then.

Short Sands Beach was one of our favorite places to explore during the summer. We walked over the trail from Arch Cape and often spent the night. A blanket and plenty of food was all we needed. One time, my brother Gilderoy burned his foot in a bonfire rather badly. We wrapped his foot and it was a painful walk for him back to Arch Cape, where we applied Vaseline to the burn. We used some other grease or ointment for cuts, abrasions and burns when necessary. There were no serious accidents and we learned to handle emergencies in stride.

After arriving from Portland in the summer of 1912, we noticed a new house under construction three lots north from our place. I remember my father taking me with him when he went to meet the new neighbor. The new neighbor, Marmaduke Maxwell, moved here from Shaniko, Oregon, where he owned a large sheep ranch in North Central Oregon about fifty miles south of the Columbia River on Highway 97. He lived there for a number of years after moving from Indiana. Prior to this he lived in Coham, Blacktorrington, Devon, in England on the Devonshire coast. He came from a prominent family there and told me that royalty visited his aunt. His father, J. G. Maxwell, a well-known writer of poetry, had been mayor of Barnstable and Sarah Siddons, the famous actress, was his cousin.

Mr. Maxwell was engaged to be married to a lady who contracted pneumonia and died shortly before the wedding date. It was then he decided to come to America, and after visiting various locations he eventually found Arch Cape. He said it reminded him of the Devonshire Coast in his native England so he purchased six lots, one on the beach front. Mr. Maxwell, considered a wealthy man, sold his ranch in Eastern Oregon for $90,000 before he moved to Arch Cape.

Mr. Maxwell's barn was the focal point of activity those days for travelers between Astoria and Tillamook. Hug Point and Neahkahnie Mountain at times forced travelers to remain in Arch Cape to wait for better weather or for lower tides. Behind Mr. Maxwell's ocean front home was a wood shed, a chicken coop and the barn east of the house with four stalls for his horse and cows. The barn originally belonged to Mr. William and Marie Adams, who built the Arch Cape Hotel in 1905 which was later purchased by Mr. Maxwell in 1914. Mr. Maxwell named his first milk cow, Cherry, and his second cow, Molly. Molly produced so much milk that Mr. Maxwell sold it to neighbors and visitors during the summer months for ten cents a quart.

Water came to the *Arch Cape Hotel* from a spring on a hill just east of the barn. A faucet constantly dripping filled a tub where the cows and horses drank. Mr. Maxwell's water supply came from the same spring. Also, on his back porch, he had a rain barrel reserved for washing dishes, pots and pans and for bathing.

Marmaduke Maxwell had no horses when he first came here. The only horse in the early days was a sorrel mare named Lil, who belonged to Mr. Millard. He and his family rented the Walsh home after Mr. Walsh lost his property and moved into the Asbury Creek cottage. Later, Mr. Maxwell purchased Lil and taught me to ride. Once, I delivered a loaf of bread my grandmother baked for Mr. Walsh's birthday, August 12, riding Lil for the first time away from Mr. Maxwell's yard without his supervision. With a bridle on the horse and no saddle, I found my way to Mr. Walsh's place, delivered the bread that had been placed in a paper bag, and returned home without mishap. I was about seven at the time. On occasion, I received 10 cents for my efforts riding to Cannon Beach for mail. For ten cents, one could purchase a root beer float at Lampheres' store. I didn't know at the time, but Mrs. Lamphere had suffered a stroke. It took her a long time to make a float but it was good and worth waiting for.

Mr. Maxwell often built a huge fire in his fireplace and invited us over for the evening. My brother and I enjoyed looking through his Montgomery Ward catalogue. Our host always served a bowl of raisins from his cupboard for me and my brother, and we thought they were the best raisins we had ever eaten. Mother and Grandmother carried on conversations with Mr. Maxwell about what was happening in England during the war years. The Arch Cape population at that time was small and much of our communications then came from newspapers, often days old. Mr. Maxwell subscribed to several English publications, one being the *Daily Mail*. This was in 1919 and the Arch Cape residents were eager to share news.

One time when Mr. Maxwell was away on a trip, he left his dog, an Airedale named Rags, at home. Rags had bitten my new friend, Mr. Millard's daughter. In anger, Mr. Millard came over and shot Rags. When Mr. Maxwell returned, he was saddened over the fact that he had lost his dog. Fortunately, other animals in the house and the children who enjoyed them helped him get over his loss. He always had cats and kittens too, and we kids played with them.

We didn't know the Millards, who rented the Walsh house, very well. They had a daughter about my age and we played together on the beach and in the meadows. To get away from my brother Gilderoy, we often hid from him by going into the woods. He cried, but we didn't feel sorry for him until he wept so hard we decided it would be best to take him to Mama for consolation.

The summers at Arch Cape passed quickly. There was much to do for the children in the community. We made sand castles, waded along the seashore, sailed driftwood boats with a string attached in the tide pools and explored the meadows and the woods. As we grew older, we built rafts and floated them around in a large pool near the mouth of Arch Cape Creek. One of the activities we enjoyed most was climbing the four walls of an unfinished log cabin located on a hill north of Maxwell's barn. In the summer of 1921, we found the cabin completely finished and owned by Albert C. Patton. He was a kindly gentlemen and became a life-long friend, known to us children as Uncle Bert.

There were bears in the near-by forests and Uncle Walter decided to frighten Elsie and Marie English and their house guests at the *Singing Sands Hotel*. People talked about seeing a bear here and a bear there. My uncle always enjoyed playing tricks on people so he went to their place, crawled on the roof and got on the large spruce tree that is shown on

Singing Sands photos and made scratching sounds. Hearing the noise, Elsie and Marie gathered their guests into one bedroom. They were frightened and thought for certain that a bear was on the roof. When my uncle returned to the cottage, he said, "You can't guess what I just did. I made all those English girls get into one room." My mother asked how he did that. He said he climbed up on the roof and rattled the branches against the roof and the windows and they thought it was the bear. The next day Marie came over and said nothing about the incident of the night before. A little later Elsie came over and neither did she say anything about the noise. My uncle said, "That was terrible last night, wasn't it? Did you hear the bears?" They looked at each other but didn't say a word. My uncle was very amused.

The beach, the rocks at low tide and the many tide pools provided hours of pleasure for residents and guests gathering clams, mussels and crab. They were plentiful then, but we never took more than we could use. If a man came with us with plenty of strength, we could have rock oysters, as they were chipped out of the sandstone rocks at the cape with an ax. They are small and much like Olympia oysters and many people consider them to be a delicacy. I believe they are called piddocks. Usually, they were breaded and fried for dinner. We enjoyed clam chowder, baked clams, clam fritters and sometimes, clam soup. Mussels were always available from the lower reaches of the cape during most low tides. We liked them and were especially fond of the delicious broth left from the cooking process.

There were times when we returned with a full gunny sack of crab ready for Mr. Maxwell to cook. He would build a fire near his house and cook the crabs in sea water I carried from the ocean. When the crabs were ready, the children ran around the neighborhood inviting everyone over to eat crab. Since we didn't have refrigeration, crabs were hung in the breeze on back porches until the next meal. We saved clam necks for fish bait and often walked to Cape Falcon to fish off the rocks for perch and rock fish. We planned our fishing time to match the tides, because we arrived after a low tide and stayed over until the next low tide, then returned home with our catch. We lived off the land, especially in the summer and everyone shared with one another.

Everyone was eager to find property at Arch Cape and in Cannon Beach west of the highway. In 1925 Mr. Sam Webb, a realtor and Mr. W. A. Tyler, a banker, re-platted sections of Arch Cape. Both were from Astoria. They sold lots for $25 down with various sales prices. Those on the ocean beach front were much more expensive. People purchased lots, often sight unseen. Sam Webb and W. A. Tyler were pleased with their new development. As a result, they sold many lots and people began building.

Later, Mr. and Mrs. Harris, who formerly lived in The Dalles, opened a grocery store in Cannon Beach, and now we were able to get staples such as butter, canned foods and occasionally fresh items.

Activities increased at Arch Cape in the twenties. Improved transportation and new home owners brought new friends. The following paragraphs are memories I recall as a small child and as a young lady enjoying every summer, weekend and vacation whenever possible, with the family at our beautiful beach:

We picked salal berries when they were ripe and made salal syrup to serve on our pancakes, an Arch Cape staple almost every morning. Mother made rolypoly, a biscuit dough made like a jelly roll, baked and cut in slices like cake. She served it as dessert with a hard sauce which was made with sugar and butter, and for flavoring she added one teaspoon of whiskey—normally reserved for medicinal purposes.

In the early days, indoor plumbing did not exist and was a dream for the future. We did our laundry in the mouth of Arch Cape Creek. Mrs. E. O. Gardner, who lived in the community, had a little wagon upon which she placed her basket full of wash and then headed for the creek with her niece and nephew, Richard and Jean Kingsbury, from Carrolls, Washington. The children spent their summers here. About that time, Mother gathered her wash and we children tagged along. Other neighbors joined us along the way. The children played in the creek and the women carried on conversations while completing their washing. After we returned home, the laundry was spread on salal bushes to dry. We slept in clean white sheets and wore garments that were washed in the mouth of Arch Cape Creek and dried by ocean breezes. In retrospect, it brought the women together and made the weekly chore enjoyable. That task, along with others, was part of the Arch Cape scene.

We bathed in the ocean, since showers were not the once-a-day luxury we enjoy today. If it rained heavily and the sea was too rough for bathing, then a huge galvanized tub filled with soft rain water collected from the roof served as a bath tub and was placed near the kitchen stove for warmth.

Incoming tides were swimming time and women dressed accordingly. I recall when bathing suits were made from heavy alpaca and decorated with puffed sleeves. When worn with tightly bound corsets and with long black hose, it prevented any lady from swimming. I often wondered if they ever actually got wet. About 1912, when bathing suits styles changed, Mother purchased a long black suit and wore black stockings. I have a picture of her on the beach in front of our home. When we did go in the surf, we all went at the same time and formed a chain and often Mr. Maxwell joined us. One time, a freak wave rolled in and nearly took us all out. Fortunately, we grabbed on to each other and all made it to shore.

At times, water for drinking and for cooking came from Arch Cape Creek. We children were too small to carry water. Later, we helped carry galvanized pails filled with creek water from a deep hole under where the present Arch Cape Creek Bridge is today. Everyone kept a water container out of the sun on the their back porch.

J. Edward Simmons and his wife Josephine acquired the old Watson homestead. The date on the map shows it was homesteaded in 1893. It was about the same time Joe Walsh and others acquired homesteads between Arch Cape Creek and Hug Point. It was a cedar cottage with a living room, a kitchen and two bedrooms which sat below an orchard with apple, pear and plum trees. This homestead is about one-half mile from the mouth of Arch Cape Creek along a platted but unbuilt county road to Tillamook County. Later, the neglected orchard became brush and then alder and evergreen trees smothered the fruit trees. We children looked forward to being invited to the Simmons' place, as a spring came up out of the earth and ran into a barrel near the house. We would dip into the barrel and carry the cool clear water to the cottage. We liked being around Mr. Simmons for he was an interesting man—and often made pancakes for us.

My grandmother's deed was signed by the Simmonses. They lived in the Walsh's house for a time. They divorced and within a couple of years Mr. Simmons married a southern lady by the name of Helen Harrington. She had studied music in Europe with a famous pianist. I recall the piano Mrs. Simmons ordered from Portland. It was a large square grand and came to Arch Cape by horse and wagon from Seaside and was placed in the old Walsh house. Mrs. Simmons played and gave musicals for those who were here for the summer. After Mrs. Simmons moved to Portland, the piano was placed in the lobby of the Arch Cape Hotel. I was fortunate to be able to take lessons from her for many years in Portland.

One Easter, my mother, my grandmother, Mrs. Simmons' daughter Helen, my brother Gilderoy and I planned a trip to the beach. We took the train from Portland in the evening and arrived in Seaside about 10 p.m. We reserved rooms at the old McGuire Hotel in Seaside and in the morning took the stage to Ecola. A terrible storm came up. In spite of the rain, all the ladies insisted they were going to spend Easter at Arch Cape dressed in their Easter finery. My grandmother wore a Milan straw hat with an Alice Blue crepe rim. A red rose showed beneath the brim of the hat. Because of the storm, the stage couldn't get any farther than Ecola, so everyone decided to walk. The walk with three little children from Ecola to Arch Cape with an incoming tide and with little beach left was a struggle. We came to Silver Point and were able to climb around the rock only to find very little exposed beach, so we took the trail over Silver Point to the south side and finally arrived at Humbug Point. Along the way, I noticed that Grandmother's complexion changed considerably, but since I was a little child, I said nothing. Again I looked at Grandmother and became concerned because she didn't look well. I still didn't say anything. When we arrived at Arch Cape, Grandmother looked terrible. We discovered what happened to make her face so red. The heavy rain caused the wet red rose beneath the brim of her hat to send its red dye to her face. Her complexion remained red for several days.

We arrived at Arch Cape that cold wintry day for the Easter weekend. Being tired, we children were placed in a southwest bedroom in the Walsh's home. We slept crossways on the bed with our shoes placed on the floor. It was still raining the next morning. We found our shoes, side-by-side, full of water due to a hole in the roof. Fortunately, the rain missed our bed, but we wore wet shoes that day. Mrs. Simmons prepared breakfast for us and, as always, prepared pancakes.

Once, a man came to the door and asked Mrs. Simmons if it was all right to drink water from the creek. She said it was and that we were drinking it. My grandmother wanted to know why he was concerned and he told her there was a dead sea lion at the mouth of the creek and thought the water might be contaminated this far inland and was afraid to drink it. Grandmother said, "Don't be afraid to drink the water, for the creek runs into the sea and you surely can drink the water up this far from the ocean." He took the water and left.

For the summer vacations in Arch Cape, the usual transportation was by train from Portland to Seaside. My grandmother, my mother, my brother Gilderoy and I stayed at the McGuire Hotel. As was the custom after the long train ride, my grandmother and my mother would go for coffee. On one occasion, they took me but left Gilderoy, who was asleep. The restaurant was about a block from the hotel. Upon our return to our hotel room, we found the door was locked from the inside. Gilderoy had apparently awakened and locked the door which had been left open. They woke the hotel clerk who found a ladder to reach the second floor and crawled through an open window to open the door. My brother slept through the whole thing.

Grandmother purchased a Model T Ford for me and my brother to run up and down the beach and for shopping in Cannon Beach. I was about 16 at the time. We didn't drive it to Portland for the winter, so stored it in Mr. Maxwell's barn. Hay surrounded the car where

Molly and Cherry, Mr. Maxwell's cows and Betty, the mare were fed. The following June that old Ford started right up and ran all summer long without a problem.

Once again it was my grandmother's wish to spend Easter, April 10, 1928, at Arch Cape. There was no road to our destination so we consulted the tide tables and found them right for driving on the beach. Grandmother, Mother, Gilderoy and I planned our departure time to match the tides and had a very pleasant trip. My father and Uncle Emil Gelinsky, who had made his home with my parents since 1925, remained in the city. Our cottage was closed for the winter so we stayed with Mr. Maxwell. We had become good friends over the years and were always welcome in his home. After a wonderful weekend, we left Arch Cape on an afternoon tide and arrived home in the late evening, tired but happy and ready to retire. Grandmother passed away at 3 a.m. The date was April 11 and many days of sadness followed. I'll always remember Mr. Maxwell's reply when he learned of our bereavement. In it he wrote: "to believe as the Gypsies did, that the time to mourn was when we were born, and to rejoice when we died. The trials and tribulations of life would then be over."

That year, 1928, Mother and I as well as family and friends, enjoyed another summer at Arch Cape. Gilderoy was in college and came to the beach for weekends. College students discovered that working with the salmon seining crews in the Columbia River made for a profitable vacation. They were employed by the Barbey Packing Company in Astoria, but worked from Sand Island, located near the mouth of the river. Long nets were strung out into the river by boat and when full of salmon were pulled ashore by teams of horses that were stabled in barns built on piling in the river. I always felt sorry for the horses that worked in the cold water for many hours. This method kept the canneries in business for years. Gill netters, later on, took over and supplied the fish.

Early one summer morning, just before Mother and I were to leave for the coast, a call came from my brother stating he was to report to work on Sand Island immediately. He asked that we pack a bag for him and said he would pick it up before the departure of the *Georgiana,* the steamboat leaving Portland for Astoria. It still amuses me when I think of what I did to a pair of my six-foot two-inch tall brother's shorts. I sewed by machine some wide linen lace on the edge of each leg. With the lace turned in, I placed them beneath all the other clothing. The story continues when the seining crew decided to attend a dance in Ilwaco, Washington, the following Saturday night. With the fellows dressing in their best attire, my brother discovered that he was down to his last pair of shorts. He was in dismay with the laughter that followed, but he wore them anyway.

The only means of transportation from the island to the mainland was by a row boat named the *Swamp Angel.* On the return from the dance, the *Swamp Angel* sprang a leak. With nothing on board for bailing the water, my brother's size 14 shoes came in handy. To save his best pants from getting too wet, he removed them. Years later, I met one of the crew who said he would never forget the scene—by flashlight—of my big brother, with lace on his underwear, bailing with one of his own shoes.

Elsie and Marie English always took parts of old sheets with them when they picked huckleberries. I never understood why until I discovered they tore them into strips and tied them to trees and branches so they could find their way home again. My grandmother's sister, Laura Moeller, was even more resourceful. She always took an umbrella with her. It took me awhile to figure that one out, too. She opened the umbrella, turned it upside down, and shook the huckleberry bushes. Berries fell into the umbrella. Then she picked out the leaves, placed the berries in a pail, and returned with clean huckleberries.

A new home was under construction just south of us when our family came down to spend the summer in 1928. One evening, Mr. George Arthur Brown, an attorney from Portland, came over. During that summer, Lorna, one of George's children and her husband John Conway, along with the rest of the Brown family, were frequent visitors in the new home. They all helped George with some of the construction. He worked on his home until his death, and Lorna and John inherited the property. Today, two of George's grandchildren, Shirley and Laurence (Buddy) Brown own the Conway home and property. Our friendship with George Arthur Brown, a widower, and his family continued for many years.

Another cottage, just east from Mr. Brown's house, was finished by Dr. E. E. Pajunen and his wife Grace. They had two daughters, Donna and Betty Ann. Dr. Pajunen, a well-known dentist in Astoria, was also the Vice-Consul of Finland. The Pajunens spent summers in their cottage; the doctor commuted to his office during the week. We enjoyed their friendship for many years and were saddened when the doctor passed away from a malignancy. Grace later rented their cottage to friends and Clay and I lived in it a year during World War II. Later, Clay's sister and husband, Florence and Glenn Jones, purchased the cottage. We were pleased that it remained in the family for several years. Grace Pajunen remarried and passed away in 1982, the result of a stroke.

Among other cottages built and occupied that year were those belonging to Mrs. Aletha Eldridge, her daughter Mabel Coffman and Mrs. Coffman's daughter, Helen. They built just south of Leech Avenue near the ocean front. The road at that time had not yet been named Leech Avenue. Mrs. Eldridge and the Coffmans came from Seattle and spent summers at Arch Cape.

Mr. and Mrs. Gault and their two daughters, Virginia and Jean from Camas, Washington, were in their new place on the south side of Leech Avenue near the present highway. Mr. Gault was a manager for Crown Zellerbach Corporation in Camas. Miss Arnold, a teacher and sister to Mrs. Gault, built a cottage next to Gaults' on Leech Avenue.

The Henshaw house, today the second house on the beach front north of Leech Avenue, was constructed in 1925 by Tyler Henshaw, from Oakland, California. I believe he was the brother-in-law of the Simmonses, since he married the sister of Helen H. Simmons. It was a coincidence that Tyler Henshaw and Mr. W. A. Tyler had the same names. Mr. W. A. Tyler, along with his partner, Sam Webb, sold lots in the Arch Cape Area and occupied the Henshaw house during their real estate venture. It was then sold to Mr. and Mrs. Thomas Wells. Shortly afterward, Webb and Tyler came to a sad end. Webb was killed near Spokane, Washington, when a tree fell on the bus in which he was a passenger. Tyler committed suicide. Several years later, Mrs. Elizabeth Wells was widowed and sold her property. Ownership changed several times between 1927 and 1934. Mr. and Mrs. Thomas Wells purchased from the Henshaws; Mr. and Mrs. S. R. Diefendorf purchased from Mrs. Wells; and Mr. and Mrs. Albert Leech purchased from the Diefendorfs April 20, 1934. Mrs. Leech managed and rented the Arch Cape Cabins during the summers between 1930 and 1934 for the Diefendorfs before purchasing the property at the west end of what is now Leech Avenue. It included the cabins and the large home on the ocean front. Today, the south part of that property belongs to Eric D. Meyers and Sarah J. Snell and the north part, where the old

Henshaw house stands belongs to Travis Tyrrell. Elsie Wood, the daughter of Albert and Nellie Leech, lives on the north side of Leech Avenue on property purchased by the family.

One warm night, around midnight in late September after most of the summer folk had left, Mrs. Wells came over to our place frantically calling for help. There was a fire somewhere under her living room near the fireplace. Mother and I, awakened from a sound sleep, grabbed flashlights and water pails and rushed over to see what we could do. We were in pajamas, which made it easier to get around. With an ax, I chopped a hole in the siding so I could crawl under the house, only to find that a two by six beam was burning near the fireplace. Mother and Mrs. Wells filled pails with water and handed them to me so I could splash water on the fire, which I extinguished. We watched the place until daylight, only to discover we had used all the water from the reservoir. It took all day for it to refill from the spring which supplied the area. Mr. Maxwell was quite upset for not having been awakened after he learned what had happened. He wanted to help, but we felt that we could get around more quickly without him. Fortunately, we were able to have water for our use the next day from Mr. Maxwell's supply line, as his line came from a different source.

On one occasion in 1928 or 1929, Mr. Maxwell had invited a friend, another Englishman, to Arch Cape for dinner. For many of his social engagements, Mr. Maxwell wore a tastefully designed Norfolk English tweed jacket and a red tie. He looked the true Englishman and gentlemen he was. His friend, a Mr. Dakin, lived across the street from the present Community Church in Cannon Beach. The house is no longer in existence. While Mr. Maxwell was preparing dinner, Mr. Dakin realized he had forgotten his dentures and therefore, would be unable to eat dinner. Mr. Maxwell called out to me and said: "Jeannie, Jeannie, please come quickly. Saddle up the mare. Would you please go to Mr. Dakin's place and get his false teeth out of the water glass by the sink. Crawl through the kitchen window, which is rather high. Hurry, because the tide is coming in."

It was a long ride and Betty had a work-out. I watered the mare from creeks along the way. Upon arrival at Dakin's house, I brought the mare alongside the kitchen window. She stood still while I opened the window, crawled in and found the teeth in the water glass, then crawled back out the window. Needless to say, we made tracks returning to Arch Cape to beat the incoming tide. I fed Betty her oats and Mr. Dakin enjoyed his dinner that night, too.

In later years, Mr. Maxwell suffered pain in his right leg and resorted to the use of a cane. It was then that Mother, Gilderoy and I took Mr. Maxwell to Astoria to see Dr. Forstrom for arthritis shots. We planned to start our trips after the tide began receding so we could get around Hug Point and back before the next high tide made it impossible. The tides allowed travelers from Arch Cape to Astoria and back only six hours, so it was a quick trip. In the late 20's and early 30's, the trip required much more time to negotiate Hug Point and to struggle along the primitive road to Cannon Beach. Today, it takes about 35 to 40 minutes to get to Astoria

One day, when traveling to Astoria with Mr. Maxwell to see Dr. Forstrom, we heard strange sounds all the way to town and could not figure out what was wrong with the car. It was something we had never heard before. When we returned home, Gilderoy decided to find out what was wrong. He looked under the front seat and found a mother mouse with a whole family of mice that did the squealing.

Mother and I continued to spend the summers at Arch Cape. Father came weekends, along with Uncle Emil and the rest of the family. Gilderoy helped Mr. Maxwell with his winter wood supply for the 1931-32 season. Late in October we received a call from Mrs. Page. The Page family had been friends of Mr. Maxwell long before he moved to Arch Cape. Mr. Page, an attorney, had been in charge of Mr. Maxwell's estate. He informed us that Mr. Maxwell was hospitalized in Astoria and asked if I would take her to see him. We left Portland shortly afterwards. When we arrived at the hospital in Astoria, we learned that Mr. Maxwell had pneumonia and was very ill. We stayed with him for several days until he passed away October 30, 1931 at the age of eighty-seven. Funeral services were held in Portland with many from Arch Cape in attendance. It was his wish to be cremated and that his ashes be scattered at sea. What a sad ending it was for our dear friend and neighbor. The livestock was sold and the mare, Betty, was no longer sound and was put to sleep. Later, Mr. Maxwell's home was sold to Dora Cornelieson.

Construction of the present Highway 101 south of Cannon Beach began in the early 30's. By 1934 we were able to drive as far as Austin Point, now Hug Point State Park, where we drove down on the beach to reach Arch Cape. There were only two places at the cape where we were able to drive off the beach. One was Maxwell Avenue (formerly named Arch Cape Avenue) and the other Leech Avenue (formerly named Walsh Avenue). Cars often got stuck in the soft dry sand in an effort to reach the primitive roads beyond the dune line leading to homes in the area. Mired cars were lifted by jacks, and then boards and driftwood were placed under the wheels. With plenty of pushing by many willing hands, cars made their way to solid ground.

I remember when Ed Sorenson and his family from the Big Creek Logging Camp became stuck in the sand when visiting Burt Patton. Ed conceived the idea of tying their baby's diapers around the rear wheels of their car to get traction in the soft sand. Ed's method worked and provided much laughter for those watching the action. Once off the beach, one could drive through the cleared area behind our place from Leech Avenue to Maxwell Avenue. This was not a dedicated roadway. Today, the road goes as far as the Morrisons' home and is now named Gelinsky Boulevard. A foot path continues to Maxwell Avenue.

An outstanding family event took place August 25, 1934. My brother Gilderoy and Earlene Deardorf were married in Portland at the Mount Taber Presbyterian church. Mother and I were in Arch Cape for the summer but returned to Portland for the wedding ceremony and the following festivities. Gilderoy and Earlene became the parents of a daughter, Gilda, who is now a registered nurse. Their son Steve, after military service, returned to Ontario, Oregon, where the Holderman family settled years ago.

In 1936, the highway was completed to where the tunnel through Arch Cape was to be constructed. Work was underway that year with test holes being bored into the north side of the Cape. One day when I was interested in what was going on, the foreman of the crew asked if I would care to go into the main test hole to have a look. Without hesitation, I crawled a long way into the bowels of the earth, which later was to be the path of the Arch Cape tunnel. It was an experience that I had to tell to my friends. A blast was planned to explode in the tunnel October 31, 1936, during my wedding ceremony that same day. The timing of the blast was miscalculated and it did not occur until two hours after the wedding. The bride and groom had already left on their honeymoon—only remaining guests heard the blast.

Logging operations entered the Arch Cape scene with the completion of the highway through Arch Cape and on to the south. Among the first were the Birkenfeld Bros., of the town of Birkenfeld, located in the Nehalem Valley. They rented summer homes in the Arch Cape area, including Maxwell's place, to house their crews. They logged timber in the upper Asbury Creek area which took the greater part of a year. From then on, other companies logged extensively in the area. Henry Kling had timber operations east of Hug Point as did George Van Vleet. Van Vleet logged the Ira Gaston and Pearl Gaston timber claims in the upper Arch Cape Creek area.

Writers note—This is a very SPECIAL EVENT told by Eugenia. It may have been the very first formal wedding in Arch Cape. Here is Eugenia's story:

August 19, 1936 — About 9 o'clock in the evening our neighbor, Grace Pajunen, came over to our cottage. I was busy writing letters and Mother was sitting before the fireplace. Grace asked if Mother and I would come over. She and Dr. Pajunen had guests at their home and they needed some entertainment. She wanted Mother to play the piano so we could all sing. I reluctantly said we would be there. So, we went over and met their company. Amongst them was a man named Clay Dooley. He was standing at the fireplace with his arms crossed and when he looked at me, he recognized me as the one that had given him a citation for shooting at Bird Rock below Arch Cape in 1927. (see *Oregonian* article below) He had with him Mr. Leo Malarkey from Astoria and Mr. and Mrs. Callendar. The moment was a little tense and Grace served some refreshments. When it came time for them to leave, Mother and I bid them good night and Mr. Dooley and his friends were on their way. This story will be continued after the following *Oregonian* story titled:

Pretty Girl Deputy Fish Warden Keeps
Violators in Check at Cannon Beach
(From the Oregonian, August 6, 1927)

Cannon Beach claims the distinction of having, as far as is known, the only girl deputy fish warden in Oregon. Miss Eugenia Holderman of Portland is the fish warden here and early and late she can be seen riding her gray horse, Betty, up and down the beach watching for infringers of the clamming and crabbing laws. "Men always have a good excuse when they are caught fishing without a license," laughed pretty brown-eyed Miss Holderman. "They always say, 'I left my license in my other coat pocket.'

"The other day I had to speak to an old man for infringing on the clamming laws. 'Wal, I'm pretty old,' he said, 'but I never had no girl tell me what to do, afore.'

"I have some funny experiences with people, too," she told me. "The other day I noticed a car parking on a clam bar, which is against the law, so I started after them to tell them. They saw me coming and in their haste to get away they ran into a deep crab hole and the whole rear end of their car dropped out. I thought they were punished sufficiently then, so I didn't say anything."

There is one violator, however, who laughs at the fish warden. This is Cannon, her pet dog, who dearly loves to dig clams. Whenever he goes after one, he nearly always gets it. When told of the law, limiting the catch to three dozen, he digs all the faster, throwing the sand contemptuously in his informant's face.

The young men in Cannon Beach almost hoped they would exceed the limit of clams allowed each clam digger, or perhaps catch a crab just a trifle below the lawful size across the back, so that the pretty representative of the law will find it necessary to speak to them.

EDISON I. BALLAGH
        MASTER FISH WARDEN
P. E. CLANTON
        DIRECTOR OF HATCHERIES

COMMISSIONERS:
JOHN C. VEATCH, CHAIRMAN, PORTLAND
W. T. EAKIN . . . ASTORIA
J. S. HAYES . . . BAY CITY

FISH COMMISSION OF OREGON

TERMINAL BUILDING
FIFTH AND SALMON STREETS
PORTLAND

June 3, 1926.

Miss Eugenia Holderman,
564 East Taylor Street,
Portland, Oregon.

Dear Miss Holderman:

        The writer while in Astoria last week took up the matter of your receiving an appointment as special deputy fish warden at Arch Cape, with Mr. John Larson, Chief Warden of that district.

        Mr. Larson approved of this idea very much. Therefore, if you can find it convenient to come into the office Friday or Saturday morning of this week, I would be pleased to swear you in as a deputy.

        I would suggest that you call the office by phone to ascertain whether or not I am in the office, before coming. Our telephone number is Main 0938.

                        Very sincerely yours,

                        Edison I. Ballagh

                        Master Fish Warden. X

Special Event—continued—Early the next morning Mother and I arose and we knew that Mrs. Pajunen was expecting a friend, Mrs. Arthur Anderson, who owned the Anderson Cannery in Astoria. She arrived early in the morning before Mrs. Pajunen had arisen. Dr. Pajunen had left for early office appointments in Astoria. I happened to look out and saw that no smoke was coming out of their chimney, so I went over, through the back door, took some kindling and started a fire in their fireplace, and then returned home. Nothing was said about my building the fire. Mother and I had breakfast. A short time later Mr. Clay Dooley arrived. We visited for awhile and then he left to attend a meeting in Portland.

A few days later Mr. Dooley returned. I told him I was sorry I couldn't stay to visit with him, as I had promised my good friends Irene English and her mother, Jennie, that I would drive them to Kelso to meet the train to take them to Seattle. Mr. Dooley immediately said, "Well, drive my new Chrysler." I said "No, I have my car and I planned to drive." I finally agreed that we take his car. Mrs. English was placed in the front seat with me and Irene sat in the back seat with Mr. Dooley. We met the train on time and proceeded to return to Arch Cape.

Clay said he had to go to his office in Vine Maple, near Jewell, to sign checks for his crew. It was a long way from Astoria to Jewell and back to Arch Cape. As we left Jewell, Clay noticed that the gas tank was low, but thought he could make it back to Astoria. Along the way the gas gauge dropped lower and this worried Clay. When we reached the top of the hill on the winding road from Jewell to Astoria, he turned the engine off to save gasoline and coasted wherever possible. We reached the Tide Water Logging camp, a railroad camp on the way, and Clay obtained enough gasoline to get us to Astoria, where we refueled. We dined at the Imperial Grill near the ferry landing and then returned to Arch Cape. I didn't see much of Mr. Dooley after that and I continued doing the summer activities I enjoyed so much.

On September 17, 1936, Clay Dooley returned. It was his birthday. He was sorry that he had not been to see us but there had been a death in the family. A little later in the month, Mother and I decided the summer was over and we should return to Portland. I had not told Clay where we lived in Portland, so on the way home, I thought it would be the right thing to do to stop by the Dooley Logging Company operations to let him know we were no longer at Arch Cape and were returning to Portland. I told him where we lived and a few days later he came to our home to visit. We became good friends and attended many concerts and social functions. He was a musician and had played the trumpet for dances in the Nehalem Valley and elsewhere.

Proposal—It wasn't long before Clay proposed marriage and I accepted. He asked if I knew of a good jeweler in Portland, so I took him to our family jeweler and introduced him to Mr. Harry Zell, our good friend. Mr. Zell showed us a tray of diamond rings and Clay asked me which one I preferred. I was reluctant to accept the diamond I had selected because of the price. Clay said to Mr. Zell, "Well, we had better see the wedding ring that goes with it." He purchased not only the engagement ring, but also the wedding ring. This was on a Saturday, October 17, and the engagement ring was placed on my finger soon afterwards. I was proudly wearing it to church on Sunday.

Clay returned to his logging operation and on Monday evening he phoned from Astoria and asked where my mother was born. I told him she had been born in Detroit, Michigan. He then asked where my father was born and I said, "Dayton, Washington." I asked him why he was asking me these questions. He said he had the marriage license. My reply to that was that I thought one had to go to the court house and then wait three days. Clay said, "Oh, I have been to the Clatsop County courthouse and my good friend Judge Boyington obtained the license for me." I asked why we had to be married so soon. He reminded me that the pheasant season opens next Friday and he would like to go up to his sister's ranch in Heppner, Oregon, to do some hunting. "I will be there shortly," he said. I hung up the phone and told Mother Mr. Dooley was coming in and that we were going to be married.

Preparations—When Clay arrived at our home, I asked him what he thought about a wedding and he said, "Well, since I met you down at Arch Cape, let's get married down there." I said, "But it would be rather inconvenient since everything at Arch Cape has been put away for the winter. The cottage is closed and I am not prepared." It was October and the weather was beautiful, so we began with our wedding preparations.

Next morning, Mr. Dooley went downtown to purchase a suit and I went to Charles F. Berg in Portland, a fashionable shop, for my wedding attire. It was a gray woolen dress with a long jacket and a gray fur collar. Mother had gone to Meier & Frank to order a wedding cake, which they assured her would be ready immediately. My father went down on Front Street to purchase a turkey. It was out of season and turkeys were not plentiful in those days, but he did find one. Uncle Emil decided he would go on ahead to open the cottage so that when we arrived, it would be partially ready for us. On Tuesday, my parents decided they should leave, too. Mother had picked up the wedding cake; Father, the turkey; Clay, his suit; I already had my wedding dress. In the meantime, we ordered flowers from Tommy Luke, our florist and family friend. He said, "Eugenia, don't worry. We will take care of everything. Just be back in a few hours and I will have everything ready." Upon our return, Mr. Luke came out with a floral center piece of chrysanthemums that filled the back seat of the car. Mr. Luke packed orchid corsages for me and my mother and rose buds for the men's lapels. There was little room for anything else in the back seat.

On the way from Portland to Astoria along the Columbia River Highway, we realized we were without a pastor to marry us, I was without a bridesmaid, and Clay was without a best man. I decided to ask Grace Pajunen, an Arch Cape neighbor, to be my matron of honor. She was having her hair done when we arrived in Astoria. I met her at the shop and told her what was going on and that I would like her to be my matron of honor. She said she would be delighted. The next duty was to find a best man. Mr. Dooley called Leo Malarkey, who was one of the friends whom I had met at the Pajunen house in August. Then, I remembered a Mrs. Blenkinsop who sat next to me when I sang in the Portland Symphony Chorus and whose husband had been a chaplain in World War I. They lived in Astoria so I called her and told her of our need for a pastor. She said, "Oh, do come up to our home and meet Reverend Blenkinsop." We did, and he said he would be able to marry us in Arch Cape, but it would have to be at 2:00 p.m., as he had a 4:00 p.m. funeral scheduled. We had planned it would be earlier. "Since you are a Lutheran and Clay, a Presbyterian," he said, "I will use an Episcopalian ceremony." We told him that was all right.

With all of that taken care of, Clay and I proceeded down to Arch Cape. It was late in the evening when we arrived. Mother, Father and Uncle Emil were waiting to greet us. At bed time, they put Clay on the day bed and Uncle Emil slept on another cot close by. My parents slept in their bed in the attic and they provided another cot and blanket there for me. Most of the bedding had gone to Portland. Uncle Emil and Clay arose at five in the morning and built fires in the kitchen stove and fireplace. I made the comment that I was cold all night long and my father said, "Well, tonight you won't have that problem."

We had breakfast at an early hour because Mother had to roast the turkey in the wood stove so it would be ready after the wedding ceremony. The wood supply was low and Mother needed a hot fire. She sent Clay and me down to the beach with gunny sacks to fill with wood chips. Mother decided we must have oyster stew at my wedding since she had it at hers.

Oysters were hard to find at that time of the year, but we did get two quarts of the Olympia oysters in Seaside and also purchased several quarts of cream from the dairy store. Clay decided we should have some wine and liquor, so he went to the drug store, which sold liquor in those days, to make his selection.

The Wedding—When we returned to Arch Cape, the Reverend Blenkinsop and other guests were there. Dr. Pajunen could not attend because he had appointments with patients. Since the cottage was full of guests, Clay and I went to the Pajunen's home to change into our wedding attire. Uncle Emil accompanied Clay; I was in another room. We returned to the cottage and were about to begin the wedding ceremony when Mrs. Nellie Leech passed through the back yard. I called out to her and asked her to come in for the wedding. She asked, "Who is getting married?" I said, "I am and won't you please come in." She said, "Oh I can't," and I asked, "And why, Mrs. Leech, can't you come?" She replied, "Because I am wearing a black dress." She did come in carrying her lantern as she was on her way to fill it with kerosene and sat on the daybed. Mother sat in a chair near Koco, our water spaniel, who was sporting a huge blue ribbon on her collar.

Reverend Blenkinsop played *Oh Promise Me* on the phonograph. The same beautiful song had been sung at my parents' church wedding in September of 1904. After a couple of stanzas, Reverend Blenkinsop removed the needle from the record and began with the wedding vows. During the ceremony, Grace Pajunen had tears running down her cheeks. My father reached into his pocket and pulled a long white handkerchief for her to wipe them away. We were married and it was a happy ceremony.

Everyone took part in preparing the food for the wedding dinner. Mother had the turkey out of the oven and my father carved it. Mrs. Malarkey mashed the potatoes and Mrs. Calendar helped with the gravy and everyone enjoyed the ceremonial meal. Before the wedding ceremony, Uncle Emil had harvested tall huckleberry branches and placed them around the inside of the cottage to make it look like a woodland setting. Guests and relatives took photos after dinner.

Escape—Uncle Emil was very busy. He tied every old shoe and tin can in Arch Cape to long ropes and onto our car. After we reached Cannon Beach, I told Clay that I couldn't stand the noise anymore. He handed me his pocket knife and I got out of the car and cut the rope and threw all of those banged up cans and shoes into the ditch off the highway. We were finally alone and on our way.

Clay, knowing I was to go with him to eastern Oregon so he could hunt pheasants, decided he had better sign the checks for the crew as we were going to be gone for several days. At three o'clock in the morning, we arrived in Portland at the Heathman Hotel. We arose early the next morning, Tuesday, the 22nd of October, because it was a long drive to Hepnner. The reason for this rush was that the pheasant season opened the next day. His sister was not even notified that we were coming, but he called her when we reached The Dalles.

The future—After the hunt, we returned to the Dooley camp at Vine Maple near Jewell, Oregon, where we had many acres of timber. We logged an area and then moved the crew to another location to log it. We were in Vine Maple until 1939. We moved our whole camp up on the Wolf Creek highway (now Highway 26), where we logged timber from the 1933 burn, and then late in 1939 sold out to James Shields. We experienced the 1939 burn. The fire was very near our camp for three weeks and we were ready to evacuate at any moment. The entire crew fought fire during that time.

Cutting drift logs with a cross-cut saw and packing it from the beach was a tedious job. Clay decided to haul a log from the Vine Maple operation near Jewell to Arch Cape to use for fire wood. He delivered a huge log via one of our trucks which provided us with firewood for several years. Chunks were cut off of it during the summer, but we never cut more than we needed because people took any cut wood lying around for their own use.

We had a logging show near Carlton, Oregon, during World War II where we set up a large camp. There were two cooks plus other help in the cook house and several bunkhouses for the men who stayed in camp. A truck, called a *Mulligan*, transported loggers who preferred to live at home to and from the logging site.

During this time we mourned the death of my father who passed away in his sleep October 10, 1943. He had retired from the family meat business and sold it in 1936. After retirement, he and Mother spent the summers at the coast. After Father's death, my uncle Emil and my mother continued staying every summer at the Arch Cape cottage.

Upon completion of operations near Carlton, we moved to Tillamook County and logged timber on the Wilson and Trask rivers. From there, we went to Arch Cape to live in the Pajunen house, which we had rented from Grace Pajunen. Clay continued the war effort by keeping our fleet of logging trucks hauling logs to the Dichter Lumber Co. in Warrenton from our operations in Tillamook county. We rented a large building located on the main street in Cannon Beach, east of the Ecola Inn, for our mechanics to service and maintain the trucks.

The long winter nights at Arch Cape during the war were spent in the dark, as we had to heavily curtain all windows so that any enemy at sea could not see the light. We heard the coast guard loading or unloading horses on the highway this side of the tunnel at dusk. They patrolled the beach on horseback. During the day, we watched blimps from the Tillamook hangars guarding the coast line. What a sight it was to see a blimp above Castle Rock.

Driving was also curtailed. Because gasoline was rationed, we often took the bus to Portland. Greyhound busses ran from Portland via Tillamook and on up the coast to Seaside and Astoria. It was a long way to go from Arch Cape, but it was transportation.

Mabel Coffman lived in her beach home named *Eldcoff*. Mrs. Eldridge had passed away and her daughter, Helen, lived in Morristown, New Jersey. Mrs. Nellie Leech was also a permanent resident. Her husband, Albert, came out of retirement and returned to Portland to work for the Portland Gas Company during the war. We had time to visit and became good friends during those war years. Summer folks came as usual and life went on at Arch Cape.

When the war ended, we sold our log trucks and returned to our Columbia stock ranch near Goble, Oregon, where we raised beef cattle. Clay was a sportsman. He fished, hunted and did trapshooting. I learned to do the same. For many years we traveled to northern British Columbia for big game hunting and for fishing each fall. Ducks and pheasants were a challenge. Trapshooting tournaments throughout the country were also on the agenda, but we still found time for Arch Cape.

Mother and Uncle Emil spent their last Arch Cape summer in 1965. After a brief illness, our mother passed away on Mother's Day, May 14, 1967, at age 83, only to be followed by uncle Emil, age 89, a few months later, on August 11, 1967. In 1973, the Gelinsky-Holderman property was sold to our neighbors, Mr. and Mrs. Floyd Scott. Thus ended sixty-six years of wonderful friendship and adventure for a family who found Arch Cape to be a very special place on this earth.

Retirement—Clay and I sold our ranches in Columbia County in 1970 and built a new home in Scappoose, Oregon. As a descendant of Jacob Holderman, who had fought in the Revolutionary war, I became a member of the Daughters of the American Revolution in the Mount St. Helens Chapter in 1976, while Clay, a World War I veteran, became a member of the Veterans of Foreign Wars. We kept busy. However, after a pleasant 1985 Christmas holiday and a happy new year, Clay developed a breathing problem January 6. After being hospitalized for two days, he passed away on January 8, 1986, at age 97, nearly fifty years after our beautiful wedding at Arch Cape, October 21, 1936. What memorable years they were!

Family and friends gather at the west porch of the newly constructed Gelinsky-Holderman Arch Cape home. Gilderoy is on Mother's lap and I am in the checkered dress, with the blurred face, standing beside my grandmother. Circa 1910. Eugenia Dooley collection.

Resting the horses while traveling from Seaside to Ecola (Cannon Beach) in 1912. My mother, Margaret Holderman, is standing with Gilderoy while I am on the stage with my grandmother, Elizabeth Gelinsky.

I'm with Gilderoy and our dog, Cannon, rafting near the mouth of Arch Cape Creek. Circa 1915.

Gilderoy Holderman, age 10 or 11, holding a fish he caught in Asbury Creek. The old Walsh station barn shows in the background. Circa 1919. Photos, Eugenia Dooley collection.

Marmaduke Maxwell, with Lil, on the way to Cannon Beach. The Maxwell house is in the background. 1914.

Marmaduke Maxwell, 1928. Photos, Eugenia Dooley collection.

Joseph Walsh standing a little north and east of his barn. The Gelinsky cabin shows in the background at the far right. Circa 1924.

Marmaduke Maxwell's cow, Cherry, on the beach with me in 1925. Eugenia Dooley photo.

Gilderoy Holderman helping Mr. Maxwell cut his winter wood supply. The Maxwell's home is in the background. May, 1931. Eugenie Dooley collection.

Jennie English, Eugenia and the family water spaniel, Coco. Jennie was David English's grandmother Circa 1928. David English collection.

Early 1920's Arch Cape beach scene. Note the heavy evergreen growth right down to the dune line. From left to right—friend, Paul Matthiesen, Eugenia, Marmaduke, Eulalia and Max Page (nephew in front of Max), Margaret Holderman, Elizabeth Gelinsky and Walter and Lellah Gelinsky.

Eugenia riding Mr. Maxwell's horse, Betty, at Cannon Beach, also the horse used when working as a game warden when patrolling the Cannon and Arch Cape beaches. 1929. Photos, Eugenia Dolley Collection.

Eugenia holding Betty while, from left to right, Louise and Roy E. Miller's children, Jean, Buck and Grace prepare for a ride. Queenie, the Holderman dog, is buried under the white cross. Note the heavy timber in the area then behind the Gelinsky and Maxwell homes. Circa 1928. Photos, Eugenia Dooley collection.

The firewood log hauled from Clay Dooley's logging camp near Jewell to Arch Cape. It took several years to cut the log into firewood. Margaret Holderman and Grace Pajunen stand next to the log. That is Eugenia on top of the log. Circa 1940.

Eugenia and Clay on the Beach after their wedding October 21, 1936. Photos, Eugenia Dooley collection.

Ray Morse, Bert Patton, Eugenia and Margaret Holderman and Bert Patton enjoying coffee at Short Sands Beach. 1923.

Mr. Maxwell wrote the following Valentine poem to Eugenia, for as he says, cards down here are few.

As Easter cards, down here are few
I send these lines, instead to you
But, if you think it would be better
Why later on I'll write a letter
But these few lines, must now suffice
As thanks for "Easter card" so nice
I trust that with the Lenten fare
You have not let your bones get bare
And hope you sang the Easter hymn
With truly good, and pious vim
The other day to my surprise
Why Mr Simmons met my eyes

With Helen sweet, and lady friend
In Gardners' house the night they spend.
Her tongue must have an extra muscle
As all the time its on the hustle
And like a clock that's wound up tight
She sure can talk from morn till night.
Next day she looked the old house o'er
And start north along the shore
The Ocean, I am grieved to say
Has washed the clambars clean away
So if you do not fritters get
You must not think that I forget
I hope that you to swim are striving
And how do you progress in diving
Should you come down in next July
I expect to see the billows fly.
Now having told you all the news
My further writing, please excuse
I trust that this may find all will
So now goodbye. Yours
                              M. Maxwell

The Lowell Hawkins Connection

The period of the 60's was a time of cooperation in local affairs in Arch Cape, resulting in a church, a volunteer fire department and a community club. One of the residents active in all these efforts was Lowell Hawkins. In a *Daily Astorian* article written when Lowell and Dorothy Hawkins moved away in 1974, he is described as everyone's friend. It states: "He's been everything to Arch Cape, but mainly he has just looked out for people. A community leader, builder of many of the isolated ocean beach community's most beautiful homes, community handyman, willing caretaker of vacation homes and one of the residential community's proudest boosters, Lowell Hawkins has been all of these to Arch Cape since he first moved there 22 years ago."

Mr. and Mrs. Hawkins began visiting Arch Cape in the early 1920's. Lowell remembers that only the old *Singing Sands Hotel* and a few homes stood in a "jungle" of spruce and salal. When they moved to their ocean front home near Asbury Creek in 1952, there were still only a few homes around them; of course the store and post office and the shingle mill were part of the town at the time. Aside from these, he remembers Arch Cape as "a naturally wild spot of gravel roads and thick foliage."

The next two decades brought more homes and he was glad to see that the town stayed residential. Mr. Hawkins was a leader in the effort to have sewers installed and he knew it would lead to more construction, but his main concern was to preserve the atmosphere of Arch Cape as it grew.

There were other physical changes in Arch Cape that Mr. and Mrs. Hawkins observed in the years between 1952 and 1974. The beach dropped about eight feet, Lowell estimated, since the 50's. "The sand that used to wash ashore to replenish the beach is gone." Mrs. Hawkins noted that "one winter in the late 50's the clam-filled bar washed away and never came back." The clam-filled sand bar Mrs. Hawkins describes began west from where Ocean Road meets the beach and ran several hundred yards north.

Another natural "happening" that the Hawkinses recalled vividly was the tidal wave of 1964. Lowell, who had helped bring cable TV to the area was listening to the television news. There had been high tide warnings that night but he heard the announcer say there was no danger. It was 11:30 p.m. on this moonlit night when he looked out his window and saw five or six feet of choppy water at the bank above Asbury Creek. The tide was low and the water should have been out five hundred feet or more. He remembers calling a neighbor living near the creek to tell him about the high water when the electricity suddenly went out.

Lowell remembers seeing the wave coming in at a 45 degree angle at a terrific velocity. When the wave hit the bank, foam and spray shot 150 feet into the air. The house shook and pebbles landed in their yard. Afterwards the water went out more than a half a mile and all he could see was sand. The water went in and out like that a few times before settling down.

Fortunately, little damage was done to Arch Cape and there have been no other tidal waves since then. He did see some other big ocean storms, however, when Castle Rock resembled a "white marshmallow" as the waves broke against it.

Both Dorothy and Lowell Hawkins enjoyed their years in Arch Cape. They were good neighbors and when they left they had enough offers to come back and visit with friends "to take up every weekend for the next year." A potluck dinner on July 27, 1974, was held at the Arch Cape Community Hall at St. Peter the Fisherman Church to say farewell to Lowell and Dorothy Hawkins. In the *The Daily Astorian* article of July 11, 1974, titled **Arch Cape won't be the same**, the writer states "The Hawkinses are one of the last of the Arch Cape old timers." One of these "old timers" is quoted as saying "it will be tough without them."

Mr. Hawkins said he was sorry to leave. "This is just about as good a spot as you can find to live," Hawkins said, "and one of the nicest things about Arch Cape is nothing happens."

Mrs. Ethel LeGault came to Arch Cape in 1953 and became the postmistress and owner of the Arch Cape Grocery. Here she is, admiring the hydrangea in her front yard on Ocean Road. Castle Rock shows in the background. Circa 1960's. Photo, Marni Beemer collection.

Real cowboys moved dairy stock between Clatsop Plains and the Tillamook area on the beach when tides were low. Here is Maxwell, though not a cowboy, driving six animals south while riding Lil. It was common then to move dairy stock between the two areas on the beach. Moving animals over Neahkahnie Mountain was dangerous, for trails were narrow, slippery, and in places, high above the ocean. Photo, Eugenia Dooley collection.

The Hill Connection
By Jim Hill

I first became aware of the Cannon Beach area about 1914 when my mother Beulah, my younger brother Fred and I sojourned at the old Cannon Beach Hotel for the summer while wheat harvest at our ranch near Helix, Oregon, was in progress. I will never know why my mother picked Cannon Beach. I was enthralled and captivated by the mass of ocean, streams, greenery and forest as contrasted to our dry land wheat areas where water of any kind was at a premium and the livestock had priority.

We did the *Cannon Beach Hotel* schedule for some seven or eight years until I became old enough to work on the ranch in the summer. By that time the ocean, sandy beaches, green forests and Elk Creek fishing had me hooked.

After college and graduate school I settled in Pendleton, Oregon, with my lifetime work as general manager of Pendleton Grain Growers, Inc., a farm cooperative. In 1934 I married Gertrude Hanger of Walla Walla, Washington, and she readily adapted to the Cannon Beach summer vacation routine. We met our friends from Walla Walla each summer for two or three lively summer weeks. Jim and Grace Richmond, Brents and Alice Sterling, Marjorie Stirling Harris and Jean Upton Williams comprised the basic group. The old *Cannon Beach Hotel*, a conservative hostelry, often rocked with our group parties. The Frisbees, owner-managers, often joined with us for good clean fun. When the hotel became the *Christian Conference Center*, we moved our allegiance to the old *Ecola Inn* and became regulars with "Mom" Stevens and her clan.

With daughter Susan and son Timothy, we became summer patrons of *Webb's Beach Front Cabins* in downtown Cannon Beach. Our kids became addicted to beach life, so we eventually leased a small beach front cottage on a yearly basis. It was on Gogonna Avenue in upper Tolovana. For fifteen years we enjoyed this cottage as our beach home. The die was cast for retirement time.

Gertrude discovered a house she liked and called on the phone to tell me about it. With out seeing it, I told her to go ahead with the transaction. On October 24, 1967, we purchased our Arch Cape home on 1670 Pacific Street. Upon my retirement and the sale of our home in Pendleton, Oregon, we moved to Arch Cape permanently, a truly fortunate and happy decision. In the early years the residents in our area were: Dave and Maggie Balfour; Jack and Hilda Foster; Bessie Grote; Dr. Roy and Margaret Biehn; Elmer and Fay Vick; the Lowell Hawkins Family; Mrs. Kent Price Sr.; and Dr. Campbell, the area blackberry picker. With his cane and tin can tied around his neck and belt, Dr. Campbell was a common sight in picking season One day when picking berries, he became lost and we had search crews out looking for him. We found him. He wasn't lost, after all. He had fallen in the blackberry bushes and could not extricate himself.

For nearly 80 years at this writing, Arch Cape and Cannon Beach have given me and my family much happiness and we are thankful to many—especially to the good Lord.

214

Jim F. Richmond and James Hill, Jr. celebrate their 70th birthday in the Par Tee Room at the Seaside Golf Club on Wednesday, December 6, 1978, with a buffet dinner. The Erhart Braun Trio played dance music following the buffet. This photo of the handsome pair appeared on the front of the invitation. Photo source unknown. James Hill collection.

Jim and Gertrude Hill, 1992. Jim Hill Photo.

The Cannon Beach Hotel—today the site of the conference center. Jim stayed there as a young boy and later, in his adult life, the hotel became a gathering place to meet friends. This photo is reproduced from an unnamed post card. Shirley Brown collection.

The Kindleys
As told by Jan Putnam Tarr

When I was a growing up in Cleveland, Ohio, in the nineteen-thirties, it was a slow trip by car to Arch Cape, Oregon, for vacations. Nevertheless, my family, the Putnams, often drove across the country to rendezvous with Mother's relatives, the Kindleys, on the Oregon Coast. During the war years we took the train, which was packed with servicemen. That trip took several days and I remember the long nights on Pullman beds. Until I was twelve, we lodged in Cannon Beach when we reached the coast. In 1944, however, three of Mother's brothers and her sister bought a lot together in Arch Cape. It was situated east of Pacific Avenue on Cottage Road, which is just north of the corner of Ocean Road and Pacific Avenue. Soon after this purchase, they built a small beach house on the lot for weekends and vacations. Arch Cape then became the focal point for our family gatherings. This was where I, a city child, caught my first trout in Arch Cape Creek and saw my first Oregon grown monster slug.

I was not around when the cabin was built, but I heard the story from my aunts about its construction. The major portion of the structure came from a United States government housing project connected to the Portland Housing Authority. Howard Kindley, one of Mother's brothers, was managing the Columbia Villa and University Homes section of this project at the time when fire destroyed a few of the houses in the development. These had to be removed. One of the damaged houses seemed to be in pretty good shape and Uncle Howard was given $50 to remove it. He decided to use the money to hire someone with a flat bed truck to haul the dismantled building to the Arch Cape lot. This two bedroom house also came with a heating stove, a refrigerator, a cooking stove and plumbing. These things were impossible to buy during the war years and so they, too, were carefully loaded on the truck to be moved to the coast.

It was dark when the truck arrived at the building site to unload. Arch Cape had no street lights in the mid-forties and so the work was done by flashlight, with much crashing and shouting. The Woods, an English couple in the house closest to the commotion, woke with a start. They naturally concluded it was the Japanese invading. These neighbors later housed a carpenter friend of the Kindleys, Mr. Behm, who was the workman that leveled the lot and built the foundation. By pooling their gas coupons, the Kindleys and their children traveled together to Arch Cape for weekends as they gradually reconstructed, panelled, sanded, painted, varnished and cleaned up the house. They rented cabins from the Leeches on these trips. Elinor Kindley remembers especially the building of the hearth and chimney. The bricks used were discards from the Portland Gas and Coke Company, where her husband, Wendell Kindley, worked at the time. Wendell and Elinor borrowed library books to tell them how chimneys and fireplaces were made. For some reason, the used Gas Company bricks were very heavy, weighing eight or nine pounds each. The girl cousins were given buckets to hold one brick apiece and they kept busy carrying them to the men and boys in the family who were building the chimney. They rigged a pulley and rope system to hoist the heavy bricks to the roof.

There was a lot of activity at the cabin on weekends and in the summers, especially in the 40's and 50's when my cousins were young. Unfortunately, I know only a few stories from those days. One, involving Estelle and Howard Kindley, is often told for a laugh. It seems they went out walking on the beach one spring day, although they'd been warned about big waves. Estelle had a new tweed wool coat to keep her warm and they were not concerned about the stormy weather. Suddenly, before they knew it, a granddaddy wave was upon them. All Estelle remembers is seeing her husband dash up the cliff beside them as the wave, carrying a log, broke over her. Although not hit by the log, when the wave receded she was anchored to the beach in a wool coat so heavy with sand and water she couldn't move. As soon as Howard rejoined her, she asked why he had left her alone in such danger and he replied, quickly, that he'd been making a path for her.

Such stories live for a long time.

Eventually, Howard's widow, Estelle, became the sole owner of the cabin and she continues to spend her summers there, renting it out in the winter. Estelle and her family live in California and can work on projects only during their vacations, Estelle's sister and brother-in-law, Vi and Bud Passmore from Vancouver, Washington, have been the main repairers, remodelers, painters, cleaners and caretakers. From 1970 to the present they have put in windows, doors, sinks, wiring, formica, television, linoleum, a laundry room, a deck, replaced walls, plastered, painted, gardened, hung drapes, and brought in furniture, appliances, heaters, plumbing and carpet. The guest book in the cabin chronicles four generations of Kindley relations and friends who have visited over the past forty-seven years and have left fond or humorous messages behind. There have also been interesting renters in the winter. One of these was Jean Auel, the Northwest author who wrote *The Clan of the Cave Bear* series. Her second novel, *Valley of Horses,* was written mostly during her winter in the Kindley cottage.

I was away from Arch Cape from 1948 until 1961. It was then that my husband, Dennis Cosley, and I moved to Seattle and we began to bring our children, Kevin, Kathy and Peggy to Arch Cape on summer trips. We stayed at the old *Beach House Motel* next to the store. Those years condense into a collage of bright memories for me.

I recall:

Our children, aged seven, five and three, protected by bright orange life vests, playing in the sand—at least 200 feet from the waves. . .

The murre that Kevin found dying on the beach and tried to keep alive in a cardboard box. . .

Vic Shults's rock shop. . .

Mr. Schaeffer's front yard miniature village of windmills, houses, trains and roads beside the Texaco service station across from the store and post office. . .

A garden full of plants in old shoes. . .

The rich candy assortment at the Arch Cape grocery. . .

The smell of the air on an early morning beach walk the first day of a two-week vacation. . .

Jars full of beach bouquets. . .

The raucous anthem we sang ("Oh Beautiful for Spacious Skies") at our first glimpse of ocean on our trips down. . .

The kids sand skimming on a round wooden board that was heavy to throw, tricky to ride and which stopped with a suddenness that sent them flying. . .

The stars, the beach fires and the phosphorescent surf in August. . .

The books read on the sand with the sound of the ocean in our ears. . .

I particularly recall the time I spent in the Beach House as the only adult with six teenagers. There was one morning at Short Sands that week when, having scrambled up a cliff at their heels, I discovered myself six feet from the top, twenty feet from the beach and fresh out of handholds. When Kevin came back to find me, he calmly assured me he could guide me up as soon as I leaned back from the rock face against which I was frozen. He said it was essential or I would fall when I climbed. Still frightened and against every instinct, I forced myself to follow his instructions and reached the top, with a new understanding of trust.

Occasionally our time in Arch Cape was spent with my Cleveland family: My sister Shirley Schneerer, her husband Bill, and their children, Carol, Ellen and Dinah. Mother and Dad (Freda and Russell Putnam) often came as well and after mother's death, my stepmother Gene (for Genevieve) came with Dad.

From the time Dwight Goffinet and I were married in 1971 until his death in 1980, we brought his children, Lance, Renee and Michele along, too, adding new adventures, friends and family to the picture.

Arch Cape for me as a child was where the Kindleys gathered, and where I was welcomed by my aunts and uncles from Portland. I am still grateful for that. Now their children and grandchildren and mine are making new collections of Arch Cape memories, giving greater dimension to my own.

Arch Cape 40 Years Ago:
A Child's-Eye-View
by Jeff Kindley

Arch Cape was the one place in the world where I seemed, at 6, to be related to almost everyone. Kindleys, Kents, Putnams—all my uncles, aunts and cousins came together here in the summers, often crammed into one cabin, and it felt to me as if this were our true family birthplace. My father and his brothers had built the cabin themselves. They painted the appliances cherry red and the furniture sky blue, just as if they were fulfilling some childhood fantasy of Home.

Babies (including myself) were bathed in the kitchen sink. Cold toes, numbed by the Pacific, were warmed up in front of the fireplace my father and uncles had put together brick by brick. On the big red stove, Aunt Stelle made the world's best pancakes, which we wolfed down at the big round sky blue table. When we looked in the kitchen cupboards for marshmallow toasting-rods, we found mouse-traps. Mouse traps! Were there mice? We kids lay awake at night in our sleeping bags listening for them.

During the day we dug holes on the beach as deep as we could dig in dry sand until we hit water, and then covered the hole with driftwood twigs; we laid newspaper over the twigs, then covered the newspaper with a layer of sand. Then we waited for some unsuspecting person to come along and plunge into the hole. Did they? No. Or if they did, it was only to oblige us, feigning alarm because they'd seen our expectant faces and knew we'd engineered a disaster.

Or we fished. My older brother Bobby was a true fisherman. He tied flies and practiced how to cast his line. I didn't get it, really—didn't have the patience. I'd pick apart salmonberries and toss the pieces in the water, watching the trout jump at my fake bait.

I liked standing on the edge of Strawberry Creek, the miniature sand-cliff above the stream, and sinking slowly, slowly into the water.

I liked the mysterious sandbars that would appear from time to time, creating warm pools of water on the beach.

I liked the tide pools between the rocks, liked poking the anemones with a driftwood stick and seeing them close up.

I did *not* like being slathered with sun lotion by my mother, however, or having my swimming trunks pulled down in full view of everyone to check how red I was getting!

We kids explored everything: An almost-hidden private trail hacked out of salal, with its slippery, slug-infested single-board bridge over a trickle of rusty water flourishing with skunk cabbage, which led from our back yard to the Arch Cape Grocery, where we could buy red licorice and jawbreakers and bottles of Nehi Grape; the fascinating little place across the way, which was built to resemble a ship's cabin, complete with portholes; the mysterious house behind our own, inhabited by an old lady we seldom saw, who kept her Christmas tree up all year round, decorated with Japanese fishing floats.

We took treks up Arch Cape Creek, made sand castles, picked buttercups at Sally's Alley, built driftwood forts, set off fireworks all summer long (in those bad old days when you could buy gorgeous rockets and sparklers and firecrackers everywhere), checked out the half-constructed new houses after the workmen had left, and went clamming at 4 a.m. with grouchy grown-ups who had *promised* they would take us.

Of course we roasted marshmallows and made S'mores on the beach, but almost better than roasting marshmallows was tossing them into the driftwood-fire embers and watching them turn into mutant marshmallow people, swelling, fizzing, and finally catching fire.

We loved the Pacific Coast's potential for disaster. The Church's house, poised far above the ocean, actually slid into the sea. And when those foolhardy people built their swimming pool near Sally's Alley—a swimming pool which has endured for quite some time now—we waited eagerly for its retainer wall to split apart. It's not that we wished them ill. We were just hungry for excitement.

On rainy days we painted sand dollars and put together warped and musty jigsaw puzzles that always had a few crucial pieces missing. TV was not an option. If we were lucky, we got the grown-ups to take us to Seaside, the source of everything marvelous: key-chains with tiny crabs embalmed in plastic, salt water taffy and bumper cars.

As for grown-ups. . . There was one I will always think of with special fondness when I think of Arch Cape: my Aunt Polly. She wasn't anything like Tom Sawyer's. She came to the beach with a make-up case as big as a bread box, several decks of cards, the latest "sophisticated" novels, a portable record player and her personal stash of liquor and

219

cigarettes. I don't remember that she paid much attention to us kids, but that didn't matter. Aunt Polly was fun. Our parents adored her because she was what a good time at the beach meant. She bought boxes of fudge and almond toffee in Seaside and left them around the cabin **open** for anyone to devour. She laughed (a low, dry, cigarette-cured laugh) and everyone else laughed too—even us kids who didn't understand the joke.

Patrick Dennis's *Auntie Mame* was one of the "sophisticated" books Aunt Polly brought to Arch Cape. I read her curling, slightly mildewy copy several years later (there wasn't much to read at the beach; one chose between ancient editions of *Heidi* and *Ben Hur*) and will always think of Aunt Polly as Auntie Mame. You remember Auntie Mame? "Life is a banquet and most poor sons of bitches are starving to death" she said.

Life *is* a banquet—or so it seems to me, forty years on—and I am oh so grateful for the magnificent plate of *hors d'oeuvres* that was a childhood among the Kindley clan at Arch Cape.

The Song of the Beach

I sit on the sand
I wade in the water;
I fall asleep on the gentle shore.
I listen. . .
    I wonder. . .
no more do I cry.

I just hum
to the tune
of the song
of the beach.

I hear a crash. . .
A wave,
    A wave.

I feel a sinking. . .
the sand,
    the sand.

In the center of the water I see a little crab.
It watches me,
    Mysteriously.
It too knows the song
    of the beach.

What is the song of the beach,
    You ask?
      I'm not quite sure I know.

But if you listen to the
water
the sand
and the crab,
you'll hear it clear,
you'll hear it clear.

Yes, listen to those three,
    my child.

The crab,
the sand
and the sea.
And you too will know that song. . .
if you will come
    to the beach
with me.

Colin Kindley
Age 9

The Tarrs—as told by Jan Tarr
From Recollections of Betty Tarr Schneider and Bertha Tarr Mitchell

In 1949, Mr. and Mrs. Stinson W. Tarr began building their home in Arch Cape. For several years they had been visiting whenever Stinson could take time from his job with the Post Office Department in Portland, often coming on the Seaside bus. On one of these trips Stinson and Isobel bought a lot in *Kent Price Park* and began planning to live permanently on this land as soon as he retired. Using skills he had picked up in night school, Stinson made a blueprint of the house they wanted and later a working model. They even carried lumber and nails from Portland in the Jeep and put up a garage on the property. However, when Stinson realized there were restrictions governing building in *Kent Price Park*, he rebelled. He quickly sold his lot and bought three more south of Ocean Road where he was away from any regulations. The garage was moved to the new location, but it was never incorporated into the house. After Stinson retired in his late 50's due to a bad shoulder injury, he and Isobel put up a big green tent and, as the story goes, began excavating with a shovel, a trowel and a coal scuttle for carrying off the dirt.

The new house was not like the model. The first thing built was a large new garage, which was their home then until the rest of the structure was completed. Later it was attached to the house and sheltered the school bus (which he drove every day to Cannon Beach Elementary School), his workshop, a washer and dryer and the greenhouse for Isobel's geraniums. Stinson framed and roofed the house; local builders did the rest. The yard on the ocean side was edged by large driftwood pieces and surrounded with his colorful plantings. Since the driftwood pieces were too large to move, he transformed them into animal figures by adding strategic bits of paint and adding reflectors for eyes.

Stinson was famous for his dahlias and hydrangeas. The hydrangeas were an especially bright blue which he kept that way by burying nails and old flash light batteries around their roots. Cuttings from these are in several other Arch Cape gardens today. A large vegetable garden was on the east side of the house with beds of flowers to brighten the neighborhood annually. He was also known for the "Tarr barrel" he built which he set up on Highway 101 to designate their street. It was a wooden barrel on a stump with a piece of drift wood attached, painted black to simulate overflowing tar, a landmark to many travelers.

Soon after the house was completed, the Tarr's children, Bertha, Bob and Betty, began to visit with their families. One of the favorite pastimes for the grandchildren was building a fort in the sand under the huge spruce trees by the trail to the beach from Grandpa's house. It was a hidden secret enclosure in the trees that would excite any child's imagination. Bob Tarr, Jr., one of Stinson and Isobel's grandsons, now lives a block from the old Tarr house. He says there is a house on top of that clearing today and the path to the beach is overgrown. He often goes that way, however, to recapture the smells he remembers—a unique combination of wild roses and their leaves, salal, wild sweet peas, beach grasses and blackberry vines.

Susie Tarr Lange, another grandchild, remembers all the driftwood on the beach. Some of the logs were so large that, as a twelve-year-old, she couldn't see over them. Once she walked on those logs from the beach in front of the Tarr house to Arch Cape Creek, a half-mile away, without touching the sand.

Betty remembers her mother's collection of glass balls and describes petite Isobel running on her short legs as fast as they would go to beat everyone to those she spotted washed ashore by the winter storms.

The Tarrs lived in Arch Cape until 1965 and then moved into a retirement village in Gresham. The house was used as a vacation house by Stinson's son, Robert Tarr, Sr., and his family until it was sold in 1967. Unfortunately, it was never occupied after that and over the years it has become sadly neglected. It still stands, however, a reminder of good times to the family who vacationed there.

Perhaps the most lasting contribution that Grandpa Tarr made to Arch Cape resulted from his concern for the safety of children when they were walking to the store on the highway. He kept after the highway department until they painted safety stripes on Highway 101, north of the present store, and also reduced the speed limit. We appreciate his persistence to this day.

The Kindleys and the Tarrs
As told by Jan Tarr

During the 1950's the Kindleys and the Tarrs were probably on the beach at the same time, occasionally using the same pathways or shopping in the little grocery-post office together, but they never became acquainted. This state of affairs continued until 1961, when Jeff Kindley and Bob Tarr met at Grant High School in Portland and discovered their Arch Cape connection.

It seems that Bob and his younger brother Rich, while staying with their grandparents, went out one night to roam around the neighborhood. They found a seven by four foot *Squirt* billboard in some underbrush and they wanted to do something with it. After thinking it over, they leaned it against the picture window of a house where they'd noticed a party in progress earlier in the evening.

Sometime later in the journalism room at Grant, Jeff Kindley told a funny story about waking up one morning in their vacation cottage to see a *Squirt* sign filling up the front window. Bob asked him what they had done with the sign and was told it was in the brush near the cabin. Bob said a silent "aha" and the next time he was in Arch Cape he looked for it, found it, and transported it back to Grant and into the journalism room without being detected. Needless to say, Jeff was surprised and Bob confessed to being the *Squirt* sign phantom—and an Arch Cape kid, too. After high school, Bob and Jeff and his wife Louise kept in touch.

In 1981, when I bought the *Arch Cape Beach House Motel*, I became reacquainted with my cousin Jeff and met Louise when they came from New York to stay in the motel. When I visited Jeff and Louise in New York in 1984, they told me that their friend Bob Tarr was staying in the *Beach House*. The day I arrived at the beach that summer, Dorothy Meece introduced Bob to me. In 1985 Bob and I married. We sold the motel in 1988 and built our own house in 1989 on Ocean Road halfway between the old Tarr residence and the Kindley beach house. Now, Bob teaches in the area, and he and I enjoy carrying on the summer reunion tradition.

Stinson and Isobel Tarr with Bruno beside their Arch Cape House.

Susie, Rich and Bob Tarr on property now owned by Womacks.

The Kindley cabin on Cottage Road. circa 1945.

Bob Tarr, Louise and Jeff Kindley: 24 years after Bob and Jeff discovered their Arch Cape Connections.

Pauline Kindley Kent (Aunt Polly) and Jan Putnam Tarr. 1967.

The women who, with their husbands and Polly Kent, put up the Kindley cabin, and two of Estelle's children. (Left to right) Blanche Kindley; wife of Robert Kindley, Joyce Kindley Joslyn, Estelle Kindley; wife of Howard Kindley, Kay Kindley Bush and Elinor Kindley; wife of Wendell Kindley. 1990. Photos, Jan Tarr collection.

The Albert and Nellie Leech Connection
Memories by Elsie Wood, Daughter

The Leech family hails from Lancashire, England. My father, Albert, served in the British Army with the Royal Welsh Fusiliers in France for four years during World War I. He was a signal man, an accomplished wireless and semaphore operator. My mother, Nellie, owned a fabric store and saved her earnings while Dad was away in the military. Mother was the eldest of ten children and was determined to go to America. In her words, "There was nothing to stay for in England." She had four sisters already in the United States, which was an added incentive. So, in December, 1919, we left England. I had my eighth Christmas in the middle of a very stormy Alantic Ocean on the way to a new and uncertain destination.

My dad had relatives on the East Coast and my mother's four sisters lived in Oregon. The east coast relatives thought we were foolish to go to Oregon, the Wild West, where Indians and cowboys ruled the turf. After our train trip across the country and a few days in Pendleton visiting Mother's youngest sister, Mother and Dad were ready to return to the East, for Pendleton was, perhaps, the last truly wild west town around.

Portland, where most of Mother's relatives lived, was the next destination for the Leech family. We arrived in February, 1920. My father had worked for a gas company in England as a bookkeeper; this experience proved to be worthwhile, since he was hired in the same capacity by the Portland Gas and Coke Company. He liked his work at the Gas Company and was comfortable with the security it provided.

I began piano lessons at age nine in 1920, and had the same teacher, Frances von Homeyer, for my entire life until her death in November, 1990. She was not only my teacher, but was also my very good friend, who visited me yearly here in Arch Cape. I also took pipe organ lessons from Lucien E. Becker, organist for Trinity Episcopal Church in Portland. Later, membership in the Portland chapter of the Oregon Music Teachers' Association gave me the opportunity to attend master classes that were sponsored by the association for teacher members.

We first visited the coast in the early 20's, staying in facilities where the Cannon Beach Conference Center is now located. Stage tours were available for Cannon Beach tourists. The Arch Cape area, via Hug Point, and the arches just beyond the massive Arch Cape headland were popular destinations. Those visits were perhaps the inspiration for my Mother's planning the purchase of property somewhere in the Arch Cape area without Dad's knowledge.

In the later 20's, Mother purchased a one-room cabin the Oregon State Highway Department engineers used while planning the bridge and tunnel. They no longer needed the building and it was in their way. Mother, for a very nominal fee, had them move it to a lot she purchased just east of the Lee home on the north side of Mill Road. It was a one-room cabin with an added porch. No plumbing or electricity was available and the comfort facility was in the heavy tree growth that surrounded the area then. Heat came from the wood stove used for preparing meals. Pure clear water, carried in buckets, came from Arch Cape Creek near the Stills' house.

I have many precious teenage memories associated with Arch Cape. How lucky I was to have a visionary mother. We spent all summer there and Dad came down weekends and during his vacation time in 1929 and 1930 to share the tiny cabin with us. We stayed in the Arch Cape Cabins the next two summers when Mother managed them for the Diefendorf's. We still used the cabin on Mill Road to house friends and to provide for extra sleeping space.

The Stills, who were Finnish, lived across Mill Road from Mother's cabin. They had a sauna building, which we all used. First, we heated a huge pile of rocks. Then, we threw creek water on the rocks to make steam. We sat in the buff, on a choice of three benches soaking up the moist heat. Of course, the higher the bench, the more intense the steam and heat, thus relaxing tired joints after the day's beach activities.

I remember the Pajunens, who lived one lot north from where Bridget Snow lives today. The home now is owned by the Hendricksons. Dr. Pajunen, a dentist in Astoria, was also the Finnish Consul for Oregon. The Pajunens had a piano, and often when I was in Arch Cape, I practiced my lessons. Dr. Pajunen's first request of me: could I play *Finlandia*? I couldn't, and it was a shock to him.

My uncle, Fred Westhoff, had a Star automobile which he drove through the arches. That was before the huge boulders crashed down from the cliffs above the arches after a very wet and stormy winter in 1940. Fred was my favorite uncle and also a cousin of my piano teacher. He was a great fisherman, who often fished on Arch Cape Creek in his secret deep holes and under the logs along the banks where the trout liked to rest and hide. One time he went out on Bird Rock, off Cove Beach, to fish and remained there throughout the entire tide, although I can't recall whether he caught any fish that day.

Clams and crabs were very plentiful and easy to harvest in those early days. Our family specialty was clams, and they were always cleaned outdoors. Clam chowder was a favorite treat and I remember the men getting theirs served in vegetable bowls; women used soup plates. We enjoyed the fried clams my mother prepared on the wood stove. These wood stoves also helped heat the house. Kerosene and oil lamps provided light. Mother heated rocks in the oven and placed them in our beds at bedtime providing a makeshift electric blanket. Electricity didn't arrive in Arch Cape until after the tunnel and bridge opened in 1941.

A number of families spent summers at Arch Cape in their own homes or in the Arch Cape Cabins. Mothers and children remained all week and the dads drove down each weekend to be with their families and to enjoy the many Arch Cape beach activities. On Friday evenings, we built a huge fire on the beach and watched for car lights on the highway coming out of Cannon Beach and waited for them to negotiate Hug Point. Depending on the time of low tide, this waiting could stretch to midnight. Usually, someone walked ahead of the car over Hug Point to be sure no one was coming from the other direction and to be certain it was safe. Then we guessed whose dad's car or boyfriend's car was on the way. Sometimes, the final chore for us was to help get the cars through the dry sand up to Leech Avenue. Many would get stuck. Gunny sacks, shovels, boards, sweat, and, at times, some choice words helped rescue the stuck cars. It wasn't until 1933 that a rough and primitive road reached Arch Cape from Cannon Beach.

Smitty, who lived at the end of Mill Road, was a hunter and a beachcomber. He brought Mother clams and venison and cared for beach front homes in the winter when owners were away.

The depression came along just when I graduated from Washington High School in Portland in 1929. I began teaching piano when I was 18. Money at that time was scarce so my fees were in kind. Instead of money, payment came as chickens, eggs, potatoes, produce from the farmers, and grocery products from a store owner. One mother did ironing for me. It was truly a barter system then.

I married in 1931. Not long afterwards, we moved in with my parents, since work wasn't available. Dad lost his job with the Portland Gas and Coke Company. They cut their staff by letting the older men go first, and Dad was about fifty-five at the time. My husband finally found work and we lived in our own home during those lean years in the early 30's. Later, Mother and Dad moved to Arch Cape full time and we purchased their Portland home.

My parents differed in many ways. Mother was a visionary who could see value in a place like Arch Cape, and her thrifty ways allowed her to finance such a venture. Dad was very cautious. He never jumped into anything until after much thought. By respecting each other's traits, my parents made a great pair and were wonderful parents for their only child.

Mother managed and rented the Arch Cape Cabins during the summers between 1930 and 1934. She convinced Dad it would be a good move to purchase the property at the west end of what is now known as Leech Avenue. S. R. and Winifred Diefendorf owned the property when Mother and Dad purchased it on April 20, 1934. They assumed Diefendorfs' $1,500 mortgage to Mr. W. C. Parks, plus $10 cash for the four cabins and a large home on the ocean front. Within a couple of years, Mother and Dad decided to make what we called *The Big House* their permanent home.

The tunnel project began in 1936 and my parents rented the cabins to loggers and tunnel workers. During that time, the shed roof garage on each cabin was enclosed to make a bedroom, thus enlarging the cabins to about double their previous size, and making them easier and more desirable to rent. Mr. Frank Lee, a local handyman, did the work.

World War II brought changes. Mother rented one of the cabins to the Coast Guard. There were six men on duty, but only four at a time stayed at the cabin. The main Coast Guard station in Cannon Beach trained patrol dogs. The dogs, donated by local residents, were taught to be vicious and mean. If they mellowed a bit, they were returned to Cannon Beach for retraining. I remember a German shepherd, a boxer, a Doberman, and an Airedale. One wonders if they were ever able to return to civilian life and be safe family pets again.

During the war everything had to be blacked out. My mother even had special black-out curtains as a mere cigarette light could be seen for several miles out to sea. My cousin, Doris, was a smoker and went out one night for a walk on the beach. She stopped and sat on a log, and lit a cigarette. Two coastguardsmen and their dogs on patrol gave her a frightful time. The guardsmen gave her a strong lecture and the dog appeared menacing, as if wanting to teach her a lesson.

The Conways lived next door and were very close friends. Mother lived alone when Dad returned to work for the gas company in Portland during the war years. After the war, he resumed retirement and returned to the coast.

Mr. and Mrs. Larry Ward's home, barn red in color today, on the northeast corner of Ocean Road and Pacific Avenue, was built by my husband's aunt and uncle, Charles and Elizabeth Wood, originally from Yorkshire, England. They lived in Arch Cape for many years. Larry Ward is Ethel LaGualt's brother-in-law. Ethel owned and operated the Arch

Cape store and post office for 18 years

　　　Mother died in 1949 at age 70 and Father two years later at age 72. They shared twenty wonderful years at Arch Cape. Mother had the tea kettle on all the time, as neighbors visited daily. Dr. John Countryman, a retired physician and surgeon, and his wife Irene lived a few houses north of my parents. They were always helpful to everyone in Arch Cape. When my mother became ill, Dr. Countryman referred her to a cancer specialist in Portland.

　　　I inherited the property and continued to rent the cottages. A few years later, Della and Frank Lee took over the management for me. Della took care of the rentals and Frank kept the property maintained. The Lees were good friends and cared for the cottages as though they were their own. Mr. Lee kept keys to most of the homes in the area on a board in his home.

　　　Bob and Ellen Womack have been close friends and neighbors to me and my family since the 30's. They, with their children, vacationed in the cottages in the late 40's and grew to love Arch Cape. They purchased their Arch Cape property in 1963 and built their original cabin in 1964. In 1976 Bob and Ellen enlarged their Arch Cape home and became full-time residents.

　　　My husband and I built the home now owned by Dr. Eric Meyer and Dr. Sarah Snell. It was a small concrete block structure then. In April of 1966, we sold the entire parcel, including the cottages, to Travis Tyrrell. He sold the lot with the new house to Brian and Tina McDonough in 1974. They used the home as a vacation home until Brian's retirement in 1983 and then made a major addition to the structure. Brian and Tina sold the home in the summer of 1991 and now reside in Warrenton, a few miles west of Astoria.

　　　My present home, also on Leech Avenue, was purchased by my daughter and son-in-law in 1975. It originally was a beach cabin, partially built by tunnel workers. We added on and remodeled, so now there is plenty of room for our families to visit. Part of that structure sits close to where Joe Walsh built his homestead cabin in the mid 1890's. I moved here permanently in September, 1979.

　　　I have a daughter, Marsha, a son, David, and seven grandchildren. All have enjoyed Arch Cape through the years as children and now as adults with their own children. My son and daughter-in-law chose to spend their honeymoon here in December, 1965. They stayed in the newer house we built in 1964.

　　　Each of the cottages had its own personality and we enjoyed staying in all of them, but our favorite place was the little upstairs apartment in *The Big House*. It had a wonderful view of the beach and of Castle Rock. Because we reached the upstairs by an outside stairway, it became a special hideaway, particularly to younger family members who enjoyed reading and dreaming away the hours. Through the years, the following anonymous poem hung framed on the wall in the upstairs apartment. I now have it on the wall near the window in my bedroom that overlooks Arch Cape Beach.

> *I LIKE a window looking out upon the sea,*
> *Where ships pass up and down the world,*
> *And bellying sails and steamer smoke signal me*
> *To leave my narrow room*
> *And search the maze of ever-changing patterns made*

By sun and cloud and wind and wave,
And far-off skies call me to go adventuring
In lands I do not know.

I LIKE a window looking out upon the sea,
Where I can stand and watch the storm,
And on a quiet night
Sense the lifting tide beneath the stars, and in
The whispering of the waters to
The sands, hear the still, small voice of Him
Who holds the oceans in His hands.

I WISH that there might be for me a window where
My soul could look upon the sea,
And know the meaning of these things, that reach
So far beyond the range of mortal sight —
That wonders of the infinite might tempt me from
My narrow earthy room to search
God's maze of mysteries and go adventuring
In worlds that no man knows.

I LIKE a window looking out upon the sea.

Elsie Wood, 16, modeling her Jantzen bathing suit just after the famous Jantzen logo became so popular.

Albert Leech pointing at the new "Leech Ave." sign that replaced "Walsh Ave." in the '40's. Photos, Elsie Wood collection.

The Log Cabin
By Irene (Christie-Mosby) Tyrrell

Albert Clarence Patton — 1878-1963

I believe that Bert, as we all knew him, grew up in Tennessee. This may be correct. However, an employee record from Crossett Western Company lists his birthplace as Leetonia, Ohio; and his birthdate as July 22, 1878; and his name as Albert Clarence Patton, son of John H. Patton and Esther McLoughlin Patton. Perhaps his family moved to Tennessee where he spent his youth. I do not know why he came to Oregon.

Our close friendship with Bert came about because he knew my dad's sister, Edna Christie. I do not know how they met, but through this friendship, our family became his family. Bert spent Christmas and Thanksgiving holidays with us, and in return, he welcomed us into his Arch Cape log cabin home. As a child, I remember he went on trips with our family to Mt. Rainier, Crater Lake, and other interesting destinations.

Bert worked as a blacksmith for Crossett Western Company in Scio, and for the Roaring River Logging Company and the Big Creek Logging Company near Knappa. The years our family was closely tied to Bert were the years he worked for the Big Creek Logging Company. He retired from there and moved permanently to the beach. I have no record of the date. His unusual artistic touch in items he made for the cabin, as well as for other early Arch Cape home owners, remains part of the decor in many Arch Cape homes today. The andirons in many fireplaces are made from railroad rails have large decorative brass balls—parts from a locomotive governor. The fireplace poker is attractive as well as practical. A wiener roaster is cleverly constructed to open for inserting hot dogs and closes to hold them tightly when roasting over the fire. He handcrafted much of the cabin furniture. We still use the hutch, corner cupboard and the three foot by eight foot sawbuck style table. He used benches on each side of the table; rawhide chairs are used today. Bert's work is decorative as well as functional

The deed for Bert Patton's Arch Cape property (Lot 1, Block 15, Cannon Beach Park) dated September 2, 1921, shows the name James Finlayson as trustee for Cannon Beach Park. I do not know if the following is true, but I have been told the property Bert bought had the beginning of a log cabin built from spruce trees cut from the lot. I have pictures of the cabin without a roof, windows and chinking. The stone fireplace and chimney were only partially finished. Bert completed the cabin working weekends from his job in Knappa. It wasn't easy in those days to travel to Arch Cape.

The small one level log cabin, in which the family spent vacations from 1921 to 1939, had a kitchen with a wood stove for cooking. Kerosene lamps furnished light and a Coleman lantern hung over the dining table. Beyond the back door was a screened sleeping porch just large enough for a bed. It had a wood wainscot halfway up the walls. The top half of the walls could be covered with wood panels that slid up to cover the screens for privacy and for protection from the weather.

Water from the Dichter system piped to the back porch of Bert's cabin supplied "cold" water, so it was necessary to heat water on the kitchen stove. No in house "comfort" facility existed at the time, so the outhouse in the back yard served that necessary function.

A guest book started in 1925 by Bert records those who enjoyed his hospitality and his log cabin home. We continue the guest book tradition and have a second book up to the present time. Early entries often mention Bert's wonderful food—clam chowder, fried clams, and crab feeds. Many feasts came from the beach and were supplemented by the plentiful huckleberries and blackberries for pies and cobblers. And one must not forget the salal berry jelly.

An entry by Bert read "lost car October 28, 1931." He told us he came down off Hug Point after dark in the fog and thought he was paralleling the ocean; instead, he was headed slightly to the west. A wave engulfed the car and that was that. The next morning he went back and the car was upside down in the surf. All that Bert salvaged were the four wheels and tires.

Visitors could stay at Arch Cape later in the year after the road was completed to the tunnel construction site. An entry dated October 21, 1934, by Mr. V. D. Kilborn tells of a terrible wind storm. He writes about a three foot snag going down not fifty feet north of the log cabin. Another spruce across the street fell twelve feet from the cabin, striking the middle of the house adjacent to Bert's cabin and breaking rafters and sheathing. When replacing the roof of the house several years ago, we found evidence of repaired rafters. Kilborn walked down the "Creek Road" to the Stills' place where a tree blew down on Smithie's garage and pinned the car parked there. The next day, Mr. Kilborn went to Tolovana and counted 46 trees across the highway. There were eight in one bunch with two large spruce about four feet in diameter just north of Shank's place. He wrote: "Mr. Walker came from Portland last night and could get only as far as Hug Point. The Stills came on Saturday leaving their car over on the end of the grade. They are now clearing Walker's private road to give access to the beach, allowing them to get out."

Entries dated December 31, 1938 and January 1, 1939, indicate there had been other strong storms with trees down all through the woods and over the road. A tree fell through Powell's house, located west of the bridge on the Arch Cape Creek Road.

Another story from January 14, 1939, tells about Charles Britton and his son Walter helping George Christie remove the cabin floor. They did this because a rotten log rolled out of the east side of the old cabin. Before the cabin completely fell apart, Bert arranged for cedar logs from the Big Creek Logging Company for construction of a new cabin. The front room is made of log in the same dimension as the front room of the old cabin, but the kitchen and upper level are framed and shingled. The original fireplace, modified by adding a fire brick lining and glass doors, provides year-long enjoyment. Old growth vertical grain fir flooring replaced the old surface, and today, the mellow glow and warmth of that floor greets all who enter our home. I don't know the dates of such modernization as indoor plumbing and electricity in Arch Cape, but in 1939 during the new cabin construction, wiring was installed along the logs within the chinking. A December 29, 1940, entry reads: "Bert has a radio and the music sure sounds good—civilization!"

I made an entry dated August 17, 1941, which reads: "We drove through the just opened tunnel and on to Wheeler over the new road. It was much different from the overnight hike Bert, Mary Henderson, and I experienced over that very same route three summers ago." I well remember that 1938 hike. Men worked on the road just south of the tunnel and the trail was up and down hill all the way. The workers told us we couldn't stay on the beach at Short

Sands State Park. The park ranger was there, in his cabin. We hid from him, ate a cold supper, and slept on the trail. The next morning we brazenly went down to the beach, only to be met by the park ranger who said he hunted for us the night before. The workmen told him we were coming and he wanted to offer us a place to sleep in his cabin!

An August, 1944, log book entry reads: "Mickeys and Stinsons tried to fish out the ocean—caught sea perch better than fourteen inches long; dug about nine dozen clams, caught four crabs and saw about 18 elk...Harry E. Christie."

Even though we now enjoy a more modern cabin, memories of the early days linger. We kept many of the furnishings and decor from the old structure. A replica of one of Columbus's ships, the *Santa Maria*, handcrafted by Bert stands on the mantle. The lamp in the big brown bean pot, the iron kettle, the fireplace bellows, the glass floats, many of the pictures and other articles are still with us. My dad, George Christie, made the wrought iron supports for the mantle. He was an accomplished blacksmith, too. The elk antlers are still over the mantle holding a musket. The bearskin and deer's head are gone, but I don't miss them.

This story is about Bert, his cabin, the people he loved, and the events that happened involving him rather than about the man—Bert Patton. But I think all of this is Bert. He loved to have people enjoy the cabin, and the hundreds of names entered in the guest book plus all those who did not write, indicate how many did indeed enjoy his bit of heaven. If the cabin was full when we arrived, we slept on the beach. We took turns at Bert's huge dinner table when there were too many for one "sit down" gathering. We played cards in the evening, sat around the fireplace roasting wieners and marshmallows, and listened to old songs on the wind-up gramophone. Evening beach fires were common during summer time. The big Fourth of July fireworks celebration became a special Arch Cape tradition each year bringing, perhaps, the largest beach crowds of the summer. We loved all of it, and especially loved Bert. Bert died January 8, 1963 at age 84. He is gone and the "old days" are gone—but they are not forgotten.

George and Clarrie Christie

Bert Patton was the link between my parents, George and Clarrie Christie, and Arch Cape. They were close friends and Bert considered us his family. In the summertime from 1921 to 1963, the family traveled from St. Helens, where we lived, to Bert's Arch Cape log cabin. Those early day beach trips were mostly weekend excursions. At times we stayed for a week or more, often with aunts, uncles, cousins and friends. In the early years it took four hours to get to the beach from our St. Helens home; now it takes less than two hours.

We usually drove to the beach on a Friday evening, but sometimes we left in the early hours on a Saturday morning. My father, George, as everyone called him, including me, checked the tide tables to plan the trip. It was necessary to drive on the sand from Cannon Beach to Arch Cape at low tide in order to get around Hug Point. That was the only way to get to Bert's cabin in those days. Many times, in our eagerness to get to the beach, we built bonfires on the north side of Hug Point to help pass the time while waiting for the tide to recede. George usually left Sunday night to return to work at the Creosote Plant in St. Helens and the rest stayed at Bert's cabin until George returned the following weekend.

We built a bonfire on Friday night to welcome George and other returning fathers and husbands. Their headlights shone as far away as Cannon Beach where we could watch them drive onto the sand, down to and around Hug Point, and to the beach below the log cabin. George backed his car as far as possible above the high tide mark to remain until time to return home.

Few cars traveled the beach in those days. One Friday evening, while anxiously waiting around the bonfire for George to arrive, a car appeared and seemed to slow down as it reached our area. My mother was sure it was George and rushed down to meet him as the car stopped. The two were almost in each other's arms before it was realized they weren't husband and wife.

George built the small boats we sailed down Arch Cape Creek and made the kites we flew. Those kites were not at all like the colorful fancy models you see in the beach skies today. But they flew and we had fun. George and Bert took us fishing, crabbing, clamming and hiking over and around the Arch Cape headland. George loved surf fishing. He made a triangular shaped "sled" with a hinged board that flopped down as the waves came toward shore and then became vertical when the wave action reversed seaward. The sled carried the fishing line far out into the surf. We relaxed on the beach with the line securely anchored, and later with great effort, we pulled in the sled and found fish on the many hooks attached to the line. Cousins and friends often tagged along with me when George and Bert drove to the vicinity of Sunset Beach near Ecola Park. We hiked down to the rocks where the men fished and we played in the surf, built sand castles and searched for shells. Other hikes over the Arch Cape Headland took us by Dichter's wooden water storage tanks on the slope south of Arch Cape Creek, to the Arch Cape Falls, over and around Hug Point, and at times, all the way to Cannon Beach.

My dad loved to take me clam digging. I walked ahead to find and circle the clam "hole" for him to dig. We made a super team! My cousins and friends did the same for Bert or any other adult who dug clams. Clam digging usually took place early in the morning. Clams were plentiful in the 20's, 30's, 40's and 50's. We always took along Bert's crab rake and usually brought home several crabs each time from the deep holes around the rocks. Clams and crab were regular fare for beach residents. It was time for breakfast when we returned to the cabin. George, known for his delicious pancakes, served breakfast to the hungry diggers and hole finders. No one made pancakes like George.

I remember large tide pools along the edge of the surf north of Arch Cape creek. These depressions, visible at low tide, became grand swimming pools. The trapped water warmed by the sun provided a safe and fun place to play. A deep hole in Arch Cape Creek near the highway bridge became another favorite play area for us.

Bert fell and broke a hip in 1962 and entered a Rockaway nursing home. My dad retired from his master mechanic job with the Creosote Plant in St. Helens and Mom and George moved to Arch Cape to care for Bert and his property. For years, Bert rented the log cabin and lived in a primitive, but comfortable, home next door. After moving to Arch cape in 1963, my parents, George and Clarrie Christie, made extensive additions to the structure next to the log cabin where Bert lived; they added to the back a bedroom, bathroom and a utility room. They remodeled the kitchen and finished the upstairs into three comfortable bedrooms. A fireplace completed the comfortable downstairs living area.

Bert died January 8, 1963, and my folks continued to live in the house and rent the log cabin. They purchased additional property north of the lot with the two houses, which gave them space for a garden, a garage and a workshop.

George loved animals and soon made friends with the neighborhood raccoons. The raccoon families came every night for a handout. Mr. and Mrs. Cory, who had the Cannon Beach Bakery, saved all the crumbs from the bread slicing machine which supplemented the bags of dog food George purchased. We found the garbage can that served as a container, for their food, needed a hinged lid with a good strong fastener to keep out the inquisitive raccoons' fingers. Soon, neighbors began arriving each evening to see the "raccoon show." One night, George put on a great spectacle. He had an old drop-leaf table on the east side of the house he used when feeding his animal friends. It held a pan of water and as George headed for the table to feed them, about a dozen raccoons moved in unison to his side of the table. This was too much. The table overbalanced. Water, food and raccoons were all over George. No harm done, but it generated hearty laughs from the audience. I have a picture in the cabin showing fourteen hungry little faces. For many years my mother and dad sent Christmas cards with raccoon designs.

My son, Dale Mosby, spent summers with his grandparents beginning in 1962 when he was eight years old. He loved the beach and George helped him make boats, fly kites, dig clams, rake for crabs and hunt for glass floats, just as he had done with me and my friends. Logs and drift were plentiful in those days and Dale and his friend, Bob Shaw, constructed many forts on the sand and spent countless hours in the surf. Dale was an eager participant when raising and lowering Lorna Conway's flag.

Dale's father, Art Mosby, and I spent many happy vacations at Arch Cape. We made our first visit together in 1938 when we were high school students. We married in 1942 and continued to vacation one or two weeks every summer in Bert's cabin, missing only two summers from 1942 to 1968. Dale and I moved to Arch Cape when Dale's dad died in 1968. We lived with my parents while my dad and my cousin's husband, Jay Potter, remodeled the cabin. Dale graduated from Seaside High School in 1972 and was one of the very few young people living here at the time.

On the night of April 6, 1970, Dale and his grandfather were beachcombing for glass floats when a sudden heart attack took George's life. It was a very difficult and sad time for my mother, Dale, and me. In retrospect, I'm certain this is the way George would have wanted it—quickly, on the beloved sands of Arch Cape. My mother died June 19, 1983. My parents, George and Clarrie Christie belonged to the era of early Arch cape property owners: the Conways, The English girls, Countrymans, Leeches, Mrs. Archer, Gelinskys, Mr. Maxwell and Bert Patton—all gone now but in memory they will never die.

Travis Tyrrell

After a thirty-five year forestry career with the U. S. Forest Service and with the Bureau of Land Management, much of it in the mountains and deserts of Oregon, my wife Dorothy and I wanted to live on the Oregon coast. We had vacationed in the early 40's several times at Cannon Beach, so looked for coast property in that area. Several places were for sale from Cannon Beach south to Arch Cape. Of all of them, the most desirable was the Arch Cape Cottages owned by Elsie Leech Wood and Marshall Wood. We purchased the property and moved there in 1966. We continued renting some of the cottages, primarily to clients who had rented from the Woods. Most of the cottages and the owners' dwelling were of historic significance, having been built in 1925 and having housed Coast Guard personnel during World War II.

Dorothy brought her antiques business, Cold Comfort Farm Antiques, from our farm in Cedar Mill, Washington County, and relocated it in Cottage No. 1. Many of her clients continued to visit her.

Dorothy suffered a heart attack while walking the beach in 1969 and passed away at the Rinehart Hospital in Wheeler a few days later. Some two years later I met Irene Mosby, who also recently was widowed, and we were married. I moved to her home, the Bert Patton log cabin, and became part of her family. Her son, Dale, also lived there while attending Seaside High School and later Oregon State University.

My service to the community has included the County Planning Commission, the Southwest Coastal Design Review Committee, and the Sewer and Water Boards. I was one of the original members of the Arch Cape fire crew and assisted in the building of the fire hall. I also served on the Arch Cape Volunteer Fire Department and was on the Cannon Beach Fire Department board.

Dale Mosby, my son (as told by Dale)

My first memorable visit to Arch Cape in 1962 with my grandparents, George and Clarrie Christie, exposed me to a bit of the Oregon Coast I will cherish forever. It was a full summer of explorations, learning experiences, and memories eight-year-old boys never ever forget. I moved to Arch Cape in 1968. By comparison to other places along the coast, Arch Cape may still seem rural; however, when compared to nearly thirty years ago, there are many changes. Sand covered most of the rocks toward the dune line then. Logs and drift were everywhere. I could walk from Ocean View Avenue to Arch Cape Creek on logs, never touching sand or water. Asbury Creek, a little to the north, was a trap for driftwood. One could always cross the strong-flowing creek over the many large logs the high tides and west winds stacked there. As the logging practices changed, the great quantities of logs and drift no longer flowed down the rivers, so driftwood on the beach was dramatically reduced. The many years of bonfires and wood cutters with chain saws after firewood removed just about all drift and logs from the Arch Cape beach. Only large stumps remain, and they keep moving north helped by strong winds and high tides.

Drift seemed infinite to a small boy thirty years ago, for I believed it would fuel beach fires forever. The great quantity of wood was wonderful for building monstrous bonfires, windbreaks and forts. The forts provided shelter for many nights spent on the beach. The logs also allowed for the construction of bridges across Arch Cape Creek. In the summer, these bridges might last for weeks, depending on the rains and tides. On the north side of the stream, where three new homes were recently constructed, a thick grove of trees with interlocking branches created an area in perpetual shadow in its center. A huge pile of drift to the west of the grove hid a fort. A small opening allowed adventurous children to wiggle down through the logs and hide in a cavern with a sandy floor large enough for two or three young boys to sit hidden from all who passed by. A trail of boards led through some swampy land to Cannon Street where it made a turn and ran under the bridge where Highway 101 crosses over the creek.

I enjoyed walks on the beach with my grandfather, especially to Arch Cape Creek. Sometimes my grandfather used his sharp pocket knife to quickly turn driftwood into small boats, which my friends and I sailed in the stream. I recall his carving some spears once and constructing some sort of stick and rope apparatus which allowed us to hurl them a long distance down the beach. One summer he made some wonderful wooden swords for us. They had large curved wooden blades resembling the swords we imagined pirates used.

Our explorations of the Arch Cape area took us to the shingle mill. I remember walking through the mill with my grandfather and thinking how amazing the big equipment and huge saws all were. We went target shooting just east of the shingle mill, the area then being unpopulated. The mill burned in 1967 and the log holding ponds were drained and filled.

My friends and I enjoyed hikes up the stream bed and often camped a day or two above the falls. We also hiked in the hills south of the creek where the wooden water storage tanks were located. It was great fun to climb to the top of the tanks and peer in at the water.

I walked the beach in search of glass floats when the strong winter west winds blew for several days and made the surf wild. I left late at night or very early in the morning to be the first person on the beach to find floats. Boots and heavy rain gear kept me sheltered from the elements. I kept a watchful eye for sneaker waves during high water and ran for the rocks when necessary.

Grandpa and I clammed during the early morning summer minus tides. We'd hit the beach more than an hour before the tide changed and follow the tide out for the last hour of its westward journey in our search for razor clams. The limit was 24 clams per digger. On those first trips, I hunted and marked the clam holes for my grandfather, but soon learned to dig my own. Grandpa taught me how to dig clams without cutting my fingers on the shells or breaking the shells with my shovel. When one faces the prospect of cleaning two dozen clams, the difference in cleaning them with whole or broken shells becomes very apparent. I was told one could dig unlimited numbers of clams in the early days. Little did I know on those trips back from the beach with our easily reached limit of two dozen clams each, just how wonderful an accomplishment that would be today. Some mornings our clam digging took us to Falcon Beach where I stopped to examine the tide pools around the arches and Bird Rock. Our dug clams were rinsed in a small tide pool on our way home and then placed in buckets of clean sea water for an hour or two so the clams could pump sand from their systems.

I attended Seaside High School, and for a time, was the most southerly student in attendance there. I was never bored living in Arch Cape as there were many things to do, such as exploring the beach and the surrounding foothills.

I learned photography, both picture taking techniques and darkroom film and photo processing skills, by working for the school newspaper and for the high school annual. I did free-lance photography for Seaside and Wheeler newspapers, and built my own photo processing facility at home to process my work. At times, those papers sent me on special photo assignments. During summer vacation I distributed papers to news stands and had the challenge of computing how many had been sold the past week and how to estimate accurately how many to leave for the next week. It became a game, for the goal was to come as close as possible to selling all the papers without actually running out before the next week's delivery.

I entered Oregon State University in 1972, graduating in engineering, and presently work for the *Sequent Corporation* in Beaverton.

I find time to visit Arch Cape often on vacations and weekends. I became a white water kayaker and explored many Oregon rivers before playing in the waves on the coast. The kayak is at the beach now and is used often. I have kayaked around Castle Rock and observed the coastline from the rock's perspective.

The 4th of July brought bonfires and fireworks displays then just as it does now. Displays often seemed quite large and impressive for many more fireworks items were legal then. One year, the family staying a few houses to the south of us had many fireworks, including a shopping bag full of firecrackers. The kids grabbed handfuls and ran around the beach lighting them. Some years later I began working on the Fort Vancouver 4th of July celebration and learned how to set off the large fireworks used in commercial shoots. For a few years I obtained a permit to hold a shoot at Arch Cape and enlisted the help of a few friends. We held fireworks displays on the beach at the end of Ocean View Avenue to celebrate the 4th of July. The first year we placed the mortars which launch the shells a bit too close to the ocean and had to haul them up higher on the beach as the tide came in midway through the show. The following day my mother, with others who watched the show, cleaned the debris left on the beach from explosions bursting paper to bits. It was a thankless job but the area was always left impeccable. I am now a licensed ham radio operator, and in 1991 several of my friends and I held the annual field day trials at the Tyrrell property on Gelinsky Avenue.

I chose an engineering profession that keeps me in a metropolitan area. Still, like my parents and grandparents, I spend all the time I can in Arch Cape just as they did in those early days and look forward to the time when I can become a full-time Arch Cape resident.

Bert Patton's cabin, facing south, before the chimney was finished. Note the heavy growth of timber and the size ot the tree on the right side of the picture. Circa 1921.

Albert C. (Bert) Patton on the beach at Arch Cape. Circa 1921.

Photos this page and the next page, Irene Tyrrell collection.

Bert Patton and Edna Christie. Circa 1940.

Front room of Bert's first log cabin.
Table, benches, hutch and corner
cupboard were made by Bert and are
in use today.

Dale Mosby in Arch
Cape in 1991 during the
ham radio operators'
field day.

> *George and Clarrie*
> *Christie in front of*
> *Castle Rock. Circa*
> *1963.*

Irene Christie Mosby
Tyrrell, Edna Christie and
Art Mosby in 1940 during
construction of the present
cabin.

Spoondrift
The Maddison-Reynolds Connection
By James M. Reynolds and David Maddison

James Reynolds

T he Maddison and Reynolds families have Arch Cape roots beginning about 1932. The connection starts with Clinton and Jessie Reynolds. Their sons, Robert and James, entered Lowell Middle School in Tacoma where Elsie English was principal. Also, our mother's best and closest cousin was chief surgeon at the Northern Pacific Hospital in Glendive, Montana, where Irene English was head nurse. It was these early associations that brought attention to Arch Cape. The Reynolds family always gravitated to the coast. When a child, my mother spent a summer in Chinook on the Washington side of the Columbia River, about 1912.

The Reynolds family were summer *Singing Sands* visitors in the 30'. *Singing Sands* was the hotel purchased by Marie and Elsie English from Marmaduke Maxwell in 1929 and it became a desirable destination for those wanting isolation, good company, and a beach that sang when one walked on the dry sand. I remember my first visit to Arch Cape, at age six or seven, in 1933 or 1934. My first drive around Hug Point was outside the point on a very low tide rather than driving over the carved out rugged cliff road with steep entry and exit grades that challenged 1930 automobiles. Most had to negotiate the rugged road, for it was a rare low tide when one could drive around Hug Point. I vividly recall a trip in a 1935 Ford with my grandmother at the wheel using language I had never heard before.

Kerosene lamps, candles, the English girls, the lovely sand used to build endless sand castles, the falls up Arch Cape Creek, elk in the wild surf are all memories never to be lost. The memories are many—a bull elk near the mill, the famous falls on the creek, a huge surf tossing sixty-foot logs like match sticks and the water coming in the front door of *Singing Sands* and out the back door. (We opened the back door to let it out.) The Reynolds family visited the cape and the arches at least twice a year. The trips to and from Tacoma and the cape were always interesting and a kind of history of the urbanization of the United States.

I was always aware of the desire of my parents to somehow get a lock on the area. I can remember the day my father announced that they had a chance to acquire Dora Cornelieson's house. I'm sure it was prior to 1944 and that it had to do with Dora's will: if her heirs did not wish to have the house, then the Reynolds family had the first rights to buy it. It is at this point that Dr. Frank and Betty Maddison enter the picture. I believe my father involved them to defray costs. At the time, Doctor Frank was the family physician and the two families were on close terms. I ended up marrying their daughter, Patty, in 1950, but for the life of me I do not remember her in connection with Arch Cape. I do not have any real recollection of Dora Cornelieson except of an elderly lady, large, and dressed in white who sat a lot.

I do recall my disappointment in about 1936 or 37 to find that the road had been cut through the head at Hug Point and you got down to the beach just south of Hug at the "orange and blue trimmed motel." I can remember walking to Hug Point and not being aware of any houses. The road and tunnel ended all that. In the spring of 1942 my brother, our mother and

I stayed at *Singing Sands* for a week. The war was on and we were in the dark at sunset. The water temperature was up in the 60's, the surf was huge and the skies were blue. My brother and I dug a great pit into which all the tin cans left over from the tunnel workers were thrown into and then buried. The workers had tossed the cans and other litter out the kitchen window of *Singing Sands*. It was the first time any of us had been to Short Sands Beach and over the trail to Cape Falcon. It was a very memorable visit. My father, Clinton, was in Washington, D. C., fighting the war.

(John Conway and his wife, Lorna, had a home three lots north of Leech Avenue. Here is an entry from John's diary: "1948—Uncle Sid tried to purchase the Maxwell house from the Cornelieson girls. He offered them $3,500. The house was sold to the Maddison and Reynolds families from Tacoma, who are friends of the English girls, for $5,000.")

I can remember when the first crab pots were allowed offshore, in 1948 or so. There was a time in 1937, I believe, when Marie English said, "We've got 14 people coming to dinner. Bob, Jim, you go get seven crabs and be quick about it. Make sure you get only male ones and be sure they are all about the same size. Now scoot." We were back in less than one-half hour with the crabs.

It was seldom that the Maddisons and Reynoldses were at the cape at the same time even before they bought Dora's house. It was named *Spoondrift* and was a **time share** arrangement. They were involved with the water system and repair to neighborhood rose gardens. Both Frank and Clinton were avid and competitive rose growers and both used the beach as a place to restore their roses and themselves. We all did. I am happy to see my children doing the same. (Authors' note. Frank and Clinton shared their prize-winning rose bushes with Elsie and Marie English and with Irene and John Countryman as well as with others in the neighborhood. Those rose bushes were part of area gardens for years until a bad freeze destroyed many of them.)

I would say that the Reynolds/Maddisons could be considered itinerants. Their involvement in Arch Cape was minimal. As the years went by, they relied heavily on Floyd "Scotty" Scott to look after their interests and pretty much followed his lead.

In the late 60's my mother suffered a stroke and my father sold his interest in the property to the Maddisons about 1969.

In 1968, Patty and I divorced. Since then I've had few contacts with the property, but my children have been there off and on.

(The co-author has a vivid memory of Jessie Reynolds. I returned from Japan, in September, 1945 and was at the Madigan Hospital near Fort Lewis, Washington, when Mrs. Reynolds appeared beside my bed. We had a great visit discussing my aunties and the beach. I had been away for five and one-half years. When she left, a box of chocolates was placed on my bed-side table.)

David Maddison

My recollections of Arch Cape are of a young boy thoroughly enjoying a carefree time at the beach. The transition of staying at the *Singing Sands Hotel* to *Spoondrift* must have been an insignificant event to me. I recall from family discussions that our first visits must have been in the late 40's or early 50's when I remembered Dr. John and Irene Countryman and Elsie and Marie English.   They played a significant role in the Maddison interests in Arch Cape.

My wife and I remember that my father bought out Jessie and Clinton Reynolds' interests in *Spoondrift* sometime in the late 60's. After my father's death, my mother continued to care and enjoy *Spoondrift* until her health no longer allowed to care for the place as she did in the past. Today, the house is, as best I can recall, the same as it was years ago. Windows have been enlarged and replaced, the back porch was enlarged and became part of the kitchen; the ice box was replaced with a refrigerator; heaters were installed in the bedrooms and in the bathroom; and a hot water tank furnished water. Before, hot water came from pipes behind the fireplace and from coils in the kitchen wood cook stove. Later, the cook stove was converted to gas surface burners and a gas oven.

After a number of years, since both Frank and I are still a long distance from Arch Cape (I'm in Idaho and Frank in Wisconsin), my brother decided he would like to sell his half interest in *Spoondrift*. After several months went by with no reasonable offers, my nephews, Adam and Aaron, were together for some occasion and Adam told Aaron about the house being on the market. Aaron became a half owner of Spoondrift in 1989 thus establishing again, much to my delight, the Maddison/Reynolds presence at Arch Cape.

The Maddison family at Spoondrift. From left to right: David, Betty, Frank, Pat and Frank Jr, in a '49 Olds. The east side of the Singing Sands Hotel shows in the background. Circa 1950. David Maddison collection.

This is the pathway between the Scott and the Maddison homes that led to the beach at the end of Maxwell Avenue. From left to right: Dr. Melvin Beemer, his son Scott, Floyd "Scotty" Scott, Elsie English, Marie English, Polly Beemer, Ella Scott, Jessie Reynolds, Irene Countryman and Clinton Reynolds. Photo, James Reynolds collection.

The Markham Connection
Memories by Mamie Markham

My husband, Wilbur "Bill" Markham, came to Clatsop County as a logging engineer for the Crown Zellerbach Corporation in 1933. At that time, the company was known as the Crown Willamette Paper Company. Bill graduated from the University of Washington with a master's degree in Forestry. Each weekend he roamed and explored the beaches and forest lands around Cannon Beach and southward toward the Arch Cape headland. It was 1935 when I saw the northern Oregon Coast for the first time, and I, too, fell in love with the area despite arriving in drenching rain, getting stuck in the sand, being pulled to safety, and then drying out in the Hug Point cave. I graduated from the University of Washington with a degree in math and physics and worked in the Actuarial Department of the Northern Life Insurance Company. When in Arch Cape, Bill and I walked the beach many times, often in the rain, while admiring the solitude, isolation, and incomparable beauty. We loved the green growth from the seashore to the hills rising just east of this spectacular bit of paradise.

We married in May, 1936. We loved Arch Cape and decided we wanted to live near the beach close to this very spot. Bill constructed a garage on land we purchased from Dow Walker at the foot of what is now Marshall Avenue and Pacific Street. A gigantic branched spruce beautifully sculptured by the winds framed the path to the ocean from our new home site.

Mr. Walker lived where the Williamson's house presently sits at the west end and north side of Ocean Road. Ocean Road is the route from the Arch Cape store and post office to the beach. Mr. Walker's garden was on the south side of Ocean Road just off of the beach, and it was a beauty, featuring vegetables along with spectacular formal garden plantings. The only roads open at that time were Ocean Road from the highway to Pacific Street and up Pacific Street as far as our home at the foot of Marshall Avenue.

Dow Walker owned most of the property in the area at that time. Running water came from a spring located on the east side of the highway. In 1939, this same spring furnished water to the old post office and store. Ernest White later purchased that system, along with all of Dow Walker's property. Later, he sold the water system to the Dichter brothers. There were only two homes on the system in 1936—ours and Walker's.

With a bathroom added to the south end, the original garage became our first home. Our furniture was Spartan in our newly converted garage: two chairs, a card table, a mini-stove, a few kitchen utensils, powder (dynamite) boxes for kitchen cabinets, and more powder boxes propping up a spring and mattress. The well-made powder boxes with dove-tailed corner joints were strong, uniform in size and easy to arrange for many purposes. Our first purchase was a kitchen range with hot water coils feeding into a hot water storage tank. The exterior boards dried and allowed wind to whistle through cracks, bringing dampness and considerable discomfort. Friends who came to visit, and you have many when you live at the beach, helped us shingle our shiplapped house. The tar paper and shingles made a great change in warmth and comfort, which was a blessing during stormy periods.

Both grocery stores in Cannon Beach made deliveries to the Arch Cape area. One store delivered two times a day and the other store delivered *The Oregonian* while making their deliveries. That first year was a great "rabbit" year. Bill often shot a rabbit on his way to his job. We soon found out that one could tire eating rabbit every other day. Razor clams were plentiful at Seaside and we dug every other Sunday when tides were right. We stopped at Haystack Rock on our way home to gather littleneck clams from under rocks and seaweed and crabs from tide pools.

We rented a house in Seaside for the winter because days were too short without electricity. It was a difficult drive from Arch Cape to Cannon Beach, especially over the unsurfaced road from Arch Cape to Hug Point.

We installed a floor and added a room to our house during the '36-'37 winter shut-down at Crown. Bill was off work much longer than he expected because of the labor unrest at the time in the logging and sawmill industry. It was a cold winter; snow and ice added to our discomfort.

Bill received an offer, at three times his previous salary, to go to Mindanao, Philippine Islands, as a logging engineer for the Philippine Cabinet Timber Company. He left in March, 1937, and I moved back to Arch Cape to complete the carpenter work we had started so we could rent our cabin. Mr. and Mrs. R. B. Jennings lived there while their home was under construction.

I sailed on the *President McKinley* in August of 1937 for the Philippine Islands. The ship stopped first in Shanghai on its way to Hong Kong to load refugees fleeing from the advancing Japanese. Then, the ship continued to Manila. My introduction to the Philippines was on the aftermath of an earthquake that wrecked many buildings. A small inter-island boat took me to Cebu, where Bill met me for the last part of my journey to Cabadbaran, Mindanao. We lived in town until the company built nipa huts for us on a spit that sheltered a bay, where we enjoyed many evening swims. Our huts were on stilts and really quite comfortable. The cook and caretaker had smaller nipa huts in back of our place and the whole area was blessed with many tall palm trees. We experienced a typhoon, the kind you read about in books and newspapers, that almost took us apart. We were just off the center, or the eye of the storm, and were wrapped in about 270 degrees of almost total destruction. The palm trees suffered, but survived.

Bill logged *lauan* (Philippine mahogany) for a Japanese company. He was superintendent and was in charge of the logging operation. He also mapped out the roads for the American-built gas-powered log trucks that moved the timber to the coast for shipment to Japan. The job terminated when the Japanese war with China expanded. Perhaps money was not budgeted to continue this operation or it was diverted for military use.

We moved to Baguio on northern Luzon where Bill worked for the Benget Consolidated Gold Mine. He supervised cutting pine timber into shoring material used in mine shafts. We remained in Baguio for about six months and sensed that Japan and the Philippines were heading for a showdown. Japanese were infiltrating and coming ashore with every ship. We knew a problem was coming and wanted to get home as soon as possible. Our son Jim was born in Baguio in 1939. Our doctor told us he should be at least six weeks old before leaving, but he was six months old before we were able to leave. We experienced so much red tape and graft and had to pay this fellow and that fellow so we could get out of the country. We returned to the United States on a Canadian vessel belonging to the Empress Line via Vancouver, Canada. The Empress boat, a coal burner, stopped in Nagasaki, Japan, to load coal. No men were left to do the loading, so women and children did the job hauling coal by the basket to the ship. It took them three days. The Japanese moved portable toilets on board for all passengers to use so they could collect the waste for fertilizer. They required passengers to supply a stool sample to validate that their waste was clean.

We returned to Arch Cape late in 1939 and remained here until winter set in and then we moved to Cannon Beach. We also lived for a time in Olney, Valsetz, and Glenwood, where Bill worked in the logging industry. We had short stays at Arch Cape in between these jobs, which continued until 1944. The government asked Bill to supervise an operation in British Honduras to log genuine mahogany for the war effort. We returned to Arch Cape for four months while paper work was being resolved.

I completed arrangements to purchase our present Arch Cape property while Bill was in British Honduras. I managed to be with him in Belize for five months after the war ended in 1945. After spending some time visiting relatives, we returned to Arch Cape in June, 1946.

A census was taken when Bill was in Belize, Honduras, and the census taker wanted to know where we were born. I told him my husband was born in Angola, Indiana; I was born in Walla Walla, Washington; Jim was born in Bagio, Luzon, the Philippine Islands; and John was born in Hood River, Oregon. The census taker wanted to know how we all got together!

We lived in the original Arch Cape house, with several structural additions, from 1946 until 1960. After the war, Bill decided to work for himself as an independent engineer doing land surveying and timber cruising. We wanted to remain in Arch Cape and raise our children without the constant moving we experienced in the past. Much of the property was not surveyed in those days, so among other jobs, Bill reset section corners and ran section lines for the Van Vleet Logging Company.

We finished our second home in 1960 on the property I purchased when Bill was in British Honduras. He moved an old house on the edge of our property to the lot June Murphy now owns. She purchased the lot and building, and in 1968 a fire badly damaged the home. June rebuilt and resides there at the present time. Joseph and Lynne Angel, from Portland, own our original home at the end of Marshall Avenue.

Bill put in the road from the highway to the house—formerly called *Hug Point Avenue*, which shows on the original plat map, and now named *Markham Avenue*. It became *Markham Avenue* in 1985 when house numbers were established so fire and medical vehicles would have an easier time finding a location during emergencies.

My husband was in business for himself until his death in 1981. His personality shows throughout the home. His exotic hardwoods are all over the house: the fireplace mantle, all the window sills, the walls and floors, and in many pieces of his own handcrafted furniture. Bill loved all woods, but he was especially fond of those woods that made him work hard to master and control. And he did it.

Our two sons are products of the Cannon Beach and Seaside schools. We were proud that an Arch Cape resident could be the valedictorian of his Seaside High School class. John Markham was that boy. Jim and John went to school by school bus and for eight years only Markhams rode the bus most of the time. Mrs. Cassidy drove her car as a school bus and complained that the boys never missed a day at school. Stinson Tarr took over when Mrs. Cassidy became ill. Tarr drove a station wagon, which the district later replaced with a school bus.

Jim and John received their Bachelor of Arts degrees from Stanford University. Jim went on to earn his Master's degree in Marine Botany at the University of Washington. His thesis research was conducted at the Friday Harbor Laboratories on San Juan Island, beginning in 1962 when the old Friday Harbor Laboratories were modernized to allow winter use. Jim spent the winter of 1962-63 at Friday Harbor and became one of the first four scientists to overwinter at the Friday Harbor Laboratories. Jim earned a Ph.D. from the University of British Columbia. His doctoral research concerned an ecological and taxonomic comparison of similar kelp plants found in Oregon and Alaska respectively, and involved reciprocal transplants of kelps between Alaska on one end and Arch Cape, Short Sand Beach, and Indian Beach on the other end. John received his Master's degree from Oregon State University, where he was one of the first to do research at the Mark Hatfield Marine Station in Newport, Oregon. He earned his doctorate from the University of Miami. Both boys earned Fulbright Scholarships. To continue their research, Jim spent a year in Norway and John, a year in Denmark.

In 1972-74, while living temporarily at Arch Cape with his wife Ella and working with his father in the land surveying business, Jim completed the first ever survey of the seaweeds of Clatsop County, which was published in 1976. The voucher specimens for this survey are deposited in the herbaria of the University of British Columbia and the University of California, Santa Barbara, where Jim is the Marine Biology Librarian.

Authors' Note

Mamie Markham is a basket weaver and has many of them displayed in her home. Today, she is an expert keeping alive a very ancient skill. She had a girl scout troop when the family lived in Valsetz and felt compelled to learn so she could teach her charges. Mamie plants her vegetable garden each year and makes blackberry dessert wine from berries picked all around her place. One needs to arise very early in the morning to beat Mamie to the beach. Dressed in her ever-present hooded rain gear and with her Australian sheep dog, Kintala, she heads for Arch Cape Creek and back at a pace most younger people would envy today.
(The family pet and companion, Kintala, died in the late spring of 1992.)

Arch Cape Memories — James W. Markham

With regard to growing up in Arch Cape, I'm not sure how much of what I remember is unique to Arch Cape and how much is just isolated country/beach living. Living at Arch Cape meant I rode on the school bus for eight years of grade school (Cannon Beach) and four years of high school (Seaside), whereas many of my classmates walked to school. It also meant that I rarely saw any classmates except in school. Some years there were two to four others close to my age living in the area and some years there were no others. Few working parents stayed very many years at Arch Cape.

I never had any marine project as such while in school (except for the time I extracted salt from sea water for a chemistry class) but a great deal of my free time was spent on the beach. Whether alone or with others, I played mostly on the beach, rarely in the woods. I dug clams, collected crabs, explored all of the beach, and did a lot of hiking and beachcombing. It was always interesting and every once in a while something exciting washed in. I found my first glass ball on a calm afternoon in July, which is not to be expected. I found a lot more after storms, when they are expected. I remember visiting Portland or Seattle occasionally and wondering what city kids did all day, especially in summer, and where in the world they played.

I really liked the Hug Point caves and got to know them very well. I still like to look at my favorite ones when I come to Arch Cape.

The arches had been buried and hidden by a slide (connected with the tunnel construction) before I came to Arch Cape. I listened to the stories of how people had walked and driven through them, had picnics near them, etc. I spent a lot of time climbing around and trying to figure out exactly where these people had been. The stories were conflicting, but I decided where I thought they had been, because I could see depressions in the rock of the Cape. When a big storm opened them up again (circa 1950), it was quite exciting to see them at last. It also turned out that I (and some of my informants) had been wrong about where they were. They were much farther east than I had expected.

Most of the time when I wasn't on the beach or in school, I read books. After all that, I became first a marine botanist, and then a marine biology librarian, so I have continued the way I started at Arch Cape.

Recollections of Life at Arch Cape — by John C. Markham

While writing this account, I have not felt constrained by any need for historical accuracy. This is intended to be a recollection of impressions which struck me, a growing, but not necessarily discriminating, boy, watching the Arch Cape scene and interacting with its changing cast of characters. Thus, it is essentially a series anecdotes, many of which I acknowledge to be trivial, but which have lodged in my memory. I leave it to my mother to provide a more accurate account of the family history, complete with dates and even some explanations of what was happening.

I arrived in Arch Cape, I am told, first in November, 1944, and again in the summer of 1946 as an involuntary, but uncomplaining, immigrant all of three years old. My parents, my older brother Jim, and I, with an oversized black cocker spaniel named Jackie, lived in the little house at the end of Marshall Avenue facing the ocean across a weedy lawn beneath two huge contorted spruces. Only later did I learn that my father began with a garage some ten years earlier and gradually added rooms as needed; that would explain our having a single entry into the house, through my bedroom, and down the stairs from the living room. Somehow, though, the arrangement seemed normal at the time. In a few years, my father doubled the size of the house by adding a kitchen with a door replacing the one in my bedroom. A second story made space for an office and a guest room. A formal front door on the south side and a fireplace completed the home then. Now, in effect, our back door led to the front yard and the front door to the back yard, so everything was in order. While at it, he built a separate garage and later expanded it westward to accommodate a shop.

It took awhile for me to learn exactly what it was that my father did at work. When he was home, though, he was always building. As soon as he had our house far enough along, he acquired a house two blocks north in Kent Price Park (now 1597 Pacific Street). Someone finished the exterior and my father took over the job of finishing the interior. Though too young to contribute, I did a lot of serious watching. One detail I especially remember was the installation of his trademark, a shiny red tindalo mantelpiece on the fireplace. Tindalo is a species of tree that has deep red wood so dense it does not float. Dad brought the tindalo boards from the Philippine Islands. Charles Wood, a ruddy-faced retiree who lived down the street, helped on the project and made a strong impression on me. He demonstrated how the belt on the cement mixer, in which he was preparing concrete for paving the driveway, could snap a strong stick, and would do the same to errant fingers. When that house was finished, my father sold it to the Borquists, who stayed there in the summers.

My father had a block of property down the beach on which stood a little house, and which was built on two levels to fit the sloping ground. This house, thereafter, we referred to as the "Little House." My father remodeled the interior, and for several years my parents rented it to tourists spending a week or longer when visiting the beach. Among the regular renters were the Rognesses, who many years later built a home in Arch Cape. My father also constructed a cabin for Mary Walsh on the south side of Maxwell Avenue. Then he undertook the building of a larger house on some of his own property east of the highway and south of the store. This time I was able to help, particularly on parts of the interior. When finished, the house stood unused until the Congers bought it, also as a vacation retreat. That done, all of us launched into building a home for ourselves, of which I'll mention more later. At various times, my father did partial or extensive interior remodeling for neighbors. His final house, near the highway on Markham Avenue (formerly Hug Point Avenue), eventually became Jim and Ella's home, across the street from the Watsons' house today.

Arch Cape always was a one-dimensional world. Because the ocean blocked the front and the hills the back, we could move along only a narrow line north or south. As a result, I have always had trouble finding my way around any community where I have to contend with two dimensions. Similarly, the ocean defines "west" so emphatically, that I have a strong sense of direction at home and severe disorientation elsewhere, to say nothing of total confusion when living on the east coasts of Florida and Mexico.

Our particular part of Arch Cape was probably the most densely inhabited. Most of the houses were always occupied so we had numerous neighbors. Just to the south lived the Pomfret family. He was a professional builder and left a significant mark on Arch Cape, as the houses he built remain distinctive. The next house belonged to the Mellingers, who lived in Arch Cape off and on for many years. South of them lived the Lensrud. Mr. Lensrud was our own concert violinist and Mrs. Lensrud, the doting grandmother to all of the neighborhoods's children. Mrs. White ran the store and post office with her son, Ernest , formerly a surveyor with the army engineers in The Dalles, Oregon.

On the corner was Blanch Mellinger, known to us as "Bee," so we called the street to the store "Bee's Road." Even now, I have trouble remembering the name Ocean Road, its real name. Blanch Mellinger was a retired teacher who occasionally was a substitute in the Cannon Beach grade school.

On the opposite corner lived the Woods, who were both from England. Next, in a large house that she had built herself, lived Mrs. Williams. She was extremely memorable, sufficiently eccentric to keep any child wide-eyed. Whenever a tide covered the beach with *Velella* , an excellent but smelly fertilizer for her very productive vegetable garden, she plodded down in her shapeless raincoat, sloppy wool socks and heavy hiking boots to fill her homemade sideless wheelbarrow. She periodically assured me that she was "crazy"; I was unsure what the term meant, but it seemed an entertaining condition. I certainly never feared her. Beside her house was a deep thicket of blackberries and she claimed credit (or blame) for introducing the species to Arch Cape.

Farther south, and not so properly in my neighborhood by my reckoning, lived Eva Benson, a likable, bookish woman. East of her house in a bachelor's nest lived Bert Patton with his loyal German shepherd, Ginger. Bert cut a familiar figure as he sauntered to the post office with his hands clasped behind his back. In the next block south lived Dr. and Mrs. Countryman. Beside them in the Arch Cape Hotel were Elsie and Marie English. South of Leech Avenue was the home of Rubena Cassidy, a sometime professional singer. I heard her perform a time or two in the Cannon Beach Presbyterian Church. It was difficult, however, for a small boy to make an objective assessment of a lyric soprano. There were some people who lived along Arch Cape Creek, but I never knew them very well.

To the north of us in Kent Price Park lived the Overtons, and east of the road and farther along on the ocean front, the Deacons. Westall Deacon was a professional portrait photographer who must have had difficulty making a living in a place as small as Arch Cape. We have pictures of Jim and me he took in his studio.

The next house, a small one on a large lot next to Sally's Alley, belonged to Kent and Dorothy Price. They had a poodle named Molly that, I understand, closely resembled the dog Sally that belonged to the Kent Price Sr. family. The path from Pacific Street to the ocean beach was named after the poodle, Sally. The only other permanent residents of Kent Price Park, so far as I knew, were the Huntleys on the hill. On the east side of the highway were the Tuttles and, in their new duplex, the Ericksons. I didn't know of any permanent residents north of Asbury Creek.

There were other houses in Arch Cape and I knew some of the nonresident owners. It was evidently a popular place for tourists since rentals were available. The Tuttles operated the *Skyline Cottages*; the Whites ran the apartments connected to the store; we had our *Little House;* Bert Patton rented his log house; and farther south were the *Arch Cape Hotel*, the *Arch Cape Cottages* on Leech Avenue, and Mrs. Cassidy's elegant *Stormcliff Apartments* south from where Elsie Wood lives today.

There were always a few other children in the community, some of whom were occasionally my playmates. Often though, my brother Jim and I were largely on our own when it came to playing. The beach provided opportunities for play, such as damming streams and exploring caves. We constructed forts in the front yard made of anything we could find and once experienced a heavy and very noisy hailstorm beneath an inverted copper boiler. On the north edge of the yard was a crooked spruce tree that formed an archway leading to an inviting plot of old-growth forest. It took little imagination to populate that glade with exciting characters, and it was always an adventure to follow the trails through it.

I once came up with the idea that I should run away from home, even though the only plan I had was to start out through that special bit of woods. Before my departure, my mother took me to Deacons' to have my picture taken and then duly asked me where I would go if I ran away. Suddenly I realized that if I went beyond the woods, I would wind up right where I already was. I saw my scheme collapse and promptly had to abandon the whole idea.

For some years, my parents had only one car, which my father took to work. On a few occasions, my mother with me in tow boarded an Oregon Motor Coach bus for a ride into Seaside. After stops at Safeway, Piggly Wiggly and wherever else, we had lunch in a cafe and then returned home by bus.

There was no such thing as kindergarten, so first grade was the start of my formal schooling. Transportation to school was by Mrs. Rubena Cassidy in her new car, a wooden-paneled station wagon. She had a convertible before named *Stormy* because it was labeled "*Stormcliff Apartments*" on the sides. She always had enough capacity for the few pupils in Arch Cape and Tolovana Park. As a special bonus, she annually invited us to stop by on Halloween for her fine pumpkin pie. When she moved, the operation of the grade school bus passed briefly through the care of Graydon Pace, the *Oregonian* deliverer from Cannon Beach. Then it came into the hands of Stinson Tarr. Mr. Tarr had originally built a garage near the northeast corner of Columbia and Pacific in *Kent Price Park* and then moved it to the north of Markham Avenue where he built a full-time residence. He erected a cleverly designed tar bucket at the edge of the highway and labeled it "S. W. Tarr," leading some people to think it meant Southwest Tarr Street. His bus was a 15-seat van painted proper school bus yellow; there were now enough pupils south of Cannon Beach to require two trips in and out each day.

My teacher in first grade, Grace Hendrickson, also taught the second grade. The six upper grades occupied the other two rooms in the Cannon Beach Grade School, and Jim's fifth grade shuttled back and forth between them. Miss Hendrickson maintained order and productivity for her first and second graders. The next year she remained as the Wolds came to rescue the rest of the school: Ole Wold was principal and seventh and eighth grade teacher, while his wife Mary taught the fifth and sixth grades and all of the school's music. Miss Hendrickson taught first and second grade in the mornings and third and fourth grade in the afternoons. The result was that I was out of school just after noon, so I attended every meeting of the Garden Club, the Library and Women's Club and a course in home nursing with my mother, though I can't say that I benefited much from that exposure. The next year Emma Gene Miller was added to the faculty as teacher of my third and fourth grade. Fifth and sixth grades were taught in the main building of the Cannon Beach Conference grounds, while a new classroom was built adjacent to the school and served the next year to house the seventh and eighth grades.

Finally, in 1954 when I was in the fifth grade, the new school was complete with four classrooms and a principal's office. District 37 was a masterpiece of personnel efficiency, consisting of five employees: a principal who also served as teacher of the seventh and eighth grades and boys' basketball coach; three other teachers, each teaching two grades; and a part-time janitor. The regular substitute for all teachers was Mrs. Dunne, who replaced Miss Hendrickson full-time after she left. Only much later did I learn that it was unusual for two grades to share a room, an arrangement that always seemed fine to us. In the lower grade we learned our own materials and had a preview of the grade to come; the next year we could show off our mastery to the grade behind us.

Mrs. Miller, who remained at Cannon Beach until after I graduated, had been an avid traveler since being widowed several years before. She also took movies, so we saw her visits to Hawaii and Europe and also starred in some of her films. All the time I knew her, she was also studying the history of Clatsop County, on which she published a book in 1958, *Clatsop County, Oregon, Its History, Legends and Industries.*

At first, music instruction was informal. Mrs. Densmore, a Cannon Beach resident, came in once a week to play the piano for our singing. Mary Wold, an accomplished pianist, provided music for the whole school, and using the tune of *On the Good Ship Lollipop*, helped us write a school song:

> *In our own school, Cannon Beach,*
> *By the Elk Creek and the ocean beach,*
> *We work and play with the friends we hold dear . . . . . .*

The entire student body once spent a whole school day repeatedly singing that song for a tape recording, on which each pupil also announced his name. When I was in the eighth grade, Mrs. Covey was engaged to start a school band. So, I received the required year of music instruction that was needed to join the high school band.

Recreation facilities at the school improved through the years. At first, we had a set of swings, a merry-go-round, a set of three horizontal bars and a "play-shed" with climbing bars inside. The new gymnasium was built when I was in second grade. This let us stay out of the bad weather during recess and gave us a proper court for basketball. It provided a setting for school programs, which had earlier been held in the Commercial Club building on the edge of the school grounds and near the highway. That building was later moved to the present site of the new Chamber of Commerce, whose function it served until it was torn down in 1989. In its final site, it was also Cannon Beach's first city hall.

A popular game in the gym was prison ball, played with a volleyball hurled against opponents and bounced off the walls. Because the nails securing the shingles extended through the walls, we wiped out many balls in the course of a few years. One year, out behind the new gym and the Commercial Club building, there was a huge pile of loose dirt. Most of the students spent their recesses burrowing and tunneling in this dirt to build *Groundhog Town*, a fine, if dirty, place to play. The teachers let us know that they didn't approve of our construction; however, as long as we were out of their sight behind the buildings, they could arrange not to see it. After all, we hadn't left the school grounds. Another time, as a preliminary to playground landscaping, the school yard was covered with conical shaped dump truck loads of topsoil, which served as blinds for hide-and-seek. Somebody came up with another use for the dirt, the dirt bomb: Pile the dirt high beneath a swing, then stand up and pump the swing as hard as possible, sit down quickly on the back swing, extend one's bottom below the swing seat and collide with the dirt pile to send it flying. Strangely, the dirty pants that resulted from these undertakings never seemed to perturb my mother.

With few exceptions, the Cannon Beach Cougars basketball team consisted of all the boys in the seventh and eighth grades. The cheerleaders were the girls in that same room. For home games, the entire student body turned out. For games away, the teacher-coach-principal simply took his whole class along to games, enlisting the help of a few parents, including my mother on occasion, to help with transportation. We once played a baseball game against Gearhart, and there were also some infrequent intramural girls' volleyball games. Also in our basketball "league" were Hammond, Gearhart, Seaside's Broadway, Manzanita's Pine Grove, Nehalem and Rockaway. All were pretty evenly matched except for our nemesis, Broadway, which we never managed to beat.

One summer afternoon, probably in 1952, some of my school classmates showed up at our door with Mr. Goldon, a man from Vancouver, Washington, who was promoting accordion lessons for children. My mother signed me up. Once a week a teacher came to our house to give lessons to George and Marilyn Mellinger and me. All through our lessons, our cocker Inky and Mellingers' terrier, Duke sat outside the door and both howled their displeasure over the sounds of the accordions inside.

After about a year I was the only accordion player left and the teacher stopped coming. We found another teacher, Mrs. Buehner, who lived behind the cemetery near Neahkahnie. She instructed me for awhile and then I switched to John Locke, who ran the store at Tolovana Park. I continued taking lessons from him all through high school.

During those years there were many changes in Arch Cape that affected me. Neighbors died and some moved away. Many newcomers arrived. House owners retired and became full-time residents. Perhaps the most disturbing happening was the destruction of the beloved woods north of our house to make room for a new house.

Kent Price decided the intake pipe in the Asbury (Astbury on old maps) Creek culvert under the highway wasn't adequate for his water system. We watched as he built his dam farther up stream. That done, he retired the old Shanks water tank beside the creek and I persuaded him to give me the pointed wooden spire from its top.

I discovered a good way to pick up a little money. I scrounged the beach and the highway for returnable bottles. They came in three denominations: beer (one cent); coke (two cents); and other pop bottles (three cents). Cans were worthless, but quite rare. Occasionally, tourists on the beach felt sorry for that ragged waif so they hurriedly emptied their bottles to donate to him. The community forest park on the north edge of Arch Cape Creek's mouth was often a good hunting place, though I was once astounded when a woman ran out of the woods there and accused me of wicked behavior. Only later did I learn there was an outhouse tucked into the woods and she must have been using it. The pickings along the highway also were often good and had the added benefit of a stop at the gas station, where Sally Brown always had a supply of her peanut butter cookies on hand. Mrs. Peckover, who then ran the store, gamely bought all my bottles, even when I presented a couple containing the liquefied remains of drowned mice. When Mrs. LeGault later took over, though, she refused to accept my bottles on grounds that I had not bought them there, so I had to have them shipped to Seaside. On mornings when I went out walking the beach, Inky always went with me; otherwise, he had his own private patrol that kept him away from home for an hour or so each morning.

Over a period of many years, the winding highway to the north was gradually improved. The cut through the backbone of Tillamook head reduced the climb and the number of sharp curves on the road. The Cannon Beach bypass sped the way south. I do not remember the first telephones in Arch Cape; they were serviced by a switchboard in Seaside. The first one I knew was the automatic-dial Cannon Beach exchange using three numbers, with Seaside a long-distance call away to the old switchboard system. So far as I know, all Arch Cape numbers were in the 300's. When the seven digit numbers came in September, 1957, HEmlock 6-2xxx was affixed to our three digits. For some years it was possible to identify old Arch Cape numbers by their former HE (later 43) 6-23xx.

Sometime around 1950, my mother decided Jim and I should witness television. At that time, there were no stations in Oregon, but a pioneer cable system in Astoria permitted reception there of Seattle stations. She took us to the John Jacob Astor Hotel, where the maitre d´hôtel ushered us into the lobby and ceremoniously seated us before a tiny set, enhanced with a magnifying lens, which he turned on for our private viewing. When Portland stations were on the air in the middle 50's, some of our neighbors erected tall spindly antennas to catch the signals. Somehow, we resisted the allure of television until the 1970's, when a reliable cable system was in place and the telecasts were entirely in color.

In the spring of 1957 my father bought a power mower, and suddenly I was a professional lawn mower. I don't know what the neighbors had done before (Jim had handled some lawns, using an antique hand mower), but the demand for my services seemed remarkably great. To the north, I mowed for Miss Jepsen and Berkeley and Betty Snow, who had just moved to Arch Cape. To the south, I mowed for Ralph Forbes and Dr. Carter. Elsie English coordinated the mowing of the extensive lawn around her two houses, the Countryman's, the Maddison/Reynolds's and Mary Walsh's small lawn. That was also the first time I met Emil Gelinsky and his sister, Mrs. Holderman. When I first mowed his lawn, Mr. Gelinsky pointed out that his house, the oldest in Arch Cape, was exactly 50 years old. He proudly showed off the electrical wiring which had just been installed. Farther down that same street, I mowed the lawn for Frieda Billings at the edge of Leech Avenue. I did other lawns occasionally when their owners were gone and unable to keep them up. Within a few months, with the aid of parentally furnished transportation, I took on several lawns in Tolovana Park. With a succession of mowers, I continued those jobs through my high school years, even though I was severely allergic to airborne pollen.

In the fall of 1957, after some years of planning, designing and redesigning, we finally started building our "dream house" at the end of Hug Point Avenue (now Markham Avenue). First, it was necessary to fell the dead spruce trees still standing on the property. Some of their wood was sound enough to be cut into lumber, which came back from the mill to be installed later as ceiling material. The first major construction occurred one day in mid-September, when the concrete was poured for the basement wall foundation. It was such an exciting event that my father, brother and I, furiously helping with the job, completely forgot that it was my mother's birthday. I think she eventually forgave that oversight under the circumstances. Though my father did hire several people for various parts of the job, he was the main builder of our house, and the other three of us, under his supervision, contributed a lot. Any sound pieces of cut beachcombed lumber went into the house's framing. Some archeologist of the future will have an agonizing time analyzing the components. One fine piece of beachcombed oak, when properly shaped, became the threshold at the front door. Combining Philippine hardwoods with a great variety of exotic paneling found for sale in Portland, my father produced a showplace to display rare and unusual woods. After too many times repainting the trim that the wind had sandblasted on our old house, we decided to put only natural cedar on the outside of the new house and let it weather. Shingles from the Arch Cape Mill covered the roof. We did all the plumbing and put water in all parts of the house. Dozens of electric circuits serve many outlets and lights, greatly reducing chances of overloads. My dad hired specialists to install tile and sheet rock ceilings in those places not featuring wood. Paul Bartells, who built the Gelinsky fireplace in 1907, came out of retirement to build the face of the fireplace. The great advantage of participating in all the construction is that we know exactly how the house went together, so when anything does cause trouble, we can track it down and make our own repairs. When I decide to add more lights and switches, I know where to tap into existing circuits. The drawback was that the house was not finished enough for us to move in until the spring of 1960, just in time for my father's birthday.

Despite its supposedly limited resources, Cannon Beach Grade School gave me more than enough preparation for high school, and Seaside High prepared me for any university. My freshman year, 1957-58, was the last for the old school, which had been built in 1914. After watching construction for a year, we moved into the new school the next fall, that being the second time I had helped initiate a new building. A cousin once asked me when had I decided to become a marine biologist. That made me realize that there was never any conscious decision. As long as I could remember, I had spent many hours poking around tide pools. When I started asking "What is that?" there were books at hand to help me find out. One of our regular renters gave me copies of Rachel Carson's books as they appeared, and they proved eye-opening. At Seaside High, the teacher I had for biology, Orrice Adler, was an inspirational instructor who would tolerate no nonsense. As a high school freshman, I did not realize that she was actually teaching a college course in both style and content, but only in retrospect can I fully appreciate that it was exactly the background I needed to start me on my career.

Jim and John Markham, 1948. Photo by
Westall Deacon, a photographer who lived
and had a studio in Arch Cape.

The Markham tree.

Bill and Jim in 1944. The same crab ring is hanging in the garage today.

Bill and Mamie. 1981.
Photos, Mamie Markham collection..

Arch Cape Memories—the Store and Post Office
By Dorothy Meece

It was a perfect September day for a drive to the Oregon Coast. Many fond memories of the south Clatsop beaches brought us from Spokane, and the grocery and post office for sale in Arch Cape was the lure.

As a youngster, I remember that our family stopped for candy or soft drinks at the Arch Cape store. During the 30's the store was part of the post office housed in what is now the motel. Mr. Ernest White, Doc Collingswood, Mrs. Peckover and Ethel LeGualt are a few of the proprietors recalled by long-time residents. Ethel LeGualt was the creator of the present facilities. You found more milk and soft drinks in the cooler than beer at that time. Residents like Betty Bridget Snow shopped "Safeway Specials" to help stock the shelves and Floyd Scott helped out in the morning serving customers while Ethel took care of the daily mail.

In 1971 Ron and Yvonne Rothert purchased the store. Their son George and his wife Marcia became managers. George had many innovative ideas and made changes in the total operation of the store. As a wine connoisseur, George established a reputation for the store in Arch Cape. It became known for its selection of domestic and imported wines. His delicatessen was another first here and attracted many tourists, often whole bus loads on the way to somewhere. That all led to the catering pickle logo designed by Joannah Carlson Hagland, the granddaughter of long-time resident Myrle (Nonnie) Grohs. The logo can be described as a large dill pickle which carries a tray high in the air, ladened with gourmet delicacies and wine.

George Rothert installed a row of school desks in front of the store facing the highway and the hills to the east for customers to enjoy the morning sun and fresh air as they read their mail or visited with friends. Today, a long bench, sometimes used by highway travelers as a bed for the night, has replaced the desks.

Marcia Rothert ran the post office Saturdays. When postal clerk Cliff Harrison retired, the Rotherts were awarded the U. S. Post Office contract. George added two Texaco pumps after Berry Miller closed his Texaco station across the highway. After ten years and two daughters, it was time for a change for the Rotherts and that change was their move to Portland.

On January 2, 1981, the Arch Cape store became our four-faceted business: a grocery store, a deli, a post office and a gas station. For an industrial engineer and a home maker, it was a challenge. Jack stayed one week, as he had to return to terminate his sales position in Spokane. After a week's training for me on post office regulations, George headed for Portland. With Marcia as my guardian angel, along with Cheri Lerma, now the owner of the Cannon Beach Cookie Company, and Jack Shields, chair of the Clackamas Community College Drama Department, who was on sabbatical, we made it through the seven days each week that first January and February. It took me that long to learn how to open the temperamental old safe in less than forty-five minutes and how to clean the meat slicer without cutting a finger.

Pumping gas was a feat of its own. I forgot to release the pump lock on the nozzle when removing the nozzle from the car I was filling with gasoline one morning. Gasoline ricocheted off of the side of a pick-up truck and splashed all over me from my hair on down to my shoes. I was alone at the time. Fortunately, Marcia arrived and took over while I went home and showered. We learned to let motorcycle owners fill their own gas tanks, for they resented having a single drop spilled on their machines.

Jack terminated his job and returned in March; by that time we had experienced our first power outage and our first break-in. A dream helped me understand the baffling finance question. "The money I held in one hand paid the bills I held in the other hand, and the books balanced." That's all there was to it—a **sweet dream.**

Jack and I moved into the motel in July, then owned by Jan Goffinet Tarr as Viviane Karney wanted her home, which we had been renting since January. We managed the motel during the winters for Jan for several more years. We liked the convenience of living close to our place of business so began building our home directly west of the store the following September in 1981.

Our days began at six a.m. on weekends when I baked pecan rolls in my home to accompany the morning coffee at the deli. The Twinkie men didn't deliver this far south of Tolovana nor did they deliver this far north of Manzanita. The day I sold all my rolls, even before they came out of the oven, was the day I changed to fresh apple turnovers and muffins. I had to watch myself when rounding the corner of the store with a tray of hot turnovers. They were known to slide off. Log truck drivers and craftsmen were regular customers.

On passing the telephone booth early Sunday morning on a three day weekend to do the baking, I came upon nine-year-old Eric Woods with a distraught Mexican migrant worker who was trying to make a call to his employer. Lorenzo had been accidentally left by his friends. We had a problem; none of us was bilingual. With hand signs and information on his green card, we made his call. Someone would come to Arch Cape for Lorenzo. After giving cookies and milk to Lorenzo,and putting my sticky buns in the oven, I called Ed Cornelius in Falcon Cove. Ed is owner of Pace, which produces materials to teach English as a second language, and he spoke with our Mexican friend..

Eric took Lorenzo to the beach for awhile, as he was trying to promote a ride home from shoppers in the store. A second call to his employer was bad news: No ride was coming for Lorenzo. Just then, a Greyhound bus whizzed by. A Greyhound bus! That would have to be the answer. Jack drove our stranded friend to catch up with the bus, and in Tillamook, Lorenzo boarded the bus and was on his way home to North Plains, Oregon.

Arch Cape, located between two outstanding state parks, welcomes many vacationers and surfers searching for action. Jack and I had the only post office on Highway 101 with no turn-off necessary. We served many vacationers from all over the world during the summer Olympics in Los Angeles in 1984; and the World's Fair in Vancouver, British Columbia, Canada, in 1986. One letter arrived at our Post Office in 1985 addressed: **Dad, General Delivery**. This was a mystery, but the return address gave us a clue. It was simply **Roz,** followed with a five-pointed star. With a bit of thought, we delivered it to Ron Summers, father of figure skater Rozlynn Summers, a United States silver medal winner in the 1984 Winter Olympics. Ron was a temporary Arch Cape resident while writing a book.

The store almost made *People Magazine* when Jean Auel, author of *Clan of the Cave Bear,* was interviewed there. This novel was number one on best sellers' lists and she was living in Arch Cape while writing her second book. Apparently, the film shot during the interview in the store was not used.

The store attracted many "street people" who traveled the highways with the seasons. They stopped to return beer and soft drink cans for their Oregon deposit or just to beg. We helped them when we could by giving them leftover food, fruit, cans without labels and dented cans.

One young man came several times a summer for several years. We referred to him as "Nature Boy" and there was no doubt that he lived on the road. Jack suggested he clean the cans he wanted to return and that he should also cleanse himself. From then on, he was squeaky clean when he came to our store. He used the refunds from the cans to purchase bread, milk and lettuce. He stopped at least four times each summer and probably headed south each winter

Being proprietors of a small mom and pop store is a twenty-four hour "eight" day a week occupation. It takes the cooperation of the hired help. Our niece, Liz Woods, was with us for the first two summers. It took three of us on weekends and two the other days. Lori Carey was our **Girl Friday** during winters and during special times in the summer. Julie Bangs gave us double duty. She helped in the store and was also our silk screen artist. Our Castle Rock logo on the tee shirts, sweats, hats and wine glasses was designed by our daughter, Peggy Meece Sigler. Marnie, Susanna, Mitzie, Annie, Julie II, Thomas and Nancy were just a few of the friendly faces who greeted our customers. Many residents helped in their own ways, too. Ted Ethgrave made a bank stop for us each Friday for change for the weekends. The newspaper and pay telephone could run us out of quarters quickly and June Murphy's piggy bank helped out a few times on desperate Sundays. Bob Tarr checked out the local laundromat for much needed quarters. Jack Shields stepped behind the check-out counter on extra busy times to help shorten the line of waiting customers. Their help was greatly appreciated. Others pumped gas or stayed in the store if there was a questionable person loitering.

Vacations were taken separately after our first one was cut short the very first morning with a call from Liz. The upright freezer malfunctioned. "Save what you can in the chest freezer and give the ice cream away," was our answer. Our vacation ended when we returned to Arch Cape that day to make repairs.

Jack and I were at the store for six and one-half years. We still speak of that time as fun and really enjoyed it, even the hard work. We received much support from the residents and from those strangers who touched our lives, but decided it was time to sell the business to a younger couple. Barbara Bangle and Jim Perna from Arizona became proprietors in March, 1987. After two years, they realized they missed the southwest and sold to two Seattle couples. It is difficult to be an absentee owner, but the people they hired will be remembered for their pleasant mannered management.

The little store known by local residents as the **Deli** is here to stay. It is the hub of this small community and a meeting place for the lunch bunch and the morning coffee clatch waiting for the mail.

We enjoyed participating in the local activities when residents of the Arch Cape Community. Jack was an active member of the Design Review Board. At a later date he was asked to serve on the Water and Sewer Advisory Board. His engineering education gave him a solid background. Upon the sale of our business, I was asked to serve as treasurer of the

Arch Cape-Falcon Cove Beach Community Club. I enjoyed mailing the newsletter to all members—most of them customers and friends from the store. I also enjoyed helping organize the annual September picnics and working on other activities associated with club meetings

It was time for a change. At the end of 1992, we moved a short distance north to our new home where we can enjoy all the fruits of true retirement. We will always recall with pleasure the eleven years we resided in the ever changing, ever growing community of Arch Cape, Oregon.

A 1987 post office scene shows residents waiting for the mail. Stamps were twenty-two cents then. From left to right—Mary Ramsey, whose idea it was to write a history about Arch Cape; Jean Coughlin, a friend of Jean's and Maurie Clark. Dorothy Meece photo.

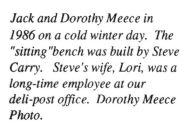

Jack and Dorothy Meece in 1986 on a cold winter day. The "sitting"bench was built by Steve Carry. Steve's wife, Lori, was a long-time employee at our deli-post office. Dorothy Meece Photo.

The Morrison Connection
By Noanie and Jim Morrison, daughter and Son-in-Law
of Fred and Betty Morrison

Although the *Arch Cape Chronicles* story begins with area homesteads in the 1890's, the Morrison connection has roots in this area extending back to 1845 and continues to the present day. The following story is from the morning *Oregonian,* Monday, August 27, 1894:

Prince of Pioneers
The Life and Services of Robert Wilson Morrison
By J. Minto, grandson of Robert Wilson Morrison
(Unedited story furnished by Jim Morrison)

Journey Across the Plains—Homestead in Clatsop County
A Conspicuous Home-Builder

On May 15, 1894, just entering on the 84th year of his age, Captain Robert Wilson Morrison died on the home farm taken by him in 1845 in Clatsop County, some 12 miles west of Astoria. He was the son of a pioneer settler of Kentucky, born in Fleming County, of that state, March 1811, and was there married to Miss Nancy Irwin in 1831, moving to Missouri in 1833. He was a conscious pioneer home-builder and had a just pride in his life as such: a conscientious, upright, fearless gentleman, thoroughly trustworthy in every relation to others, and ready at times to give his services to his fellow citizens to the full measure of his abilities. For the peculiar work of a pioneer, crossing the plains and mountains to help to make good the title of the United States to Oregon by making his home here in 1844, he was equipped by nature in a degree above the average of his fellows. Having, fortunately for myself, in company with the Honorable Willard H. Reese, joined Mr. Morrison as an assistant in his proposed trip to Oregon, the writer had ample opportunity to weigh and observe his character. He had just sold an excellent farm in Andrew County, Mo., and was putting the price of it into an outfit for emigration to and settlement in Oregon, when we joined him on the following conditions, verbally stated by him and accepted by us: "I will haul your trunks, board you, have your washing and mending done, and you shall give me your help in getting my family and effects to Oregon in the way I judge best." He proceeded: "I don't think the work will be hard or confining, as there will be three men of us, and three of my children are large enough to be of some help in driving the loose stock. I will have but two wagons, so that one of us can hunt every day, if we like. I have four guns and suitable ammunition."

We assented to the conditions and he took us into breakfast. Immediately after eating he requested Mr. Reese to mount a horse which he himself had saddled, and giving him some gold coin, requested him to ride to "Rubadeou's Landing" (now the city of St. Joseph, Mo.) and purchase nine barrels of flour and 300 pounds of cornmeal for our journey. Thus a bargain was made in a few minutes which required more than a year to complete, and a trust of money and property was placed in the hands of an utter stranger, in a manner illustrative of the trustworthy character of Mr. Morrison himself. The action, however, did not escape the notice of Mrs. Morrison, who, a few moments after Reese's departure, came to the cabin door and remarked: "Wilson, you'd feel mighty queer if that man should play you a Yankee trick, and go off with your horse and money." The thought had evidently not occurred to Mr. Morrison as it was some time before he replied: "Well, if he does, he'd better not let me overtake him. That's all I've got to say." The lady laughed and returned to her housework. That night the family entertained, on a visit of friendship and farewell, the sheriff of the county, together with his wife and daughter, and from the day we joined the family until we crossed and left the Missouri River, there was a continuous stream of visitors from neighbors, friends, and family connections.

As preliminary to starting, the services of three resident citizens were enlisted to make examination into the sufficiency of provision made by each head of a family, for the journey, which was estimated to require at least six months of time. The writer was busy about the wagon which was loaded with provisions chiefly, when this committee came to the front of it, and the member who seemed to be the head of it remarked: "Well gentlemen, I don't think it is worth our while to meddle with these wagons, for if he is not amply provided for the journey, not one of them ought to start." The committee made no examination into the larder of these wagons. On the Sunday preceding this incident—the last day the family spent in their Missouri home—the visitors were numerous and largely of kinfolks. After dinner the older men formed a group and were talking over the nature of the journey—the tribes of Indians to be passed, and the reported number of those to be settled amongst, when Judge Irwin (Mrs. Morrison's oldest brother, in evident sympathy with her feeling against the great, and to them unnecessary venture) said, addressing Morrison:

"Well, Wilson, why are ye going, anyhow?" Mr. Morrison's reply was very deliberate, and as I recollect was as follows: "Well, I allow the United State government has the best right to that country, and I am going to help make that right good. And I suppose it is true, as you say, that there are a great many Indians there who will have to be civilized, and though I am no missionary, I have no objection to helping in that. Then, I am not satisfied here. There are few things that we can raise here that will pay for shipment to market. Tobacco and hemp are about all, and unless a man keeps niggers (and I won't) he has no even chance with the man who owns slaves. There's Dick Owen, my near neighbor, who has a few house slaves and few field hands. They raise and make about all his family eats and wears and a surplus besides, which he can sell or hold over if the market is low. I have to sell everything I can spare every year to make ends meet. I'm going to Oregon, where there'll be no slaves and we'll all start even." Such was Mr. Morrison's declaration of purpose and the reasons given for it. It was received in silence and reflected upon some time before conversation was resumed. No attempt was made to dissuade him. They all seemed to know him as a man of few words, but of steadfast purpose and determined action. He was just entering his 34th year, stood fully six feet high, carried no surplus flesh, but was a strong man. In movement he leaned slightly forward, the result of habit in carrying a heavy gun and close observation in the woods. He was a good hunter and an excellent chopper. He was also a good judge of livestock, and was especially fond of a good horse. His family of children when he left Missouri were six in number—three girls and three boys. His wife had no equal in General Gilliam's companies, except it might be Mrs. Sally Shaw (sister of Gilliam's) in capacity to manage her own affairs and render needed assistance to the sick, the destitute or those otherwise distressed. In addition to what was deemed ample provision of food for the journey and clothing necessary, Mr. Morrison had the irons of a plow, some field and garden seeds, a flax wheel, the spindle and sheaves of a wool wheel, the sleighs and shuttle for a loom and a supply of wool and dressed flax and flax seed. In a word, the outfit was as complete as could be loaded into two wagons so this worthy couple would be self-dependent for re-establishment in Oregon.

Shortly after leaving the Missouri River a military organization was effected, at which Cornelius Gilliam was chosen general; M. T. Simmons, colonel; R. W. Morrison, William Shaw (Gilliam's brother-in-law) and A. Saunders and R. W. Woodcock were chosen captains in the order named. Amongst the officers thus elected, the plan of movement agreed upon was that Morrison's steady teams should always set the pace, and he himself should limit the day's movement by selecting the camping places. This placed him generally several miles in advance of the moving trains, and consequently, in the most exposed position. This arrangement lasted only until the trains reached the buffalo range on the main Platte, where Gilliam, who was an ardent hunter, lost his head and gave opportunity for discontent, with his dilatory orders, to manifest itself, with the result of his resigning all control over the trains, after which such generalship as we had was exercised by the combined minds of Captains Morrison and Shaw, who kept their companies within supporting distance of each other and maintained discipline and guard as long as it was deemed necessary. Many good and brave leaders in addition to General Gilliam have failed to meet the requirements of commanders in crossing those plains, but Morrison and Shaw, of the movement of 1844, maintained their positions, and did all that courage and patience combined could do, to get their followers and their property to Oregon. Only one little trouble with the Indians occurred east of the Rockies, when some hungry Sacs and Foxes drove out in the night some six or eight head of cattle. Captain Morrison was foremost on the trail next morning, but six of the beeves had been slain before they were overtaken, and the Indians fled to the reservation. The agent and chief compromised the raid by replacing the slain cattle with six of the choicest the United States government had but recently purchased for the Indians. Under guidance of these two natural captains, the people and property got to the west side of the Blue Mountains without loss. On the Umatilla, Morrison's most highly prized mare was stolen within a few feet of his hand, while he slept in his wagon, by the Cayuse Indians, and the same Indians it was believed, followed the trains to The Dalles and took the next best horse—a choice gelding of racing stock. The emigrant trail from the Blue Mountains to The Dalles was literally lined with Indian thieves. Especially was this so at the fords of the John Day and Deschutes Rivers. The villages here were largely populated by renegades from surrounding tribes, gamblers and thieves, and it required a constant vigilance to guard against their driving off stock and pilfering clothing from the wagons. At the John Day, one of the oxen received from the Sac and Fox Indians was driven off. Captain Morrison attempted to recover it by following the trail, and while so following it several miles from camp, two Indians on horseback came to him and after fruitlessly trying to confuse and delay him by signs, one of them leaned forward and adroitly took his knife from its sheath on his hip. He had no other weapon and could not even find a rock to throw at them. At the Deschutes the pillaging was done in a systematic manner by collusion between the Indian guides who extorted all they could for showing the ford; so delaying the movement in crossing as to give opportunity to the pilferers stationed amongst the broken sand hills between the ford and the great hill, to ascend which required the doubling of the wayworn teams. It was while Captain Morrison was detained at the river settling with the extortionate guide that a mounted Indian attempted to turn the leaders of the team which Mrs. Morrison was driving so as to turn the wagon over and so create an opportunity for theft. She made him desist by thrashing him with the whip. When he attempted to ride her down, she redoubled her blows and put him to flight. This was a great indignity to even an Indian thief, and this one and his friends followed the teams to their camping place, watching an opportunity for revenge, and were driven from there by Captain Morrison and Reese resorting to their rifles. Through this gauntlet of thieving the trains reached the Dalles—

> *"But there is still the river trail,*
> *Or the Cascade Range to scale."*
> *Before rest from the weary journey can be attained.*

Captain Morrison detailed Mr. Reese with others for the attempt to get the cattle across the range via the only trail then used, which passed the north base of Mount Hood, but the rains had set in at Oregon City on the 18th of October, and had fallen so copiously that the Willamette river rose by the 1st of December higher than it has been since, except once. This meant snow on the summit of the Cascades, and the cattle were only urged to the head of Hood river, till they were scattered to the hemlock thickets for shelter from a furious storm. The drivers made their way out of it by following the stream down to the Columbia river.

Captain Morrison, who had got his family in a boat, was descending the river, and seeing camp-fires of the party on the bank, hailed them, and, of course, landed to learn the cause of failure. He exchanged places with Reese, called for volunteers, and made his way to the cattle, extricated all that had not perished by eating laurel, and drove them back to The Dalles, where they recuperated very rapidly during the winter and whence the writer drove them the next March via the river trail to the Washougal bottoms, and whence they were driven the succeeding summer through the lower Willamette valley across the Coast range to Tillamook, and thence along the coast to Clatsop plains. This episode of extricating the cattle from the snow was the most trying short experience Captain Morrison had, as the live stock of others, as well as his own, were in great danger of being utterly lost. Then for food the party had to kill the only dog they had to save themselves, they being temporarily separated from the cattle by the swollen river, occasioned by an unusually warm "Chinook" wind, suddenly melting the fresh-fallen snow.

He always spoke very highly of the kind treatment received from Rev. A. F. Waller, the Methodist missionary at The Dalles. This was so different from the total ignoring of myself and party when we arrived at the mission, on the second Sunday of October, that I have since surmised two reasons for the difference. First, we arrived at the mission at the very hour Father Waller was teaching the Indians to regard Sunday as a holy day. Second, courage and devotion to others made R. W. Morrison subsequently, during the Indian war, refuse to be left to guard Fort Wascopan at The Dalles with a pitiful force of six men. This was the only time, I believe, he ever showed impatience. He always felt revengeful toward the Indians along the Columbia, the Cayuses included, and when they murdered Dr. Whitman and others, in 1847, he dropped his own affairs immediately, took down his gun (the gun that furnished the first buffalo meat to Gilliam's trains and that shot the last buffalo seen as we crossed the divide of the Rockies), and told his wife "the Indians had murdered Dr. Whitman and some 20 people, and he was going to help punish them." And he went. He had been selected as deputy sheriff under Thomas Owen the previous year (1846) and made the first arrest on the Columbia River under American law, the lawbreaker being a man named Fellows, who was trading liquor for salmon to the Indians, at Woody Island, thereby placing in jeopardy the isolated settlers of Astoria and Clatsop plains

Captain Morrison seems to have chosen his location under a preconceived determination to be near a highway of commerce, induced thereto by reading the journal of Lewis and Clark, which was one of the few books he had. It is believed that his chosen location covered the very spot whereon Lewis & Clark men boiled the Pacific waters to get salt—at all event, many an elk and bear has fallen by Captain Morrison's gun amongst the hills crossed by Lewis & Clark's party in the winter of 1805-6.

He was, as an individual, almost a complete representative of the American winners of the west shore of the United States, in all except the commercial spirit for which he had no talent whatever.

The first important labor he did after getting his family located was to build a large log structure as a wolf trap. The large mountain wolf was then a destructive enemy to stock raising. His next building was for a school house, and in that the first preaching to the white settlers and the first marriage ceremony after his arrival occurred. He and his noble wife gave the first land donated for church and cemetery purposes in the country. His residence became the main (it might almost be said the common) place of entertainment of visiting strangers as the hospitable customs of frontier life were maintained. Captain Morrison, at home, was a mild-spoken, quiet gentleman, a good listener to any stranger who called upon him, who was able and willing to talk on the subject of public measures calculated to advance the development of the country, a subject which engaged his own thoughts much more than did his own private affairs.

Illustrative of this, Mrs. Morrison used to enjoy telling of his actions on the brig Henry, which arrived in the Columbia River for a load of supplies of food and lumber, in 1849. The passengers and crews of such ships always came in on short rations of stale provisions, and willingly paid big prices in gold dust for fresh articles, like eggs, butter and cream. The report of the arrival of this ship caused their making up a party of the scattered settlers to board her with such food stuff, and Mrs. Morrison charged her husband with a five gallon can of cream. He got it on board and was relieved immediately by the ship's steward while he was engaged in conversation with the captain about the great prospective advantage the people of Oregon would derive from the market these gold mines would furnish. This theme engaged both captains till the ship, with wind and tide favoring, got above Tongue Point and Morrison's company hurriedly called him to their boat to return home. Arrived there, Mrs. Morrison demanded an account for her cream, when, in confusion, he had to confess he had entirely forgot all about it, and the can, of much more value than its contents, had gone up to Portland on the ship.

Captain Morrison made a mistake in the location, so far as his own business adaptations were concerned. Stock-breeding on a roomy range was much more to his taste than dairying, to which Clatsop plains are best adapted. When the gold discoveries made an extraordinary demand for lumber, Captain Morrison joined General John Adair in the ownership of a sawmill, and later built a small grist mill, but this was not congenial business. After another result of gold discoveries, Clatsop plains was overstocked with cattle, so that the turf covering was worn through in many places. What had once been nice pasturage became extensive stretches of blowing sand. Mr. Morrison led the way to a local organization to arrest the effect of this destructive agency by keeping cattle off the sea ridge, as the land near the beach was termed. On the other hand, the inside of these sand dunes is a strip of lake and marsh land. Forty years ago Captain Morrison conceived a canal to drain these marshes and to freight the produce of the farms to Astoria. Last winter his sons and grandsons, with their neighbors, realized the canal could float sawlogs from the boarders of Culaby Lake into the Columbia. So far as the freighting of the farm produce is concerned, the railroad (an agency never thought of by Captain Morrison in his day of 50 years ago) gives daily opportunity to reach Astoria within an hour's time with produce or passengers. The living and active of today can feel the ground tremble under the passing train loaded with visitors to the beach near which this elderly man was a pioneer and where he lies in his last rest. An inborn gentlemen, owing just enough to education to enable him to note intelligently the growing results of the action he represented 50 years ago, he closed his days in quiet contemplation of his day of leadership through dangers "seen and unseen" of honest counsel as a legislator, of firm devotion to public duty, in executing the law; always caring more for the common weal than he ever cared for his own part of it. He closed his days with great satisfaction in the fact the realization following the consummation of his purpose for which he left Missouri 50 years ago had been greater already then and his co-workers could possible conceive of.

He died also in the knowledge of leaving a healthy, numerous progeny to share in the result of his labors as a pioneer. In addition the six children he had when starting to Oregon, three others were born at Clatsop plains subsequently. One day, the eldest son died in early manhood. The others (as of 1971) are still living and named and located as follows: Mrs. Martha A. Minto, of Salem; Mrs. Mary E. Carnahan, of Clatsop; Mrs. Hanna M. Hamlin, of Astoria; T. H. Benton Morrison, of Astoria; James T., William I., Robert J., and David C. are residents of Clatsop Plains, where they were born.

(From the *Daily Astorian*)
The Pioneer Women of Oregon
by
Mrs. Owens-Adair, M. D.

Nancy Irwin Morrison

(Some of this story has been eliminated since it would be repetitive of portions of Mr. Morrison's story. Mrs. Owens-Adair, in the 1860's at age 20 taught school in the Clatsop Plains Presbyterian church. She was to receive two dollars from each of her sixteen pupils to teach them for six months.

A part of this sketch of that remarkable pioneer woman, Mrs. Nancy Irwin Morrison, was furnished me by her second daughter, Mrs. Mary Ellen Carnahan. The remainder is from the pen of Honorable John Minto, husband of Mrs. Morrison's eldest daughter, Mrs. Martha Ann Minto. Mrs. Carnahan says:

My mother was born April 27, 1809, in Anderson County, Mo. She was the mother of nine children, thirty-one grandchildren, and eleven great-grandchildren.

Mother brought a little flax wheel, a bunch of flax and a sack of wool: but no cards. We children picked the wool from which she spun yarn and we knit stockings, and from the flax she spun sewing thread.

When father went to the Cayuse war and was gone from December till May, Mother managed everything: putting in the crops, making butter, and doing everything that was to be done. And, in addition, she did any work that she could get to do for the support of the family. I remember that she worked for many days, with the help of two children, untying a net that had been woven too coarse, for which she only charged 25 cents per day. I also remember that she paid the taxes for one year by knitting socks.

At the eighteenth reunion of the Oregon Pioneer Association, held in Portland, June 17, 1890, Mr. Minto read the following interesting sketch of Mrs. Morrison:

It is the labor of love on the part of the writer to attempt thus to convey to others the character of this estimable woman, as seen in the toilsome action and trying inaction, the sleepless vigilance and constant readiness to meet and overcome or endure the trials in which her duties as a wife and mother placed her as an emigrant to Oregon and as a settler in the country upon her arrival. My point of observation was as a member of her family—at first by temporary adoption as an assistant during the journey to Oregon, and subsequently by marriage of her eldest daughter three years after arrival. I state this to show the reader I had excellent opportunities to know what manner of woman it was that crossed the plains and mountains with ox teams (when the entire distance from Missouri to the Willamette was in possession of the Indian race) to become, with her husband, a home builder in Oregon.

Nancy Morrison had another acquirement not usual to womanhood. She could use a rifle with effect. As a frontiersman's daughter, she was left in early girlhood to be her father's housekeeper by the death of her mother. She had been taught the use of the rifle, but never effected it in mannish ways. I have heard her tell of killing a hawk in defense of the poultry, but never saw her handle the rifle we called her gun, although I did overhear her asking where it and its accoutrements were, one night when the camp was in alarm, expecting a night attack from Indians.

Here I wish to note the fact that I presume was true of a large majority of the wives and mothers who crossed the plains as pioneers. The movement was against the judgement and feelings of Mrs. Morrison; she told me so in so many words, but never alluded to the subject again until she had been several years in Oregon, and then told me she was satisfied with the change on her husband's account; but she believed he himself was not. No person seeing Mrs. Morrison in her daily routine of duties would have supposed she was engaged in an enterprise her judgment did not endorse. She was no complainer; while sociable, not an excessive talker. She was at this time in the prime of life, and thinking for words to characterize her in her relations to her family and others, those of Prov. XXI:25 comes to mind. "Strength and honor are her clothing." Her neighbors and friends must have been very numerous.

The following are excerpts from *Clatsop County, Oregon*, Its History, Legends and Industries, by Emma Gene Miller published in 1958.

The Robert Morrisons came to Oregon in 1844, moved to Clatsop Plains in 1845, taking 640 acres for their farm. The first Presbyterian church in Oregon and west of the Rocky Mountains was organized on Clatsop Plains in September, 1846 by the Rev. Lewis Thompson, Mr. and Mrs. Alva Condit, and Mr. and Mrs. W. H. Gray at the Gray house. Robert Morrison gave 10 acres for the church grounds. When several bodies were found on the beach from a shipwreck, he gave two more acres behind the church for the pioneer cemetery.

The first public school started in the county and the third in Oregon was in the winter of 1844-45 in a log building furnished by Robert Morrison, on Clatsop Plains. The Morrison and Solomon Smith children attended. Smith taught school, while his wife Celiast acted as interpreter of the Indian language.

Robert Morrison raised flax in 1845 on his place on the Skipanon River from the seed he brought with him across the plains. Practically all the settlers planted large quantities of potatoes. The Morrison farm was divided among his surviving children, William later buying most of his brothers' and sisters' land. Some of his land was sold to the Oregon National Guard for "Camp Clatsop." It is said that he sold the farm because he couldn't handle his beef cattle crossing the highway. Mrs. Harold Tagg, granddaughter of Robert Morrison, still in 1958 owned 100 acres of the original acres her grandfather owned in 1845.

Noanie and Jim Morrison

James Hayes Morrison, a grandson of Robert Morrison, and his wife Alice lived in Astoria. His brother Irwin was proprietor of the Johnson-Morrison grocery store on Commercial Street and was also a town constable.

James Haring Morrison was the son of James Hayes Morrison. When the young son was three weeks old, the family was forced to flee their home because of the catastrophic Astoria fire in 1922, a fire which destroyed most of Astoria. Much of the town afterwards was rebuilt on pilings out over the river. The area was then filled and became what is now part of present-day Astoria. Young Jim attended grammar and high school in Astoria. It was in high school that he met another Morrison, Noanie, and they became "steadies." This Morrison family had just moved to Astoria in 1939 where Fred was to have a Gilmore Oil Company distributorship. His wife Betty became Astoria's "artist-in-residence."

In 1941 Jim was given an appointment to the Merchant Marine Academy in Great Neck, New York. He completed his college education there and graduated as a Third Officer in the United States Merchant Marine. He later obtained an unlimited Master's license [Captain]. Jim made his first trip as a midshipman in 1942 during World War II. He sailed to Dutch Harbor, Alaska, shortly after the Japanese bombed it. He was 19 then. Many trips to the South Pacific followed: Guadaicanal, New Guinea, and New Caledonia. For 126 days at anchor in a lagoon of Ulithi Island, his ship acted as one of many supply ships for the Pacific

Fleet. He also made trips in 1942-43 through the Caribbean and up the Atlantic Coast.

In 1945 Jim and Noanie were married in Astoria upon Noanie's graduation from Stephens College in Missouri. After Jim spent several more years at a sea career, the young couple with their two little boys, Jim and Vince, moved to Seattle. There, Jim began his thirty-six years with the Boeing Company.

Jim's long career with Boeing flourished. He had responsible management positions on the Dyna Soar program, the Minuteman Missile program, the Supersonic Transport and the combined 707, 727 and 737 operations. He and Noanie were in Iran four months doing planning and programming for the Imperial Iranian Air Force before the Shah fell. This occasioned a hasty evacuation from Mehrabad Airport in Teheran where a Pan Am jet, staffed by a volunteer crew, came to the rescue. The last eight years of his career at Boeing were spent in labor relations, where he was first a director and then a corporate vice-president. Jim made a very positive impact on the relations between Boeing and their unions. Upon his retirement, he was given a plaque honoring **Gentleman Jim** from the Machinists Union. Jim and Noanie have had numerous friends from both the management and the union who visited with them in Arch Cape.

Arch Cape came into the Morrisons' lives in 1945 when Betty purchased property there. Fred felt it was quite far from Astoria, but grew to love it and spent much time there. An unwelcome piece of news was that there was some doubt as to the real location of the piece of property purchased. Platting in the early years seemed to have been sketchy, at best.

Betty expected the lot where a small modest house sat and where the family had several outdoor picnics was the one she purchased, even though they had no key to the house. Final papers transferring ownership were not complete at the time. To their dismay, a legal looking letter arrived from someone named Gelinsky, informing them that the lot with the house belonged to the Gelinskys. After much negotiating, it was determined the lot just to the south was the one purchased and the small modest house was two feet over the property line onto the Morrison lot. In a gesture of goodwill, one and one-half feet of the property on the north side of "Betty's lot" was deeded to the Gelinskys.

Betty and Fred began clearing salal accompanied by their very pregnant daughter, Noanie. Thus it was that Jim (Rip), who now lives in San Francisco, spent a lot of time at 1242 Gelinsky Boulevard, well before his arrival into the world.

After clearing a reasonable space, Fred and Betty purchased a construction shack from a site near Oney's Tavern on Highway 26 (formerly the Wolf Creek Highway) and had it moved to Arch Cape in 1946. Originally, it was moved on rollers to the rear of the lot, but as more clearing occurred, it was moved toward the ocean front to take advantage of the view.

The one-room shack, about 500 square feet, had a stove but lacked running water. The whole family adored it. One could sweep the sand down through the cracks in the floor, cook great pots of spaghetti on the wood stove and fill teakettles of water at the outdoor standpipe that was connected to the Dichter water system. The toilet was outside, a true "chic sales," a one-hole familiar contraption, quite clearly in view.

As the young Morrison family grew, Fred built a small bunk room for four on the back of the shack and a small living room with a Franklin stove on the north end. Eventually, a **real** operating toilet was installed in the tiny room at the south end of the cabin. What luxury. Jim Morrison and sons Jim (Rip) and Vince worked hard helping Fred install a septic tank and digging the ditches and laying the pipe for the connecting drain field.

It was not possible to spend overnight there during the winter since the cabin was loosely constructed and allowed wind to blow through the many cracks. Mice and bugs became winter residents. Each spring opening of the cabin began with a thorough scrubbing with bleach and soap. "Smells like an operating room," Jim would say.

Fred and Betty always welcomed the growing family during the summers and many friends of both families felt it was their summer place, too. Jim and Noanie's daughter Melissa, born in 1954, joined the group during this time.

Fred and Betty found it difficult to maintain and operate the cabin, so deeded it to the young Morrisons. In 1962 the family had a tearing-down work party to demolish the very over-age structure, saving only the small living room as a bedroom. The old structure was replaced by an A-frame house which still stands today. A number of years later the final "old part" was removed and replaced by a larger addition. Another six-foot addition pushing toward the ocean followed a few years later.

Over the years, though, no one has lived full-time in the old cabin or in the newer A-frame home. It became an integral part of our family for the three children and their families. All share in the enjoyment of this wonderful environment. It was a major part of Rip, Vince and Melissa's youth. Vince's skateboarding through the tunnel and Rip and Vince's taking their surfboards out around Castle Rock (which has always been Queen Vic to the Morrisons) to Betty's dismay; Melissa and a long-time school friend spending the summer as housemaids at the Surfsand Motel in Cannon Beach and bicycling both ways; overflow tenting in the back yard; huge bonfires on Fourth of July along with a great fireworks displays, are all fond memories never to be forgotten. There were enormous "house on fire size" beach fires for Labor Day and for New Year's Eve. One must not forget the annual and revered New Year's Day swim where Betty Snow, through her 90th birthday, put everyone to shame if they did not "nerve" themselves to plunge into the ocean.

One of the most dramatic events occurred in March of 1964 when the earthquake in Alaska created a tidal wave on the Oregon coast. The whole family was in Arch Cape and it was a beautiful moonlit night. Rip and Vince came up from the beach laughing and said, "Some drunk on the beach says there's going to be a tidal wave." Jim and Noanie laughed too, and then decided they had better check with the radio, which seemed to confirm the event. No firm estimation of time of wave arrival was given.

Since the A-frame had no telephone, it was necessary to go to the pay phone at the Arch Cape store to seek further information. Jim's brother-in-law, Delwin Larson, was chief engineer on the Peacock, the Columbia River pilot boat stationed in Astoria. A call was made to him. While talking to Del, whom he had awakened around 11:30 p.m., the phone went dead and the lights went out.

Jim raced back to the cabin to see if the family had survived. Rip and Vince had the memorable experience of seeing the wave coming. Noanie was upstairs with young Melissa, who was nine at the time. The wave heaved foam into the yard but caused no damage. With the phone dead, Del assumed all the family had drowned or had washed away, so he loaded all kinds of rescue gear into his car. With Jim's sister Eva, they headed for Arch Cape. It was not easy to do, for bridges were out everywhere and forced them to travel the long way around through Jewell.

Meanwhile, evacuation began in a hurry at the cabin for fear of aftershocks. First, the family drove to Neahkahnie lookout, which is the highest accessible land around. It was still a beautiful night, although uncanny, with radio reception from Hawaii completely free from static or interference. We then drove to the Cannon Beach Junction where the Crab Broiler Restaurant had opened in the middle of the night as a refuge. Many frightened and excited people gathered, some in pajamas and coats. Free coffee and hot chocolate were available to everyone.

The next stop was at Silver Point, where people tried to find each other. A large crowd rushed around searching for family members and other loved ones. Here, Del and Eva Larson encountered all the Morrisons and their dog, Louie, a meeting accompanied by much hugging and crying.

Finally, everyone returned to the cabin. The power was off so everyone sat around a fire roasting hot dogs and marshmallows about three o'clock in the morning. Rumors of aftershocks found the whole group too tired to leave again. There was damage in Cannon Beach and Seaside, but Arch Cape was spared. A family of five sleeping on the beach at Depoe Bay was tragically drowned.

Summer Christmas was another tradition for several years. The whole neighborhood gathered at the Birkbys' back and side yard, decorated a Christmas tree, gave silly presents and had a cookout. Seaside merchants were dumfounded by the number of people asking for Christmas wrapping paper in the middle of summer. Berkeley Snow played his guitar and everyone sang at these jolly occasions. It was a great way for giving people who didn't see each other during the Christmas season a chance to share the fun and joy from the make-believe mid-summer holiday. One wonders what people thought when the music of "Silent Night, Holy Night" echoed across the Arch Cape sands in the middle of summer.

Fond Memories—Beginning the Summer of 1946

We remember the 4th of July picnics when family and friends gathered at long plywood tables. Lola Kelly, a long-time Astoria friend of Betty's and Fred's, brought four-dozen cupcakes. Grandma Betty made a giant pot of baked beans to add to all the other holiday specialities. And then, we remember the kids spitting watermelon seeds into the salal bushes. One wonders why we have no watermelon growing today. Mrs. Laverne Kittilson, Lola Kelly's daughter, seemed to be pregnant every 4th of July with one or the other of their six children.

Razor clams were memorable breakfast fare, especially when we could get them on **our** beach early in the morning.

Unbelievably, a favorite memory was getting up at four or five in the morning when it was still dark to caravan in a group to Garibaldi to dig butter clams and cockles. Vince stood thigh deep in water with a pitchfork digging for quohogs, a type of clam brought to this coast in sand ballast from the East Coast. At Arch Cape, volunteer cooks butterflied them and then deep fried or sauteed them for a gourmet treat. The Beemers and the Birkbys joined us with this activity.

One of the nicest of surprises was to read Bridget Snow's poems written in the sand every morning along with her little logo—a swingy-skirted stick figure with a smile.

There were summers when the Velella, often called Portuguese man-o-war, made the beach smelly and uninhabitable.

One year there was a tall shingle of rocks almost to the water. The beach, made of rocks with a narrow sand portion near the water, allowed one to sit on the sand and lean back against a rock wall.

Everyone learned to harvest and to eat and enjoy mussels. Rip may have been instrumental in starting what we called "mussel delight."

Grandma Betty enjoyed painting pictures of the rock, the cape, the trees and the "deer" driftwood that stayed on the beach for so long. The "deer" driftwood was a long log with root structure resembling a deer's head with many antlers. It was a great log to climb upon, too.

One year Jim, Melissa and Vicki Caulkins, Melissa's life-long friend, garnered thirty crabs at Nehalem, so there was another huge neighborhood feast.

Grandpa Fred often sat out on the back step of the old cabin talking to the blue jays who talked back to him. He also fed peanuts to the chipmunks, who ate them off his ears and shoulders and out of his hands.

Several wonderful dogs were part of our beach history and all of them loved it. Chiefer, a Samoyed/Brittany cross, looking more like the former, was the first. He thought the beach was great, but hated the 4th of July. Then came Louie, a big yellow Labrador retriever, a truly noble dog remembered not only by family but by most of their friends also. He dug monster holes on the beach, properly dubbed **Louie Craters.** Night-time beach walkers soon learned to watch out for Louie's excavations. One time, Louie surprised a sea gull on a wave, caught it, and heard our whole family yelling at him to let it go. The family held a wake when Louie died at age thirteen. Brandywine, another yellow Lab, was next. He was a lovable, rascally fellow who also lived to age thirteen. Pirate Lady, a chocolate Lab, is the current Morrison canine, and at two years of age, is blessed with a sweet and natural disposition all of her own and continues the tradition of love for the beach that her predecessors so much enjoyed. The Morrison family has always felt that seeing dogs romping on the beach is an expression of pure joy.

Today is 1993. Jim and Noanie have nine grandchildren ranging in age from two years old to 25 years of age, all of whom share and love Arch Cape. Family members live all over the country from California to Alabama, but the Arch Cape retreat remains a permanent focal point for gathering and for sharing. Grandma Betty, who died in 1991, would be proud at what she had brought about.

Jim and Noanie are retired now [for five years] and have become world travelers, but always—there is the return to Arch Cape.

A copy of a water color by Betty Morrison shows the original Arch Cape Morrison home. Circa 1947. Morrison collection.

Grandma Betty with Rip, age 10; Vince, age 8; and Melissa, age 2 on the driftwood we called "The Deer" at the Arch Cape beach in 1956. Photo, Morrison collection.

Fred Morrison in 1962. The new A-frame home
shows in the background.

Rip and Vince in 1954.

Noanie and Melissa, age 3, out on the plank walk in
front of the cabin in 1953.

Jim and Noanie at the
Astoria High School
Senior Prom, 1941.

Melissa with Louie digging
"craters" in 1972. Photos,
Morrison collection.

The Mersereau Connection
Memories — by John Mersereau

In the mid-seventies, when hiking the section of the Coast Trail between Arch Cape and Falcon Cove, I admired the house and property on Arch Cape Creek at the trail head on Third and Webb Avenues. My wife Deb and I were living in Cannon Beach and looking for a place to purchase away from the commercial hustle-bustle of that town. We happened to be hiking the trail the same day the house we wanted went up for sale. We signed the papers that afternoon.

The house had belonged to Randall McLoughlin, a resident of Arch Cape since the early forties. We never met Mr. McLoughlin, but heard stories about him from Iva Delaschmitt, Angelo Costanzo and Frank Lee, his contemporaries on Shingle Mill Road. He was a semi-retired plumber, and the remnants of his trade, various homemade contraptions like dirt sifters and garden carts made from plumbing parts, are still in evidence on the property. He also painstakingly hand-laid a 600 foot water line to a small spring up on the hill across Arch Cape Creek for his water supply, which is still in operation.

As a child, I have fond memories of Arch Cape. My grandmother, Lucille Mersereau, lived in Gearhart during the summer and took us on picnics. One of her favorite places to visit was Short Sands beach and then we'd stop at the Neakahnie golf course clubhouse for a great burger and shake. On the way back, we stopped in Arch Cape to visit Dr. John and Irene Countryman and Elsie and Marie English. I remember the amazing glass float collection in the *Singing Sands* living room. They gave each of us a float every summer. My parents also took us for outings to the mouth of Arch Cape Creek which I often do with my family today.

I am an avid fisherman and became interested in the salmon and steelhead runs in Arch Cape Creek. Living right on the creek, the kids and I often hike along the banks watching for fish during the winter months. Arch Cape Creek is a healthy, relatively short stream designated by the Fish and Wildlife Department as a spawning creek and therefore, closed to fishing for salmon and steelhead. In 1986, I started raising fish through the volunteer Salmon and Trout Enhancement Program (STEP). I received fertilized eggs from the North Fork Nehalem River Hatchery and incubated them in two hatch boxes which were fed with a constant flow of water from a tributary of Arch Cape Creek. This system is designed to imitate an egg nest or "redd" in a gravel bed of a stream. The eggs hatched in three weeks, and then in another six weeks, I released the two inch fingerlings into various small tributaries of local coastal streams including the Necanicum, Nehalem, Short Sands Creek and Arch Cape Creek. In the five years I raised fish, I planted close to 90,000 fingerlings in Arch Cape Creek. Even with less than one percent survival rate, these fish added to the existing run in the creek. The fish I planted are not marked, but I have noticed an increase in fish in the creek over the last three years. Oregon Department of Fish and Wildlife spawning surveys on Arch Cape Creek have indicated there was a healthy run of salmon and steelhead, an important fact considering today's concern over dwindling salmon stocks. The Arch Cape Creek should remain a clean, healthy spawning stream for future generations of fish.

Deb and I have two children, Ashley, age seven and Taylor, age five. When we first moved to Arch Cape, there were no school age children in the town. Now I count 18 kids and the school bus makes a number of stops in town. Arch Cape is a wonderful place to raise a family. Our kids never tire of going to the beach, fishing in the creek or exploring the extensive woodlands and wildlife that surround our home. May it always be so.

The bridge across the Arch Cape Creek guides travelers toward the Oregon Coast Trail when traveling south. David English photo.

Four year old Taylor and six year old Ashley exploring the arches with their mother Deb. 1992. John Mersereau photo.

Taylor, age 4 and Ashley, age 6, 1992. John Merseruea photo.

The June Murphy Connection
As told to Jan Tarr

In 1962 June Murphy and her husband bought a cabin in Arch Cape. June says she saw the little house one weekend when she came down on the bus with a friend. It was 20 feet by 20 feet, the size of a double garage. When June returned to Portland she told her husband about it and he agreed she should buy it for their retirement. On Monday June withdrew money for a down payment and called the realtor. By Thursday she had her transaction completed and owned a piece of Arch Cape. Later, her friend, Alice Manning Rosseau, who owned a house in Arch Cape across from Marian Rall, sold her place in three hours. It seems that real estate deals were easier then.

After June's husband died in 1965, she continued working at the University of Oregon Medical School and weekending in Arch Cape. June knew several people connected to the medical school that also had homes in Arch Cape: Dr. Roy Biehn, Dr. James Speros, Dr. Edward West, Dr. Michael Baird, Dr. David Baird, Dr. Archie Pittman, Dr. Vessie and Caroline Pommarain, the registrar for the medical school. June's friend, Alice, a lab technician, was in charge of the clinic laboratory for 20 years. June ran the electrocardiograph department for 12 years, worked in the X-ray department, and also in pediatrics during her years of service with the medical school, a "jack of all trades."

Sadly, in 1969, fire completely destroyed June's Arch Cape house, which she had just remodeled, burning everything, including pictures of the Dalmatian show dogs that she and her husband raised and other irreplaceable personal treasures. Because there was a moratorium on building then, it looked as if she would not be able to replace her home; another tragedy for June. Bob Moon, a local builder, convinced the county however, to allow her to put up a structure the exact size of the original building on the same site. That is what she did with the fire insurance money so that when she retired after 26 years, she had a snug house waiting for her in Arch Cape, just where she wanted to be.

June has always enjoyed walking with her dog along the beach; first Cindy and then Susie. By observing the local environment, she has collected a store of information, particularly about the birds in Arch Cape, many of which she feeds daily. She also knows the best places to find Japanese floats when they wash ashore following storms. She found her largest float on Mother's Day, 1981, a few hours before her daughter arrived to give her a book about identifying Japanese floats.

Because of her friendly manner and the size of Arch Cape when she first came here, June knew everyone in town. She says it was impossible not to, since everyone, even weekenders were being recruited to work on St. Peter the Fisherman Church and the fire station. When she tried to tell Monsignor Smith she couldn't drive a nail, he countered with, "Well, you can carry brush, can't you?" So, she worked clearing ground with others. She remembers these neighbors, now gone, and how well they worked together.

June still has many friends of all ages who chat with her over coffee every morning at the Arch Cape Deli/Post Office. They discuss the local, national and world news with the morning *Oregonian* spread all over the table, sparking the conversation. Those present enjoy her common sense and easy going attitude.

A Newcomer from Seattle
by Elizabeth Forsyth Forbes

Ralph Forbes and I were married in Seattle in September, 1948, at the *Meany Hotel* in the University District. We left Seattle about two o'clock that afternoon and headed for Arch Cape. We had our wedding dinner in Astoria at the Stevens restaurant, which at that time, was nothing special. We then drove to Arch Cape. The next morning Ralph wanted me to meet the Arch Cape neighbors. Our first stops were at the Countryman's home and then to Elsie and Marie English's home. After the introduction, Ralph said to Dr. Countryman, ". . . and what do you think of my Koko?" Dr. Countryman said "Well, we will have to wait and see." That was my introduction to Arch Cape. Then I met some of the other neighbors—Jule Kullberg, Orlena Harsh, Frieda Billings, Jessie Faire, and many others. Our honeymoon in Arch Cape lasted only a few days because Ralph still worked, so we returned to Seattle.

When Ralph retired in 1954, we moved permanently to Arch Cape, and I was invited to join Elsie and Marie's *Tuesday Club*. The club consisted of Elsie and Marie English, Irene English Countryman, and Ella Scott, along with other neighbors and me. At our meetings, each of us would contribute something educational. Marie reported on things she found on the beach, such as sea shells, driftwood, and perhaps the new log washed in by the latest tide. Ella, a retired librarian, would discuss a book she had recently read and the rest of us would talk about gardening, cooking, and any other newsy things of interest.

We all looked forward to the Meier and Frank specials, called "Friday Surprise." Almost every Friday was a shopping trip to Portland for new furnishings for our house. The English girls traveled with us since they were building the new *Singing Sands* home which replaced the old early-day *Arch Cape Hotel* stage coach stop. We left them at the *Heathman Hotel*, after which they fanned out to the different department stores to shop for drapes, carpeting and furniture, pricing the needed items. About noon, they met back at the hotel to compare prices, and after lunch, went out to make their purchases. Usually, it was a very productive day. We met them at *Heathman* about four o'clock and returned to the beach. Whoever stayed home that day, whether it was Irene or Elsie, had dinner ready for us.

We played bridge often, but not on a regular basis. We usually had two tables and rotated from house to house. Dessert was always served and all of us enjoyed the companionship, especially on those long winter nights during the '50's and '60's. We made our own entertainment then.

At Christmas time, Mabel Lensrud would tell the story and present the ritual of the *Lucia Bride*. Marie English always managed to get a young lady to play the part of the bride. Real candles attached to the bride's hairdress were lit as Mabel told the story. Marie stood behind the bride with a wet towel, ready to spring into action if necessary.

The Forbes family had built their beach home for summer recreation and for vacation use. It was a wonderful place for Barbara to come during the summer with her friends. She was in charge of the household duties. Ralph appointed Miss Eva Benson, a neighbor, as the chaperon for Barbara when she was a college freshman. Miss Benson laughed at that because she wasn't sure of her authority, if it was ever needed. Miss Benson, a spinster librarian, had built her own little house next door. She drove a Model A Ford.

Our house had a living room, kitchen, bath, bedroom, and a garage with a storage shed. We later closed in the patio with plate glass windows and installed a glass windbreak on the ocean front. This was a great addition, as we now not only looked out on the ocean, but on the lawn and landscaped area, too. Beautiful flowers grew all around our patio. The lush bouganvillea and jade plants became major attractions and people enjoyed them every winter. The patio, with all the plant growth both inside and outside, became our living area. Ralph painted the concrete floor fire engine red every year. People who knew Ralph were well aware of his love for red. He wore red ties, a red Pendleton jacket, red socks, and decorated the trim of the house in red. A dear friend, Lucille Scarborough, dedicated the following poem to Ralph on his birthday:

Ode to Ralph or
"As You Like It"

Paint It Red, he said-
Any color, as long as it's Red!
Perhaps he has a secret,
To get more out of living
    and
When we see our friend
Approaching "four score and ten
With such gusto
Perhaps we should all
Use a great deal more Red!

Ralph was vice president of the Northwestern Mutual Fire Insurance Company of Seattle and was responsible for underwriting insurance for the sawmill industry. Mr. L. D. Brill was president at the time. The Brills were long-time friends and Barbara's god parents. Ralph's job covered five western states where he evaluated sawmills and plywood plants for fire insurance requests and needs. He took an inspector with him. I enjoyed the exciting and adventurous trips with Ralph. It took us to many primitive and isolated places where sawmills were located in those days, close to timber sources. Personally, it was a wonderful education for me. We traveled all over Washington, Oregon, Idaho, California, Nevada and Canada. Ralph was a very dedicated fire insurance person and was always cautious and concerned about the possibility of a fire.

I lived in Arch Cape from 1954 until 1973. The adjustment from busy Seattle city life to quiet Arch Cape was made easy because of the many friends in the area. Elsie and Marie English, John and Irene Countryman, Floyd and Ella Scott, Hoken and Mabel Lensrud, Jule Kulberg, Orlina Harsh, Frieda Billings and Jessie Fair made me feel like I belonged here. I truly appreciated those people and I learned so much from them. Each had special qualities and they were eager to share their knowledge and talents with me. We all worked hard doing our yard work, planted gardens, painted and cooked. On weekends we played bridge games, had picnics, visited friends and neighbors, or relaxed with a good book.

We kept busy with guests during the summer. We often commented about how the sheets were always hot from taking them off the beds and putting them back on for the next group. After Labor Day, the locals joined together for a flag salute to everyone returning to work and to give thanks for having the beach all to ourselves again.

Bert Patton was a very interesting person whom we always enjoyed. He managed to dig clams when others seemed to have difficulty. Clams were much larger and more plentiful then than they are today. His recipe for clams called for one egg for each clam. He would roll the clams in flour and then dip them into the egg. He would come over with a whole platter of clams for us. Ralph's favorite drink was *Jack Daniels* and when Bert would come over with the platter of clams, Ralph would set the bottle beside Bert and let Bert enjoy himself. I never saw Bert inebriated or out of kilter. He loved children and sometimes rented his cabin so parents could bring their children to the beach. One mother who took her child to the beach sat up on the dry sand reading a book while her child played in the water. Bert couldn't stand watching this so he went up to the lady and said, "What did you do, bring this child down to drown him?" The mother, Bert thought, would not be able to save the child if he fell in the waves. Bert always looked after the young people. He loved sharing his vast outdoor knowledge with everyone, especially the younger ones. Bert was a good chaperon and people felt safe having him around. He was a great man, a good woodsman, a mechanic, and was well-known for his skill as a blacksmith.

Our boxer dog, named Pepper, gave us lots of joy. Ralph trained him to carry messages from him to me and vice versa. When Ralph worked in the yard and I wanted him to come in for lunch, Pepper carried a message to him and returned back to me with a message from Ralph saying he was on the way.

The Friendly Path began at the Christie's house and ended at the Scotts' house. It ran down the trail at the end of Ocean View Road, through the meadow, wound between the Countryman's house and garage, through Irene's rose arbor, behind Singing Sands and on to the Scotts'. We didn't have the open paths that you see today; the path allowed enough space for one person to walk single file. If a person in front of you walked fast, you lost site of him because the path was not straight and because of the heavy growth. The path had character and required work keeping it open through the tall salal. A sign along the way reminded those users that this is "*The Friendly Path.*"

Ralph installed his own fire hydrant on the east side of our house. When June Murphy's house caught fire, Dale Mosby, George Christie and Ralph pulled a fire hose from our place to June's place to put out the fire. The fire was too advanced to save the house, but the hose did help in protecting other homes near by.

Ralph loved keeping things neat and would use a sickle to keep the grass cut on our property below our house, and he also kept the grass mowed off Ocean View Road. That space became a great play and sun bathing area because it was well protected from the wind. Badminton and volley ball nets were often part of the scene there. Ralph loved doing this kind of work and working up a sweat in the process. It made him feel good to see the results of his work.

In 1973 we sold our house to Claus Sinai's parents and moved to Gearhart. This move was for health reasons. We spent our years in Arch Cape with many good friends and I look back at those times with fond memories. Ralph died in 1976.

Top left—Ralph and Elizabeth Forbes with Bob and Jim Shaw, 1958.

Top right—Jim and Barbara Shaw with son Bob, 1991.

Left center—Jim Shaw and his son Ben with Polly Beemer Wellman, 1985.

Lucy, Ralph and Barbara in the garden, 1947. Photos, Barbara Shaw collection.

Arch Cape Memories
By Emma Rogness

O ur introduction to Elsie and Marie English came through our neighbor and good friend, Doris Keeler. Doris' son, Doug, and our son Earl Robert, were the same age and were good friends. One day I told Doris that my husband Earl and I wished to take Doug to the beach. Doris said, "Why don't I call the English sisters? They have a guest house and a hotel and maybe you could stay there."

We drove to Arch Cape and into the English driveway and there was Marie waiting for us. She examined us, as she did all new guests, to see if we would fit in with the Arch Cape scene and guests. I had brought down cookies and banana nut bread. Needless to say, that began a long tradition, as I always came with a good supply of baked goods, mostly cookies, for my Arch Cape friends and guests. Marie took us to Mabel (Marie's sister) and Hoken Lensrud's guest house on Pacific Avenue. Mabel had fresh flowers on the table and we were introduced to a squeaky-clean accommodation. Mabel, who was the Arch Cape expert regarding all growing things, was sitting outside working with her plants. It didn't take long to unpack and become acquainted with our surroundings and with Mabel and Hoken.

We stayed often at the Lensrud guest house, and when it wasn't available, rented High Tide, the upper unit behind the Singing Sands guest house. Marie was in charge of that project and she often supervised Earl Robert as he helped with chores around the territory.

We stayed at Singing Sands, too, and loved it very much. Breakfasts were memorable occasions where guests and hosts had many leisurely morning visits. I helped with the preparation of meals, washed dishes and helped with the clean-up afterward. All guests had various tasks and responsibilities, which made us feel more attached to Singing Sands, a one-of-a-kind hotel.

Two home economic agents whom I knew in South Dakota were guests of ours one summer, for they wanted to see the ocean. I called Elsie and Marie to see if we could stay at Singing Sands. These guests, Agnes and Harriet, had never seen the ocean. We enjoyed all of the usual day-time activities, and in the evenings we had beach fires for roasting wieners and marshmallows with the Lensruds and English girls. Elsie and Marie seemed to do all the roasting. Harriet took off her socks and somehow one of the girls caught it on a marshmallow stick and it ended up in the fire. It gave us all a good laugh, but Earl Robert, who was nine then, didn't see any humor at all. He said, "Mom, that was one of her good socks," and he never forgot it. Today, whenever I write to Agnes and Harriet, I mention those great days at the beach and keep them informed about what is new there.

Earl was the cost accountant for the Pendleton Woolen Mills. One day, when I had a scheduled PTA board meeting to attend, Earl's boss and plant manager, Mr. Bishop, called and asked that I come to his office. I asked if Earl was sick. (Earl had a heart attack at age forty-five and we both worried about that.) Mr. Bishop said Earl was all right but to please come to his office. When I arrived, Mr. Bishop's conference table was surrounded by people. He told them that the company needed a Home Economics Department and that I was going to manage it. What a surprise! I developed the Home Economics Department and was in charge of testing woolens for washing and for care instructions. I also prepared bulletins about wool for school use. Another responsibility of mine was escorting tour groups through our facility. Mr. Bishop would not allow these tested items to be sold and asked if I knew anyone who would want them. I made lap robes out of the blankets and gave a number of them to my Arch Cape friends and to various churches. Dr. John and Irene Countryman, Elsie and Marie English and others, were probably the areas best-dressed beach residents. I stayed with the Pendleton Woolen Mills for twenty years and Earl worked for them for thirty-seven years.

One time when I was visiting Arch Cape, space was not available at the hotel. Elsie suggested staying at Jule Kullberg and Orlina Harsch's place, which was a block or so south of the hotel. Earl Robert was in college then. It was raining and friends of Earl Robert showed up and didn't have a place to stay. We arranged sleeping space for them in the lower level, where they warmed up with showers and spent the night. We told Orlina about this and wanted to pay extra for giving the boys a place to sleep, but she thought it was a neat experience for them and wouldn't take the money. Recently, at our granddaughter's wedding, some of those boys were there and said to me, "Do you remember the time we came to Arch Cape and how you put up with us and cooked all that bacon?" Those are memories one never forgets.

After Earl and I retired, we took many voluntary assignments for the International Executive Service and traveled all over the world. Our assignment was to share with them our knowledge about textiles, merchandising and to help them with financing problems. We taught them how to buy, price and sell their product.

Our first trip was to San Salvador, then to Iran, to Brazil, two times to Malaysia and then to Chili. We stayed in each country about three months and were always met by an American representative, except when we went to Chili. When we arrived in Iran, a man named Jack met us. We were in a desert and we asked him where our apartment was and where the plant was located in which we were to serve. We had been told when we left New York that we would have an apartment, but Jack said we would be lucky to have a bed with straw in it—and that is what we had. Our experiences were varied, often trying, but a part

of our life that was very rewarding in many ways. Our Arch Cape home was built by Steve Erickson, a local builder, after we sold our Lake Oswego house in 1972. After twelve years living at the beach, making new friends and enjoying the ever-changing ocean, we moved to an apartment in Portland. We returned to the beach for weekends and on other occasions and intended to have another ten years of beach life. Not so. Earl passed away in 1985. Today our son Earl and his wife Mary spend many weekends in Arch Cape. At times, I am with them and I still enjoy the beach Earl and I loved so much.

Earl, Emma and Earl Robert in front of Hoken and Mabel Lensrud's cottage. Circa 1944. Emma Rogness photo.

Harold Schaeffer
Service Station Manager, Local Fixit Expert and Artist

I can't tell you when Harold Schaeffer (others spell it Schaffer or Shaffer) came to Arch Cape or when he left the area. Local residents and visitors remember him in the 50's and 60's as a strong force in the community. Harold operated the Union Oil service station across Highway 101 from Ethel LaGault's store and post office. He maintained power lawn mowers, outboard motors and mechanical devices in the Arch Cape area. He also repaired and serviced automobiles, for he had a supply of belts, filters, fuel pumps, hoses, and could fix most problems that came his way.

Hundreds of tourists who visited his Arch Cape Union Oil Service Station remember his miniature scenes in front of the station. With scraps of lumber and skill, Harold created a representation of western history among native plants, shrubs and small pine trees in the front yard of his home and gas station.

In this make-believe world of props and imagination, there were wagons, horse teams, pioneers, an old fort, a log cabin with a deer's head over the door, a church, hotel, cafe, saloon and a farm house with the sign "West Coast 1858" on it. He constructed a house with a picket fence where a saddle horse stood outside the gate. There was a trading post with four horses hitched up outside. Besides these was a geyser which was the source of a tiny creek that ran off a little cliff to form a lake where a colorful stern wheeler floated. At one side was a village with tepees and Native American figures. A mail rider rode up a small hill. On a cliff, a prospector stood beside his tent and mine shaft. At the edge of it all was a small light house with the name "Arch Cape," and in front of the station stood a wishing well. Later, he added windmills, a railroad, an airship and put lights inside the buildings to make them come alive at night.

The whole display was an unforgettable attraction for adults and children when they visited Arch Cape, thanks to Harold Schaeffer's imagination and cleverness in planning and construction.

The end of an era. The service station that served the Arch Cape community for a long time was burned—used as a training exercise for the Arch Cape volunteer fire department. Photo source unknown.

283

The Scott Connection
Recollections by Marney Scott Beemer, Daughter

My father, Arthur Floyd Scott, was born in Eldora, Iowa, and died early in 1980 at the age of 90 in the Seaside, Oregon, hospital. When he was young, his family moved to Cedar Rapids, Iowa. After he graduated from Iowa State College in Ames, Iowa, in 1913, he moved to Buffalo, Wyoming, for his first job as a Wyoming county agent.

My mother, Ella Williams Scott, was born in 1894 in Buffalo, Wyoming, and in 1979 at the age of 87 died in the Wheeler, Oregon, hospital. Ella graduated from the University of Nebraska and taught in a country school in Buffalo, Wyoming, where she met and married my father, Scotty. They moved immediately to Wenatchee, Washington, and then to Tacoma, Washington, where he again was a county agent.

The home economist in his office was a friend of Elsie English, who told the Scotts about Arch Cape and the old hotel, *Singing Sands*. The Scotts spent several summer vacations there in the middle 1920's. As their only child, I well remember those trips around Hug Point, driving down the beach at low tide and up the board planks laid on the dry sand to reach the road to *Singing Sands*. There were always other families with children my age in the area. We all loved the crabbing, clamming, berry picking and riding Mr. Maxwell's white horse. Elsie and Marie English, both educators, loved children and seemed to have unlimited energy for the many Arch Cape activities involving children and guests.

We moved to Longview, Washington, in 1923, which made it easier to visit Arch Cape. My parents, however, bought a lot and built a cabin at Ocean Park, Washington, in the late 20's. We did not return to Arch Cape until the late 40's when Mother and Dad rented a cabin for a month from the Huffs, who lived in Portland, Oregon (now Jack Birkby's house). I brought my three little girls from Iowa and stayed with them. My husband, who was a busy veterinarian, joined us later. We all fell in love with Arch Cape again. My parents eventually bought a lot, built their home at Arch Cape in 1951 and retired there permanently in 1956. Later, they bought the lot just south of their home. The "Sitty Hall" behind the house had been built in 1951 for the carpenter from Longview, Washington, to live in while he built the house.

After being a county agent in both Wyoming and Washington, Scotty became one of the original real estate agents in the planned city of Longview, Washington, which opened to new citizens in 1923. The Scotts moved to southern California twice for short business ventures and to Deer Lodge, Montana, for a phosphate mine venture in 1930. Scotty owned a Texaco service station in Longview for several years and worked there for the Federal Land Bank of Spokane. Scotty found his real calling when he entered the life insurance business in 1938. He worked for the Oregon Mutual Company which is now the Standard Insurance Company. He sold over a million dollars' worth of life insurance each year for many years before he retired. Scotty sincerely felt he had done something wonderful for a family when he sold them a life insurance policy.

Everyone wondered how Scotty could ever adjust to retirement at the beach. His only hobby had been civic work. True to form, though, he involved himself in civic work in a new area. He was elected to the school board in Cannon Beach, attended Rotary regularly in Seaside, and worked on many important committees for the Seaside Episcopal Church.

Scotty was a strong leader in Arch Cape affairs. He helped organize the Arch Cape Community Club, worked long and hard promoting the fire station, sewer and water service districts, as well as other programs for the benefit of the Arch Cape community. For years, he worked the counter and cash register at the Arch Cape store while Ethel LeGault sorted the mail so box holders could get early morning delivery. Later in the morning, Scotty delivered mail to the neighbors around his home. He helped build the St. Peter the Fisherman Catholic Church in Arch Cape. The flag that was flown over the Capitol in Washington, D.C., in honor of Scotty's 90th birthday is displayed in the church community hall.

Not only was Scotty known by his neighbors and friends as the "unofficial mayor of Arch Cape," he had been raising the Stars and Stripes over his ocean-front home for 25 years, no matter what the weather. The flagpole was on the dune in front of the house for all to see as they walked the Arch Cape beach. The flag was raised at dawn and lowered each evening precisely as the sun set. Arch Cape residents could set their clocks by Scotty's daily walks on the beach and around the neighborhood.

For their 50th wedding anniversary in 1967, my family gave Ella and Scotty a miniature poodle named Goldie. Scotty and Goldie were the "official" investigators and watchers for the local property owners when they were away from Arch Cape, especially in winter when storms or cold temperatures caused problems. Scotty had keys to many homes of those who were not full-time residents of the area. Goldie was such an important part of Scotty's life that he sent out "death announcements" when she died, so saddened was he to lose his loyal friend of eleven years.

David English, nephew of Elsie and Marie English, and his wife Alma, tell how Scotty, after a severe storm cut power for several days, checked out their house. The freezer was a mess! Meats, salmon, pastries and fish bait were all soft and beginning to smell. The fish bait was special. Something strange had happened late that previous summer. A windrow about a foot wide and several hundred yards long of dead anchovies had appeared on the beach. The fish were apparently driven onto the beach by sea gulls and sea birds because many had visible bird bite wounds. David had sorted through the fish to select undamaged ones to package for fish bait for salmon fishing the next summer. Fifteen packages, each with a dozen anchovies, went into the freezer. The gulls, in the end, had the freezer contents for a special dessert—compliments of Scotty. He hauled everything to the beach for them. It must have been some sight, as every gull in Clatsop County probably got into the action.

Scotty was a "superman" and did the work of a ten-man county crew when it came to road maintenance. Most Arch Cape area roads are private roads so area residents are responsible for their upkeep. Maxwell Avenue entered our area of eleven homes from Highway 101, so Scotty kept the entry road clear of side brush, the drainage ditches open and the roadbed surfaced with crushed rock for all home owners to enjoy. He did this for years.

Perhaps Scotty's greatest claim to fame was his New Year's Day dips in the cold Pacific Ocean from 1968 until 1978. He and Betty Snow did this together and persuaded many others to join them. They were often featured on Portland television channels. Scotty was called "The Old Man of the Sea" by television announcers.

Ella Scott was an intellectual, an avid reader, a librarian in Longview, Washington, for many years, and a whiz at doing crossword puzzles and playing Scrabble. She worked often by giving reviews of books and plays as well as having a radio show about new books at the library. These talents were part of Ella's life at Arch Cape. Her book reviews were special events when her turn came to perform for the local literary club. Ella was also an artist. She specialized in embroidery, primarily on shirts and blouses.

Ella had diabetic neuritis for her last fourteen years at Arch Cape, so many local residents did not get a chance to know her for her graciousness and talents. Probably her greatest joys were her five grandchildren, who were raised in Iowa, but loved to be in Arch Cape for vacations. Two of them attended college in Portland, Oregon, so they could be near their grandparents and Arch Cape.

A few weeks before Scotty's 90th birthday, October 5, 1979, he was involved in a tragic accident a mile north of the Arch Cape store. His car collided with a motorcycle and a young woman passenger on the motorcycle lost her leg. Scotty never recovered from the shock of this incident and lived only four more months. His estate was sued and his family lost everything. His wife, Ella, had died two months before the accident. It was a sad ending for a man who dedicated his life to working with and for the public, a man respected and loved by everyone who knew him.

My husband and I purchased the Scott home in Arch Cape so it could continue to be used by our entire family. It is a shrine to the memory of Ella and Scotty's life in Arch Cape, the place they loved for so many years.

Ella, Scotty, and and their poodle Goldie, given to them on their 50th wedding anniversary in 1967. They also celebrated their 60th anniversary in 1977. Arch Capers could set their clocks by Scotty's walks on the beach with Goldie at 11 a.m. and 3 p.m. every day, rain or shine. Goldie had her own custom-made rain coat. Photo—Marney Beemer collection.

Grace Miller is at the lower right with Jean and Buck Miller next on a huge stump behind Singing Sands in 1928. Marney Beemer is at the top and their "baby sitter" Arthea is at the lower left. There are fences and gates to keep the cows and horses in the barnyard. Note the stand of timber in the background..

Marney, the Scott's daughter, and husband Blackie Beemer celebrated their 50th wedding anniversary in July 1992 by having a family reunion on Maui, Hawaii. They and their five children, spouses and grandchildren came from Australia, California, Colorado, Germany, Iowa and Hawaii. Their nineteen T-shirts had printed on the front: "A FAMILY IS—A CIRCLE OF FRIENDS—WHO LOVE YOU." Left to right: Detlev Lüdtke, Justin Halterline, Bob Wellman, Scott and Scotty Beemer, Scott Halterlein, Lynne Beemer Halterlein, Gayle Beemer Lüdtke, Blackie Beemer, P. J. Halterlein, Barbara Beemer Moritz, Marney Scott Beemer, Polly Beemer Wellman, Jan Beemer, Allen Lüdtke, Ella Wellman, Laura Lüdtke, Mary Wellman and Jay Wellman. Photos—Marney Beemer collection.

The Snow Connection
Memories by Bridget Snow

I was born November 1, 1898 in Portland, Oregon, on 15th and Hancock Street in a little house that is still standing.

I began school at age six in Astoria, completed the first and second grades there and lived with my great Aunt Devlin on 16th and Exchange Street. She was a German immigrant and married John Devlin, an early cannery man with a cannery in Astoria and one in Alaska. Mr. Devlin had a Chinese native working for him who let him know that the cheeks of the salmon were worth something. His cannery was the first in Astoria to market salmon cheeks.

I returned to my home in Hood River and began the third grade in a country school where the first eight grades were in one very large room. The children had small desks and graduated to the larger ones as time passed. We had two outhouses—one for the boys and one for the girls. The teacher arrived early to start the fire just as they did in pioneer days. We used a bucket for water and everyone used the same dipper. No one worried about "bugs" in those days. I returned to Astoria for my seventh and eighth grades and then went back to Hood River to finish high school. I think I was the first girl cheerleader ever to be voted by the Hood River High School, or any other high school student body, to lead the school cheers. Cheerleading at that time was a male responsibility, for discrimination laws were something off in the far future.

Our Hood River home, shared with two younger brothers and two older sisters, was two and one-half miles out of town. We lived and were raised like a Bohemian family when my father was home. Father was a musician with a wonderful voice and our home was often filled with music and people. We raised and processed all of our own meats and had ham and bacon slabs hanging in the attic storeroom. We did considerable bartering and we cured our meats at the Hood River Market. Salted butter and eggs were our staples for cooking. Eggs filled the water glass. The water glass for storing eggs was usually a crock with a lid. A mixture consisting of sodium silicate or potassium silicate or a combination of the two mixed with water made a syrupy liquid, sometimes called soluble glass. Eggs stored in the water glass kept for a long time. A great variety of food was stored at home. Hood River is a farming community where great apples, pears, and Marshall strawberries grew. Marshall strawberries are no longer on the market because they spoil much faster than newer varieties.

I remember when folks came to visit and to play Whist, a very popular card game in those days. Guests put their horses in the barn. One time, when the guests were ready to leave, they found a foot of snow outside, so they stayed the weekend. There were no snow plows in those days. I was sent to town on horseback to get more food. I had to plow through snow deep enough to reach the belly of my horse all the way out our long drive to the main road. The two and one-half mile trip to town was easy because traffic packed the snow, which made the ride enjoyable for me.

Folks put wagon boxes on sleigh runners in the winter. The horses had bells on their harness and when we heard them, we knew a neighbor was on his way to take us to school.

Aunt Devlin died in 1918, the year I graduated from high school, and she left each of the nieces $1,000. I wanted to be a nurse, but Mother convinced me to go to college, so I enrolled at the University of Oregon in 1918. I attended college for one year, joined a sorority, and had $300 left when, in 1920, I met a man named Berkeley Snow. He convinced me to give him the $300 and marry him, and in exchange he would give me the equivalent of a college education. Berkeley was with the 4th Engineers in World War I and I did volunteer work for the American Red Cross. We married June 18, 1921, and as promised, I began receiving my equivalent education spiced with a lifetime of joy and happiness. Berkeley owned a Model T Ford, was a Cornell graduate, and had a good job as manager of Pacific Power and Light in Hood River.

We lived in Hood River for a few years. Berkeley had an opportunity to move to Portland to become editor of a trade magazine called *Electrical West*. The magazine was distributed throughout western United States and British Columbia for those connected with producing and distributing private electric power. We built our first home in Green Hills in Portland and then the depression came and hit us very hard. We managed somehow. During the depression, I read palms at Lipman's Tea Room for a year. The depression wound down and the economy improved. Later, Berkeley worked for the hotel industry in Portland organizing conventions based on contacts he made when he was editor of the trade magazine.

One day, we answered an ad in *The Oregonian* for vacation rentals and found Bert Patton's log cabin in Arch Cape. Our time there convinced us that was the place for us.

We moved to Arch Cape in 1956, and that is when heaven opened its doors for us. We lived in our first home on Carnahan and Hemlock for twelve and one-half years. One of the reasons we moved here was to take advantage of the great fishing in the area, as Berkeley was an avid fisherman. We had salmon and perch from the ocean, salmon and trout from the streams, and clams and crabs from the shoreline. We didn't know anyone in Arch Cape but knew about some of the people, especially the English girls. For a long time we thought the English girls were from England. We soon found out that was their name. Gradually, we met others. The first people to call on us were Floyd and Ella Scott.

Each summer we built a shelter on the beach in front of our house on Carnahan Street with driftwood that came in the past winter. Our sign stated that this was the "Snow's Annex: make yourself welcome but please leave it clean." We have three sons and are blessed with eight grandchildren and six great-grandchildren. We have pictures of our grand children in the Snow annex.

We chose Arch Cape for a number of reasons. We eliminated Gearhart, Seaside, and Cannon Beach to live in, even though we knew Cannon Beach quite well. We liked the Arch Cape scenery and the closeness to Portland where our children and friends lived, so we could visit them and they could come down here. We walked to the store and knew at the time Arch Cape had many retired people about the same age we were. We soon became acquainted with many great people. There were the Crowleys, Coopers, Scotts, Jule and Orlina, Frieda and Jessie, the English girls, the Forbes, and many more.

We were here before the television cable arrived. Berkeley was a knowledgeable and talented musician and soon found people here were interested in good music. There was an occasional concert in Astoria. The roads to Portland were rugged and not easy to negotiate during the winter. Berkeley had a wonderful music system and a very complete library of records, so he decided the thing to do was to have concerts at our place. Our home had a huge living room with a high ceiling, so the acoustics for listening to music were excellent. Berkeley let it be known we planned to have these concerts and that anyone interested could come. We had as many as thirty-five attend, and our house, at times, was a little crowded. We had concerts once a month between October through the following April, when people became involved with gardening and other outdoor activities. Cannon Beach residents heard about the concerts and asked to come, so we became acquainted with many people from Cannon Beach, as well as the Arch Cape and Cove Beach residents.

Those that came were starved for good music. Berkeley selected the music and typed a program for the guests. He gave a résumé about the music to be played and some background on the composer. He would follow this with an explanation why the composer wrote the music. An intermission about half-way through the program allowed guests to pass through the kitchen for a glass of wine. Lucille Costanzo remarked that the concerts at the Snows were the most enjoyable and memorable Arch Cape event for her and she looked forward to each one with great anticipation. This was Berkeley's contribution to Arch Cape for eleven years.

But this was not the only thing that made Berkeley's presence felt here. He had a terrific ear for music and needed little excuse to share his talents. Berkeley played a guitar and composed many songs. He wrote a terrific ditty about Ella and Scotty after they went to Australia. The ditty equates what they would see there with what they had in Arch Cape. We made our own fun in Arch Cape. Any gathering was an excuse for Berkeley to get out the old guitar. All one had to do was to whistle a few notes of a melody and Berkeley would go from there. The group sang along with Berkeley and appreciated his leadership while enjoying those folk ballads he was so famous for.

Later, television was instrumental in breaking up the family gatherings we enjoyed so much. Two residents had television, Dr. Rockey down at the Cove and the Weibensons. This was before the cable came in and reception was very limited.

Scotty called one day and said a big band was coming to Portland and we should go hear it. We went to the Mallory Hotel for cocktails before the concert and Ella said, "I did bring my allergy medicine with me." I said "I didn't know you had allergies." Ella replied "I have an allergy for a weak drink" and then pulled a bottle out of her purse and poured reinforcements in each of our drinks.

The Markham boys, Jim and John, were commissioned by the Oceanography Department of the University of Oregon to take water temperatures and test for salinity once a week at high tide. First, it was Jim's job, and then, when he left for college, John took over until he entered college. I continued with this project for several years. I missed a few times in the winter when stormy weather conditions made sample collecting unsafe.

Winter storms with strong westerly winds were cause enough for Arch Cape residents to race beachward to be the first searching for the treasured glass balls floating shoreward from Japanese fishing grounds. These hand-blown glass floats supported fish nets, and when separated from their nets, began an odyssey that carried them from Japan via the Japanese Kuroshio current across the northern Pacific Ocean. The current bent southward from the Queen Charlotte Islands, off the west coast of Canada, down to northern California, where the California current took the floats southward to the equator. The North Pacific equatorial current carried its floats westward along the equator until curving northward just east of the Philippine archipelago. The floats were now homeward bound toward the southeast coast of Japan where they, again, entered the Japanese current. Severe storms all along this great egg-shaped route caused floats to be found on beaches all over the North Pacific Ocean. Storms out of the Gulf of Alaska and off the coast of Oregon and Washington brought thousands of floats to our shores. The 60's were very productive years for gathering floats. Now, new fishing methods and machine made plastic floats have virtually eliminated the thrill of finding the old hand blown treasures.

One early morning long before sunrise, I saw many flashlights on the beach. I ran back into the bedroom and told Berkeley to hurry—others beat us to the beach. Glass floats were easy to find in those days. At times, we found more than could be carried home in one trip. We hid them behind drift and logs hoping they wouldn't be found by others. Gooseneck barnacles and marine growth covered some floats and made them heavy. The hunt for floats was tremendous fun. One time when I had a dinner planned for the Scotts, the English girls, and others, the glass floats were coming in with each wave. The dinner waited while my guests were harvesting floats. Since I was a "Johnnie come lately" to Arch Cape, I suddenly realized how important it was to harvest these glass balls and learned the rules of the hunt. No one bothered to tell me that my guests would rather collect glass floats than eat dinner on time.

I received a call one day informing me there was a pink sea gull near Asbury Creek. Naturally, I had to see for myself, and surely enough, there was this pink sea gull with all those beautiful white gulls. I did research regarding pink sea gulls. It took me six weeks and much run-around before I found that the sea gull was dyed pink so they could keep track of migration patterns. My information came from the Colorado Wild Life Department. They dyed gulls in Alaska and one found Arch Cape. I haven't seen a pink gull since, (nor a purple one either).

Berkeley died in September, 1969. I sold our house and bought the home I now occupy and have been here for 23 years. Frieda Billings and Jessie Faire, the former owners, had a price of $27,000 and they sold it to me for $25,000 because they believed I would take care of it and that I would never disturb Walgrem, their French poodle's grave. Walgrem is under the Rhododendron tree in the back yard. We had a habit of planting a tree over our pets when they died so no one would ever disturb them. Frieda and Jessie were in a nursing home in Seaside when their Arch Cape home was listed for sale. My home sold immediately so I purchased theirs. It worked out beautifully and was a good move.

One morning when I awoke, I looked out the window and all I could see were logs. Logs were all over, covering Leech Avenue, Travis's yard, everywhere. I was the only one around at the time so I had to alert all the people who owned houses in the area to come down with their chain saws. I walked to the bridge and saw logs everywhere. They washed up the creek from the ocean. It became a contest to see if the logs won or if the bridge held. This had to be a terrible storm, but I did not hear anything from my bedroom the previous night. Travis invited people to gather wood from his yard after these storms.

Jule Kullberg and Orlena Harsch came down every summer in the 70's. Both were teachers. Jule taught art courses at Seattle Community College and Orlena was a Seattle high school counselor. We began writing messages in the sand to each other and found out that other beach walkers became interested in our messages. Orlena, to confuse people, wrote messages in Spanish that none of us could understand. A young girl, Joan Herbert, who was a nurse, suggested we take turns doing the beach message. It just happened that summer vacation ended on Labor Day, so we quit. The next summer I began writing my original rhymes and messages, depending on the weather. I selected a location at the high tide mark just north of Arch Cape Creek. The sheltered sands there below the rocks protect the sand dunes. It is an area cleansed by a new high tide and made ready for my next message which I continue to do to this day for special occasions.

I remember a bad storm when logs were up to the second story of Jule and Orlena's house. A young man who lived nearby opened the back door to let the water out. Had he not done so, the whole house would have collapsed. I had keys for most of the homes around here and was responsible for looking after them, a neighborly gesture.

It is interesting how the street, *Gelinsky*, got its name. Scotty had this dog called Goldie and he would say to Ella, "I am going to walk Goldie down Gelinsky" because the Gelinsky family had a house down from Scotts. At that time, the Gelinsky house was half collapsed and my grandchildren named it the *Haunted House*. Betty Morrison Moran and I talked about Gelinsky and I said, "I have this nice piece of driftwood here—why don't you make a sign and let us call it *Gelinsky Boulevard*"? The sign has been here for years and the Gelinsky name is now on the county plat maps. There really ought to be a street named after the English girls.

I remember being in Singing Sands once. I think we were looking for a place to rent and we looked it over. I recall the big kitchen with the huge stove and the spacious living room. I was told that if you put a tennis ball on the floor, it would roll down hill. It reminded me of my old home in Hood River.

I have always been involved in all aspects of community affairs. I love Arch Cape and have done what I can to make it a more viable and livable place. Arch Cape should always be a residential community. I realize growth and development will continue to be a part of this area and the community should monitor this growth and development. I was president of the Arch Cape Community Club twice. In May, 1977, I received a **Certificate of Merit** from the Cannon Beach Chamber of Commerce for devoted service to the Community. Many Arch Cape residents took an active part in Cannon Beach affairs and belonged to their Chamber of Commerce before Arch Cape formed their own Community Club.

Probably my greatest "claim to fame" began January 1, 1957 at the house on Carnahan when I took my first annual New Year's Day ocean dip. This tradition spans 32 years with the exception of two times when the ocean was too rough: one year when the doctor forbad me to go, and another time when I was stranded in Portland. Floyd "Scotty" Scott joined me in this tradition when I moved to my present home in 1969. The last several years drew large crowds with many local families, including my own family, both as bathers and spectators. Television crews from Portland and photographers from the local newspapers also were present for the event. There were fifty in the water and a hundred or two watching January 1, 1989, when I announced my retirement. The water temperature was about 46 degrees and the air temperature somewhat the same. It was a dry day with high scattered clouds allowing splashes of sun to reach the beach.

Huckleberry season was an excuse for the locals to gather in the hills near the Manzanita Cemetery. It was a wonderful place for huckleberries, and when we finished picking, we would gather at Singing Sands to clean the berries. The berries were placed on a woolen blanket and tossed and rolled back and forth. The stems and sticky leaves stuck to the blanket, and when the process was finished, we had clean huckleberries. It is said that errant husbands were given the berry cleaning blanket so to prickle them and make them uncomfortable all night long.

Ocean traffic was much more active in the early days. Ships of all sizes crossed the horizon on their way to and from the Columbia River and tugboats with barges traveled north and south daily. Today, you would be lucky to see a large ship or barge once a week. The huge container vessels and highway trucks are partially responsible for the reduced ship traffic.

The Christmas season was always very special to us. We gathered together to collect greens and then ended up at someone's house for a Wassail celebration. We sang Christmas carols going from house to house and then drank hot spiced wine to our health served from a Wassail bowl. This was an early English family tradition. Later, we carried our greens home to do our own decorating. This wonderful Christmas activity demonstrates the strong bond developed over the years by the early Arch Cape residents. We always cut our own Christmas tree, usually in the Manzanita area, where pine grew in abundance. Sometimes the men searched for fir trees in the hills east of us. We were real greenhorns when we arrived here. We decorated our whole house with hemlock greens the first year, including a tree on the deck and one in the living room. Four days later needles were all over the place. We learned to gather pine, fir or spruce in the future, for they would last through the holiday season without shedding their needles.

One of the most exciting sights each fall was the migrating shearwaters heading south from Alaska. They are a long-winged bird related to the petrels and the albatrosses and usually skim close to the water. At times, the horizon would be black with these fast traveling birds destined for a warmer climate. We haven't seen them in the great flocks or numbers for the last five or six years. One day we were on a bluff watching the shearwaters feed on anchovies very close to shore when my brother and a friend tried catching them with a lace tablecloth. The gulls were feeding on wounded anchovies left over by the shearwaters and regurgitated them right over our heads.

The wildlife was prolific when we first arrived. We could hear coyote screaming. Quail were daily visitors to our yard. Deer bedded down in the yard next to us, and at times I would be lucky enough to catch a mother with her fawn through my camera lens. Nan Law told me a story about a deer named Sally. Every year Sally appeared with her fawn. People would say "Hello Sally," and Sally would turn around and bow in acknowledgment. I saw Sally for two more years. We were told that Sally was shot. One time I thought I heard a baby cry and called Berkeley. There were no babies around here at this time and discovered we heard a cougar, which sounds just like a baby. Some girls who lived near where Jack Foster's house stands saw a large animal chasing a deer. (The Fosters sold their home in 1992) I walked to Hug Point that morning and saw the tracks of a large cat and that of a deer. I saw where they met and could see where the deer got away up the cliff. I was told that the cat must have been very sick to let the deer get away. We saw an occasional bear and many elk. They did not come into our yard like the deer, who were less bothered by people. Many residents in the area fenced gardens to keep deer from eating their produce.

Scotty and I formed a warning system for the Arch Cape area. We worked together to do many things for our community and were called "the promoters." We wanted a system so everyone in Arch Cape could be warned should a tidal wave alert, illness, or any other emergency arise. We used the telephone. This was before television, and since we knew everyone here, we knocked on doors to alert people and to get help when needed. It was an excellent system and residents respected the use of the telephone for emergency use. A very suspicious man came into Ethel LaGault's store one day. Ethel told the man she had a gun and he had better leave or she would use it. He left but she believed he might come back so she notified us and we got the word around to home owners to be on the lookout for a stranger. The police found him in the area. He had escaped from the Tillamook Correction Center.

The following material by Betty (Bridget) and Berkeley Snow is presented here exactly as written Friday night March 27, 1964.

TIDAL WAVE

On Friday night March 27 I was upstairs in bed, Berk working at his desk. This was a beautiful moonlight night, no wind, the ocean clean and shimmering, stars and the full moon made it a night of beauty.

Several times I left my story just to look at the beauty of the night, it was so bright you could read a newspaper.

We were called around nine o'clock, asking if we had heard about the earthquake in Alaska. Not having a television, and poor reception on radio, we seldom listened to the newscasts and depended on the morning Oregonian for our news. No more calls came in so we promptly dismissed it from our minds.

Shortly after eleven o'clock Ron Enna and three young people came over and asked if we had heard anything about a tidal wave. Now I am second to be notified in case of an emergency, Floyd Scott is first on the list. We have a good system of warning along the coast, and have twice evacuated on false tidal wave alerts. So I assured the boys that I am sure we would have heard if we were in any danger. We chatted for some time, the boys left, it was now about eleven twenty p.m.

I went upstairs, saw the Campbell's light was still on, called them up and asked about the earthquake and tidal wave. They then told me about the quake, how awful it was, but no alert on the wave. No danger—the latest report. It was now about 11:30 p.m. so we tried for the news. We listened to the quake reports when we heard and felt a bump and the house shake as though someone has thrown a heavy sack of cement, with great force, against the house. It came again in matter of seconds. Berk and I rushed outside and heard the noise again, like an explosion up north, and then the lights went out and Berk yelled "Tidal Wave." We rushed out front and there was a great mass of ocean, six to eight feet or more of swirling water around the foot of the bank, with good size choppy waves coming in on top of it. A sight to see, fascinating, exciting and very SCARY. In a matter of minutes I turned tail and ran. I was scared and ready to head for the tall timber. I will now let Berk give his version, for everyone has a different account, then I will come back to finish. Bridget Snow.

My version of the evening's entertainment varies particularly not at all from Betty's. Our fear in observing the turbulence at the foot of the bluff was not that the waves would splash up over the top and rush toward the house, but that they might undermine the bank and drop us down into the swirling waters. We rushed back to the house but shortly noted the noise abating and I went out to look over the bank again. The waters had receded somewhat and soon the beach and the sea took on a more normal aspect. We decided the show was over and went back to compare notes with neighbors who had gathered. No casualties—No damage—No hysteria—But lots of talk. - Berk.

Soon, all the neighbors gathered, Bill Kane, Lura Graham, Estelle Campbell, the Bradburys and Mr. Foster and his son. We all talked at once, but the decision was reached that all was clear and we had nothing to fear. The Bradburys went to Cannon View Park, which is very low, to see if anyone needed help. Bill Kane, Berk and I went south to check on our friends in the lowlands, the Scotts, the English girls, and Freda and Jessie and others. All was well there, and no evidence of water over the sand dunes or on the road at Leach Avenue was evident. So, home to bed for a good night's sleep after a hectic night.

The next day we found out that another wave came in at 3 a.m. but we were not alerted. A few people who rushed to the high timber were stopped by the State Police and were not allowed to return to their homes until 4 a.m.

Gearhart, Seaside and Cannon Beach were alerted for the second wave, which was not much higher than a good storm at high tide.

On the next day, Saturday, we traveled out and around to see what damage was done. Very little here in Arch Cape, and in the past, we have experienced much more damage by some of our winter storms. Cannon Beach was another story, for extensive damage was done to many places on the waterfront, especially around Elk Creek. Water surging up the creek carried a duplex 400 yards and laid it down as though placed there by a giant hand, along with the highway bridge crossing the creek near the school. Fences around the school were down, playground equipment damaged, and water reached the building with mud and sand all over the playground. Logs of all description spread everywhere. Across Elk Creek, several houses were damaged. A motel with logs and debris piled high and soaked with water and sand all through the place suffered much damage. A house in the area had logs in the living room.

There are many versions of what people saw when the wave hit, or by those who saw it coming in. We were extremely lucky that the wave hit on an angle instead of coming in directly. If we had a direct hit, the story would be one of horror and disaster. WE WERE VERY LUCKY.

It took a week to write this because Spencers' two youngest children visited us. The weather was so divine we spent all our time on the beach, and tumbled into bed at night exhausted from the fresh air and fun on the beach.

Back to the tidal wave once more. In summing up, we saw about 8 to 10 feet of water with waves on top; another person saw the sea rise 7 feet in 7 seconds, with the waves on top, then receding way out and rushing in again; another saw a wall of water 16 feet high which came rushing in and just dropped; another reported the same thing and everyone reported the terrible noise and some noted the pounding we felt. Harley Sroufe saw it come up Elk Creek: a wall of water 15 feet high, lifting everything in its way and carrying it on top of the wave. Others slept through it all.

Arch Cape residents are special. They must love nature and be able to take the weather, especially the storms, in stride. One must be able to adjust from city activities, enjoy quiet times, be able to read a good book beside the fireplace when the winter storms are with us, and to have strength within oneself to not have to depend on others for contentment. I could sum it up with these words: Being in Arch Cape is about as close to Heaven as you can get.

Authors' note — We have known Bridget for many years. She is a lady with strong convictions, beliefs, morals, and one willing to stand against opposition for what she believes is right and proper for the benefit of her community. We know of no other person who commands as much love and respect from those who know her.

Bridget, for years, wrote messages during the summer at a very special place in the sand just a little north of Arch Cape Creek. And then, the next high tide would smooth the sand again for the following daily message which would be an excuse for all of us to see what Bridget could come up with next. She never faltered. Bridget created special beach material for guests and relatives of friends on request, usually before retiring at night. It was prepared and ready early in the morning for all to enjoy as the sun rose over the eastern hills. Here are a few of her sand writings just as she wrote them for all of us to enjoy.

I have the sea
The sun and gulls
The hills--the stream.
All this
I call mine.
Things of which
Others dream.

Buds Bursting
in the sun.
Daffodils nodding
in the breeze.
Buzz saws buzzing
Lawn mowers mowing
Spring is here.

Winter storms
Waves ride high
Spin drift blowing
Sand in eyes.

A little rain
A little mist
Lift up your face
By heaven be kissed.

Don't turn your back
Upon the sea.
Or you'll get smacked
As it smacked me.
It smacked me right
Upon my fanny.
Do not laugh
It was not funny.

The tips of the hills
Are hidden with mist
Making trails of magic
Near the tree tops
Drink in their beauty
Let your imagination soar
Let it fly with the mist
From hills to shore.

Smoke from chimney.
Leaves dropping
To the ground.
Smell of autumn
In the air.
Natives walk
The beach alone.

I write of the hills.
I write of the sea.
But most of all
I write of thee.
Thee who come
To read my verse
To see if it is
Sublime or worse!

Ah! the glory of
The early morn
When I walk the
Beach alone.
Alone? Not alone.
There is David
With mug in hand
Along with Rufus
His canine friend.
Together we watch
The early morn
The joy of seeing
A new day born.

The lovely land
Between the hills
And the restless sea
Trees stand
With misty caps
Silhouetted against the sky.

Sugar snaps are planted
A row of carrots too.
Travis says
The seeds will rot.
If so, I'll cry.
Wouldn't you?
(this after a very wet spring)

Hey diddle diddle
The cat and the fiddle
All the fish in the sea
Looked on with glee
Watching me
Trying to empty
The sea
With a spoon.

The sea today
is pearly grey.
The sky is light blue.
Tips of the waves
Are OH so white.
The gulls fly high
 A dot in the sky.
Down on the shore
A child flies a kite.

Changing sea
Summer calm
Water blue
Surfers surfing
Children playing
On the shore.

Waves running high.
Trees blowing with the wind
Leaves dropping to the ground
Rain pouring from the sky.
Do I have to tell you
Summer has gone by.

Some say the sun.
Does not set.
Tis the earth that
Turns around
Don't spoil my dream
My fantasy.
I know the sun
Sets in the sea.

Share
I share with thee
The murmur of the sea
And the treasures she
Brings to me
As I walk
The shore.
I share with thee
The cry of the gull
As he seeks his food.
I share with thee
The singing sands
I share with thee
The hills
And all the wonders
That we see.
Thank him
Who has given
This beauty
To you and me.

Without the rain
To make things grow
We would have none to eat.
Without the rain
To make the streams
We would have none to drink.
So rain must come
To help all things
Or we would end up with none.

The sun of slugs
Came after my snaps
I got my Cory
And gave him a smack
He went back to his den
Told the rest of his friends
She's a bad wicked woman
I won't go there again.

And then, Bridget often helped welcome guests and family of her many friends with a special sand message. Here is a sample.

From Seattle come Heidi, Michelle and Tami
To visit aunt and uncle and to explore
Our Arch Cape shore.
Sand dollars you may find
Along the low tide line.
Watch sea gulls bathing in the creek,
The pelicans diving for their fish,
A water ouzel I did spy,
Let your imagination fly.

Mrs. Berkeley Snow, center, is flanked by friends and family as she steps out of the surf New Year's Day. Mrs. Snow, 86, takes an annual dip at Arch Cape on the first day of each year. Identified from left in the foreground are Vince Morrison, Ray Niebuhr, Berkeley Snow III (Mrs. Snow's grandson), John Markham, and Tom Hanlon. Seaside Signal photo by Fran Keating, January 3, 1985.

Berkeley and Bridget Snow, August 13, 1962. Photo, Bridget Snow's collection.

Peggie Steinauer
As Told to Alma English

Peggie lives east of Highway 101 on Ocean Road. She and her husband, Bill, moved to Arch Cape in 1977 after Bill's retirement from a Kenai oil refinery in Alaska. Prior to their move, Peggie worked as the first secretary to the steering recruiting committee for the Alaska Methodist University from 1959 to 1961. This school is now the Kenai branch of the University of Alaska. Later on, Peggie worked for the Kenai School District.

Peggie and Bill moved here to treat Bill's arthritis. He was in pain and the Wheeler Clinic was well-regarded for treating those suffering from chronic arthritis. They liked the area and purchased property in Arch Cape east of the store and post office and had a modular home assembled on the site. They became acquainted with many of the citizens who stopped occasionally to watch the home assembly.

Bill was active with the American Legion in Kenai and transferred his membership to the Cannon Beach American Legion organization. Peggie became involved with the womens' auxiliary and spearheaded a program that served lunches on Tuesdays and Thursdays to Senior Citizens.

Bill died in 1980 and Peggie regrets his having only three years in Arch Cape. She continues to speak fondly of her late husband and often interrupts her conversation with "I wish you could have known my Bill. You would have loved him."

In 1981 Peggie and her son, Don Shaw, purchased the old Texaco service station. Shortly after the purchase, Peggie wanted it destroyed. She made arrangements with the Arch Cape Fire Station to burn it to the ground. Peggie hired Don Boehm, a general contractor from Cannon Beach, to get the required permits to remove the two gasoline tanks. The Cannon Beach Fire Department kept one of the tanks; the other had no value. Neighbors and friends in the area observed the burning, the excavation, and the removal of the tanks. This gave Peggie an excuse to have a party on her deck.

Peggie's love for animals is well-known in our town. Often area residents see her taking her three dogs for a ride in her easily recognized red car. Her latest addition, Abby, is black and white Japanese Chinn (or spaniel). Abby is ten months old and often outruns Bonnie and Casey. When Peggie lets them out for exercise and wants them back, she shouts, "Here ABC," and all three respond. Peggie also has three cats that give her joy with their antics chasing the dogs and seeking attention.

Elk visit Peggie and often destroy her hanging baskets, the potted plants on her deck, and flowers in her garden. They eat most shrubs, but shun rhododendrons. A year ago Peggie contacted Fish and Wild Life personnel for help. They gave her **Magic Circle,** a product which comes in pouches or which can be mixed in the soil. The odor is offensive to the elk but not harmful or offensive to pets. Since this application, the elk do not come into her yard. Peggie does, however, see them in the area.

Peggie's warmth, her laugh and smile add sunshine to our day. The authors have experienced many suppers at Peggie's home enjoying exotic preparations, including "camouflaged" frog legs—and who knows what else at other times. Maybe elk!

Summer Infatuations
By Elisabeth Speros McCrea

Although I was born and raised in Portland, I can't remember a time when Arch Cape was not a part of my life. My parents were vacation visitors long before I was born, and they looked for a place to buy whenever we were in the area.

I can remember staying in the Singing Sands Hotel. I half-remember stories of buried treasure, perhaps under the floorboards, and can recall dim, vast interiors dominated by a rough-hewn stone fireplace. There was an industrial-size kitchen and an intimidating corridor on the second floor which was long and shadowed. Many doors led to bedrooms and to a bathroom.

In 1954, when I was eight years old, my dad, Dr. James T. Speros and stepmother (named Margaret, but called Fibbie) bought the house at what is now 10 Ocean Road. It was built by Mrs. Williams herself and was a spectacular place. The second floor was a great room with sleeping lofts on the east and west sides. The attached garage had a dirt floor, a year-round "creeklet" and a stuffed, standing sea gull. After remodeling the garage, it became the only official bedroom in the house. The bathroom featured a parallelogram bathtub made of concrete which I thought was sensational. When it was replaced by a boring, standard-type tub, I was the only one who missed the old one. One outstanding architectural detail was the "Hollywood Staircase," made of wood that curved up the exterior wall on the east to the side porch on the second floor. I thought it was a perfect set-piece for Loretta Young in beach togs. The stairs were declared a security risk, however, and torn away. Years later we added the present garage to the east side of the house.

Our first years in the *Cape Cottage* (our name) were spent removing and rebuilding. I spent several summers side-stepping old lumber and rusty nails. Once I misstepped and drove a nail into the sole of my foot. Of course, Dad had a syringe set and tetanus vaccine in his black bag.

Is there a doctor in Arch Cape? There were always a number of doctors in residence in Arch Cape. My brothers, Tom and Mark, and I were sure that the local chapter of the AMA could gather in Arch Cape and have a quorum without anyone's having to drive to the meeting. Besides my dad there were Drs. Baird, Biehn, Uren, West and Poppe from Portland and Dr. John Countryman, a permanent Arch Cape resident from Grafton, North Dakota.

We purchased *Cape Cottage* as a vacation retreat, but it soon became the residence of my maternal grandmother, Maude Hughes. She lived in Arch Cape "half-years" (April through October) from the mid 50's until her death in 1969. It was through Maudie that I knew the Mellinger girls, the English sisters, the Countrymans, the locally famous Ethel LeGault, and Lowell and Dorothy Hawkins. I also came to know the simple, secretive pleasure of listening in on the party-line telephone and the "Arch Cape Yodel"— Knock twice, open the door, stick your head inside and warble, **Yoooh Whooo**. In the early 60's, my uncle, John Hughes, moved into the house. John was a charter member of the Arch Cape Fire Department, and lived in Arch Cape until his death in the early 70's.

In 1975 my dad retired and he and Fibbie became full-time Arch Cape residents. Fibbie died in January, 1976. Dad lived in the house until late 1991 when he moved to Iowa, close to me and our family, where he died in May, 1993. His retirement years in Arch Cape were quiet and happy, spent puttering around the house and in the yard with his dog, Kilgore. He took pride in his flowers, constantly battling moles and slugs that threatened his garden.

It is not the *Cape Cottage,* however, that holds my heart. It is the beach. I was given free rein while growing up in Arch Cape and learned most of the important lessons of life by listening and watching and walking along the tide line. As a child and as an adolescent, a young adult and as a middle-aged matron, I know a wholeness of spirit just by being on the beach.

There are gifts from the sea for those who discern their value: Jellyfish and kelp in their season, sand dollars, starfish, sea anemones and the ubiquitous sea gulls and sandpipers. There are the secrets given to the adventuresome who wait for a very low tide to walk around the headlands to the next beach. There is the singing sand, so fine that scuffing feet on dry sand produces a melodious squeak. The sand that looks white while walking looks quite different when one lies basking on a towel. The grains are white, and also coral, and jet and amber: surprise!

The most highly prized treasures washed onto shore during late winter storms in February and March were the glass floats torn from fishing nets of the Japanese fleet. Residents made sure their binoculars were handy, and people who were always polite could become downright unfriendly when confronting another collector at the in-coming tide.

Some of my best treasures are memories of the friends of summer. I remember the kids from the Markham, Tarr, Law, Kindley and Rall families. Most, like me, were children and grandchildren of residents, and we enjoyed a freedom of thought and movement unusual for the times. We walked up in the hills to check out the source of water, paddled about in the pools of Arch Cape Creek as it flowed under the highway bridge and played chicken in the tunnel. We went into Seaside and strolled the midway and the beach front. After exploring tiny Cannon Beach, we were amazed that the whole town didn't just disappear from lack of interest. Of course, Arch Cape was even smaller; if we could count more than a dozen people on the beach, it was crowded. We played on the driftwood, built windbreaks out of driftwood, and watched out for driftwood rolled about by shallow sneaker waves.

There are summer infatuations that were fleeting, lasting only a season, and there are some that endure. The affection with which I hold the community of Arch Cape endures.

Dr. James Speros on the Arch Cape beach. Circa 1955.

Elizabeth Speros McCrea and Billy Ward, nephew of Ethel Legualt, the long-time store and Post Office owner, in Arch Cape, 1954. Photos, Elizabeth Speros collection.

The Walsh-Berry Connection
The Story of Mary Louise Walsh at Arch Cape - 1891-1985
Memories — by Coryell Berry

Miss Mary Louise Walsh was born in Tacoma, Washington on August 14, 1891. She attended Washington State University and later the University of Washington, graduating in Home Economics. She taught school in Tacoma and Seattle for her entire professional career. Mary never lived full time in Arch Cape, but owned property there, and was always considered part of the community.

Records are unclear as to the exact date, but it is known that Mary visited Arch Cape in the early 1930's. During this time she taught school in Tacoma and met Elsie English, a Tacoma school principal, and Elsie's sister Marie, also a school teacher, who taught in Seattle. The English sisters owned the *Arch Cape Hotel* they named *Singing Sands*. Mary was a frequent guest of the English sisters, who opened and ran the old hotel every summer for many years. It did not take much persuasion by Elsie and Marie to convince Mary to purchase a small parcel of land close to Singing Sands.

Communication and travel to and from Arch Cape in the mid-thirties was limited. One summer day in 1936, Mary's niece, Marilynn Walsh Berry and a friend rode their bikes to Cannon Beach at low tide. This was an adventure, for they had the responsibility of picking up the mail and delivering it to everyone staying at *Singing Sands*. It was a great shock that this batch of mail included a telegram from Marilynn's brother, Bill, which told of their father's heart attack. At that time Western Union delivered only as far as Cannon Beach and messages, no matter the urgency, had to be picked up there with the rest of the mail.

Mary purchased a parcel of property on the southwest corner of Maxwell Avenue and Cannon Street in 1945. Floyd and Ella Scott had property to the west, now owned by their daughter, Marnie Beemer and her husband, Dr. Melvin Beemer. The Huff property to the south was owned by Jack and Dorothy Birkby for many years. They sold and moved to Seaside in 1992.

After acquiring the lot, Mary hired Wilbur Markham to construct a small cottage on the property. Two structures placed together formed a 400 square foot building. One part of the building had less head room than the other part of the building, which resulted in inadequate head space for adult male members of the family; but, the tiny house was complete. The kitchen had a sink with hot and cold water taps, a two-burner hot plate and a portable oven. A full-sized refrigerator sat beside the dining table. Counter surface was minimal, as was drawer and cabinet space. Still, Mary loved to prepare gourmet meals and share them with her many friends. The living area became sleeping space and a bath with shower was available. Activities centered around the dining table in the neat and tidy house. Besides Mary's delightful meals, happy times are remembered playing Yahtzee, Hearts, Scrabble, and other games of that era. The table also served as a work area and for writing post cards to unlucky friends who had to remain in the city. The house was tiny but comfortable.

The exterior walls sheathed with cedar shingles soon turned to a marvelous driftwood gray. A flat roof had just enough pitch to allow heavy rain to dissipate. The cabin sported a picture window with a pleasant garden view from the dining area. The landscaping around the house looked neat all of the time with a mix of native growth and planted flowers. Mary always had a flower arrangement on the dining room table.

She lovingly named the cottage *Breffni* which she explained was an Irish name meaning "little house beside the sea." A visitor quickly recognized the affection Mary had for the small cottage and for Arch Cape.

BREFFNI

There is a place that I adore
Tis down beside the ocean shore
It is so tiny and so small
It's hardly any house at all

But in spring when flowers bloom
The golden sun rides high at noon
There I lie out upon the sand
And try to get a summer tan

Then autumn with its gentle rain
That beats upon my window pane
The grass grows tall, the leaves come down
A crimson carpet for the ground

In winter when the north winds roar
And tides race high along the shore
It is so cozy, warm as down
I have no wish to live in town

That's why I love you Breffni
My tiny house beside the sea.

Eva Walsh, Mary's sister-in-law

Mary was a great one for entertaining. The fact that *Breffni* was really too small to accommodate her many friends did not matter. There were many luncheons, afternoon teas, and dinner parties held there. In fact, she frequently would invite Seattle and Tacoma friends down for a few days. She was truly a "space" engineer.

Mary Walsh was an extremely generous person and wanted to share *Breffni*, the ocean, and Arch Cape with her family. For many years, her sister-in-law, Eva Walsh; her niece, Marilynn Walsh Berry; her nephew, William J. Walsh, Jr.; and their offspring benefited from her vision and generosity. Deer visiting in the early morning light, the roar of the ocean, the squawking of the sea gulls, the fresh air of the salty breeze, the twilight hour with Queen Vic looming over the breakers: All were treasures for all to enjoy when visiting Mary's wee bit of heaven. And then, of course, wonderful people like Marie and Elsie

English, John and Irene Countryman, Floyd and Ella Scott, Bridget Snow, the Maddison family, Ralph and Elizabeth Forbes, Nan Law, Frieda Billings, Jule Kullberg, Orlena Harsch, plus many others helped make Arch Cape so precious for Mary, her family and for her friends.

She deeded her property to Marilynn and Bill in 1971. In 1976, they purchased a small adjoining parcel from Floyd Scott which made the total area owned by them a simple rectangle. *Breffni* was happily used by the family until 1980 when it was determined that dry rot had taken over and it was best to have it demolished.

In 1983, Mary's niece, Marilynn and her husband, Coryell (Cork) Berry with her nephew, William Walsh and his wife, Mildred (Mitzi) joined forces to build a replacement house on the property. *Breffni II*, designed by architect Cork Berry, meets the needs of the two families.

The "little house beside the sea" had been cherished by the family. The grand nephews and nieces, Scott, Caroline and Joan Berry, and Kathleen and Marilynn Walsh loved to come to the beach, stay at *Breffni*, and enjoy the endless fun and beach activities. They enjoyed gathering driftwood to build evening fires for hot dogs, marshmallows and *s'mores*, jumping the waves, picking berries, hiking around Hug Point, searching for glass balls and sand dollars, sailing kites and gathering those delicious razor clams and mussels. When these children were youngsters, the trip from Bellevue, Washington required up to eight hours— a long hard drive—but always worth the effort.

Mary Walsh's great-grandnieces and nephews, Eva and Madeline Huffman (parents Caroline Berry and Bruce Huffman); Stephanie Caldwell (parents Kathleen Walsh and Bob Caldwell); and Drew and Tyler Gregg, (parents Joan Berry and Bob Gregg) represent the fourth generation at Arch Cape. The oldest two are not quite five years old and already are expressing their love for Arch Cape. In this respect, they are very much like their parents, their grandparents and their aunt and uncle, Marilynn Walsh and Martin Rothen.

The devotion that Mary Walsh had for Arch Cape has had a major impact on her family. Thank goodness she found it when she did.

THIS GLASS BALL

I've hunted high
I've hunted low
Wherever western winds do blow
I've looked for miles along the shore
They may not make them anymore.

But someday on an ocean beach
I'll find one lying at my feet.
Right there upon the shining sand
Where it came in from old Japan.

But I will find one never fear
And it will be for you, my dear
Now here it is, at long long last
Be careful for it's made of glass.
Eva Walsh

"Breffni", the cottage constructed for Mary Walsh by Wilbur Markham in 1946. The Huff house is in the background with the original log siding that was replaced in 1962 with shingles from the Arch Cape Shingle Mill.

Mary L. Walsh on the beach at Arch Cape in 1934 wearing white shoes and white gloves. Photos, Marilynn Berry collection.

The Bill and Ruth Watson Connection
As told to Alma English

Bill came to Arch Cape as a child in the early 20's with his mother, Lucille, and his grandmother, Rose Woodard. They were introduced to Arch Cape by their friends and neighbors, the Gelinsky-Holderman families, and often stayed at the Leech cottages. Bill's mother purchased property in 1926 from Sam Webb and W. A. Tyler, local real estate land promoters. It was not unusual then to think you had purchased a certain parcel of land to learn later that this was not the case. This happened to Bill's mother, Lucille. When Bill and Ruth wanted to build their present home, they discovered the highway department had taken twenty feet off of Lucille's property without her knowledge and without compensation. They struggled with the necessary permits and the usual problems one faces building on a nonconforming lot. This caused sacrifices to their building plans and gave them a lesser house than they wanted. In 1975, Bob Moon from Cannon Beach constructed their home. Ruth and Bill became full-time Arch Cape residents in 1979.

On January 1, 1974, Bill retired from the U. S. Postal Service after 32 years. In May, 1993, Bill received his fifty-year gold pin from the national Association of Letter Carriers.

Ruth worked most of her life at various jobs. She worked twelve years in the garment industry in the Twin Cities, where she made athletic clothes. She moved to New York and was a chef in a private home which employed thirty people. It was not unusual to serve a five course meal to as many as thirty guests. Ruth's experience as a cook remains with her today when preparing food for large groups. Not only is the quantity there, but the quality causes your taste buds to jump with joy.

In March of 1947, Ruth moved from New York to Portland where she met Bill Watson. They married the following September and Ruth stayed home for the next twelve years with their children, a daughter Julie and a son, Terry. They now have four grandchildren. Ruth worked for G. I. Joe, a job she loved, until their retirement.

I recall when Ruth prepared several dozen butter cookies for a Cannon Beach Library fund raising affair. According to her, they were priced much too low. What did she do? She purchased them and gave them away, one package to us, and as with all of her baked goods we have enjoyed, they were delicious.

Ruth is an active member of the Garden Club and the Cannon Beach Library Women's group. Besides cooking and baking, she enjoys gardening. Her landscaping and garden plants attest to her love for native growth around their home.

On September 12, 1989, Bill walked the beach with his dog, Skip. He turned to run with him and fell, breaking his hip. The tide was coming in and Bill lay at the water's edge. He tried desperately to move away from the rising surf by digging into the sand with his hands and pulling his body shoreward. Jan and Bob Tarr were walking on the beach, saw Bill, and realized he had a problem. Jan rushed to the Markham home for blankets and to call 911, Bob held the dog, Barb Shaw dug a trench to keep the water away from Bill while John Markham went to get Ruth. Mike Graham, our local EMT, arrived soon and rushed Bill to the Astoria Hospital. It was a frightful experience for Bill, for he grew up with respect for the ocean and for the power it commands.

Today, Bill enjoys walking with Skip to the beach and up and down Markham Avenue. He can be seen every day on his way to the post office to collect his mail and to offer his assessment regarding the weather for the day.

Whitley, Forbes and Shaw Arch Cape Connection
By Barbara Forbes Shaw

The Arch Cape connection for the Whitley, Forbes and Shaw family began in the early 1920's when Mary Isherwood Whitley and her daughter, Lucy, moved from St. Louis to Seattle. They purchased a house in the same block where the English family lived in Seattle's Roosevelt District. My grandmother and my mother soon visited the Englishes' Arch Cape *Singing Sands* summer home and then Ralph Forbes joined them after marrying my mother, Lucy, in 1927. Mrs. Whitley, born and married on the Isle of Man, lived in Bingley, Yorkshire, England, before she and her wool-broker husband, James Scott Whitley, moved to the United States. She spent her summers on the English seacoast and Arch Cape had similar charm for her.

Mrs. Whitley began taking me (her granddaughter Barbara Forbes) for summer visits to *Singing Sands* in the early 30'. It took twelve hours on three bus lines to reach Seaside from Seattle. Elsie English met us in Seaside and drove us on the curvy road (over 70 sharp curves) to Cannon Beach. The date and time of the trip had to coincide with a late low tide. Only then could the drive on the beach over Hug Point and on down the beach to the planked route through the soft sand that met Leech Avenue be negotiated. The short drive to Mr. Maxwell's barn completed the long journey. Today, it takes four hours to make the same trip by automobile.

Most of the guests at *Singing Sands* were school teacher friends of Elsie and Marie English. Their mother, Jennie, and my grandmother (I called her Grang) were of similar age and had a special bond. I was well supervised as I was usually the only child there. Grang often sat and knitted at the Singing Sands gate that led to the beach while she watched me play in the sand.

My grandmother and I gathered bark from the Arch Cape Creek area and carried or dragged it back in gunny sacks to fuel the cook stove. This bark had less salt in it than bark gathered on the beach so was less corrosive to stove parts. Also, it provided longer lasting hot pieces to cook with than did regular firewood. The Arch Cape Creek area was our favorite gathering place, for ocean waves and currents deposited logs and drift there. One year, a small wooden dingy washed ashore and provided me with many hours of play in the creek pools.

A Cannon Beach grocery store truck delivered provisions and mail via Hug Point to Arch Cape twice a week. All perishable food was kept in coolers on the north side of Singing Sands. The coolers, made from boards and enclosed with fine mesh screen, allowed cool air to circulate. Electricity was a future dream, so coal oil lamps provided light. The shower, on wood planks on the south side of the kitchen, used water warmed in the pipes of the wood-burning kitchen stove. Warm water showers were available only when the stove was in use. The outside shower was popular in summertime to wash away sand and salt after swimming and sun bathing on Arch Cape's singing sands. The living room and dining room each had a large wood stove for heat. When electricity came to Arch Cape after the tunnel opened in 1941, a fireplace replaced the living room stove.

Constructing a wind-break was an important annual task in front of *Singing Sands*. First, three logs laid in the shape of a U facing south were rolled into place. Then, 2 x 4 uprights nailed to the U shaped logs provided support for a heavy white canvas with grommets that matched nails driven into the logs and uprights. The windbreak provided a snug space for sunbathing, for reading, or for enjoying the beach. Large logs were abundant on the beach then, as well as small driftwood pieces. When I reached school age, low tides brought much excitement to me with early morning crabbing and clamming. We first stopped at the Cape to search for crabs in the tide pools. Then, on beach bikes with gunny sacks slung over the handlebar to carry clams and crabs, we rode to Cape Falcon. In those days one could dig all the razor clams one needed, but crabs became more of a challenge. Long handled rakes pulled them from deep holes. One crabbing trip to Cape Falcon produced forty crabs. It was suggested that they be sold on the road, but the road ended at Arch Cape and was without traffic. So, we ate the crab. They were probably accompanied by Elsie's great blue or red huckleberry pies made from berries picked in the nearby woods. I still wonder why the coastal huckleberries are scarce today.

Grang put earnest money down on two lots owned by George Christie in the late 30's. After the long ride home to Seattle, we decided Arch Cape was too far away for property ownership and returned the earnest money. Two years later, at double the price, Grang purchased the same lots bordered by Cannon Street, Ocean View and the ocean. I came down during spring vacation with Elsie, Marie, Edith Countryman and her preschool son, Bob. While staying at *Singing Sands,* I planted the first garden on the Whitley-Forbes property.

I remember the war years in the early 40's: Blacked out windows, soldiers and coast guardsmen patrolling the beach on foot or on horseback, Tillamook based blimps floating up and down the coast searching for Japanese submarines, and the food and gasoline rationing. Even though gasoline rationing made it difficult to get here, Grang and I still visited Singing Sands each summer. We were here in June, 1942, when a shell from a Japanese submarine landed in northern Clatsop County, about 20 miles north of Arch Cape.

The summer of 1944, my father was able to secure enough lumber to build an 18 by 18 foot tent platform so that my mother could spend time at the beach. It was wartime, and since Dad was so familiar with the sawmill industry, he managed to locate enough lumber for an 18 by 36 foot house.

The house was positioned on the lot at an angle running from the northeast to the southwest so the cape was framed in the picture window on the ocean side. Carpenters and other craftsmen were very difficult to find during the war years. Mr. Angelo Costanzo, who lived up Mill Road and worked on the tunnel, always came to the rescue when Mom and I needed help. I lived in one of Leech's *Arch Cape Cabins* during the summer of 1945 and supervised the progress on the house and hammered many a nail. My mom returned to Seattle in early summer for Grang was not well. She passed away in July, 1945. Her good friend, Jennie English, died in December, 1942.

Dr. John Countryman, who married Irene English, moved to Arch Cape from Grafton, North Dakota, in 1940. In 1945, the two of us began a tradition of swimming in the ocean on Christmas Day. Later, Bridget Snow became an Arch Cape resident and participated in the annual swim. That became a New Year's day event, and is a popular event to this day. I have participated in the swim each year since returning in 1980.

Miss Eva Benson owned a small single-wall cabin immediately north of the Forbes property. Miss Benson, a Portland librarian, built her cabin in the 1920's with many materials salvaged from the beach. She had a brother, a Colorado miner, who unexpectedly appeared in Portland and demanded that she leave her job and take care of him in her beach cabin, which she did. The only time I remember seeing Miss Benson's brother was when he came outside during one of our rare earthquakes. Heat for Eva's house came from a wood cook stove and the fireplace. She had no refrigerator so Mom gave her the key to our house. She came over every morning to get cream for her coffee and other needed items. Mother helped Eva by purchasing clothing for her.

My mother, Lucy Forbes, enjoyed the beach and loved her garden. She passed away in 1948 after I had entered college. I continued caring for the garden with great enjoyment during my college years. I lived alone at the beach home, but shared dinners with Elsie, Marie and their guests. In turn, I would prepare dinner, and this was great training for a college girl. Also, we often played bridge after dinner, which was a Singing Sands tradition. The year I graduated from Queen Anne High School in Seattle, Elsie and Marie made a special scroll for me, a Beach Diploma. It was "in recognition of my beach education."

When James Royal Shaw Jr. began courting me in 1950, Miss Benson happily came over to the Forbes house and chaperoned us on our weekends away from Lewis and Clark College. Miss Benson drove a Model A Ford, which Jim wishes to this day he owned. Eva resided at the Wheeler Hospital for several years and died there in 1961. Her property was left to a distant cousin in Arizona, who arrived with a friend and a mother collie with ten pups. The dogs howled under my parents' bedroom window. One had to know my dad to understand how that program could not survive. Dad had an option of first refusal for the property and paid Eva's distant cousin $5,500 for the cabin and the property. Our home is on that site today.

Jim, my husband, also has roots in this area as his grandfather, John A. Shaw, was in charge of the construction and operation of the Hammond Lumber Company in Astoria in 1909. There is a model of the *John A. Shaw* in the Columbia Maritime Museum in Astoria, an ocean going tug named after him by the Hammond Lumber Company. When the tug was first built, it was powered by wood. Jim's father, James R. Shaw, was sales manager for Hammond Lumber before building his own mills in the Klamath Falls area.

Bert Patton, a former logger and blacksmith from Scio, lived in a log cabin he built just east of us. Bert often shared dinners in the Forbes home. He came dressed in a white shirt and wore a hat. When Bert entertained, he often served razor clams and his recipe for clams called for one egg per breaded clam. His clam feeds were legendary. Now, if found, clams are small compared to those dug in the 40's and 50's.

I found Ginger, a shepherd mix, at the Seattle dog pound in 1948. When college began, I left Ginger with Bert. They became instant pals and had many years together. Bert had an old carved pump organ that many of us enjoyed playing. Our sons, Jim and Bob, have many fond memories of Bert, a kind southern gentleman.

Bert had not written a will and that bothered my dad, who was an attorney. One day my dad announced he was driving Bert to Tillamook to visit an attorney. Bert left his property to Dale Mosby, Irene Christie Mosby Tyrrell's son, whose family lovingly continues to care for the log cabin.

Dr. Morgan Odell, President of Lewis and Clark College, and his wife, Ruth, were frequent guests of mine at Arch Cape. Jim and I were married by Dr. Odell in 1951. We worked in Redding, Chico and most recently in Orinda, California, where we had an accounting business.

During those years sons Jim and Bob enjoyed our Arch Cape vacations. We hiked every trail we could find. We clammed, crabbed, roasted hot dogs at Short Sands Beach, picked huckleberries and had many evening bonfires on the beach. Marney Beemer came from Iowa with her five children every other summer and stayed with her parents, Floyd and Ella Scott. We thoroughly enjoyed our shared active and adventurous Arch Cape vacation activities. Our families, including the grandchildren, still share fun times together.

Dad passed on in 1976. Jim and I purchased the Benson cabin from Elizabeth Forbes, who married my father in 1948. In 1980, we sold our accounting practice in Orinda, California. We tore down the old cabin and with help from our architect and his wife built our present home. Our brick work includes the old bricks I cleaned from the cabin plus 3,500 Jim and I hauled from the old Broadway School in Seaside as it was being torn down. We refinished and used all the old doors from the cabin, including the seventy inch high bathroom doors, which became pantry doors. Some doors have unique designs chewed into them by insects. Only a pine dish cupboard and a hand painted plate remain from the original furnishings. The latter was a wedding present to us from Miss Benson. A bronze medal found by us during the excavation is special. The face says "Insurance Company of North America, founded 1792." On the back it reads "Presented to M.V.B. Benson for long and faithful service, January 1, 1917." This may have been presented to Miss Benson's father.

When we were preparing our yard for landscaping, a small yellow type daisy, which I call Oregon Sunshine, began to germinate from seeds that had blown over from Mom's garden. I can remember when my mom was given a start of those flowers by Bill Gustin, who lived in Nehalem. Today, we enjoy Oregon Sunshine in our ocean front home, for it survives the severe winter storms and recovers every summer to put forth glorious color and beauty.

Jim and I thoroughly enjoy our Arch Cape home and life-style and love to share it with family and friends.

Mary Whitney sitting knitting at the Singing Sands gate. Circa 1932. Photo, Barbara Shaw collection.

Lucy Whitney Forbes on the south side of the arches in the 1920's. Note the laced hiking boots and the embroidered dress and hat.

Barbara Forbes Shaw by Falls Creek, just south of Hug Point, in the early 1930's. Photos, Barbara Shaw collection.

The Womack Connection
By Ellen Womack

When I met Bob, he was a professional musician who played the saxophone with several big bands. In the early 30's Bob played all over the country, including Lake Tahoe, the Olympic Hotel in Seattle, and with a ship's orchestra aboard a President's Line vessel. In 1937 we were expecting our first child. I told Bob it was time to settle down in one place. I did not want our child to sleep in dresser drawers while we were traveling with the orchestra.

Bob went to work for W. P. Fuller Paint Company in Portland and later transferred to Seattle. In 1959 he changed jobs and worked for Tektronix and remained with them until his retirement in 1976.

Bob and I were introduced to Arch Cape by Elsie Wood in the 40's. The Woods were long-time friends and neighbors of ours in Lake Oswego. Elsie loved the beach and invited us down for a visit. As time passed, we vacationed in Arch Cape with our daughter Becky and son Bob, renting one of the Leech cottages.

We purchased our present Arch Cape home site, 1381 Beach Street, from the Markhams in 1962. In 1964 we began building our beach home. Bob hired Ray Watkins, a Cannon Beach contractor, to do the framing and to finish the kitchen and the bathroom. We did the rest of the work ourselves. I became Bob's "go-fer" and admit it was a fun time for us even though we lived with bare 2 by 4 walls for awhile. We worked on the house weekends and during our vacations. During this construction period we stayed in Elsie Wood's cabin on Leech Avenue. Bob retired from Tektronix in 1976. We commuted between Portland and Arch Cape for two years before deciding to sell the Portland home and live full-time in Arch Cape. The transition between the two places was not difficult, for we enjoyed the beach, made friends and became involved in local affairs.

In 1983, the Arch Cape Fire Department requested that signs be erected to identify street names and house numbers. Ray and Rachel Hill from Cove Beach presented two maps: one for the Cove Beach-Falcon Cove area and one for the Arch Cape area. A committee made up of Barbara Shaw, Dorothy Birkby, Ray Hill, Jim and Sally O'Donnell, and Jack Foster assigned house numbers. Numbering starts at the Clatsop-Tillamook County line with 0 up to 999 south of the tunnel and with 1,001 north of the tunnel. Odd numbers go east and south; even numbers go west and north. Mike Graham supplied the materials and the street names and numbers to Bob. Using a green background and white stenciled numbers and letters, he created attractive street signs. You will see these signs when driving or walking around the area—a nice addition to our community.

I joined the Cannon Beach Womens' Club in 1980 and answered a request to work at the library and became a volunteer. To this day, I spend one day a week at the library, which I enjoy.

Occasionally, we see bears in Arch Cape, especially in the summer when the salal berries are ripe. We have a bear story worth repeating. In 1976, the roots of a large tree in front of our home were damaged when a sewer crew was working in the area. The tree trunk was partially hollow and the damage done to the root system hastened the decaying process. The hollow trunk became a haven for a queen bee and her workers. Soon there was ample honey and that attracted the visit from a bear. One evening I thought I heard a scratching sound. I looked outside the window but didn't see a thing. I was sure it was a bear. The next evening I heard the same noise. This time I told Bob. Armed with a flashlight and his camera, Bob opened the door. When Bob turned on the flashlight, the bear disappeared. The trunk of the tree was torn apart and the bear got the honey it was after. Today, the tree is topped and the bees, gone.

On September 14, 1985, Bob had an interesting experience. While sitting on a stump near Leech Avenue (a resting placc), he heard a sea lion bark. It came from behind the stump and claimed Bob's sitting spot. Jim Markham came by and took a picture of the sea lion and wrote the following poem for Bob:

> Himself sought his stump for to sit;
> Said barking sea lion, to wit:
> > "Get away from my stump
> > You can't rest your rump,
> I's sunning myself here a bit."

There is never a dull moment in Arch Cape . . .

His majesty, Mr. Sea Lion, 1985.

Ellen Womack, 1955. That is Elsie Wood's cabin in the background.

The bear tree, 1986.

Bob Womack, 1985.

Photos, Womack collection.

Memories of Cannon View Park
By Inarose Zuelke

Our house was built by Dr. Ralph Ray of Portland, and after five summers of kids and horses (the stall was still in the car port), the Ray's sold to Mrs. Dean Seabrook, who owned it for five years. We bought it in 1957. The only permanent residents at the time were Mr. and Mrs. Bennett. We envied Mr. Bennett, for his house was full of glass floats. It was years before we beat him to the beach to search for them. It meant getting out of a warm bed at four in the morning and controlling a Coleman lantern, sometimes in a raging storm, while searching the high-tide line for the elusive treasure. The reward for us one morning was five glass floats.

Our summers were full of children's laughter, wet clothes, baseball and volleyball games, wet clothes, sandy hot dogs and sticky marshmallows around sing-a-long campfires and more wet clothes. There was no clothes dryer. Al and Dorothy Illge's daughter, Barbara, drove to the beach every day in her jeep, overloaded with all the giggles and screams she could hold. Peisotta's (two doors south) often loaned their house to Catholic sisters from Portland and the children would report on their presence. How did they know they were nuns? Well, as they put it, who else would look that white in a bathing suit?

Peisottas sold to Mr. and Mrs. Wendell Sivers and as the house was disintegrating; they gave it to the Arch Cape Fire Department for a training exercise. As we were watching it burn, a lady came up, horrified, and asked, "How did it start?" Win Sivers said, "Oh, well, you know, my darn wife left the coffee pot on." The lady began to cry and rushed off down the beach. Guess she never knew the fire was intentional. Onlookers lined the highway and Carnahan Street and one was overheard to say, "Boy, am I glad I don't live in this fire district; they can't put out a fire." We celebrated the event with a buffet dinner for friends.

Al Walsh bought the lot just south of us and discovered the developer of this area had allowed the Rays, the original owner of our lot (north side) and the Davises (south side) to put their septic tanks in that lot. Mr. Goodin, the developer, considered it too low for building. We moved our tank at Al Walsh's request only to find a moratorium was placed on permits until a sewage treatment plant was operational. Al was caught in a difficult time frame as his little house just east of us was sold to the Sayers and the moratorium stopped him from building his home on his new lot. Ten years later, a permit was issued. We put a card table in the middle of the empty lot, complete with candles, silverware and a tablecloth with a sign announcing it as "Uncle Al's Kitchen."

The area abounded with relatives. The two Priers were brothers. Mrs. Walsh and Mrs. Bennison were sisters, and Mrs. De Klotz, who lived between them, was their niece. Current residents Mr. John Brosnan and Mrs. Sinnott, are brother and sister and they were related to Mrs. Illge. Mary Ellen Moore and Dick Petrone are brother and sister.

Retired navy chaplain Father George Smith, added a special flavor to Cannon View Park. He gave all the area's children an invaluable lesson in patriotism. Each 4th of July he invited them to his front yard, now the Downes' home, and appeared in his full uniform bedecked with medals. He selected one child to ring the huge bell and instructed two others how to raise the flag. The Pledge of Allegiance was followed by loud and off-key singing of the national anthem.

This area is noted for its row of flag poles, probably started by the Grohs. Not to be outdone, we augmented one of Father Smith's 4th of July celebrations with our flag raising ceremony. A visitor insisted on his knowledge of how to tie a special knot so that the elevating rope could be removed after the pole was raised. To the childrens' delight, the rope did not disengage and they had a marksmanship contest with a .22 caliber rifle to fray the rope. The flagpole sustained many bullet holes. It rotted out and had to be replaced one year later.

Memories include the surf-fishing skill of Mr. Garoff, one of the areas first residents. Bridget Snow had a different skill. To our children, Bridget will always be the **Periwinkle Lady**. She taught them how to find olive shells, which they called periwinkles.

Our neighbors to the north, one of the Priers, sold to the Randall and Sullivan families. The Clatsop County Historical Society, after some study, selected that site for the first Arch Cape Post Office marker. Upon the death of the Sullivans, the Randalls sold the house to Mr. H. A. Andersen, who then sold it back to the Randalls for one dollar. The Randalls moved the house to Castle Rock Estates and elevated it to a two-story house, which Margaret Curtis now owns. Mr. Andersen later built the present house that is on the property. Art Prier rescued the post office sign which is now posted in his yard.

In 1958 we bought into this low-key neighborhood. Today we live in an area bounded by extremely expensive homes and skyrocketing land values. Property taxes have escalated to the point where we are so wealthy, we're not sure we can afford it.

Six out of nine Zuelke children on the beach in 1959. From left to right: Lynne, Rosemary, Janet, Paul, Kathy and Bill.

Jennie, a one year old grandchild in 1977. Murphy Rock shows in the background.

"ZUELKE ZOO"
The Zuelke Family Reunion — Fortieth Wedding Anniversary — 1987

From left to right (more or less) Paul Zuelke, Paul Breslow, David Turner, Ernie Turner, Dr. Paul "Ed" Zuelke, Inarose Zuelke, Rosemary Fraine, John Fraine, Leah Fraine, Lenora Zuelke, Susie Antles, Andy Magner, Eddie Zuelke, Jennie Breslow, T. J. Zuelke, Michael Zuelke, Brian Erickson, Jeanne Albertson, Bill Zuelke, Lynne Magner, Kathy Turner, Holly Magner, Janet Breslow, Christopher Erickson, Craig Erickson, Grant Turner, Holly Magner, Janet Breslow, Christopher Erickson, Craig Erickson, Grant Turner, Jay Breslow, Danny Magner, Shayna Breslow, Diane Erickson, Kimberley Erickson, Charlie Fraine and Russ Albertson. Photos, Inarose Zuelke collection.

The Graham Connection
By Rainey Graham

Mike and I came to Arch Cape from Salt Lake City, Utah, in December, 1974 for a one year sabbatical. Both of us had a childhood dream to live by the ocean. A relative in Tolovana Park introduced us to Genevive Smith Campbell, who had Parkinson's disease, and needed assistance in her Arch Cape home. She had an extra apartment and welcomed us and our two little white dogs, Rogie and Shelly, openly. She was also enthusiastic about Mike's plans to write.

Genevieve was a long-time member of the Clatsop Weavers' Guild, established in 1959. Most members were Astorians and they ventured to Genevive's lovely home for their June meetings. Genevieve taught Barbara Forbes (Shaw) to weave when she was in her teens and lived next door for the summer. Barbara still weaves. I have enjoyed my weaving and guild friends the past 18 years.

Genevive had talent. She was a private pilot, a former administrator of Wheeler and Seaside hospitals, a professor of nursing instruction at a community college, and had published a book—*Care of the Patient with a Stroke.*

We felt very welcomed to Arch Cape by Clella Glanville, Travis and Irene Tyrrell and Irene's mother, Mrs. Clarrie Christie, our nearest neighbors. Because we enjoyed the year sabbatical so much, we sold our Salt Lake City property and bought land on Mill Road in 1976. We built a small cottage on that lot in 1977, the same year Mike went to work for the Arch Cape Service District. In 1981 he wrote full time until returning to the district in 1986.

Mike joined the fire department in 1977 and became an Emergency Medical Technician. Today he is Lieutenant in charge of the Arch Cape Engine Company as well as Fire Marshal of the rural fire protection district.

I continue helping people in their homes, working in my yard and garden and walking my dog, Zach, a three year old black lab. Mike's mom, Cleo, who has visited here many times, moved to Arch Cape in April, 1993. We all enjoy the climate and the special people who make Arch Cape a truly unique place to live.

Cleo Graham with Zach, 1992.

Rainey Graham, Rogie and Shelly, Circa 1976. Photos, Mike Graham Collection.

Memories of a Long-Time Carnahan Street Resident
By Myrle (Nonie) Grohs

I was born in Lincoln County, Oregon, in 1899. My father was the county clerk. My brother Vin, and my sisters Anna and Catherine and I had lots of time searching out new beaches and vacation spots. When my husband Fred and I set our eyes on Cannon View Park, we could see that no other beach in the state could compare with the beauty and serenity of this place. My husband retired from his career as a pharmacist and we moved to Arch Cape in 1960. We purchased the Mclaughlin home and settled down to several years of fun and hard work.

The families with vacation homes on Carnahan Street became a close-knit community. The "cocktail flag" appeared somewhere in the neighborhood around five in the afternoon almost every week-end. This meant residents headed to the designated spot with contributions for a potluck dinner.

There were about fourteen homes on the beach side of the road and only four east of the road. Not many were permanent residents, but even the part-timers fit in well and we all looked out for each other's interests. Folks coming to the beach during the produce season brought boxes of vegetable and fruits to share with neighbors. People borrowed a child's wagon to deliver the bounty up and down the street.

Our Carnahan group lobbied in Salem and were successful in getting a law passed that prohibited horses and cars on the Arch Cape beach. Both were frequent intruders, many from Cannon Beach. After the prohibition, the local kids reclaimed their beach and could play safely without worrying about being run down. My granddaughters Nancy, Julie, Rosemary and Johanna spent their entire summers on the beach coming to the house only for food, (sometimes) or for sleeping. The community residents looked after one another and always gave needed assistance to stray kids, dogs and cats.

We installed our own water system and it still remains. I remember when the wine vats from a California winery were added to the system and our water was purplish for some time. It must not have tainted the water, as the residents drank more than their allotted amount that year.

After my husband died, my sister Catherine came to live with me and worked in the Arch Cape Grocery and Post Office for Ethel LeGault, who owned it at that time. Ethel furnished laundry service as well as grocery and postal services. We were privileged to help by picking up the meat each week in Seaside for the delicatessen. Later, George and Marcia Rothert owned the store. My granddaughter, Johanna lived with me and worked at the store and post office during the summers while going to college.

No garbage service was available in the early years. It wasn't needed, for raccoons and sea gulls ate every scrap of food and bone put out for them. The county provided bins in various locations along Highway 101, but the bears ravaged them so badly that they had to be removed.

We've had many years of joy in Arch Cape on Carnahan Road in what is known as Cannon View Park. It is the most peaceful, most beautiful, and most breathtaking place on this earth to me and to all of my family.

The Natural History of Arch Cape
John C. Markham, Ph. D.

Introduction

The area of Arch Cape is small, but because of its location on the edge of the ocean, it contains three distinct habitats: the marine, the terrestrial, and the transitional region where those overlap. In a human time scale the coastline seems well-defined and essentially permanent; in geological terms this coast is very young and actively, even violently, changing. For most of the 4.6 billion years of the earth's existence, the Oregon coast has been under water, receiving a layer of sediment to a depth estimated at about 6000 meters. Only during the last few hundred thousand years has it been above the ocean to permit erosion, with the result that all exposed rocks or outcrops belong to the Cenozoic or most recent epoch, specifically, the Pleistocene, Pliocene and Miocene eras. Located on the "Pacific Ring of Fire," the Oregon coast is subject to frequent earthquakes, ranging from the undetectably mild to the severely devastating.

The dominating presence of the ocean is, of course, the single greatest control of the region's climate. Besides providing the water through evaporation to produce generous precipitation and injecting enough salt into the air to affect the composition of the terrestrial vegetation, the ocean serves as a huge heat reservoir that greatly moderates our climate and prevents deviations in temperatures very far above or below the mean.

About Measurements

Under this same title, the authors of *The Oregon Ocean Book* state "We chose to use metric units because virtually all scientific sampling uses this system." Nearly all of the sources consulted for this account, besides that highly valuable summary of Oregon oceans, including sources for local plants, coastal mammals, oceanography and astronomy, to say nothing of years of university instruction, are in the international or "metric" system, so it would be confusing to do otherwise here.

Geological Considerations

For a thorough account of the geological history of the coast at and near Arch Cape, please refer to the section of this publication, *Arch Cape Geology*. Here I want only to add a few remarks on geological conditions directly significant to the local biota, including some details not mentioned elsewhere.

The North American Plate extends nearly a third of the way around the earth, being generated along the mid-Atlantic Ridge, where it arises from a series of volcanic cracks. Moving westward about two centimeters per year, this plate carries North America into collision with the small Juan de Fuca Plate only about 200 kilometers west of our coast. At the line of meeting called the Cascadia Subduction Zone, the North American Plate overrides the Juan de Fuca Plate, which crumples and raises its leading edge, much as a carpet pushed against a wall would be pushed up into a heap. Although the rate of rise averages only about one millimeter per year (currently just enough to counter the rise in sea level resulting from post-glacial or interglacial warming, exclusive of any effects of human activity), it is not a smooth or constant rise. Rather, the ridge of hills behind us, the highest Angora Peak at 830 meters, consists of ocean bottom, which has been pushed up one earthquake at a time. Local geological studies indicate that violent earthquakes, up to 9.0 on the Richter scale, occur here, on average, about 380 years apart, the most recent having been about 1690. Because the actual intervals between such quakes have been considerably less and more than 380 years, we are now in a time of vulnerability for the next major quake, which may, however, not strike for several hundred more years.

Local rocks, as the *Arch Cape Geology* section stresses, are of sedimentary sandstone and mudstone with interbedded basalt flows. Because the basalt is much more resistant to erosion, it has become the prominent headlands such as Arch Cape (which arcs northwesterly in a series of "stacks", the last and largest of which is Castle Rock), Cape Falcon and Tillamook Head. The sedimentary rocks have yielded to erosion in between the headlands or have partially survived because of protection from adjacent basalt beds, as on Austin Point and Hug Point. Breakage of the basalt occasionally occurs along fault lines, resulting at times in the loss of boulder-size chunks. This is the process that closed the arches in Arch Cape and later reopened them. Serious cumulative erosion of the basalt cliffs occurs during severe winters, when water inside cracks freezes, expands and snaps off windrows of sharp-edged chips onto the adjoining beach. Along the landward edge of the beach are basalt rocks from cobble size up, which have been rounded and smoothed as the ocean has repeatedly ground them together. On the outer faces of both Cape Falcon and Tillamook Head are inaccessible beaches where hikers on the paths high above can see and hear the rigorous grinding of such rocks in the surf. Our shore-lining rocks originate there through fragmentation of the bordering cliffs and, after rounding in the "grinding beds," are distributed along the beaches by successive storms.

Worldwide, ocean beach sand ("sand" being a category of size without reference to its composition) is of two general types. Silicious (SiO_2, volcanic or quartz) sand predominates in temperate latitudes, such as here, while calcareous ($CaCO_3$, biogenous or shell) sand is typical of the tropics. (Local exceptions, such as the "black sands" of Hawaii and New Guinea are ash from nearby active volcanoes, whose output overwhelms regional sources of calcareous sand.) Because $CaCO_3$ is relatively soft and soluble, it becomes very smooth and makes the water in contact with it slightly acidic, with important implications for the life inhabiting beaches. Although calcareous sand is certainly generated here from mollusk shells, echinoderm skeletons, the deposits of calcareous algae, etc, when it comes in contact with harder silicious sand, the latter grinds it into silt, which is then lost by dissolving or being washed away.

The main source of our sand is granite, a volcanic rock not found locally. Microscopic examination reveals a diversity of beautifully colored particles of quartz, mica, feldspar and other minor granitic components. A quick pass of a magnet over a handful of our sand shows that many black grains are iron. The sand evidently originates well up the Columbia River, which discharges it into the ocean, where it is dispersed along the coast. Current theory postulates the functioning of "cells" defined by prominent headlands, within which sand remains resident for several years. Our "cell" extends from Tillamook Head to Cape Falcon. Under the influence of seasonally variable wave forms, the sand is deposited shoreward, usually in the summer, or transported offshore, usually in the winter, to return again the next season. A relatively small amount is lost onshore, as winds build dunes, or offshore, as storms carry it over the continental slope. An extreme example of the latter process was the effect of El Niño of 1983, when so much sand was lost seaward that it took some years for it to be replenished. The particular strength and angle of the waves prevalent at the time of deposition determine the size of particles left on each beach, and ocean waves tend to be consistent enough to produce very good "sorting," or only slight deviation from a particular mean diameter. The mineralogic source material happens to be such that the sand particles preferentially selected for our beach produce the characteristic squeak designated the "singing sands" of Arch Cape.

Catalog of Marine and Shore Environments

Shallow marine environments are characterized by the amount of ocean coverage (whether intertidal or subtidal), influence of fresh water (whether fully marine or estuarine) and substrate (whether beach of various particle sizes from silt to boulders, or bedrock of different hardness). Shore environments are dunes (shifting or stabilized), watercourses or dry land, bedrock or soil, and ocean-front or inland, all subject to the effects of elevation. At Arch Cape, two typical coastal habitats are absent or insignificant: Arch Cape Creek, our largest stream, carries too little water to produce the body of diluted sea water classed as an estuary (the closest true estuaries being those of the Necanicum to the north and the Nehalem to the south). Sand dune development occurs only to a very slight degree from about Markham Avenue to Arch Cape Creek, and even that tiny stretch is almost completely stabilized and long since converted into terrestrial soil. (The unusual, steeply sloping berm of large rocks along the northern part of Falcon Cove may be regarded as a "rock dune," which has the ecologically important effect of impounding the small dune lake behind it. The rocks themselves are not colonizable, but the rotting and disintegrating drift logs on them provide a substrate for terrestrial vegetation. This rock dune is slowly becoming a terrestrial habitat, though not as a typical sand dune would.)

Tides: Theory and Consequences

Whenever two or more astronomical bodies are large and close enough to exert a detectable gravitational effect on each other, tidal phenomena arise. The earth's solid crust rises imperceptibly a few centimeters in response to tides, and its gaseous atmosphere invisibly streams far out toward the moon, but our discussion is properly confined to the actions of water, in which tides are both visible and fairly large.

Three components interact to create tides as we experience them: the astronomical, the topographical and the meteorological. Astronomical considerations deal with the precisely predictable positions of the sun, earth and moon relative to each other; they are the basis for the predictions of times and heights of high and low tides at a specified location (in our case at Tongue Point, east of Astoria), as published in tide tables. Topographical features are the carefully surveyed fixed configurations, orientations and locations relative to the prediction location of specified coasts, headlands, inlets, etc., which are reflected in the correction table for heights and times published with the tide tables. Meteorological effects such as wind speed and direction and barometric pressure, because they remain unpredictable with any precision more than a few days in advance, are the joker in the deck; their effect can be highly significant in determining the actual height of a tide (normal variation in atmospheric pressure can vary water height by 30 centimeters), but there is no way to allow for them in tide tables.

The earth averages 150 million kilometers from the sun, whose mass is 2×10^{30} kilograms; the average distance to the moon is 384,400 kilometers and its mass is 7.4×10^{22} kilograms. The earth's orbit is such that it is closest to the sun each December, while the time of closest approach of the moon is not related to the time of the year. Tidal effects, the product of gravitational attraction between bodies, are directly proportional to the mass of the bodies and inversely proportional to the squares of their distances; even though the moon has only 1/27,000,000 the mass of the sun, it is only 1/3900 as far away, so the tidal effect of the moon on the earth is about 2.2 times that of the sun. The moon orbits the earth in the direction of the earth's rotation, that is, counterclockwise as viewed from the north pole. While each solar day is 24 hours long, the lunar "day", the time between successive crossings of a given meridian by the moon, is 24 hours and 50 minutes, because of the advance of the moon in its orbit.

Beneath the moon on the earth is a tidal bulge or crest of the tidal wave that extends half way around the earth; at its greatest, this bulge on the open ocean amounts to about one meter in height. When the sun, earth and moon are aligned (at the times of new moon and full moon, thus slightly more than twice per month), the condition called "spring tide" occurs with the bulge at its greatest; when a line from the sun through the earth's center to the moon describes a right angle (at the times of the first and last quarter moon), the condition called "neap tide" occurs with the tidal bulge at its smallest. Angular momentum of the earth-moon system simultaneously causes the formation of a second bulge (or crest of another tidal wave) on the side of the earth opposite the moon. While the two bulges are producing local high tides, the water at points 90° away is pulled down to produce troughs in the tidal waves or low tides in between the two high tides. As the earth rotates on its axis, all points on its surface pass beneath the two highs and two lows each day, while the highs and lows themselves are also moving in response to the moon's orbiting; thus there are two high tides and two low tides at every point on the earth during each lunar day, though local conditions may interfere with tidal flows enough that one high and one low tide may be greatly reduced or apparently disappear altogether. Because the circumference of the earth is 40,000 kilometers, the speed of the rotational movement of the surface at the equator is 1667 km/hr relative to a fixed point or 1611 km/hr relative to the advancing tidal bulge (diminishing to zero at the poles), but the water itself is moving at right angles (up and down) relative to this movement, not streaming across the face of the earth.

This is the basic theoretical condition for an earth rotating perpendicular to its orbital plane and covered entirely by ocean of a uniform depth. Reality imposes great variations on this pattern. First, the axis of the earth is tilted 23°28' from the perpendicular. This, of course, has the important annual effect of producing four seasons. On a daily basis, it greatly influences the configuration of the tides. As a given point on the earth passes beneath a tidal crest, it is at a different alignment relative to the sun-earth line than when it passes under the other tidal crest half a day later. Because the sun's gravity pulls most strongly on that point directly on the sun-earth line, the high tide closer to that line for a given point on the earth's surface is higher than the other one occurring the same day, and the same is true for the intervening low tides. (The difference between successive high tides and low tides is greatest at summer and winter solstices and diminishes around equinoxes.) A plot of tidal height against time produces a varying sine curve whose turning points represent higher-high, lower-low, lower-high and higher-low tides through a lunar day and then repeat.

The tidal crest of one meter is seen in the open ocean, but obstacles such as continents and local configurations of embayments serve to amplify tidal variations; at the extreme, in the Bay of Fundy in eastern Canada, the total tidal range reaches 20 meters, while here the greatest difference between high and low tides is about 3.7 meters. On the west coast of North America, the 0.0 tide datum, from which all tides are calculated, is mean lower-low water, that is, the average height of all the lower-low tides, so half of the lower-low tides will be above and half below 0.0, while all higher-low tides are above 0.0. Unlike "sea level," the datum from which land elevations are calculated, the 0.0 level is not fixed; it reflects the dynamic tidal system and moves somewhat with varying long-term weather fluctuations, such as El Niño, a decrease in barometric pressure that lets the ocean rise. On average here, it stands about one meter below designated sea level.

During the course of a year, extremes of spring tides undergo significant variations. In the summers, monthly lowest lower-low tides occur in the morning and monthly highest higher-high tides around midnight, both at the time of new moon; in the winters, monthly lowest lower-low tides occur in the evening and monthly highest higher-high tides around noon, both at the time of full moon. A reversal of these patterns occurs twice each year over a period of months around the equinoxes, when the differences between spring and neap tides and between higher and lower highs and lows all become smallest. Another variable of significance is the deviation of the moon's orbit to and from the sun-earth center line. At the time of closest alignment, when solar and lunar eclipses occur, spring tides are more pronounced than usual; in 1991, a solar eclipse with an exceptionally long period of totality occured in July, close enough to the summer solstice to give us the lowest tides experienced here in many years, in both June and July. The highest forecast high tides of the year are in December and January, and the lowest forecast low tides of the year in June and July. Because storms and low barometric pressure are much more common in winter than summer, the extreme highs of winter and lows of summer are further exaggerated by typical meteorological conditions.

Other Water Movements

Movement of the ocean is intimately related to the movement of the atmosphere overlying it. One atmosphere of pressure, the average at sea level, is 1013 milli-bars. A frequent check of a barometer shows that it rarely falls that low here. The combination of equatorial solar heating and the earth's rotation generates the North Pacific high, at 1022 to 1024 millibars, centered just off our coast in the summer and somewhat to the south in the winter. To quote *The Oregon Ocean Book*: "The North Pacific gyre is the great clockwise ocean circulation system spun from the North Pacific high. Although it encompasses virtually the entire North Pacific basin, the gyre is displaced toward the west side of the Pacific Ocean by the earth's rotation. As a result, currents along the coast of Japan are fast (40 to 112 kilometers per day) and narrow whereas those along the North American coast are slow (less than 10 kilometers per day) and wide." This weak and rather diffuse current further divides into northerly and southerly components, the latter, the California Current, passing our coast southward; in winter that current is displaced seaward, leaving the near shore surface exposed to the faster underlying north-flowing Davidson current. Thus ocean currents along our coast are weak and subject to seasonal reversals. Any object floating on the surface, especially if it extends at all out of the water, is much more subject to being blown about by the wind than carried by a current.

An important type of water movement along our coast that results from the presence of the shore is upwelling. As wind blows over water, its movement of that water is rotated slightly to the right in the northern hemisphere by the so-called *Coriolis Effect* induced by the earth's rotation. A particle of water at the surface in turn moves an underlying particle, which moves a particle below it, etc. The resultant gyre becomes weaker as it descends. The net movement of a body of water of as little as 20 meters deep is about 90° to the right of the prevailing wind. In the summer, our winds are consistently out of the north, so the ocean is pushed to the west, out to a distance of 10 to 30 kilometers. The displaced water cannot leave a void but must be replaced from the only available source, underneath. The water which comes up, from 100 to 200 meters, has lain below the reach of sunlight for a long time, so it is considerably cooled and has been too dark to maintain photosynthesizing phytoplankton. Life above has decomposed into simple chemical compounds, primarily nitrates, phosphates and silicates, as it drifts down. As this deep water is upwelled, its nutrients and sunlight meet to produce an explosion of life, which serves as the basis of our rich fisheries and feeds myriads of noncommercial animals up through food-webs along the coast. This rich life also clouds the water so badly that visibility within it falls close to zero, so would-be pleasure divers, even if they are not put off by the cold and turbulence, tend to decide it is not worth the trouble.

Studies here have shown that the effects of rainfall and the Columbia River "plume" tend to reduce the near shore salinity to about 33 parts per thousand and hold its temperature above 10° centigrade. When upwelling occurs, the salinity rises and the temperature falls, the latter change being especially noticeable to even the casual wader. It is not unusual for the onset of summer upwelling to drop the temperature of the surf from a relatively tolerable 15° to a bone chilling 7-8° over a few hours, while the salinity rises to 35 parts per thousand.

Periodically, a phenomenon called "El Niño" (now expanded in coverage as "El Niño

Southern Oscillation") occurs. The name, which in Spanish means "the child," is applied because of the typical start of the phenomenon off the coast of South America in December, so in reference to the Christ child's birth. Depending on its strength, it can be localized there and short-lived or, as in the case of the major event in 1982-83, which started in June north of Australia, it can affect weather around the world for a long period. Off the coast of Peru, there is usually a region of high atmospheric pressure, which generates westerly winds and entrains a current in the ocean, which in turn produces an upwelling (by a process different from that found here). At the time of an El Niño Southern Oscillation, the atmospheric pressure drops, so sea level along the east side of the Pacific rises, the westward wind and current diminish, and upwelling ceases. The consequences, depending on the strength of the event, can be a warming of sea water off South America to deadly levels, with all isotherms displaced poleward, destroying or moving many fisheries, producing disastrous ocean flooding, and, through disturbance of jet-streams in higher latitudes, causing droughts or torrential rainfalls worldwide.

Local Biology — General Considerations
Biogeography

All life on earth is distributed according to the climate which it favors or at least can tolerate. Local conditions, treated under the heading of ecology, determine precisely where within the appropriate climatic region a given species is found. Those species found where they evolved or spread through their own agency, are called "native." Those species brought in by human activities (intentional or otherwise) are "introduced;" if the introduced species have adapted well enough to their new habitats that they can survive there without further human assistance, they are considered "naturalized." Almost all of our marine biota is native, the few exceptions including such commercial species as oysters, which grow only under human supervision and need reintroduction of each generation, or localized estuarine populations, which are generally quite small. (One notable exception is the shad, introduced from the Atlantic coast, which migrates to and from the ocean into the Columbia River, where it has become the most populous species of fish.) On land, many species of naturalized plants have become noxious weeds, while the most serious animal pests are naturalized rodents; in both cases, problems have arisen because the introduced species have come without the predators, parasites, etc, which evolved to keep them in check in their native ranges.

Local Biogeography

The shallow-water marine temperate region, from the Aleutian Islands to central Baja California, is mostly classed as "cold temperate," which extends to Point Conception, California, delimited at the north by a winter minimum of 0° centigrade and at the south by a summer maximum of 20° centigrade. Our coast lies in the southern half of the cold temperate, the Oregonian Province, whose northern border is the Strait of Juan de Fuca.

Within this province, originally defined for the marine mollusks but now generally accepted for all taxa, there is a north-south gradient of change of species, but nearly all of the species found in any one place also occur in all other similar habitats. Thus, identification manuals written to cover Puget Sound to central California are commonly and reliably used here for all marine animals and plants.

On land, the Nearctic Realm covers all of North America down to the coasts of Mexico and southern Florida. Our coast lies in the Oregonian Province, a narrow strip extending from central Vancouver Island to San Francisco Bay, thus with both northern and southern boundaries just slightly north of those of its marine namesake. It extends inland to the Cascades, although some species do not cross the Coast Range. Because most regional field-guides to plants and animals follow state lines, the books for Oregon cover many species not found here, while coverage of the coast of Washington or California is suitable for our coast as well.

Two guides to local mammals I have consulted classify the local region more precisely in biogeographic terms. Bailey (1936. *The mammals and life zones of Oregon*) recognizes a Transition Zone between Canada and California and between the Cascades and the coast, in which he cites a "Humid Division," further subdivided into a "Coastal strip or fog belt with damp cool ocean winds..., an even climate through the year and annual rain of 80-100 inches..., almost free from frost in winter, cold and damp in summer." A more recent treatment (Kritzman, 1977. *Little mammals of the Pacific Northwest*) refers to a "Humid Transition Life Zone [with] dense, moist coniferous forest, 76-254 centimeters of rain per year, winters mild with little snow, temperatures rarely [below freezing] up to 900 meters."

Marine Animals

The marine habitat comprises two distinct but intimately interrelated parts: the water or pelagic realm and the bottom or benthic region. Among pelagic species of animals are those that can swim strongly enough to prevail against the movement of the surrounding water, collectively called "nekton," represented almost exclusively by vertebrates from fishes to mammals; and those that are passive drifters or at most feeble swimmers, classed as "plankton," including the immature dispersal stages or "larvae" of all animal phyla from sponges to fishes, spores of algae and the adults of myriads of species from unicellular organisms to microcrustaceans and ranging in size from ultramicroscopic bacteria to large jellyfish. The marine benthos is locally quite limited ecologically, consisting of rock-dwellers and sand-dwellers. (Elsewhere the presence of estuaries considerably increases the number of marine habitats.)

Pelagic Animals

T he pelagic habitat is certainly the most typical habitat of our local ocean, but at the same time it is the least experienced; we cannot easily enter it at high tide because of the roughness of the water near the shore, and even a diver would have difficulty seeing anything there because of the particulate matter and foam in the water. At low tide, the normal inhabitants of the region move out, to give us terrestrials access to an exposed region of rocks and sand devoid of its most active residents until the water is restored.

Local upwelling provides the inorganic chemical nutrients or fertilizer to meet sunlight and create the base of the food chain, the photosynthesizing phytoplankton, unicellular plantlike organisms, which collectively account for over 90% of the world's primary productivity or conversion of inorganic chemicals into food for other creatures. The most common phytoplankters in cold waters such as ours are the diatoms, microscopic brownish cells (which often aggregate into fragile chains long enough to be easily seen), which are enclosed in delicately sculptured boxes made of silicon dioxide, the stuff of glass. Certain conditions of weather and shore runoff promote "blooms" of diatoms, which can turn large patches of the ocean brown. Present with the diatoms are other unicellular algae as well as the dispersal stages of multicellular plants, all contributing to the production of organic material through photosynthesis.

Feeding on this rich supply of food are many species of zooplankton, both unicellular protozoans and many true, multicellular animals. Among the latter are representatives of perhaps 12 invertebrate phyla unknown to most people and lacking common names. One better-known taxon well represented in the micro-zooplankton is the Crustacea, especially such forms as copepods and cladocerans. In addition, dispersal of marine animals is by planktonic immature stages called larvae, which look very different from the sea anemones, worms, snails, barnacles, crabs, seastars, fishes and other well-known animals into which they will metamorphose as they settle out of the water column. It is important to keep in mind that the vast majority of this larval life does not survive to become adults; rather it serves as food for animals living in the water and on the bottom, thus playing the indispensable ecological role of passing on the matter and energy originally fixed by the phytoplankton. A specialized region of the ocean, in which plankton often becomes trapped and concentrated, is the foam layer. Sea foam is more than salty water whipped up by the wind, though that is its start. Organic remnants, especially naturally occurring hydrocarbons, from decomposing organisms produce the stickiness needed to maintain foam bubbles, whose surfaces then trap both living and dead plankters. In the words of one author, "Sea foam consists of saline water, air and a great variety of decomposed organic materials, algae, bacteria, fungi and Protozoa." The integrity of foam is such that a strong winter wind can cover the beach knee-deep and even blow ashore a pulsing mass able to remain for several hours.

Large planktonic species are mostly coelenterates, the primitive hollow-gutted animals. Although mainly tropical in distribution, the by-the-wind sailor, *Velella velella*, turns up here most years, usually in spring. Not a jelly-fish, it is a member of the Hydrozoa, the coelenterate class containing many tiny tree-like species attached to hard surfaces. *Velella* is a colony of sessile hydroids (variously modified for food-gathering, defense and reproduction) suspended from a float whose angled sail the wind pushes. Ordinarily the wind direction is such that *Velella* stays at sea, but a shift in the wind can cast huge numbers of colonies ashore, sometimes completely coating the beach with a slippery purple mass of doomed animals, which quickly die, rot and stink under the sun. In the tropics, *Velella* supports a sizeable community of predators and other hangers-on, all sharing its purple pigmentation. Because it is here at its northern limit, we see few of its accompanying animals, but the delicate purple snail *Janthina janthina*, which secretes a bubble-float for support and feeds on *Velella*, has washed ashore here.

True jellyfishes, individual animals, not colonies, in the form of pulsating bells up to dinner-plate size, are very common in our waters but, because of their transparency, rarely seen until waves cast them onto the beach to die. Two common species are the nearly spherical brown-streaked *Chrysaora melanaster* (often shredded as it washes in) and the flat colorless moon jelly, *Aurelia aurita*. Very different animals are the comb-jellies or cteno-phores, so named because of the eight rows of beautifully iridescent "combs" lining their sides. Like the jellyfishes planktonic and transparent, one of them, the common thumbnail-size "sea gooseberry" *Pleurobrachia bachei* is often stranded on the beach.

Nektonic animals along our coast are virtually all vertebrates: many species of fish, rare sea turtles and several marine mammals. A comprehensive guide to the coastal fishes of British Columbia, which is probably a very good reflection of the Oregon coast, covers 272 species in 83 families from fresh-water to abyssal depths. Many of these are never seen on shore, though they certainly occur in our ocean. Despite the common impression of fishes as active swimmers, many if not most species spend their entire lives near or even firmly clinging to the sea bottom or sometimes burrowed into sediments. All the species of commercial importance along this coast pass through our waters at some time, and some even become stranded on the beach, but fishing for them is restricted to boats offshore. The only exception seems to be the white surfperch, *Phanerodon furcatus*, a small but edible fish occasionally abundant enough especially near Arch Cape Creek to provide enjoyable recreation and even a few meals. A live-bearer, a hooked female sometimes releases a batch of fully-developed young to swim away as she is reeled in.

Jawless fishes include the lampreys, which are parasites of other fishes. The Pacific lamprey, *Entosphenus tridentatus*, is an abundant anadromous species which migrates in large numbers up the Columbia River with salmon. Among cartilaginous fishes are at least ten sharks, five skates and two stingrays. The most common shark is the Pacific dogfish, *Squalus suckleyi*, a small species formerly captured for its oil, later for vitamin A from its liver, now often used for dissection in biology laboratory courses. The larger blue shark *Prionace glauca* frequents our waters, and a dead one washed ashore in Arch Cape a few years ago. Largest is the basking shark, *Cetorhinus maximus*, a strainer of small pelagic crustaceans which grows to 13 meters. The only local shark regarded as dangerous to man is the great white shark, *Carcharodon carcharias*, implicated in two recent attacks on surfers at Cannon Beach. The big skate, *Raja binoculata*, and the longnose skate, *R. rhina*, are common and often wash up dead; their young develop in leathery pouches called "mermaids purses," which frequently are cast ashore. Most other species occur farther offshore. Stingrays are poorly known north of California.

The teleost or bony fishes account for the great majority of fish species here; nearly all are edible, and many are of sport and/or commercial value. The white sturgeon *Acipenser transmontanus*, a primitive sluggish inhabitant of both the ocean and many rivers, occasionally becomes stranded on our beach. It can reach 6 meters and 800 kilograms during a life that may last a century and provides good eating and choice caviar. The pilchard or sardine, *Sardinops sagax*, passes by here seasonally in large schools, and in the fall of 1992 thousands of them washed here. It is edible and commercially caught but not the tastiest of fish. Northern anchovies, *Engraulis mordax*, are known to litter our beaches at times with their tiny metallic silver-blue bodies. The costal trouts (discussed in more detail elsewhere as fresh-water species) are seasonally common near shore, as are their close relatives, the salmons, *Oncorhychus* spp. The Pacific lancetfish, *Alepisaurus borealis*, is a distinctive long fish (up to 1.4 meters) with a tall dorsal fin, vicious backward-pointing teeth and flabby flesh; though an inhabitant of deep water, it occasionally washes ashore here, as did several in the summer of 1991. Personal experience reveals it to be poor eating. The Pacific hake, *Merluccius productus*, which may account for a quarter of the fish biomass near our coast, was long left for the Japanese, Russians and Koreans to catch. Now it is harvested by American fishing fleets in huge numbers for use as surimi, a ground product flavored, molded and marketed as "imitation crab" and other masquerades. As it has acquired domestic commercial importance (and some accompanying political notoriety), it also gained the more euphonius name "Pacific whiting." Individuals wash in here at times; hake is certainly edible, but the taste is nothing special. Several members of the flatfish family, the Pleuronectidae, the flounders, halibuts and soles, live on the sandy bottom offshore; many of them are commercially important. Seaperches (family Embiotocidae) frequent kelp beds on moderately deep hard bottoms, as do the greenlings and lingcod (family Hexagrammidae) and the rock fishes (many species of the genus *Sebastodes*, family Scorpaenidae); these are the characteristic "bottom fish" caught from charter boats just offshore on such rocky ridges as that lying at 30 fathoms' depth next to Castle Rock. Sculpins (also family Scorpaenidae) are numerous small species often found on the bottoms of shallow tide pools. The large and bizarrely shaped ocean sunfish, *Mola mola*, about the size and shape of a large manhole cover, is better known from warmer waters, where it floats sluggishly at the surface, but it has washed ashore here at least once.

All sea turtles are tropical species, and females come ashore to lay eggs only on tropical beaches, but some of them range far seasonally. The loggerhead, *Caretta caretta*, has been reported from the mouth of the Columbia River, and, about 1985, a leatherback, *Dermochelys coriacea*, washed up dead on the beach at Tolovana Park. The known range of the green turtle, *Chelonia mydas*, extends to Alaska. Nearly all sea turtles are considered threatened or endangered because of overharvesting and destruction of nest-sites, so there are few to be seen even in the main parts of their ranges, let alone in this peripheral region.

Except for the sea otter (in the same Carnivora family as the skunk), local marine mammals belong to two orders, the Pinnipedia (the seals and sea lions) and the Cetacea (the whales and dolphins). Seven species of pinnipeds and 23 cetaceans are known along the Oregon coast, but only a few are ever seen on or near the shore; the sea otter, though becoming well re-established in Alaska and California, is still absent from northern Oregon. Our most common pinnipeds are the man-sized harbor seal *Phoca vitulina*, which frequently hauls out of the sea and spends the night on our beach; and the much larger California sea lion, *Zalophus californianus*, often seen and heard barking just beyond the surf. Less commonly seen are the Steller sea lion, *Eumetopias jubatus* and the northern fur seal *Callorhinus ursinus* (emaciated pups of which washed up here dead many years ago).

The two groups of cetaceans are the toothed whales (generally smaller and typically near-shore hunters of large prey including the dolphins and porpoises) and baleen whales (much larger filter-feeders ranging throughout the oceans). The only cetacean commonly seen here is the grey whale, *Eschrichtius robustus*, which passes close to shore from March to May on the way to its feeding grounds in Alaska or when returning in November through February to its breeding lagoons along Baja California. Strict protection, extended to all species of marine mammals, has been especially successful in restoring the population of the grey whale, now estimated at 25,000, believed to be the number before hunting started in the 1800's; unlike most baleen whales, it filters small crustaceans out of bottom mud rather than eating plankton. The killer whale, *Orcinus orca*, has been seen attacking sea lions at the Columbia River's south jetty and surely passes by here, though there seem to be no actual reports from Arch Cape. The humpback whale *Megaptera novaeangliae* has been sighted from shore in southern Oregon, but generally almost all other species of cetaceans recorded from the northeast Pacific remain too far offshore to be visible by people on land.

Benthic Animals

The benthic or bottom-dwelling animals occur in two general habitats, moveable (strictly sand, no mud here) and fixed (rocky headlands and offshore stacks and reefs). Sand, because of its instability and abrasiveness, is a very rigorous environment, with the result that few species live there (though those that do may occur in very large numbers). Plants cannot become established, and no ecological succession is possible. Fixed rocks provide sufficient stability to meet the needs of numerous species of both animals and plants, whose numbers of individuals may be relatively small; over a period of years a sequence of succession, governed by height relative to the tide, leads from pioneers to climax assemblages.

Living in our sandy beach are some of the most popular local marine animals. The razor clam, *Siliqua patula*, is keenly adapted for life in sand. When dislodged by a wave or threatened by a predator (such as man), it extends its strong foot, which it expands hydraulically and then quickly retracts to draw itself rapidly down into the sand. The water coming back out of the foot squirts out the siphon at the top end of the clam, producing a fountain in the water or a hole in hard sand, the "show" detected by a clamdigger. Its shell is enclosed by a shiny varnish-like secreted layer called a periostracum that protects it from abrasion and reduces friction. For reasons never determined, the large numbers of razor clams once dug on our beaches are no longer present; the frequent occurrence of washed-in fresh shells of various sizes indicates that there remains a viable population offshore, but it is beyond the reach of diggers. During the severe loss of sand caused by El Niño in 1983, razor clams suffered from loss of habitat; more recently a bacterial infection devastated clams, especially along the coast of Washington. Other conditions that do not damage the clams can render them dangerous to eat. Chief among these is paralytic shellfish poisoning, or PSP, sometimes called "red tide" (a name more properly applied to a different phenomenon in the tropics). The result of poisons produced by certain species of phytoplankton, PSP occurs at least briefly nearly every year, usually in the summer; frequent monitoring by state biologists along the coast leads to the issuance of alerts when levels are too high. Another problem first detected in 1991 is domoic acid: also the product of phytoplankton, it causes amnesia in human victims. Razor clams can live as least five years, but about 90% of the population is lost each year to natural causes and human harvesting. Despite the lack of diggable clams at Arch Cape, the beaches of Clatsop County as a whole produce 90% of Oregon's razor clams each year.

Another sand-dweller is the sand dollar, *Dendraster excentricus*, a flattened sea urchin that forms vast shoals some places; it is common intertidally in Seaside but almost entirely subtidal here; most commonly seen are internal skeletons called "tests", though whole or even live animals covered with spines also wash in. The Olive snail *Olivella biplicata* lives just beneath the surface of the sand, where it produces "dimples" (occasionally confused with clam shows) or ridges; like the razor clam, it bears a glossy periostracum. The mole crab or sand crab, *Emerita analoga*, is a summer resident which may be absent for many years and then return in large numbers. It rides the tides in and out to position itself always at the edge of the surf and filters food out of the water; in the summer of 1992, a huge population, molting simultaneously, produced a windrow of millions of cast skeletons along the beaches of northern Oregon. Some segmented worms and other invertebrates are also common in local sand.

Some species of crustaceans commonly scavenging on top of the sand when the tide is in burrow into it for protection if caught out of the water by falling tide. The largest of these is the commercial or Dungeness crab, *Cancer magister*; if unable to bury itself adequately, it falls prey to gulls when they start patrolling at dawn. Every spring, crabs molt to grow, and hundreds of their cast carapaces wash ashore. The sand shrimp, *Crangon nigromaculata*, whose salt-and-pepper coloration renders it nearly invisible in the sand, is another burrowing strandee. Where the sand is damp, huge numbers of small crustaceans called isopods scamper about on the sand and burrow into it; collectively, they are the main scavengers of stranded seaweeds and any scraps of animals not first claimed by birds. Further inshore, where the sand is drier, their role falls to the equally abundant sand fleas, members of the related order Amphipoda, in the genera *Orchestia* and *Orchestoidea*. Among sand-dwellers found in pools near rocks are two large sea stars, the sun star *Solaster stimpsoni* (generally orange, with about 10 rays) and the larger sunflower star *Pycnopodia helianthoides* (often purplish, with about 20 rays). Both of these flow over sandy bottoms in search of buried clams and other prey.

A habitat or substrate connected with the beach is that of drift logs. When I was a boy, I could go the length of Arch Cape beach by hopping from log to log; among the logs were many cut beams and boards. People used the wood thus available to make wind shelters, to fuel fires on the beach and in fireplaces, and to build fences and houses. Less obvious was the ecological role played by the wood, serving as shelter for some land animals, food for termites and the wood-eating isopods called gribbles, and even a place for plants to grow. A few weathered and rotting remnants of that supply remains: there is still a fair amount of old wood on the short arcuate beach just north of Cannon View Park and rotten driftwood is turning into soil on the shoreline ridges between Leech Avenue and Arch Cape Creek and along the northern part of Cove Beach. The environmental consequence of the disappearance of this wood is still uncertain, but the reasons it is no longer here are quite clear. The Columbia River has been tamed by dams and lower reaches of it and other rivers have been extensively logged, so there are no longer trees to be washed to sea or uncontrolled flooding to carry them. On the ocean, the log rafts that once passed on their way to California and were subject to breaking up no longer go by; and the exotic timbers cast overboard after use as dunnage to brace cargoes in freighters became obsolete with the introduction of metal containers.

Life on Rocky Shores

The general impression of life on rocky shores is one of little activity, but that is a result of our being able to see this habitat only at low tide, a time when the animals that can flee with the receding water have done so, and those forced to remain have ceased nearly all activity in order to withstand desiccation, stressful heating or cooling and the effects of fresh water. Essentially, the plants and nonmotile animals on the rocks spend periods of low tide doing little more than waiting for the tide to rise, so they may resume their life activities.

Studies of rocky shore around the world have shown that the assemblages of organisms found on each are distributed in patterns directly comparable to each other, their zonation being a function of the average time each level is exposed daily by the tide. In regions of small tidal ranges, the resultant zones are proportionally compressed, and, under the hot sun of the tropics and subtropics, heating severely limits colonization of rock faces. Conditions here are such that life covers the rocks up as high as the tides ever reach. Because of the rich supply of plankton in the water, food is always abundant enough, but space to attach is severely limited and leads to keen competition. At the highest levels, a blackening of the rock surface betrays the presence of encrusting lichens and penetrating blue-green algae. The highest-living animals are the acorn barnacles, *Balanus glandula*, which make their band distinctively white. Those barnacle larvae unable to find space at their optimal level may be forced to settle too far up to survive more than a few months, so many empty small barnacle shells occur there. Other barnacles desparately settle so closely together that they have no space to grow laterally; the resultant clusters of tall narrow "columnar" barnacles are so fragile that storm waves soon strip them from the rocks. Barnacles can cement themselves to any rigid hard substrate, so they also occur on the shells of mussels, the carapaces of crabs and, of course, manmade structures from piers and pipes to boat hulls, where they constitute the bulk of the "fouling" that people are forever fighting. Those barnacles managing to settle in uncrowded regions at the proper level can live for many years. A second species of barnacle commonly found here is the leaf barnacle, *Pollicipes polymerus*, one of the goose or stalked barnacles. It typically forms dense clumps among the beds of the acorn barnacles and slightly lower on the rocks.

The next lower level here is the realm of the California mussel, *Mytilus californianus*, a robust species well-adapted to life in pounding waves. Mussels attach themselves to rocks and other mussels, sometimes many layers deep, by means of flexible fibrous threads extruded as liquid from a gland near the foot and attaching and hardening when exposed to seawater. Mussels can stand continuous immersion, but their main predators, the sea stars, attack them from below and force them into the intertidal zone; in years when star populations are large, the bottom margin of mussels is a distinct line, but when those predators are less abundant, the mussels extend irregularly down into the lower tide zones. To withstand the exposure of low tide, mussels are able to clamp their shells tightly shut; this cuts off their access to oxygen in the air or water for hours at a time, but the reddish pigment myoglobin in their tissues lets them retain extra oxygen, while it gives mussel flesh its distinctive color and strong flavor. Like razor clams, mussels frequently harbor paralytic shellfish poisoning, making them temporarily dangerous to eat.

The lowest intertidal zone is home to fleshier animals that can stand less aerial exposure. The largest and most conspicuous of these are the ochre sea stars, *Pisaster ochaceus*, and the solitary green anemone and aggregating anemone, *Anthopleura xanthogrammica* and *A. elegantissima*. Despite its name, the ochre star is commonly orange or purple, with fewer individuals brown, blue and other colors. Like all members of its ancient phylum the Echinodermata or "spiny skins," it moves by means of a water-vascular system requiring it to pump seawater into its body to extend the tube-feed it uses for attachment; thus it is immobilized by removal from the water and so can prey on mussels only at high tide. It attacks a mussel by patiently pulling on its shell valves with its suction-cup tube-feet for many hours until the mussel finally lets its shell gape enough for the star to evert its stomach and force it inside the shell to digest and kill the mussel. Though farther up and so less within its reach, barnacles are also common prey for the ochre star. For unknown reasons, ochre stars exhibit wide fluctuations year to year, from near absence to such abundance that many wash off the rocks. Only one other species of sea star, the little six-rayed *Leptasterias hexactis*, is at all common intertidally here, but several species of deep-water rock-dwellers, probably dislodged from Castle Rock or its adjacent reef, frequently wash ashore. (Overall, the number of species of sea stars found along the northwest coast is the greatest of any place in the world, so specialists often come to laboratories here to study them.)

The *Anthopleura* anemones carpet large expanses of rock, and are very similar except for their size and the ability of the smaller aggregating species to split its body into new individuals to form clones spreading far across rock surfaces. Both species are green because of photosynthesizing unicellular algae in their tissues, exposed to the sun as the animals spread their disks wide; it is probable that these algae provide nearly all of their hosts' nutrition, though the anemones always stand ready to engulf and digest any animals or animal parts that land on their disks.

A current but incomplete list of the fauna of Haystack Rock contains 80 species of rock-dwelling invertebrates, while a more exhaustive list from Yaquina Head near Newport contains 113 such species, so that is an estimate of the numbers which may eventually turn up on the rocks at Arch Cape. Basalt, the rock making up nearly all of the local headlands, is too hard to permit animals to burrow into it, as many do in regions of intertidal sedimentary rock. Most animals find shelter in the protected interstices of mussel beds: sponges, hydroids, many kinds of worms, snails, limpets, nudibranchs, clams, moss animals, isopods, amphipods, hermit crabs, true crabs and tunicates among others. In response to the rich soup of plankton flowing over the rocks, the predominant mode of food-gathering of these animals is filter-feeding, as barnacles spread their nets of modified feet, mussels pump water over their gills, and smaller numbers of tube worms, porcelain crabs and tunicates are also adapted for trapping food from the water. Several species, including the chitons, limpets, many snails, hermit crabs and small sea cucumbers, graze the surface of the rocks to remove plants, bacteria and detritus. Predators on other rock-dwelling animals, beside the ochre star, are the whelks, *Nucella* spp., which drill into barnacles and other snails; predatory nudibranchs, which variously eat sponges, anemones, moss animals and tunicates; anemones and crabs, which feed less selectively, and, of course, octopuses and many species of fish present only at high tide and some birds at low tide.

Through each year, the height of the sand on local beaches varies considerably, with the result that rocky shores are variably exposed or covered. Remarkably, some species of both animals and plants attached to those rocks remain present and alive while beneath the sand, even for many months, and when the sand goes out again, they resume life functions. The advantage of this is clear: the occupants of limited rock surfaces do not lose their hard-won positions to subsequent arrivals. Still uncertain is what physiological mechanism permits the survival of such dormancy. During the winter of 1991-92, the sand did not retreat significantly, so the typical sand deposit the following summer build up on top of it and left many rocky tide pools filled in and adjacent rocks covered far higher than usual. As of this writing, more than a year later, the sands remains abnormally high; it will be interesting to determine the effects, if any, of such coverage on the rock-dwellers when the rocks are finally bared again.

Terrestrial Biota

T he dominant regulators of the local terrestrial flora are the amount and nature of moisture available. Because the ocean, through evaporation, is the source of nearly all water available for precipitation, and weather typically moves from west to east, annual rainfall along the northwest coast averages the highest of any place in the United States, over 250 centimeters. (In the same coastal band, the rainfall of the Olympic Peninsula is over twice ours, but the biota there is essentially the same.) Although not measurable as precipitation, the fogs typical of summer mornings provide an added, and remarkably large source of moisture that many plants can extract from the air during periods of low rainfall. Not all water coming from the ocean results from evaporation: winds also scoop up salt spray and blow it ashore.

There seems to be no complete catalog of local species of land plants, though its numbers would run into the hundreds. Of these, only two species of large plants dominate the narrow band of exposed coastline, the Sitka spruce, *Picea sitchensis*, and salal, *Gaultheria shallon*. Both of these require heavy rainfall and can tolerate salt exposure. A very short distance inland, the spruce yields to the western hemlock, *Tsuga heterophylla*. (A good place to see this transition is along the Pacific Coast trail over Arch Cape, which passes through virgin forest at the natural boundary between these two trees, at an elevation of about 75 meters.) Salal, while growing best on the coast, ranges much farther inland and occurs throughout the Willamette Valley. The forester's rule is that Douglas fir, *Pseudotsuga menziesii*, does not like an ocean view, and only on the Coast Range does it claim dominance from the western hemlock; efforts to grow Douglas fir or any of the true firs (*Abies* spp.), in

Arch Cape are rarely very successful. Interestingly, the tree roots visible in the eroded clay bank on the south side of Arch Cape Creek and fleetingly revealed when Asbury Creek once gouged deep into the beach, are those of Douglas fir, still in the locations where they grew some 12,000 years ago, according to carbon-14 dating. At that time, the last Pleistocene ice age, the ocean stood so much lower that the coast was perhaps 30 kilometers farther west, so the rule held that the Douglas fir had no ocean view.

The only other tree to form large stands in Arch Cape is the red alder, *Alnus rubra*, which favors disturbed areas, including logged land or road cuts, such as the area east of the highway just south of the tunnel, where it seeds in rapidly and eventually is replaced by spruce or hemlock. (A close look reveals that the latter species are already growing among the alders south of the tunnel; in a few years they will be tall enough to shade them out and succession will be complete.) Sparsely scattered among other species is the western red cedar, *Thuja plicata*, which never forms solid stands here but was formerly abundant enough to sustain the Arch Cape shingle mill. Arch Cape lies within the native range of the jack pine (also called lodgepole and shore pine), *Pinus contorta*, which is abundant on sand dunes as close as Cannon Beach and Manzanita. Because there are no developed sand dunes here, no pine occurs here naturally, though it has been widely planted around Arch Cape. It is the only tree that can withstand the severe drainage produced by loose sand; in the course of landward succession from dunes, Sitka spruce, which lives longer and grows taller, eventually displaces it as stable humus soil forms, but here that soil occurs to the edge of the beach, so the spruce seeds in at the start. Smaller native trees found around Arch Cape are the red elderberry, *Sambucus callicarpa*, the black twinberry, *Lonicera involucrata*, and, in moist locations, the coast willow, *Salix hookeriana*.

Among shrubs, one native species which was once almost as abundant here as salal is salmonberry, *Rubus spectabilis*, but it is becoming ever rarer. Two congeners, the Himalaya blackberry, *R. discolor*, and, to a smaller degree, the evergreen blackberry, *R. lacinatus*, both Old World natives, have been widely introduced and, because of their very similar ecological roles but far more aggressive growth habits, have largely displaced their locally evolved close relative. Another species, the thimbleberry, *R. parviflorus*, has a remarkable natural range from sea level to 2,700 meters, from Alaska to Mexico and as far east as the Great Lakes; it is present but not common in Arch Cape. Some other shrubs, such as the huckleberries (*Vaccinium* spp.), favor newly logged ground and were once very abundant along the highway east of Falcon Cove until succession led to their displacement by alder (on the way to a hemlock climax). *Arctostaphylos* spp., kinnikinnick and the manazanitas, are native species commonly planted as ornamentals. The wild rose, *Rosa nutkana*, found in some dense thickets, produces an edible rosehip fruit. Scotch broom, *Cytisus scoparius*, a species introduced from Europe, was extensively planted near the Columbia River mouth for dune stabilization in the 1920's and 1930's and has since spread widely; a few plants occur in Arch Cape, but, like the jack pine, it needs very sandy soil to be competitive, so it remains rare here. A highly attractive sand-inhabiting native shrub is the western rhododendron, *Rhododendron macrophyllum*, found at Arch Cape only when planted; in some cases it has remained after houses near which it was planted were removed and their lawns were otehwise overun by salal, etc.

Herbacious plants comprise by far the largest number of species of flowering plants here as elsewhere, and frequently they have considerably more restricted geographical range than shrubs or trees. Still, because conditions are relatively constant throughout the Oregonian region, there are few if any endemics near sea level along the Oregon coast. In a specialized habitat, however, the two highest elevations of Clatsop County, the volcanic peaks of Onion Peak (at 932 meters) and Saddle Mountain (at an easy-to-remember 1001 meters), relict populations left behind with the retreat of the ice-age glaciers contain several species of herbs found nowhere else. Hundreds of species of herbaceous plants occur in Arch Cape, and it is beyond the scope of this account to deal with them in detail. Many of the common weeds found in our lawns originated in Europe and were accidentally imported; thus a lawn in Amsterdam or Paris looks remarkably like a lawn in Arch Cape. Typical lawn grass here is fescue (*Festuca* spp.), and bluegrass (*Poa* spp.), both native and European species. Generally, property owners plant newly established lawns with commercial grass seed, which originates in the Willamette Valley (the source of the seed sold throughout the Unites States), and which sprouts rapidly and forms interlacing sod. Within a year, wild grass typically moves into a lawn and displaces the planted grass; although is not as good looking, wild grass has the distinct advantage of being well adapted to local climatic conditions; it tolerates salt spray well, and in summer droughts it simply goes dormant, turns yellow, stops growing and stands ready for quick revival when rain returns, so watering is necessary only if owners demand green lawns year around.

Weeds common in our lawns are the creeping buttercup, *Ranunculus repens*; the plantains, *Plantago lanceolata* and *P. major*; the coast strawberry, *Fragaria chiloensis* (named for the Chilean island of Chiloe, an indication of its long range along the Pacific coast; it is the ancestor of the domesticated strawberry); the white and red clovers, *Trifolium repens* and *T. pratense*; the seaside lotus, *Lotus formosissimus*, (which lives up to its name with very pretty clusters of bright yellow flowers); the purple-flowering menthacean, *Prunella vulgaris*, (which is so well adapted to life in lawns that it has evolved a recumbent variety that blooms low enough to escape cutting by lawn mowers); the pimpernel, *Anagallis arvensis*, (whose pretty tiny orange flowers resemble miniature jewels); the pineapple weed, *Matricaria matricarioides*, (which is evidently native to this region but has found its way to all similar temperate regions around the world); the little English daisy, *Bellis perennis*, the yarrow, *Achillea millefolium*; the seaside tansy, *Tanacetum camphoratum*, (a native species that seems to have become more common here in recent years; because it elaborates an alkaloid compound toxic to cattle, authorities on the state and county levels frequently demand its eradication, even though it appears most abundant in state parks; when it grows in lawns, lawn mowers pass over the basal leaves but prevent growth of the tall stems of dense yellow flowers often seen along roadsides); and, of course the dandelions, *Taraxacum* spp., and the false dandelion or hairy cat's ears *Hypochaeris radicata* (introduced European natives whose long tap roots let them reach deeper water to remain green throughout the summer, and whose basal involucres are pressed so tightly against the ground that they smother other plants in an effective but ecologically greedy defense of their territory); the false dandelion is called "one of the most abundant and troublesome lawn-weeds of western Oregon." Where lawns experience winter flooding, as in the floodplain of Arch Cape Creek along the Old Mill Road, they have stands of wiry rushes, *Juncus leseurii* and other species. (A relative, which grows up to two meters tall, is the water-loving *J. bolanderi*, filling much of the dune lake in Falcon

Cove.) In marshy areas, such as along the Mill Road, there are dense stands of tall grass-like sharp-edged sedges, *Carex* sp.

Outside of lawns (though occasionally in them as well) are some larger common herbs. These include false lily-of-the-valley *Maianthemum bifolium*; the cow parsnip *Heracleum lanatum* (whose hollow woody stems I, when a little boy, often made into play pipes); the western wild cucumber *Echinocystis oreganas* (whose vines, up to ten meters long, climb and drape over shrubs and trees; its large fruit is too empty to provide much food, but chipmunks often gnaw it open and remove the big thick discoid seeds); the beach morning glory *Convolvulus soldanella* (found both inshore and onto the beach); the seaside dock *Rumex maritima* (with dense clusters of tiny buckwheat flowers), the giant vetch or wild pea, *Vicia gigantea* (also found at the very edge of the beach; its lentil-like seeds are edible but require softening); the foxglove *Digitalis purpurea* (the source of the powerful cardiac medicine named for the genus; a European native, it's a biennial that covers whole hillsides farther inland and puts up a tall flower stem from its basal leaves each year); the seaside daisy *Erigeron glaucus* (whose large purple ray flowers are distinctive); the oxeye daisy *Chrysanthemum leucanthemum* (with even larger white ray flowers.)

A widespread large lily that produces numerous orange flowers in late summer appears to be *Lilium pardalinum*. The fire-weed *Epilobium angustifolium* thrives in disturbed areas. In swamps, especially near the fire station, are large stands of the skunk cabbage *Lysichitum americanum* (whose beautiful bold yellow flowers herald the arrival of spring, but whose stems and leaves do indeed stink like a skunk). One of the seemingly bravest terrestrial plants is the American sea rocket *Cakile edentula*, a radish relative that insouciantly ventures out across the beach each summer to the retracted high tide line, where its succulent leaves hold enough water to sustain it in the face of severe drainage, while it produces pretty purple flowers and dares the ocean to kill it; each fall the returning high tides call its bluff and wipe it out. Common on cliffs near Hug Point is the colorful Indian paintbrush, *Castilleja litoralis*, (whose large nectaries are always a delight to suck for a sweet treat). In some localities the common evening primrose, *Oenothera biennis* is abundant, its perennial basal rosette each spring producing a tall and rather scrawny stem bearing numerous large yellow flowers.

Some introduced cultivated plants occasionally escape and become well-established here. The English ivy, *Hedera helix*, if not trimmed back, will eventually creep across lawns and climb to the tops of trees. The European holly, *Ilex aquifolium*, produces bright red berries that some birds eat; as a result, they spread the seeds widely, so it is not uncommon to find a domestic holly bush far out in the forest.

Among nonflowering terrestrial plants, the mosses, horsetails and ferns need at least a brief mention. Local mosses are poorly known. Approximately 300 species of mosses are recorded from the coastal region from Alaska through California, so there are probably many different ones here. Unfortunately, identification requires microscopic examination of the reproductive structures present only a short time each year. Mosses often move into local lawns, and homeowners must selectively poison them to maintain good growth of grass. Several years ago, Adolf Marsa, who owned a summer home near Asbury Creek, cultivated an unusual but very pretty lawn exclusively of moss, which he considered highly preferable to grass (which he mercilessly eradicated as an unwanted weed) because it formed a uniform green carpet that never needed mowing. Lawns in swampy areas often have stands of the primitive non-flowering vascular plants called horsetails, *Equisetum* spp., which produce annual errect stems from perennial rhizomes. Because the internal skeletal fibers contain abrasive SiO_2 or glass, horsetails have been used as potscrubbers, and some species are called "scouring rushes." Their presence indicates water seepage in such places as the geologically unstable shoreline of Cove Beach.

Three native species of ferns are common here. The multibranched bracken fern, *Pteridium aquilinum*, has a perennial underground rhizome from which it sends up fiddle-necks into local lawns every spring; if allowed to grow fully, it can exceed a person's height. The rhizomes and young shoots are edible, and the leaves have seen use as bedding and thatch. The sword fern, *Polystichum munitum*, a very attractive plant, is commonly grown in rock gardens, and its leaves are used commercially in the nursery trade. The licorice fern often fills the crotches of large, branching spruce trees. Less frequently seen because of its restriction to regions of deep shade and constant abundant water is the maiden-hair fern *Adiantum pedatum*, a smaller species whose common name may derive from its fine fibrous roots, not its leaves.

Fungi

Although traditionally treated as plants, the fungi are now considered to represent a kingdom of their own. None converts inorganic materials into carbohydrates by photosynthesis, as most plants do, but all break down complex organic material into simpler compounds, a more animal-like activity, though none "eats" in the animal sense. Other aspects of their structure and function serve to separate the fungi from both plants and animals. Many fungi are parasites responsible for diseases (often hard to treat) of both animals (including humans) and plants, but their role as decomposers makes them essential to our lives. Though a few mushrooms are highly prized as food, this is much less important than the uses of some yeasts and the antibiotics derived from some species. Spread by microscopic spores always present in the air, water and soil around us, fungi are inescapable. Air movements and human activities have dispersed molds worldwide, with a single species often restricted to bread, cheese, a species of fruit or whatever. The mushrooms are less widely distributed, often being associated with a particular species of tree or other plant or limited by local climatic conditions of temperature or moisture. Mushrooms live under-ground or in the bodies of dead plants, sometimes for hundreds of years. Only when they produce fruiting bodies, typically for a short time each year, are they visible above the ground, and only then can they be harvested for eating or even identified. As with other groups, the total number of mushrooms occurring here is only a guess; it is estimated that 4,000 described species live from the Rockies to the Pacific coast of the Unites States, so perhaps one could expect at least 500 of those along our stretch of coast. Virtually every species of tree forms "mycorrhizal associations" (which facilitate the breakdown of complex compounds in the soil) with mushrooms, without which it would not flourish or, in many cases, even live. Some of these associations are species-specific for both the tree and the fungus, while others are broader. Lichens, which can grow under some of the earth's most rigorous conditions of temperature and drying, are obligate symbiotic associations of algae (to photosynthesize) and fungi (to provide support and retain water). They are common here on such varied exposed substrates as basalt cliffs, shingle walls and tree trunks.

Among edible mushrooms here, the choicest are the morels (*Morchella* spp.), found briefly in the spring in particular forests, though those people who know exactly where to find them, keep such information a close secret. The fairy-ring, *Marasmius oreades*, which produces circles of dead grass in lawns in summer, is considered edible. Species of *Amanita* are among our most colorful local mushrooms; enough of them are deadly poisonous so that all should be considered inedible. The shelf-fungi (family Polyporaceae), characteristic decomposers of dead spruce trees, are among the few species with permanent fruiting bodies, in this case hard woody shelves that may be very large; people occasionally collect the white shelves and use them as decorations, sometimes even painting pictures on them, for which they serve as good permanent "canvases". Puffballs (members of several different families), named for the round fruiting bodies that explosively eject their spores, appear in lawns in the fall; some
are edible.

Terrestrial and Fresh-Water Animals

Although the vast majority of local animals are invertebrates, especially insects, they are only poorly documented. On the other hand, the vertebrates, particularly the birds and mammals, are quite well catalogued for western Oregon and even Clatsop County, if not precisely at Arch Cape. Among non-arthropod terrestrial invertebrates most commonly seen here are the earthworms essential for turning over and aerating soil, and the slugs, *Limax* spp. (their name derived from the Latin word meaning "slimy"), whose herbivorous habits make them the bane of gardeners. Incompletely adapted to terrestrial existence, both of these must stay in moist shady spots to avoid desiccation; their mucus or slime is secreted to reduce the volatility of the moisture covering their bodies and thus retard its dangerous evaporation. The land snail, *Helix* sp., characterized by a very delicate tan shell, appears occasionally. Of importance in the soil are numerous species of free-living hairlike nematode worms, rarely seen unless they burrow into such root-crops as radishes, turnips or carrots. A common millipede is a hard-shelled black one with yellow spots (genus *Harpaphe*) which eats detritus. A frilly red centipede (genus *Stenophilus*?) is commonly found locally in rotting wood.

Many species of flying, crawling and burrowing insects, some harmful, some beneficial, but most neither toward human interests, occur here, but their documentation is very poor. An entomologist's rule for estimating the number of species in a region is that there are about ten times as many species of insects as of terrestrial plants. The latter number is also only an estimate for Arch Cape, but there are probably at least 300 species of land plants here, so one could expect to find some 3,000 species of insects. (The total number recorded from Oregon is 25,000 to 30,000.)

There is an insect fauna found on and around spruce trees, a different one associated with hemlocks, yet others with alders, willows, etc. Some of these insects gain only shelter for themselves or their offspring, some hasten the decomposition of cut or fallen trees, and others selectively feed on the leaves, buds, bark, roots or sapwood of their live hosts. Because the insects and trees evolved together here, they are generally in a dynamic balance, though human activities, such as monoculture planting, may disrupt that. There are occasional outbreaks of the spruce aphid, *Elatobium abietinum*, which defoliates and kills spruces along the coast, especially the older ones. Thus many of the magnificent saltspray-deformed monarchs lining our shore, on the order of 200 to 500 years old, were killed or seriously injured in the 1950's. (Professional treatment of our "Big Tree" at the end of Marshall Avenue, managed to save it that time, but most of the other large spruces in that area are now gone.)

The cedar elaborates chemicals that give it unique resistance to insect attacks, with the result that dead cedar snags can remain standing for many decades; this, of course, also accounts for cedar's durability in external construction and the use of cedar chips to keep fleas out of dogs' beds. (Prolonged exposure to the wood can produce allergic reactions from these chemicals, as I discovered when wearing shorts while applying our shake roof.)

A dedicated amateur collector in Elsie, on the Sunset Highway, has turned up 300 species of moths alone there; because most of those live only in a narrow band near the coast, the number of species in Arch Cape should be similar. Their close relatives, the butterflies, prefer warmer and drier conditions, so they are rare on the coast; the current unpublished count for all of Clatsop County is 46 species. None has been documented for Arch Cape, though at least three species of butterflies are expected here along "partly shaded roadsides with moist areas and lush vegetation," to quote John Hinchliff, a Portland lepidopterist. (To distinguish them, note that moths at rest spread their wings out to the sides, while butterflies hold theirs straight up; species of either may be drab or brightly colored.)

The great majority of insect species are beetles, and we certainly have our share here, both flying and nonflying species. Some blind beetles live in forest litter; a leaf beetle (Family Chrysomelidae) feeds at night on salmonberry leaves; ladybugs (Family Coccinellidae), which hibernate but are often very abundant in summer here, have been widely introduced because they are beneficial predators on harmful pests such as aphids; and the large black beetle, *Scaphonotus angusticolus*, often seen plodding through local forests, preys on snails and slugs.

Insects commonly seen in houses include the long highly flexible primitive wingless silverfish, *Lepisma saccharina*, an innocous but unattractive resident of cupboards; the house-fly, *Musca domestica*, a nonbiter that can spread many diseases by contact if it has access to them; and the European earwig, *Forficula auricularia*, harmless to people despite its formidable appearance and folklore about its entering ears, though it can damage some crops. Cat and dog fleas, (*Ctenocephalides* spp.), are common in nearly any house where the pets live, and, despite their common names, readily attack humans as well; their larvae overwinter in lawns and are particularly numerous in summers following mild winters. Local mosquitoes (Family Culicidae) are small in both body and bite and not known to bear any diseases; ocean spray and shore winds confine them to sheltered inland areas of the community.

Many species of ants (Family Formicidae) occur here, most unseen in forest litter, where they are important recyclers of plant matter; the carpenter ants, which swarm in the air each summer, can seriously damage wooden structures, as nearly all of our homes are.

There are a few species of bees (essential pollinators of many flowering plants) and wasps (at least one of which builds beautifully delicate paper nests inside house walls), whose stings are quite harmless except to people with pronounced allergies. Some insects are better known from their larvae than their adult forms; the woolly-bear caterpillar, commonly seen in fall, becomes an inconspicuous tiger moth (Family Arctiidae); and, in summer, a leaf miner, the caterpillar of the moth *Lithocolletis gualtheriella*, riddles many salal leaves, especially higher up along the Arch Cape trail.

Numerous species of spiders, present in huge numbers though often out of our sight, occur here, but they are not well catalogued. They include web-spinners, stalkers, jumpers and others, all keenly adapted to capturing particular prey, mostly species of insects, including such serious pests as the spruce budworm. Mites and ticks, both freeliving and parasitic, are common but poorly known.

Vertebrates, because of their size, activities, conspicuousness and frequent use for food, are by far the best known terrestrial and fresh-water animals, even though the numbers of their species are relatively small. The rainbow (steelhead) and coastal cutthroat trout, *(Salmo gairdneri* and *S. clarki,)* and coho (silver) salmon, *(Oncorynchus kisutch,)* occur in Arch Cape Creek (where they are subject to fishing regulations of size, season and number) below the barrier of the waterfall. As the operators of the Arch Cape Water District are well aware, a water-right claims nearly all of the flow of Arch Cape Creek for maintenance of these populations. There is an installation of the statewide Salmon Trout Enhancement Program (STEP) in Arch Cape Creek. The trout species, after hatching in the creek, spend two to three years at sea before returning to spawn, while the salmon comes back after a single year. Because of its smaller flow and the barrier to migration presented by the "hanging" highway culvert, whose lower end is improperly located above stream level, Asbury Creek no longer serves as habitat for these seagoing fishes. Above the barrier in each creek, populations of resident (nonmigratory) cutthroat trout are known. Personnel of the Oregon Department of Fish and Wildlife make frequent (sometimes weekly) surveys of fish populations and habitat in the creeks. Records from reports on file at the regional office provide interesting insights. One for Arch Cape Creek dated April 11, 1952 (author unrecorded) reads:

"BARRIERS: Two log jams and one fifteen foot falls.
FISH OBSERVED: Steelhead (both young and adults), cutthroat trout, and two age classes of young silver salmon.

The first mile of the stream has good spawning gravel most of the way. The gradient becomes steeper in the second mile and the spawning areas become fewer. The last half mile surveyed consisted of a very steep gradient with large boulders and terminated by a fifteen-foot falls.

Three steelhead adults were found about two miles upstream in a large pool below a log jam. Apparently that is their upper limit. The first log jam is about one hundred yards above the shingle mill at the end of the road. At the present time it does not block fish migrations but may in the future. The second and last of any consequence is about two miles upstream. There is little spawning gravel above the jam so it is not considered detrimental to fish migrations."

The destruction of the shingle mill and the complete removel of its mill pond were clearly beneficial to fish habitat. A second report by Aarron Currier, dated December 18, 1990, reads in part:

"The first one-half mile (up to log bridge) was excellent coho spawning habitat. There were about five three foot by five foot holes and about five areas two feet by three feet along the side of the bank. One [tributary] entered the creek from right next to the log bridge. The habitat immediately changed to a higher gradient. Many deep three foot by five foot pools, a lot of boulders with one to three foot falls for the rest of the survey. . .One dead male coho was found. . ."

A species of small sculpin (Family Cottidae) resides in the Falcon Beach dune lake, where it aggressively defends its territory. It is unknown whether the sculpins reproduce in the lake, and thus whether the individuals currently there or their ancestors were the ones cast over the rock berm by storm waves; at any event, they probably eliminate both frog tadpoles and mosquito larvae in the lake.

Amphibians are represented by frogs and salamanders. It is uncertain how many species of true frogs occur here; at least the red legged and bull frogs *(Rana aurora* and *R. catesbeiana)* are known. The former, smaller species starts calling at night as soon as springtime air temperatures rise enough to rouse it from its winter torpor. In the early 1950's, just north of Maxwell Avenue, a contractor dug a hole to accommodate the basement of a house, which was never built. Winter rains turned the hole into a fine pond, in which frogs deposited eggs each spring. Several summers I netted tadpoles from the pond and took them home, where I could keep them alive until they metamorphosed into adult if minute frogs, providing a good back-porch lesson in natural history. The bullfrog, though not native west of the Rocky Mountains, has been widely introduced, often to the detriment of local native species of frogs. The Pacific tree frog, *Hyla regilla*, is a small species more often heard than seen.

The rough-skinned newt, *Taricha granulosa*, whose tough leathery skin is handsomely colored brown above and orange below, is our most common salamander. It used to be abundant during springtime breeding in the quiet backwater on the south side of Asbury Creek just west of the highway, but that habitat has been destroyed without a trace to accommodate building. (When in the first grade, I once captured a few specimens, which I took to school and kept as class pets for several months in an aquarium; except for the time the janitor found them roaming around the piano in another room, they were no trouble.) Its body is slightly poisonous, so it shows little need to hide from predators; only by eating the animal would a person suffer harm. Outside the breeding season, the rough-skinned newt lives on forest floors, where it remains inconspicuous until the breeding urge sends large numbers plodding determinedly across the ground toward water. Another salamander occasionally seen in Arch Cape is the soft-skinned dark Pacific giant salamander *Dicamptodon ensatus*, which is not always so large as its common name implies. Distribution maps show at least seven other species of salamanders in this region, though I do not know of their documented occurrence in Arch Cape.

Reptiles are very poorly represented here, there being only two species of snakes, both nonpoisonous, commonly seen. These are the northwestern and common garter snakes,

Thamnophis ordinoides ands *T. sirtalis*, which are difficult to distinguish and so handled as one species in this account. Because its favored food is the garden slug (which, as a boy, I enjoyed watching it engulf), local gardeners often encourage it to keep that pest in check. Unlike most reptiles, it bears live young rather than laying eggs, so nesting areas, on hillsides exposed to warming afternoon sun, are masses of miniature wriggling snakes. (One spring, before vegetation overgrew it and made it too shady, garter snakes nested on the clay bank just below Ralph Forbes' house on Ocean View Avenue. I collected a fistful of young ones and took them to school, where my classmates and I had fun watching them swallow earthworms.)

Lizards seem undocumented from Arch Cape; I once found one in Cannon Beach, probably the northern alligator lizard *Gerrhonotus coeruleus*; and there is a report of the western skink, *Eumeces skiltonianus* at Arcadia. There is evidently no turtle found here.

By way of contrast, it is interesting to compare the herpetofauna of Portland. A recently published list includes 13 amphibian species and 10 reptiles, including all of those mentioned above in and near Arch Cape. The larger numbers probably reflect Portland's much greater area and more varied habitat as well as its distance from the ocean, to say nothing of better documentation.

Birds are everywhere observed by numerous avid amateur watchers, many of whom can provide highly reliable identifications, so their occurrences are well documented. Various groups of birders prepare and frequently update sighting lists at the state and local levels; the one best covering this area is the Lower Columbia Birding Association, headed by Mike Patterson in Astoria. Its most recent list, derived from many years' observations in Fort Stevens State Park, includes 206 species, of which 74 species are known to breed there. As with other taxa, the bird fauna of Arch Cape lacks those species restricted to estuaries, large lakes and sand dunes, perhaps up to half of the list (especially ducks and geese), though a few species common in those habitats do occasionally appear here. There are probably no species recorded from Arch Cape that are not on the Fort Stevens list. Local birds are roughly divisible into four categories: year-round residents, summer residents, winter residents, and migrating passersby.

Among year-round resident birds, the most conspicuous deserve special citation. The song sparrow, *Melospiza melodia*, calls before dawn on spring mornings so loudly as to be audible far out onto the beach. The white-crowned sparrow, *Zonotrichia leucophrys*, which occurs over most of western North America, has a simple song that shows distinct dialectual differences. The Steller's jay, *Cyanacitta stelleri* (usually, but not quite accurately, called "blue-jay") is more common slightly away from the shore. The common crow, *Corvus brachyrhynchos*, has always been here, but it has become much more common and bolder in recent years. The western gull, *Larus occidentalis* (some of whose numbers migrate seasonally inland as far as Yellowstone Lake, but which is never absent), is by far the most common gull here. The yellow-shafted flicker, *Colaptes auratus*, though a woodpecker, prefers the ground. The American robin, *Turdus migratorius*, leaves completely only in severe winters. The common starling, *Sturnus vulgaris*, is a good insect catcher but messy and agressive, and it has caused the reduction in numbers of many native bird species as its populations crossed North America; it was first seen here in the 1970's. It was introduced from England to Central Park, New York City, in 1890 by a physician who had the bizarre notion that every species of bird mentioned by Shakespeare should be in North America; only once, in Henry IV, part 1, does Shakespeare mention the starling, and there it is in quite disparaging terms: "I'll have a starling shall be taught to speak nothing but 'Mortimer'..." Another introduced European species common here is the house sparrow, *Passer domesticus*; released in Brooklyn, New York, in 1852, it has since spread across North America and evolved into distinct geographical races. Also here year around are such strictly marine species as the western grebe, *Aechmophorus occidentalis*; the pelagic cormorant, *Phalocrocorax pelagicus*; the common murre, *Uria aalge*, and the pigeon guillemot, *Cepphus columba*.

Among the many birds seasonally present in Arch Cape, some are especially noteworthy. The brown pelican, *Pelicanus occidentalis*, the same species found along the coast to Chile and along the Atlantic and Gulf coasts to Venezuela, appears here most summers and falls, gliding just over the waves in small groups or rarely standing on the beach. The great blue heron, *Ardea herodias*, mainly an estuarine species, turns up sometimes on the beach. Bald eagles, *Haliaeetus leucocephalus*, occasionally perch on tall trees or fly over and have been seen attacking nesting sea birds on Castle Rock. The American oystercatcher, *Haematopus palliatus*, distinctive because of its bright red bill, visits Arch Cape Creek at times. Large flocks of least sandpipers, *Erolia minutilla*, run tightly bunched together along the beach. An oceanic gull, the black-legged kittiwake, *Rissa tridactyla*, catches insects on the wing, sometimes quite high above the beach, while the Bonapart's gull, *Larus philadelphia*, stirs up small crustaceans with its feet in the surf zone. The band-tailed pigeon, *Columba fasciata* comes in large flocks in summer and may strip the crops of elderberries; it is easy to frighten, probably because it is the only local species of bird for which there is a legal hunting season.

Two hummingbirds, Anna's, *Calypte anna*, and the rufous, *Selaphorus rufus*, are attracted to red flowers, especially *Fuchsia*. Barn swallows, *Hirundo rustica*, nest on the eaves of houses, though they are becoming ever rarer as a result of loss of habitat in their wintering locations in Latin America. Piliated woodpeckers, *Dryocopus pileatus*, by far the largest of their kind, can noisely rip large strips off spruce snags. The rufous-sided towhee, *Pipilo fuscus*, and the varied thrush, *Ixoreus naevius*, are harbingers of winter; the latter species is the local bird most likely to kill itself by flying into windows. The red-wing blackbird, *Agalaius phoeniceus*, which we first saw here about 1950, used to nest in willows of local swamps in large numbers and filled the air with its distinctive four-note call; it readily frequented winter-time bird feeders during its stay. As abrupt as its initial arrival was its disappearance from this area several years ago.

As with birds, there is no comprehensive list of mammals found strictly at Arch Cape, but there is very good documentation of the species known from Oregon as a whole and in the coastal region of the state. Thus one may judge which species are probably here in addition to those with reliable anecdotal reports. One old field guide lists 54 terrestrial species likely, if not actually known, to occur here, while the recent book *Natural History of Oregon Coast Mammals* reports that "Nine...orders and 31 families...live along the Oregon coast. A total of 96 species, representing 65 land and 31 marine mammals, inhabit the coast. Of these, five of the land species have been introduced, and one species of marine mammals has been reintroduced."

The lone species of marsupial native to North America, the opossum, *Didelphis virginiana*, was first introduced from the southeastern United States into Oregon about 1910 because of its food value. Another introduction in 1939, evidently by southerners here for Depression-era employment, brought it to northwestern Oregon. Though rarely seen alive because of its nocturnal habits, the opossum is a frequent road kill here.

The smallest mammals, the insectivores, are represented by nine species along the Oregon coast. Their ordinal name is deceptive because some species eat many kinds of small animals and even plants besides insects. Although rarely actually seen, the insectivores that make their presence the best known are the moles. Two species occur here, Townsend's mole, *Scapanus townsendi* and the coast mole, *S. orarius*. The two species, which often occur in the same habitats, are difficult to distinguish, even when captured. Evidently the more common here, coast moles, which are much smaller, tend to favor better drained soils and dig shallower borrows, often just beneath the surface, sometimes resulting in ridges along the ground; their hills are smaller, less conspicious and generally less numerous. Lawn owners understandably curse the moles' hills, but their large (more than their body weight daily) consumption of insects and other small invertebrates, as well as their reworking and aeratin, the soil make them beneficial overall. Four species of shrews (*Sorex* spp.) are reported from the northern Oregon coast; they are probably common here, but their nocturnal habits, small size and preference for sheltered areas make them rarely seen. Similarly elusive is the American shrew-mole, *Neurotrichus gibbsi*, whose range also includes Arch Cape.

Bats (Order Chiroptera) are well-represented along the Oregon coast, where ten species, most in the genus *Myotis*, are known. It is not unusual to glimpse bats flying at dusk here, but lighting conditions at that hour make it virtually impossible to distinguish species. Local bats are beneficial consumers of insects, the different species favoring slightly different localities, elevations, times and size of prey to avoid undue competition. Because many bat species are known carriers of rabies, it is never advisable to try to trap or handle them.

In the order Lagomopha are two local species, the snowshoe hare, *Lepus americanus*, and the brush rabbit, *Sylvilagus bachmani*. The brush rabbit, also called cottontail, is the smaller species (about 30 centimeters, in contrast to 40 centimeters) and lacks the black ear-tips of the snoeshoe hare; it is evidently the more common, often seen scampering about lawns or raiding inadequately fenced gardens on early mornings. The snowshoe hare, (not properly a rabbit) has been introduced several places because it is a highly edible game species; its fur is considered to be of little value. It typically changes from brown summer pelage to a white winter coat and so is also called a varying hare. In contrast, the local subspecies, whose range is western Oregon and western Washington, remains brown all year. Neither species hibernates.

Twenty-five species of rodents (four of them introduced), ranging from tiny voles to the beaver, occur along the Oregon coast; at least thirteen occur in this area. Most are native and, when seen, regarded favorably. Those species that give the Order Rodentia a bad rap are the three introduced from Europe, the house mouse *Mus musculus*, and the black (or roof) and Norway (or brown) rats, *Rattus rattus* and *R. norwegicus*. Native mice species, genus *Microtus*, called voles, are small, nocturnal and secretive, so people are rarely aware of them, even though they are quite numerous here; the three species known from the northern Oregon coast are very difficult to distinguish. A similar species is the deer mouse, *Peromyscus maniculatus*, also rarely seen. The packrat or bushy-tailed woodrat, *Neotoma cinerea*, is an attractive furry animal sometimes considered a good pet and called "excellent to eat;" it is rarely destructive, but the huge nests it builds of wood, paper and other debris in attics and garages to which it gains access can pose severe fire hazards.

The rodent most often seen in Arch Cape, and nearly everyone's favorite mammal, is Townsend's chipmunk, *Eutamias townsendi*. It is a conspicuous and noisy ground feeder easily attracted with edible crumbs and seeds during daylight hours. It nests in trees and attics, where it probably serves the useful function of keeping destructive rats away. (We have had a colony in our attic since shortly after our house was completed in 1960, and its entry holes are so well concealed under the eaves that I am happy to let them be.) Our chipmunks do not actually hibernate, but in severe winters they are occasionally torpid; even then they rouse themselves frequently to eat stored food or even to raid bird feeders. Often seen here is the California or Beechey ground squirrel (also called "gray digger"), *Spermophilus beecheyi*, a rather wary animal that typically stands tall on its hind legs to spot threats and flees quickly when alarmed. It hibernates through most winters. Arch Cape is within the ranges of the chickaree, *Tamiasciurus douglasi*, a small squirrel originally collected at the mouth of the Columbia; the North American jumping mouse, *Zapus trinotatus*, which spends much of the year in hibernation; and the northern flying squirrel, *Glaucomys sabrinus*, whose nocturnal habits keep it out of sight.

Several larger rodent species are native here. The mountain beaver (appropriately named except that it occurs at sea-level and is more closely related to the squirrels), *Aplodontia rufa*, also called "boomer" because of the sound it produces by gnashing its teeth, is considered a nuisance because of tunnels it often digs in sloping sections of lawns; it is considered edible, and its fur saw use as blanket-like robes by Amerinds. The true beaver, *Castor canadensis*, is known from Arch Cape Creek, where it has been seen cutting trees but never seems to build a dam; lengths of beaver-gnawed alder trunks often wash up on our beach. The muskrat, *Ondatra zibethicus*, though a common water-dweller along much of the Oregon coast, including the Columbia River, seems not to occur in Arch Cape. Another large rodent, the nutria or coypu, *Myocastor coypus*, a South American native imported to Oregon in the 1930's for a fur industry that never quite developed, is well established in rivers as close as the Necanicum and Nestucca but not known in Arch Cape.

Mammals of the order Carnivora are often hunted and thus of reduced numbers or even exterminated; those that remain are understandably wary of people, so they tend to move away from human habitation or at least remain well concealed. Up to fifteen species are recorded from northwestern Oregon, but it is doubtful that most have been seen around Arch Cape, even if they do still occur here; this is especially true of the wild cats, the bobcat and mountain lion, as well as the red fox. Our most observed carnivore is the raccoon, *Procyon lotor*, a species found over nearly all of North America, from Canada to Panama. Because of its considerable intelligence and great manual dexterity, the raccoon is a very entertaining night visitor, but it can also be a nuisance by overturning garbage cans, attacking domestic poultry and othewise damaging property. Well into the present century, the grey wolf, *Canis lupus*, a species native to the entire circumboreal region of the world, occured in Oregon, including the local area. It has since been hunted to extinction in the state, one result of which is that a prey species, the ever-opportuinistic coyote, *C. latrans*, extended its range west from

347

eastern Oregon and is now occasionally spotted, usually in early morning hours, around Arch Cape. Another common carnivore, more often smelled (usually after being struck at night by a car) than seen, is the striped skunk, *Mephitis mephitis,* which is a beneficial predator of rodents and insects, though considered the most common carrier of rabies in North America. It prefers to face a threat and raise its tail to make its body appear large; only when cornered is it likely to turn around and spray. Other members of its family, a species each of spotted skunk, mink, otter, weasel, fisher and marten, though known from western Oregon, seem to be absent here.

Our largest carnivore is the American black bear, *Ursus americanus*, which occurs through nearly all of North America. It is usually brown rather than black here and thus commonly called the brown bear. Sightings of bears are fairly frequent east of the highway, but only rarely do they cross to the west side. The deep scratches on the handle of the screen-door at the Arch Cape store record one such visit.

The two domestic species of carnivores, the dog (*Canis familiaris*) and cat (*Felis catus*) deserve mention here. The beach is a popular place for dogs to play, and they pose little harm to wildlife there unless they needlessly harrass shore birds, a common misbehavior of two or more dogs in unsupervised packs. An adequately fed dog typically becomes too lazy to hunt and so does not endanger native animals. Cats are a different matter; shunning the beach, they stalk and kill birds and small mammals (millions per day nationwide) in the undergrowth, even when they receive good care and feeding in homes. Self-sufficient feral cats can survive well in our mild climate, so they turn up frequently around Arch Cape.

Only two native species of hooved mammals occur on the Oregon coast; both, the North American elk or wapiti, *Cervus elaphas*, and the mule deer, *Odocoileus hemionis*, are very commonly seen here. Our elk, which goes under a number of common names, was, until recently, considered distinct from the Eurasian species and called *C. canadensis*, further divided into regional subspecies. Now only a single species, ranging from Canada to Mexico and from Korea through Europe into northwestern Africa, is recognized. It is, of course, a major game species in Oregon, so it tends to be wary of people. Nocturnally active, it commonly browses along the old Mill Road, where it is easy to hear clomping over the pavement or crashing through the bushes if one frightens it in the dark; its large tracks riddle lawns along that road and frequently show up on the beach.

The mule deer, also called black-tail deer and other names, is considered "the most important big game mammal of the West." Because it prefers open areas where its predators are more visible and its herbaceous food more abundant, the mule deer was more common here just after the logging of the nearby hills, first in the 1930's and again in the 1960's. It still appears east of the highway and often west of it as well, and can be an annoying pest in gardens because of its penchant for certain vegetables and even flowers and its ability to jump fences readily. It is one of the most commonly seen road-killed mammals here.

References for Further Reading

Astronomy, Geology and Oceanography

North, W. B., & J. V. Byrne, 1965. *Coastal landslides of northern Oregon.* The Ore Bin, 27 (11): 217-241.
> Accounts of the causes and effects of local landslides, including those at Ecola Park and Falcon Cove.

Pattullo, J. G., & W. Denner, 1965. *Processes affecting seawater characteristics along the Oregon Coast.* Limnology and Oceanography. 10 (3): 443-450.
> Observations on salinity and temperature of the surf along the coast, including Arch Cape (as recorded by Bridget Snow and John Markham) and conclusions derived from them concerning the fate of the Columbia's outflow and the effects of upwelling.

Zeilik, M., 1982. *Astronomy: The evolving universe.* Third Edition. New York: Harper & Row. xv + 623 pp.
> A university-level text, now superseded by newer editions as knowledge in astronomy rapidly expands.

Marine Environment and Biology

Bacon, R. L., & J. C. Markham, 1992. *Invertebrate and fish species found at Haystack Rock.* Unpublished typescript prepared for Haystack Rock Awareness Program. 4 pp.

Kozloff, E. N., 1983. *Seashore life of the northern Pacific coast.* An illustrated guide to northern California, Oregon, Washington and British Columbia. Seattle: University of Washington Press. 370 pp.
> A nice compromise between popular and technical coverage.

Kozloff, E. N., 1987. *Marine invertebrates of the Pacific Northwest.* Seattle: University of Washington Press. 511 pp.
> One of the few books specifically covering the whole coast of Oregon, extending into British Columbia. It strives to be comprehensive, with keys to all species known from the region. Written at a more technical level than most guides.

Link, T., 1981. *The ups and downs of razor clams.* Oregon Wildlife, May 1981. 4 pp.
> A summary of what is known about the biology of razor clams with tips for diggers.

Maser, C., R. F. Tarrant, J. M. Trappe, & J. F. Franklin, editors, 1988. *From the forest to the sea: a story of fallen trees.* General Technical Report, U. S. Forest Service, PNW-GTR-229. 153 pp.
> The historical and current fate of trees living and dying along the Oregon coast and later washing ashore as logs.

McConnaughey, B. H., & E. McConnaughey, 1985. *The Audubon Society Nature Guides: Pacific coast.* New York: Alfred A. Knopf. 633 pp.
> A well-illustrated guide to much of the life in and near our ocean.

Morris, R. H., D. P. Abbott, & E. C. Haderlie, 1980. *Intertidal invertebrates of California:* Stanford, California: Stanford University Press. 690 pp.
> A thorough guide to the identification of most of the species found here, including descriptions, line-drawings and hundreds of color photographs. For each species, there is a summary of what is known about its distribution and biology and what remains to be learned.

Parmenter, T., & R. Bailey, 1985. *The Oregon ocean book: An introduction to the Pacific Ocean off Oregon including its physical setting and living marine resources.* Salem: Oregon Department of Land Conservation and Development. 85 pp.
> This large-format low-priced paperback book provides a superb concise compilation of current knowledge of the ocean in our front yard. Written for the intelligent layman, it should be in the library of every curious coastal resident.

Ricketts, E. R., & J. Calvin, 1968. *Between Pacific tides.* Fourth Edition. Stanford, California: Stanford University Press. 614 pages.
> One of the most important and durable guides to marine invertebrates of this coast. Organized by habitat, not taxonomically, it is both informative and highly readable.

Schlichting, H. E., 1971. *A preliminary study of the algae and Protozoa in seafoam.* Botanica Marina 14: 24-28.

Smith, R. I., & J. T. Carlton, eds., 1975. *Light's manual: Intertidal invertebrates of the central California coast.* Third edition, Berkeley: University of California Press. 716 pp.
> Another classic field guide valuable here despite its emphasis on California. It is taxonomically arranged, with each section of this edition written by a noted specialist.

Yamada, S., 1992. *Species list for mouth of lower quarry, Yaquina Head outstanding natural area.* Unpublished typescript. 17 pp.

Terrestrial Plants and Fungi

Chambers, K. L., 1973. *Floristic relationships of Onion Peak with Saddle Mountain, Clatsop County, Oregon.* Madroño 22: 105-160.
> Catalog of the higher plants of Onion Peak, just behind Arch Cape, with remarks on their origin.

Franklin, J. F., 1961. *A guide to seedling identification for 25 conifers of the Pacific Northwest.* Portland; Pacific Northwest Forest and Range Experiment Station. 65 pp.

Frye, T. C., 1934. *Ferns of the Northwest.* Portland: Binfords & Mort. 177 pp.
> This seems to be the only such book. It should still be in print, because it has been reissued a number of times.

Gilkey, H. M., 1929. *A spring flora of northwestern Oregon.* Oregon State College? 153 pp.
> Although out-of-date, and probably long out of print, this thin volume has the advantage of homing in on our particular region. Strangely, details of its publication are lacking.

Gilkey, H. M., & L. R. J. Dennis, 1967. *Handbook of northwestern plants.* Corvallis: Oregon State University Bookstores. 505 pp.
> An easy-to-use book with line-drawings of many species.

Harthill, M. P., & I. O'Connor, 1975. *Common mosses of the Pacific coast.* Healdsburg, California: Naturegraph Publishers. 114 pp.
> Although covering only 68 of the reported 300 species of this region, this little book handles them nicely with keys and drawings.

Larrison, E. J., G. W. Patrick, W. H. Baker, & J. A. Yaich, 1974. *Washington wildflowers. The trailside series*, Seattle: Seattle Audubon Society. 376 pp.
> Though emphasizing Washington, this book also covers our part of Oregon, with color photographs of many species.

McCarter, M. A., 1986. *Plants of Neahkahnie Mountain.* Astoria: Unpublished typescript.

McCarter, M. A., 1988. *Plants of Short Sands Area.* Astoria: Unpublished typescript.
> These two checklists cover the most conspicuous terrestrial plants in these two habitats just to the south of Arch Cape.

Peck, M. E., 1941. *A manual of the higher plants of Oregon.* Portland: Binfords & Mort. 866 pp.

>   A rigorous technical coverage of ferns and flowering plants, striving to include all species known from the state, but lacking illustrations. There is a newer edition.

Randall, W. R., R. F. Keniston, D. N. Bever, & E. C. Jensen, 1981. *Manual of Oregon trees and shrubs.* Corvallis: O. S. U. Bookstores. 305 pp.

>   A convenient pocket guide to Oregon's larger plants, periodically revised.

Ross, C. R., 1978. *Trees to know in Oregon.* Extension Bulletin 697. Corvallis: Oregon State University . 96 pp.

>   A picture-book guide to the trees with anecdotal notes about the species, uses of the woods and history of Oregon forestry. Revised a number of times.

Ross, C. R., 1983. *Ferns to know in Oregon.* Extension Bulletin 785. Corvallis: Oregon State University Extension Service. 17 pp.

>   This is an extract of the book by Frye (1934) with more usable illustrations of a few species.

Smith, A. H., 1975. *A field guide to western mushrooms.* Ann Arbor: The University of Michigan Press. 280 pp.

>   One of the few mushroom guidebooks available. Though it covers only 201 of a possible 4,000 species, it has good color photos and useful notes for them.

Thompson, P., 1992. *Our green home: the resources of Portland, Oregon, 1992.* Portland: Portland Environmental Commission. 101 pp.

>   A summary of current knowledge of the natural and human environment of Portland for planning purposes. Appendices list the city's amphibians, reptiles, birds, mammals and higher plants.

Wiedemann, A. M., L. R. J. Dennis, & F. H. Smith, 1974. *Plants of the Oregon coastal dunes.* Corvallis: O. S. U. Book Stores. 117 pp.

>   A nice coverage of a restricted habitat.

Terrestrial Invertebrates

Borror, D. J., & R. E. White, 1970. *A field guide to the insects of America north of Mexico.* Peterson field Guild Series, 19. Boston: Houghton Mifflin. 404 pp.

>   A well-illustrated guide as far as it can go; the sheer number of species of insects found in the United States restricts a handbook's coverage to little beyond family level.

Furniss, R. L., & V. M. Carolin, 1977. *Western Forest Insects.* U. S. Dept. Agriculture. Forest Service Misc. Publ. 1339. Washington, D. C.: U. S. Government Printing Office. 654 pp.

> A compendium of nearly all that is known about insects in forests of the western United States.

Hinchliff, J, 1993. *Butterflies of Clatsop County, Oregon.* Unpublished typescript. 3 pp.

> Annotated list of the 46 species recorded here, extracted from a database for Oregon.

Kaston, B. J., 1952. *How to know the spiders.* Dubuque, Iowa: Wm. C. Brown. 220 pp.

> A guide to common species throughout the United States.

Kevan, D. K. M., & G. G. E. Scudder, 1989. *Illustrated keys to the families of terrestrial arthropods of Canada, 1. Myriapods (Millipedes, Centipedes, etc.)* Ottawa: Biological Survey of Canada. 88 pp.

> Evidently the only coverage of these groups, unfortunately only to family level and not quite local.

Vertebrates

Fishes

Bond, C. J., & A. J. Beardsley, 1984. *Field guide to common marine and bay fishes of Oregon.* Extension Manual 4. Revised edition. Corvallis: Oregon State University Extension Service. 59 pp.

> Literally a pocket-guide, this little book presents good identification drawings for the relatively few species it covers.

Clemens, W. A., & G. V. Wilby, 1961. *Fishes of the Pacific coast of Canada.* Bulletin No. 68. (Second Edition). Ottawa: Fisheries Research Board of Canada. 443 pp.

> A more technical guide than most and one of the few striving to include all the species known from the region, including those from deep water. A newer edition has appeared.

Gotshall, D. W., 1981. *Pacific coast inshore fishes.* Los Osos, California: Sea Challengers. 96 pp.

> A nice little book with a key to fish families, a drawing of a representative of each family and a photograph in the habitat of each species discussed.

Lamb, A., & Edgell, 1986. *Coastal fishes of the Pacific Northwest.* Madiera Park, B. C.: Harbour Publishing Co. 224 pp.

> A convenient guide for the sports fisherman, diver, beachcomber and the gastronomically

venturesome. It features 174 photographs of fishes in their native habitat and careful drawings with diagnostic features highlighted.

Love, R. M., 1991. *Probably more than you want to know about the fishes of the Pacific coast.* Santa Barbara, California: Really Big Press. 215 pp.
> This book is a flippant as its title sounds, but it is still a useful guide to the identification of many common species.

Amphibians and Reptiles

Stebbins, R. C., 1985. *A field to western reptiles and amphibians.* Second Edition. The Peterson field guide series, 16. Boston: Houghton Miffin. 336 pp.
> The standard field guide for our herpetofauna.

Zim, H. S., & H. M. Smith, 1956. *Reptiles and amphibians:* A guide to familiar American species. A Golden Nature Guide. New York: Golden Press. 160 pp.
> A brief account that is incomplete but still useful. There is a newer edition.

Birds

Austin, O. L., 1961. *Birds of the world.* New York: Golden Press. 319 pp.
> This beautifully illustrated volume is not the best for use in identifications because of its worldwide coverage, which must be incomplete for any particular region, but it provides a tremendous amount of information about the species considered.

Baptista, L., 1977. *Geographic variation in song and dialects of the Puget Sound white-crowned sparrow.* The Condor 79: 356-370.
> A study of one of our local birds, with sampling of its song as close as Tolovana Park.

Gabrielson, I. N., & S. G. Jewett, 1970. *Birds of the Pacific Northwest, with special reference to Oregon.* New York: Dover. 650 pp.
> Originally published in 1940 as Birds of Oregon, this book provides a wealth of information about the state's avifauna.

Patterson, M., 1991. *Checklist for birds of Fort Stevens.* Astoria, unpublished.
> Evidently the closest bird list available.

Peterson, R. T., 1990. *A field to western birds.* Third Edition. The Peterson field guide series, 2, revised and enlarged. Boston: Houghton Mifflin. 432 pp.
> The newest edition of this good guide, with new drawings and distribution maps.

Mammals

Bailey, V., 1936. *The mammals and life zones of Oregon. North American Fauna.* No. 55. United States Department of Agriculture. 416 pp.

> Although clearly out of date in some respects now, this book offers a still very useful account of the state's mammals by region. Besides mammals, it presents valuable discussions and regional lists of plants and breeding birds of Oregon, and it has a thorough account of Oregon's natural habitats and biogeography.

Burt, W. H., & R. P. Grossenheider, 1976. *A field guide to the mammals of America north of Mexico.* The Peterson field guide series, 5. Boston: Houghton Mifflin Co. xxv + 289 pp.

Daugherty, A. E., 1966. *Marine mammals of California.* Sacramento: California. Department of Fish and Game. 87 pp.

> A convenient pocket-size volume that covers all the species of marine mammals known from Oregon as well.

Ingles, L. G., 1965. *Mammals of the Pacific states.* Stanford, California: Stanford University Press. xii + 506 pp.

Kritzman, E. B., 1977. *Little mammals of the Pacific Northwest.* Seattle: Pacific Search Press. 120 pp.

> By limiting its scope, this book does well what it announces. It also contains good concise characterizations of local life zones.

Larrison, E. J., 1976. *Mammals of the Northwest: Washington, Oregon, Idaho and British Columbia.* Seattle: Seattle Audubon Society. 256 pp.

Maser, C., B. R. Mate, J. F. Franklin, & C. T. Dryness, 1981. *Natural History of Oegon Coast Mammals.* United States Department of Agriculture, Forest Service General Technical Report PNW-133. Pacific Northwest Forestry and Range Experimental Station. xix + 496 pp..

> A very readable account that serves as a highly usable guide to the identification of all of the mammals, both terrestrial and marine, of the Oregon coast and a treasury of entertaining insights into their biology.

Nowak, R. M., 1991. *Walker's mammals of the world.* Fifth edition. Baltimore: The Johns Hopkins University Press. Two volumes. xlv + 1629 pp.

> The definitive guide to all of the world's living species of mammals, periodically updated.

Acknowledgments

Many people generously provided information and helped me track down both obvious and obscure references as well as furnishing published and unpublished reports they had authored. Frequently one person referred me to another, whose knowledge I would otherwise have missed entirely. The conversations that resulted proved as valuable for the chance to share a common interest as for the information I learned (and was regrettably forced to condense, I hope without undue distortion). While trying to make this list complete, I surely have missed some names that belong here; I apologize to those inadvertently omitted.

Paul See (formerly with Clatsop Community College) refined my interpretations of local geology. Neal Maine (Seaside School District) recounted his extensive experience with the natural history of Clatsop County, provided publications and referred me to other helpful people. Terry Link, Russ Stauff and Robert Buckman (Oregon Department of Fish and Wildlife) provided data on razor clams and the fishes of Arch Cape Creek, respectively. Robert Bacon and several colleagues (Haystack Awareness Program) helped document rocky-shore invertebrates. Margaret McCarter (Clatsop Community College) gave me copies of her local plant and animal lists. Michael Patterson (Astoria High School) furnished a specially annotated list of the birds of Clatsop County. Robert Pyle contributed from his broad knowledge of butterflies and referred me to John Hinchliff, who sent me a summary of the documentation of butterflies in Clatsop County.

Many essential contributions came from members of the faculty of Oregon State University in Corvallis and Newport: Jefferson Gonor told about his study of logs on the beach; John Lattin and Paul Hammond answered questions about coastal insects and other terrestrial arthropods and guided me to library materials; Bruce Mate discussed marine mammals and provided a copy of the book on coastal mammals that he had coauthored; Sylvia Yamada sent copies of her lists of the biota of Yaquina Head; and curators in the herbarium of the Department of Botany shared their knowledge of coastal plants and located publications for me.

Librarians at Oregon State University, Clatsop Community College and the Portland office of the Nature Conservancy freely gave assistance and access to their libraries. People who read parts of the manuscript made suggestions for its improvement. I deeply appreciate the editorial assistance and unflappable patience of David English in the face of my delays and alterations. And finally, my warmest thanks go to my mother, Mamie Markham, for her encouragement and support at our home, site of the **Arch Cape Marine Laboratory**, of which this report is publication number 25.

The End of the Story
1893—1993

Negotiating Hug Point, Circa 1907. Reproduced from an old post card. Photo source unknown.

Ten of the eighteen "new generation" living in Arch Cape today. Could they be part of our volunteer Arch Cape fire crew in the future?

From left to right: Elisa Campbell, 11; Grace Hughes, 10; Ashley Mersereau, 7; Taylor Mersereau, 5; Micah Cerelli, 5; Vito Cerelli, 7; Clay Henry, 9; Alan Anderson-Priddy, 12; Ian Anderson-Priddy, 10 and Luke Henry, 7. David English photo.